JOHN WILSON CROKER

John Wilson Croker, painted by William Owen *c.* 1812. Reproduced by kind permission of the National Portrait Gallery.

John Wilson Croker
Irish Ideas and the Invention of Modern Conservatism 1800–1835

Robert Portsmouth
The National University of Ireland, Galway

IRISH ACADEMIC PRESS
DUBLIN • PORTLAND, OR

First published in 2010 by Irish Academic Press

2 Brookside,	920 NE 58th Avenue, Suite 300
Dundrum Road,	Portland, Oregon,
Dublin 14, Ireland	97213-3786, USA

© Robert Portsmouth 2010

www.iap.ie

British Library Cataloguing in Publication Data
An entry can be found on request

ISBN 978 0 7165 3071 8 (cloth)

Library of Congress Cataloging-in-Publication Data
An entry can be found on request

Printed by MPG Books Group, Bodmin & King's Lynn

Contents

Acknowledgements

I have to express thanks to a number of individuals and institutions for the generous assistance I have received during my research. The most important financial award was a three-year Irish Research Council scholarship, and the other, from the Clements Library, at the University of Michigan, Ann Arbor, for part funding the two months I spent examining the Croker archives. The staff at the Clements, in particular their curator of manuscripts, Dr Barbara De Wolf, were tirelessly hospitable and helpful. I am also obliged to the librarians and other staff at the Perkins Library, Duke University; the Regenstein Library, the University of Chicago; the Bodleian, Oxford; the Hardiman Library, NUI Galway; the Cumbria National Records Office, Carlisle; the National Library of Ireland and the British Library for their assistance. Professor James Sack of the University of Illinois, not only provided me with specialist advice on the Tory press and party of the period, but also insisted I stay at his home when I visited Chicago. I am also indebted to Professor Jacqueline Hill of NUI Maynooth for her valuable assistance on a number of occasions, and to William Thomas of Christchurch College, Oxford, who broke much new ground with his own Croker studies, for his advice at the commencement of mine. Brevity prohibits me from mentioning a number of other scholars and friends who I have thanked already in person, but I am particularly indebted to Simon and Eileen Lee for their hospitality in Dublin on many occasions; Louise Willems and Martin Byrne for the same in Galway; Caroline Haslam for technical advice; Lisa Hyde at Irish Academic Press, 'positive' in all things, and my ever helpful daughters, Marie and Maxine. My greatest debt, however, is to Professor Gearóid Ó Tuathaigh, of NUI Galway, whose wide knowledge of both British and Irish political, social and cultural history combined with his cheerful guidance and acute insight provided me with invaluable assistance throughout my research.

Abbreviations

Add. MSS	British Library Additional Manuscripts
Blackwood's	Blackwood's Edinburgh Magazine
Carlisle MS Records	Lowther Papers, Carlisle Public Office, Carlisle
Chicago MS	Manuscripts, Regenstein Library, University of Chicago
Clements MS	Manuscripts, Clements Library, University of Michigan, Michigan
Croker Papers	*The Correspondence and Diaries of the Right Honourable John Wilson Croker LLD, FRS, edited by Louis J. Jennings,* 3 vols (London, 1885)
DUM	*Dublin University Magazine*
Duke MS	Manuscripts, Perkins Library, Duke University, North Carolina
Fraser's	*Fraser's Magazine for Town and Country*
Hansard	*Hansard's Parliamentary Register*
Iowa MS	Croker Manuscripts, University of Iowa
Wellington New Despatches	Arthur, Duke of Wellington, *Supplementary Despatches Memoranda and Correspondence of Arthur Duke of Wellington,* ed. 2nd Duke of Wellington, 8 vols (London, 1867)

Introduction

In August 1857, the high society gossip and diarist Charles Greville noted that the Whig historian and politician Thomas Babbington Macaulay had been ennobled in the same week in which his most accomplished Irish opponent had died:

> While Macaulay is thus ascending to the House of Peers his old arch enemy and rival Croker has descended to the grave, very noiselessly and without observation ... He had very considerable talents, great industry, spoke in Parliament with considerable force, and in society, his long acquaintance with the world and with public affairs and his stores of general knowledge made him entertaining ... He was particularly disliked by Macaulay who never lost the opportunity of venting his antipathy by attacks upon him.[1]

Greville's epitaph has remained an enduringly appropriate one, for although John Wilson Croker had a more significant and extensive career than all but a handful of his Irish and British peers, his work and ideas have remained largely within the grave. The son of a Corkonian customs officer and Hester Rathbone, a Galway clergyman's daughter, Croker was born in 1780 at Craughwell, County Galway, and entirely educated in Ireland, within a few years of graduating from Dublin University his precocious talents as a political writer won him a seat in the House of Commons. In 1809 he was appointed to the highly responsible wartime post of secretary to the Admiralty, making him effectively the general manager of the Royal Navy, and over the next four decades he became a celebrated parliamentarian; a highly respected historian and literary reviewer; the founder of the Athenaeum Club; committee member of the Royal Society, and as a royal consultant on architecture, a planner of regency London.[2] All of which would have been an impressive career for a west of Ireland man from a relatively humble background, but his work as a highly valued advisor to three prime ministers and as one of the most influential political thinkers and pressmen of his era would be of much greater historical significance.

Croker's ideas and the development of his political and press career from when he was a young pamphleteer in Ireland promoting reforms to improve the state of Ireland, his relationship with political leaders like George Canning, Wellington and Sir Robert Peel, and his 'invisible predominance over the Tory daily press' up until 1835 will be the main subjects of this study. As we will see, he established a London *Guardian* in 1819, the notorious *John Bull* a year later, and remained the chief political writer and theorist for the Tory/Conservative press flagship, the *Quarterly Review*, for over forty years. In this capacity he was long accredited in dustier political dictionaries for having first invented the term 'Conservative party',[3] but much more importantly, and the main hypothesis of this study, together with what I describe as his circle of predominantly Irish pressmen, he was most responsible for 'inventing' and first promulgating its political philosophy. This was some years before the famous *Tamworth Manifesto* of December 1834, when modern parliamentary Conservatism is commonly seen as having been, 'to all intents and purposes, invented by Sir Robert Peel' to defend the 'traditional institutions' and resist the 'restless spirit of innovation', but 'promote the reform of proved abuses: in fact, to combine the Burke of *Reflections* with the Burke of the Economical Reform Bill'.[4]

In the first and second chapters we will see that these were essentially the same principles Croker had first promoted as a young man in Ireland with a group advocating Emancipation and other reforms in the hope of establishing a political *via media* between intransigent Protestants on the one hand and their Catholic rivals opposed to conciliating concessions on the other. The former of course are normatively described in most Irish and British historiography as 'ultra' Protestants; and not without justification often with the prefix 'fervent' or 'bigoted'. But such adjectives are rarely used to identify an 'ultra' Catholic equivalent, whereas Croker and his circle saw them as equally responsible for exploiting atavistic prejudice and exacerbating sectarian division. Furthermore, they believed that Daniel O'Connell, although not an 'ultra' himself, cynically played a leading part in this after 1813, in particular after 1819, by aligning himself with the ultra Catholic clergy and petty elites who were diverting popular disaffection onto religious issues in order to empower themselves. Thereby in the circle's view, ultimately destroying their ambitions to improve the state of Ireland, unite its people within the Union and relieve the poor.

Croker took some satisfaction in believing that his political ideas represented something of a tradition of Irish thought opposing 'extremes' and promoting reform and 'protectionist' social unity since Molyneaux and Swift, reaching its apogee within the writing of his hero, Edmund Burke. His press circle shared most of the same views, and would constitute one of the most successful groups of press writers in Britain and Ireland during the first half of the nineteenth century. Notable among its members were William Maginn of *Fraser's Magazine*, Stanley Lees Giffard of the *Standard*, George Croly editor of the *Guardian* and *Monthly Magazine*, Mortimer and Samuel O'Sullivan of *Blackwood's* and the *Dublin University Magazine*, and Theodore Hook of *John Bull*. As we will see, they were early campaigners for radical social and economic reforms in both Britain and Ireland, and many of their ideas had much more in common with modern perceptions of good government and social interventionism than their rivals. But as one of the few scholars familiar with some of their publications remarks, although representing a strong current in popular politics in the 1820s and 1830s, their work has 'suffered the neglect and misunderstanding of most lost causes',[5] after being subsumed beneath the triumphal twin orthodoxies of Catholic proto-nationalism in Ireland and free-trade economics in Britain.

Between 1810 and 1840, their periodicals and newspapers were highly popular in Britain and Ireland; and like many of their political antecedents, their talents as satirists and often acerbic literary reviewers helped win them an even greater readership. Unfortunately for their reputations, however, many of their targets would later become some of the most iconicised figures of literary, political and cultural studies. In Croker's case, as one admirer of Lady Morgan describes, initiating a tradition of vituperative literary defamations 'of the kind few men have ever had to endure in a single lifetime'.[6] Percy Shelley furiously denounced him for having murdered Keats with a cruel review; William Hazlitt and Leigh Hunt caricatured him as an evil Tory press 'svengali' and 'talking Irish potato', and even a young Conservative admirer, Benjamin Disraeli, later famously portrayed him as Rigby, a 'political toady' with a 'malevolent spirit' and 'restless instinct for adroit baseness'.[7] Harriet Martineau perhaps best captured this enduring enmity, when despite Croker only reviewing one of her publications many years before, she published a coruscating obituary in a national daily in 1857 celebrating the departure of 'the unhappy old man' with a 'malignant ulcer of the mind' and the 'knock-down temperament' of an 'Irishman at a fair'.[8]

Together with the lively political activities of the press circle, such passionate rivalry makes any study of them not only entertaining, but academically rewarding, because rather than rouse much curiosity among successive generations of scholars, there appears to have been a convention of largely unexamined disapproval rather than research into their ideas. When Croker is mentioned at all today it is usually as a 'slashing' reviewer with reiterations of him as 'the python of humbug' who 'hated [George] Canning and his liberal Toryism' and 'opposed Catholic Emancipation'; 'no-one could lash a woman like Croker',[9] the 'sworn enemy of reform in every shape'[10] with an almost 'fanatical detestation of anything modern'.[11] The only extracts of his extensive writing re-published within an Irish academic work remain a few sections taken from his early Dublin pamphlets in the *Field Day Anthology of Irish Writing* (1991). This is to the credit of its editor, but the remarks he made in two other publications perhaps better illustrate why some Irish figures continue to remain beyond the pale in most areas of Irish studies. Croker was a 'consistently bitter opponent of the Catholic claims', sharing Peel's 'acrid views on these issues',[12] and 'when Yeats told the Senate that the Anglo-Irish were "no petty people", he was evidently not thinking of the John Wilson Croker type': a man who 'reduced Burke's thought to the mean proportions of his own intellect – a considerable feat'.[13]

But if one looks beyond the campaigns of his early detractors, and as any fairly rudimentary examination of *Hansard's*, the newspapers of the period or Croker's own writing will illustrate, almost all of the specific accusations listed above are inaccurate, and most of the more subjective assessments difficult to sustain. Croker would deservedly earn his reputation as the leading Commons opponent of the Great Reform Act (1831–2), and Whig historians like Macaulay barracked him accordingly, but an important feature of this study will be to show that the promotion of reforms was a vital element of Croker's political philosophy. In 1820 he drew up a plan for extensive parliamentary reform, but his political leaders rejected it. In 1822, 1827 and 1828 he continued to press them 'to lead and control the Reform movement rather than be controlled by it', but with little more success.[14] As he argued near the end of his life in an effort by then left too late to correct his detractors, he had 'never been a *Retardataire* ... I have always advocated, and *pro-viribus* advanced all progress that I thought improvement, but I always wished *improvement* to be based on *experiment*.' Like Burke, who he praised as 'that wisest statesman, that patriarch of rational reform', Croker argued that corrective reforms were 'wholesome and indispensable' and that good government should lead them before popular disaffection was exploited by radical extremists threatening the established political framework.[15]

When examining Croker's relationship with Peel, we will see that while the latter was certainly a dedicated enemy of Catholic Emancipation, and toasted 'three time three' as the young 'Protestant Champion', Croker, rather than being a 'bitter' opponent, was in fact among the most active campaigners for it. In his earliest Irish pamphlets he argued that Emancipation was a justice in itself as well as a unifying inclusive measure; presciently insisting that it should be led by government before ultra-Catholics made it an emotive 'panaceatic' for all the misery suffered by the Irish masses. In 1817 he compiled the first successful post-Union measure of Catholic Relief: for 'near-equal' status in the armed forces, described in *The Times* as a 'wise, temperate and conciliatory measure' designed to herald full Emancipation,[16] and in 1819, he seconded Henry Grattan's ultimate Emancipation bill with a much more extensive series of arguments (occupying twenty-eight columns of *Hansard's*). Rather than 'hate Canning' the 'liberal' Tory, in 1827, when most others resigned from his ministry because he was pro-Emancipation, Croker served as one of his closest advisors. Having advocated the measure all his life, he had few political qualms about doing so other than another Burkeian one of concern for party unity and fear of parliamentary factions. All of which will be examined in the first and second chapters, and of particular significance for the main hypothesis, within his long 1819 pro-Emancipation speech, Croker would make his first extensive parliamentary statement of what would become Conservative party principles when mocking ultra-Protestant notions of the fixity of the constitution.

In March 1825 he seconded another Emancipation bill and campaigned for it behind the scenes with Canning and a mixed party group.[17] Among the latter was Daniel O'Connell, the 'Catholic Champion', who Croker had known personally since they were young lawyers, and was, he believed, finally willing to support conciliatory concessions because his opposition had made him by then the unchallengeable 'Alpha and Omega' of the Catholic movement.[18] Voted down in the Lords, Croker later saw this as the last opportunity for 'conciliatory Emancipation'. Robert Peel was probably most responsible for its failure, and as with his view of O'Connell, Croker would have rejected what would become the posthumous promotion of Peel as a proto 'liberal' and most 'sagacious politician of his day'.[19] Their relationship will be a continuous feature of the main study examining Croker's role and interpretations of events in British politics between 1812 and 1835. A closely associated lesser one will be his and the press circle's refutations of the orthodox interpretation of the Catholic Association as a 'progressive' and enlightened development in Irish history. While they were particularly well placed to judge these events, and, of course, their testimony should not necessarily be given any more weight than others, its continued neglect and dismissal has been to the detriment of Irish historical studies of this period in much the same manner the 'whig interpretation' was in concealing a broader understanding of political history in Britain.

The British view of their determinist tradition has been much revised, but despite the efforts of many 'revisionist' Irish historians, as one respected European scholar of literature and nationalism recently described 'for all the post-modern, post Marxist or post-colonial theoretical insights, Irish critics on the whole' continue to 'evince no desire to query, and indeed choose to follow and confirm the patterns of self-definition formulated by nineteenth-century nationalists'.[20] Something additionally appropriate for this study where literary and cultural studies are concerned, because Croker and the circle would be early and indignant challengers to what Joep Leerssen goes on to describe as the 'appropriation' if not 'invention' of an Irish cultural tradition that would eventually exclude their alternative discourse. Some of the circle's views of what they saw as a conspiracy of 'ultra' Catholics are naturally unappealing and encourage accusations of bigotry, but this has distracted attention from their more extensive work calling for a radical programme of social reforms, such as Poor Laws for Ireland, taxation of landowners, rentiers and manufacturers; most of which were opposed by their rivals. Rather than getting too bogged down in speculations of who was or was not a bigot, this study will seek to assess their ideas and opinions in their historical context and concentrate on their more important associated campaigns between 1829 and 1835 when they had their greatest influence in 'inventing' and promulgating the principles of the new Conservative party.

Croker was the leading authority on the early period of the French Revolution, and his collection of Revolutionary newspapers, pamphlets and personally gathered testimonies (numbering over 58,000 items, and the largest in the British Library)[21] illustrate his concern that the press was the main vector of revolution. But he also believed it was the best antidote, and although it must always be borne in mind that he was well able to 'spin' for his party, as William Thomas, one of the few scholars familiar with his writing and his archives describes, in his histories Croker's 'central preoccupation and his strongest instinct was the presentation of the record'.[22] Herbert Butterfield dedicated a chapter of his own canonical study to Croker's eighteenth-century history, praising him for having the 'specialised outlook of the technical historian',[23] and today most political historians would find themselves more in agreement with Croker's view of political events in Britain than with the 'whig interpretation'. However, in contrast to Macaulay's hugely influential work, until recently most of Croker's substantial collection of correspondence and diaries had remained within the auction boxes delivered to their US university purchasers in the 1920s. They have only ever received any extensive attention from three or four scholars, and together with his almost equally neglected *Quarterly Review* articles, their contents when examined here will, I believe, contribute towards a better understanding of a number of contested issues in British political history.

In January 1830, eleven months before Reform agitation drove the last Tory ministry from office, the term 'Conservative party' was used for the first time within a *Quarterly Review* article: 'We always have been, decidedly and conscientiously attached to what is called the Conservative party ... Some of this party object to all change whatever,' whereas 'we have no hesitation in stating it to be our conviction' that we 'are as anxious to promote prudent and practicable amelioration of the state as any of their fellow subjects'.[24] The sentiments it represented were essentially the same Croker had advocated since he was a young Dublin pamphleteer, and after 1831 he would promote the same political ideas in the *Quarterly*, the most authoritative publication of the new Conservative party and the theoretical flagship for the other publications of the press circle. As we will see in the final two chapters, with his first speeches against the Whig Reform bill Croker introduced what would become the basic policy and tactics of his party's parliamentary opposition. Over the next sixteen months he led a filibustering battle against the bill, but as a corollary he used this tactic to build support for his new party in the Commons and in the press during a period when no political event had been more avidly followed and the 'electorate responded with a new degree of inter-election partisan loyalty'.[25] In the three years after 1831, and before Peel and their leaders publicly acknowledged them with the *Tamworth Manifesto* in December 1834, Croker and the press circle were 'inventing' the principles of the new Conservative party and promoting them to their readers as a *via media* where moderates could unite against 'Ultras' and conciliate popular concerns with the reform of proven abuses. The conflict was between two parties: the '*Conservative* and *Destructive*' Croker emphasised, and

Edmund Burke 'has left us in clear beautiful words the safe rule of conduct' for reform: '"a disposition to preserve and an ability to improve"', 'of remedy and reparation' rather than 'subversion and revolution'. This was 'the legacy of Burke, Windham, or even Grattan and Fox', and any moderate Whig or moderate Tory ought, by 'the principles of those great men, to be now Conservatives'.[26]

NOTES

1. H. Reeves (ed.), *The Greville Memoirs, A Journal of the Reign of King George IV, King William IV and Queen Victoria, by Charles Greville*, 8 vols (London, 1888), vol. viii, p.122.
2. See John Summerson, *Georgian London* (Middlesex, 1969 [Pelican edition]), p 201.
3. Myron Brightfield, *John Wilson Croker* (New York, 1940), pp.91–2, 403. This remains the only biography of Croker and deals mainly with his literary career. In 1940 Brightfield first refuted Croker's responsibility for inventing the term; we will examine the validity of this in Chapter 3.
4. R.J. White, *The Conservative Tradition* (London, 1964), p.11. See also Duncan Watts, *Tories, Conservatives and Unionists: 1815–1914* (London, 1994), p.54. It is important to note here that a number of political historians have challenged the significance of the Tamworth Manifesto, some of whom will be cited below, but it is still commonly seen outside, and within some, academic circles as the founding document of the Conservative party.
5. Harold Perkin, *The Origins of Modern English Society* (London, 1969), pp.239–40.
6. Lionel Stevenson, 'Vanity Fair and Lady Morgan', *PMLA*, 48, 2 (June 1933), p.547.
7. Taken from Benjamin Disraeli's *Coningsby* (London, 1959 [1844]); see in particular pp.7, 8, 9, 13, 23.
8. See my PhD thesis, 'The Intellectual and Political World of John Wilson Croker: Ideas, Circles and Conservatism' (NUI Galway, 2007), Chapter 9, Section 5 for a fuller account and *The Press*, 15 August 1857 for the Martineau obituary.
9. Jane Ridley, *The Young Disraeli* (London, 1995), pp.38–45.
10. Gamaliel Milner, *The Threshold of the Victorian Age* (London, 1934), p.70.
11. Fergus Fleming, *Barrow's Boys: A Stirring Story of Daring, Fortitude and Outright Lunacy* (London, 1999), p.10.
12. Thomas Moore, *Thomas Moore: Memoirs of Captain Rock*, ed. Emer Nolan with annotations by Seamus Deane (Dublin, 2008), p.212.
13. Seamus Deane, *Celtic Revivals: Essays in Modern Irish Literature* (London, 1985), pp.22, 30.
14. *Croker Papers*, II, p.54.
15. Ibid., Croker to John Murray, 24 October 1851, III, pp.244–5; and *Quarterly Review*, 'Sir Robert Peel's address', February 1835, pp.278–83.
16. *The Times*, 11 July 1817; and see *Parliamentary Acts*, vol. 7, 57, George III, cap. 9.
17. *Hansard*, XII, 785, 28 February 1825. See also *Croker Papers*, 12 March 1825, I, pp.279–80; Duke MS, box 3 misc. uncatalogued.
18. J.W. Croker, *State of Ireland: Letters Re-published from the Courier* (London, 1825), pp.11–14.
19. Norman Gash, *Reaction and Reconstruction in English Politics, 1832–52* (Oxford, 1965), p.184; see also Boyd Hilton's famous challenge, 'Peel: A Reappraisal', *The Historical Journal*, 23, 3 (1979), pp.585–619 and Ian Newbould, 'Sir Robert Peel and the Conservative Party: A Study in Failure', *The English Historical Review*, no. 98 (July 1983), pp.529–57.
20. Joep Leerssen, *Hidden Ireland, Public Sphere* (Dublin, 2002), p.20.
21. See A.C. Bradhurst, 'The French Revolutionary Collection in the British Library', *British Library Journal*, vol. 2 (1976), pp.138–58.
22. See William Thomas, *The Quarrel of Macaulay and Croker: Politics and History in the Age of Reform* (Oxford, 2000), pp.177, 187. Thomas is one of the only scholars to have studied the Croker archives, and I am indebted to him for the generous advice he gave me at the start of my own research. See also Chapters 2, 4 and 6 of his study for Croker's role as an historian and an analysis of his political views and influence.
23. Herbert Butterfield, *George III and the Historians* (London, 1957), pp.119–20, and see his chapter entitled 'John Wilson Croker and the Tory View'; see also Thomas, *Quarrel of*

Macaulay and Croker, p.180.

24. *Quarterly Review*, 'Internal Policy', January 1830, pp.276–7.
25. John A. Phillips and Charles Wetherall, 'The Great Reform Act and the Political Moderniza-
    tion of England', *The American Historical Review*, 100, 2 (April 1995), p.427; John Cannon,
    Parliamentary Reform: 1642–1832 (Cambridge, 1973), p.245.
26. *Quarterly Review*, 'Sir Robert Peel's Address' (February 1835), pp.278–83.

CHAPTER ONE

The Power of the Pen and the Press: An Introduction to a Political Life: 1800–21

An author ambitious of *fame* should write the history of transactions that are past, and of men that are no more; [and if] desirous of *profit*, he should seek it from the prejudiced liberality of a party. But he whose object is his country must hope for neither; and shrouded in disinterested obscurity should speak of sects and factions not what they desire, but what they deserve to hear ... This style of writing – least popular, least profitable – is at all times the most difficult; and in bad times the most dangerous, [for] power, always quick in revenge, is quickest in reaching its literary opponents; and the populous is never more slanderous than in arraigning the motives of him who would curb their violence. (J.W. Croker, *A Sketch of the State of Ireland, Past and Present*, 1808)

I. FORMATIVE INFLUENCES

John Wilson Croker spent most of his early childhood in Galway and Newport, County Mayo where his father was stationed as an excise officer.[1] In an attempt to cure a 'most distressing stutter' he was sent to 'an academy kept in Cork by one Knowles, who had married one of the Sheridans, and professed to remedy cacology and teach elocution'.[2] It appears to have been a success, and as the author Sheridan Knowles recalled, the opinionated verbosity Croker would later become famous for perhaps first flourished as his 'dear lamented mother's favourite ... she loved you for your constant good spirits and cordial frankness'.[3] By 1792 he had moved to Willis's school at Portarlington, where a junior boarder 'placed under your protection' reminisced that he was 'at the head of the school, and *facile princeps* in every branch of our course'. The headmaster and 'Mr Doineau, the French teacher ... were proud of your talents and acquirements, as being likely to rebound to the character and credit of the school'. It was here that he attained a 'perfect facility' in 'reading and writing French'[4] from his enlightened but anti-revolutionary émigré schoolmasters, and also what would prove equally lasting lessons on the 'Reign of Terror'. Something he was already receptive to, prefacing a collection of historical essays a few months before he died in 1857:

> I was in my ninth year when the Bastille was taken; it naturally made a great impression on me, and the bloody scenes that so rapidly followed rendered that impression unfavourable. Such also was the view of my wise and excellent parents, and an alliance between our family and that of Mr Burke helped confirm us in that great man's prophetic opinions, which every event from that day to this appears to have wonderfully illustrated and fulfilled.[5]

Just before his sixteenth birthday he entered Trinity College Dublin, and soon distinguished himself as a scholar and a debater in the Historical Society, winning one of its first gold medals for a series of historical essays and establishing lasting friendships with, among others, Thomas Moore, the poet, Bartholomew Lloyd, his tutor and later provost of the college, Percy Clinton Smythe, later Lord Strangford, and George Croly, press-man, poet and early biographer of Edmund Burke.[6]

Jonah Barrington described Croker as looking strikingly like Wolfe Tone,[7] and like Tone he was also a declared Irish patriot, but when his lookalike was attempting to make Ireland independent of the British connection, Croker was a student volunteer standing guard outside Dublin Castle defending it as best for his country. According to Moore, he had been sympathetic to the United Irish ambitions and probably an early signatory, but in 1798 he became a dedicated opponent of political extremists who exploited 'evils, real or imaginary', when the spirit of the 'French Revolution, having filled its own country brimful with misery', ignited divisive 'monstrous and inevitable' evils in ours. In Ulster, politics, 'elsewhere bigotry: the Dissenter fought, the Papist massacred, the Loyalist cut down both'.[8] One of his earliest published works was a song published after the conflict, together with two by Thomas Moore, containing the harmonic repetition: 'All bards' should 'raise the song and strike the harp ... the fields of Erin are glad in peace once more, raise ye hundred bards the voice of peace'.[9] Its simple lines an early illustration of the conciliatory ambitions both the 'Tory' Croker and the 'Whig' Moore would share throughout their lives for a peaceful united Ireland.

By the time of the Act of Union, Croker's father had been appointed surveyor of Dublin Customs on a salary of £800 pa. Described by Edmund Burke as 'a man of great abilities and most amiable manners; an able and upright public steward, universally respected and beloved in private life',[10] his rise in fortune, however, was more the result of lobbying by the Beresford family and Lord Shannon in return for assisting them with an accomplishment his son appears to have shared at the remarkably precocious age of nine:

> I was an early dabbler in political squibling. There happened to be an election for the County Cork severely contested; and prolific of a deluge of lampoons. I forget the date: I suppose about 1789. There were three candidates: a Mr Morris was one. He was my father's and, I suppose Lord Shannon's friend, and I wrote at least one piece of prose on his side, which was printed; it was a dialogue. I wish I could recover it. As I was born on the last days (20th) of Dec. 1780 it was probable that this election had something to do with my father's visit to Castle Martyr, and Lord Shannon's notice of me.[11]

Like many other talented Irish 'parvenus' of his class, Croker clearly had early ambitions for a political career and saw his pen as the best vehicle to attain it. His family connections with the dominant Pittite parliamentary group gave him an advantage, but he was clearly welcome in wider Irish political circles. In October 1799 William Drennan, the United Irishman and poet, received a letter from his sister Martha saying she had heard interesting reports about young Croker, and in August 1800 he told her that Croker had just visited him: 'very agreeable, genteel and fashionable, just from London, full of paradox, and natural good principle, put into proper training in Mr Beresford's, his father's patron'. This was in contrast to a fellow guest, 'the boldest, most ill-bred boy I ever saw is Mrs Emmet's son – in jail with his father is the very place for him, he is indeed a liberty boy.'[12] Maria Edgeworth praised Croker's precocious literary talents, and when he joined the lawyers on the Munster circuit in 1802 he had what he called a 'sharp encounter' with Daniel O'Connell who attempted to 'try my mettle' at their reception. After which, and despite being on opposite political sides for most of their careers, Croker continued, 'we were always on the most good humoured terms ... and the very last time I saw him ... the year before his death, [O'Connell] opened his arms and enveloped me in a strict embrace *à la Francaise* to the astonishment of his own tail.'[13]

Croker's first successful political pamphlet was a defence of Lord Hardwicke's handling of the Emmet rebellion in July 1803. Within it he ridiculed the political opposition and their newspapers for exaggerating the threat[14] and condemned revolutionary violence and agitators in the same manner as his hero, Burke. They were 'political hyenas ... eager and insatiable' to 'propagate calumnies ... I know them, and the causes of their anger'; a 'very brigade of bad passions' and a 'terrible self-devouring malignity' inspired their deadly ambitions. Hardwicke was praised for responding resolutely to extra-parliamentary threats, as good government should, but also for his 'prudence, circumspection, clemency and the justice of his government' for having tried to win 'back the hearts of the seditious ... and enabled our most happy escape from a repetition of the horrors of 1798'.[15]

As we will see, Croker would be a patriotic advocate of reforms to improve the state of Ireland, and felt some sympathy for Emmet as victim of his own deluded obsessions, but a significant feature of his writing would be criticisms of the 'making of the legend'[16] around figures like Emmet, viewing it as both historically fraudulent and calculatedly divisive propaganda:

> It is absurd ... about Emmet, I knew him and until he came to be hanged, I do not believe he was suspected of being a great man – he was a party zealot and a poor fellow, and a victim, and, of course, his party will swear he was Demosthenes and Brutus. But I confess I thought him no very uncommon person. The only thing I thought remarkable was with all his (now known) turbulence and enthusiasm that he seemed so quiet and dull.[17]

While Emmet would become a 'Demosthenes' of Irish nationalist history, Croker saw his own political philosophy of support for a conciliatory *via media*, but resolute opposition to 'abstract theorists' literary radicals and 'ultras' of any political or religious kind as part of a much more neglected 'tradition' of Irish polemics and political thought.

Jonathan Swift was one of its foundational writers and thinkers, and his *Battle of the Books* and more famous *Tale of a Tub*, written in the late 1690s, was inspired by Swift's own experiences of the twin 'extremes' of 'Dissenter' and 'Papistry' when he had been a young curate in Ulster. The 'frenzy and spleen of both, having the same foundations', and in contrast to the favoured Anglican tradition, seen as the moderate tolerant alternative to both, each extreme was playing the other's divisive and 'murderous' game.[18] Almost twenty-five years before Gulliver's mockery of deluded Laputans, Swift was ridiculing the Cartesian solipsists for weaving 'venomous' webs of their own substance in order 'to set their own philosophical systems, the creations of their own individual faculties, over the accumulated wisdom of the past'. It was from such 'Grand Innovators' that the 'disposition arises in mortal man, of taking into his head, to advance such systems with such an eager Zeal'. They are 'the parent of all mighty revolutions that have happened in Empire, in Philosophy and in Religion'; for when 'man's fancy gets astride his reason … common Understanding as well as Common sense is kicked out of doors'.[19]

Burke later adopted similar arguments, and they are of course famously evident in his *Reflections on the Revolution in France* wherein he railed against 'political theologians and theological politicians', 'arch innovators' and 'literary caballers' on behalf of moderation and what is usually described today as a conservative political philosophy of custom. 'The pretended rights of these theorists are all in extremes, and in proportion as they are metaphysically true, they are morally and politically false. The rights of men are in the *middle* … in compromises sometimes between good and evil … and the first of all virtues, prudence'.[20] Throughout his political life Croker would draw upon Burke to promulgate and adapt these same political principles, and to a lesser extent the legacy of Swift, William Molyneaux and Oliver Goldsmith, to represent his conservative political philosophy as a 'middle' way firmly opposed to the 'ultras', but a moderate reforming tradition encouraging social unity in deference to custom over abstract ideological innovation.

In the same pamphlet defending Hardwicke, Croker also criticised the developing literary tide of what has been described as the 'invention' or 'appropriation' of what would become modern Irish popular culture.[21] 'The art which is practised by almost every comic playwright of the present day [is to] introduce an Irishman … and a complete *Paddy* starts up to entertain the delighted audience.' They are 'are in a

national respect, real insults' and 'would become an object of indignation to Irishmen, were it not seasoned by fulsome affections of praise
of Ireland and the Irish character ... surely we should repel the insult'.[22]
In his more successful 'anonymous' *Familiar Epistles to Frederick E.
Jones on the Present State of the Irish Stage* (1804), and representative
of the tone of many of his later more famous *Quarterly Review* articles,
he continued these arguments when ridiculing Jones's contrived pro-
ductions by calling for an Irish national theatre to replace such 'maudlin
farce and melodrama' so that works of 'natural Irish good taste', such as
Sheridan's and Congreve's, could 'grace our stages'.[23]

His pamphlets ran 'through Ireland like fire and smoke causing
consternation on every side',[24] and Drennan wrote to his sister that
Croker was 'a genius and, I hope, he will not flag in any future publications'.[25] Not surprisingly, Frederick Jones, a leading figure in Dublin's
Whiggish *beau monde*, found this slur on his abilities and the potential
damage to his highly profitable dominance of a number of Dublin's
playhouses much less appealing.[26] The *Freeman's Journal* launched
some appropriately melodramatic attacks on the 'infamous scribbler' of
the *Familiar Epistles*, who had delivered a literary 'stab', even putting
one actor (who had apparently died from drink) in an 'untimely bier'.[27]
Whereas the rival *Dublin Journal*, whose ultra-Protestant editor, John
Giffard, was a Custom House colleague of Croker's father, praised it
for drawing attention to the 'degraded state of national drama'.[28] But
a much more intensive and serious counter-attack provided Croker
with an early lesson in the personal risks of engaging in controversial
polemics, and perhaps the riskiest of all, offending literary egos. Sydney Owenson, later famous as Lady Morgan, and her father were members of Jones's circle, and she orchestrated or played a leading part in
a more sinister campaign against the 'anonymous' author whose 'ambition to gain celebrity' had broken 'all the bounds of modesty and
decorous behaviours' with 'cowardly indecent expressions of hatred
against the female part of our performers'.[29]

While Croker was certainly pursuing an ambition to gain celebrity,
references to 'indecency' or 'hatred' against the female performers were
hardly an explicit part of his pamphlet. However, those readers left
wondering at these references soon discovered why, when she instigated what the only other scholar who appears to have studied Croker's
archives as well as Owenson's side of the story described as a 'violent,
indecent and contemptible affair' designed to destroy Croker's personal reputation[30] and even raise deadlier attention of Dublin's many

eager duellists. In a pamphlet entitled *Cutchacutchoo or the Jostling of the Innocents*, young society ladies were identified in all but name as being manipulated by the sinister 'Cr—er' who had invented a corrupting new dance encouraging them to wind their 'petticoats tightly round themselves and bend into a posture as near as sitting as possible' and then jump around until they are bowled over; whereupon 'Cr—r cries God damn my eyes! Let each squat down upon her ham, jump like a goat, puck like a ram.'[31] Croker rushed into print with a refutation, and fortunately for him such accusations appeared too exaggerated to be believed, but a remark that he should move to London where 'if he went to Grub Street ... he might earn half a guinea per week by writing verses' was much more accurate.[32]

Owenson socialised in many of the same circles as Croker, and knew that when attending the Inns as a young articled lawyer he had written for the London newspapers despite it being a disbarring offence. His pamphlet criticising Jones was in the style as William Gifford's mockery of early Romantics, or 'Della Cruscans', and Gifford had been the editor of the *Anti-Jacobin or Weekly Examiner*, established in 1797 by Pitt's most talented political protégé George Canning, to counter the Foxite Whig press.[33] In 1809, Gifford would become the first editor of the *Quarterly Review*, founded by John Murray, Walter Scott, George Ellis and Canning, with Croker as a junior member, but they had first met in London in 1800, when Croker had written his first article for *The Times*. This was a satirical account of imaginary conversations between the French revolutionary and regicide, Tallien, who Croker portrayed as a sinister ghoul obsessed with insurrection on a tour of London with his increasingly nervous Whig hosts. Tallien admired London's 'boulevards', but only for their facility '*pour les fusillades*'; at the Tower of London he was delighted by the places of execution, and when they visited the zoo the savage tigers purred in deference to one of their own kind, and to the horror of the now trembling Foxites, he bought a pet dog from a passer-by and flung it as a tit-bit to his ferocious admirers.[34]

Croker also wrote for a 'Church and King' organisation called the 'Pic Nic Society' run by Henry Francis Greville. In one of the few letters surviving identifying Croker's early connections with the press, Greville described an article he had written as 'so good humoured and delightful, it will be almost thrown away putting it in the *Oracle*, I shall send it to the [*Morning*] *Post*'. They also produced plays together that were, apparently, little more original and clearly more overtly propagandist than those Croker would criticise in Dublin two years later. One, a French play, 'the Smiths, you and I have to take an act each and "englishify" it instantly and then get [undecipherable] to act it for the benefit of volunteers or by subscription'.[35] The Pic Nic Society produced its own weekly paper, the *Pic-Nic*, and when its editor, William Combe, was gaoled for debt in 1803, Croker was in London again and Greville called a meeting of the contributors and declared his new plan:

> He had engaged a young Irishman of surpassing talent, who for a weekly honorarium, not exceeding what was paid to Combe, would undertake to get up and edit the whole paper. So saying he left the room, and returned with Mr John Wilson Croker, who under the impression that he was to be intellectually trotted out before the company, began instantly to exhibit his conversational powers, which were even then of a high order, with all the ardour and copiousness of an aspiring Hibernian.[36]

The title was changed to the more politically ambitious *Cabinet*, but 'want of aim, of method, of money, and even of the talent and political intelligence that give popularity to a newspaper, were impediments to the success which not all the abilities of the new editor' could overcome. 'After a sickly existence of a few months', and despite Croker recruiting the assistance of some other young tyros like Thomas Moore, the *Cabinet* closed. [37]

He returned to Dublin and, according to Maria Edgeworth, his next major pamphlet, *An Intercepted letter from J—— T——, esq. writer at Canton, to his friend in Dublin* (1804), contained 'one of the best views of Dublin ever seen, evidently drawn by the hand of a master, though in a slight playful and unusual style'.[38] Written in the style of letters from an oriental traveller reporting on Ireland that Goldsmith had used and in parts also evocative of Swift's *Modest Proposal* and *Drapier's Letters*, it was re-published seven times in the first year, and represented Croker's first successful advocacy of social and economic reforms to improve the state of Ireland. The authorities were criticised for allowing public works to be mismanaged by cronies and erecting public buildings on a grand scale while people lived in hovels; the water supply was broken down; the quays in ruins, and the university failed to encourage scholarship. Dublin shops sold inferior English goods at high prices, and although the character of the Irish people, both Catholic and Protestant, was 'adorned by the purest blaze of virtue and wisdom', it was also 'marked with the extremist shades of folly and wickedness':

> A hundred thousand of them will take the field for an abstract question of religion or politics, which not ten of them understand and not one cares about ... They are so generous that their houses and hearts are open to the stranger [yet] nothing will awaken their public spirit but evil knocking at their own door ... They will suffer any privation for you, but will embark on no action but for themselves ... Nothing could be more ridiculous than that two neighbours should be willing to cut one another's throats because one chooses to travel one path to God and their neighbour another.[39]

Enlightened education to encourage tolerance and unity, and even 'dances, bands and music ... and football are better preventives of civil disturbances than the threatening of penal laws and the example of capital punishment.' If the government wished to win the loyalty of the Catholics for the Union, then 'apply all your spare land to the production of provisions ... make all your people rich, and then they will have something to fight for' and then we 'need not fear the influence of foreign emperors'.[40]

Although willing to criticise the establishment, Croker clearly had his eye on winning patronage to achieve a parliamentary seat. In 1806, he married Rosamund, one of the many daughters of William Pennell, deputy comptroller of Waterford Customs, and according to William Drennan, neither 'handsome, nor fortune'.[41] Whatever the truth of this ungracious remark, they would remain devoted to each other all their lives, and despite having 'no fortune' to fund it, later that same year Croker nearly fulfilled his ambition to become an MP while serving as a solicitor for the Rowley family at the Downpatrick election when their son, Josiah, a naval officer, was called to sea and they offered him the opportunity to stand in his place. He lost by just thirteen votes, but in February 1807 the Mayo MP and Irish 'Leviathan' of patronage, Denis Browne, a family friend since his childhood, wrote saying he would try and get him a seat, and that 'there are few opportunities of my life I would value more than any that would enable me to serve you.'[42] This proved unnecessary, when in June following the fall of the 'Ministry of all the Talents', Sir Arthur Wellesley (later the Duke of Wellington), the new Irish chief secretary, solicited the funds for him to run again at Downpatrick. Following a violent contest Croker won by just a few votes as the 'Pittite', or what he would later describe as the fore-runners of the 'Conservative party', the 'Enlightened Tory' candidate, initiating a close political and personal relationship with Wellington that would last until the latter's death in 1852.[43]

Croker delivered his maiden speech on his first day in the House of Commons by making a combative response to Whig members of the opposition for taking up the time of the House 'in hearing contest for places and power' and encouraging division 'when the map of Europe was only another word almost for the map of France'.[44] He then addressed Henry Grattan, a Whig, but a compatriot he had long admired, arguing that he too 'wished for the inhabitants of Ireland the full benefits of the constitution ... but that was a thing not to be won in half a session of Parliament' and 'without unanimity nothing could be effectual there'. However, like Grattan, he too defended Irish Catholics, arguing that the recent rebellions were more the work of 'demagogues and Jacobins and French emissaries' than 'genuine Roman Catholics', but it was not unreasonable for Protestants to seek proof of their good intentions with a temporary moratorium on Emancipation.[45]

A parliamentary reporter later described Croker as having never lost his Irish accent and 'the very finest speaker, but his elocution is some-what impaired by the circumstance of his not being able to pronounce the letter R', and sometimes by becoming overly emotional making 'violent gestures, sometimes theatrically so'.[46] Croker claimed that he had not planned to make a speech on his first day; he had been roused by the ill-informed comments of the opposition, but his passionate declarations won him the immediate attention of his party leaders. 'Canning whom I had never seen before, asked Mr Foster MP [and former Speaker of the Irish Commons] to introduce me to him after the division, was very kind, and walked home with me to my lodg-ings.'[47] Croker's reputation rose rapidly within the first year. Arthur Wellesley, not noted for casual effusions of praise, wrote to the Duke of Richmond in Dublin: 'It is impossible to describe to you the interest which the latter has created in the House.'[48] Around this same time, he also sent Croker a memorandum dealing with a proposal for the Crown to have the right to veto Catholic episcopal appointments as part of a plan to facilitate Catholic Emancipation. Following this, and with Wellington's assistance, Croker wrote his most significant single publi-cation on Irish affairs.[49]

His *Sketch of the State of Ireland, Past and Present* (1808) would be republished at least twenty-two times in legitimate editions alone over the next two decades, and it has deservedly been described by one of the few scholars familiar with it as the first directly applied Irish 'national history' that sought to 'demolish the sectarian myths cherished by various parties in Ireland' and promote national unity 'as clearly as Tone or Emmet had done the common name of Irishman'.[50] Croker argued that ultra-Protestant hostility to Catholic Emancipation was half the problem, but militant Catholics who opposed conciliatory concessions such as the right of episcopal veto that was freely accepted by the Anglican Church were equally intransigent and divisive. 'All men write and speak' of Emancipation, 'but few candidly – its supporters and its opponents are equally injudicious or unjust; the reason is that the parties of the state have divided the question between them'. Like the two political factions of the Roman Empire, 'the green and the blue distracted the civilized world ... they bled for their party not for its symbol. Catholic emancipation is the green and blue of Ireland, the colour of division not cause rather than the real object of the war between the religious parties.'

> How else could half a nation so pertinaciously seek, and the other half refuse, an almost empty privilege? How else can it have happened that every concession has produced such a commotion, and complaint increased as the grievance disappeared? ... yet to the Catholic code is attributed all our misfortunes. The truth is the parties have made the question and not the question the parties.[51]

The neglect 'of the conquerors, the degeneracy of the colonist, and the obstinacy of the natives', 'Orangemen and Defenders, coercers and revolutionists ... the English administration and the Irish director have divided between them, the press and the nation'.[52] All shared some responsibility for retarding Ireland's unity and development. Catholic Emancipation was a necessary component of an enlightened programme, for then might 'one torch of discord at least be extinguished'. It was, however, essentially a 'panaceatic' and must be accompanied by more practical reforms if the divided communities were to unite and play a shared part in the Union. For '*Who* can be emancipated from *what*?'

> At most six Lords, one hundred and fifty commoners, and twenty ecclesiastics – from four or five disabilities, which reach not, interest not, the mass of their community. Theorists trace from the political exclusion of the peer the

mental debasement of the peasant ... I reason that ... there are previous paramount duties; that enlightening two millions of Catholics is more important than indulging two hundred.[53]

The Catholic clergy should be paid by the state and a property tax established to replace Church tithe payment rather than let it become the focus of religious contention. The condition of the peasantry 'is still almost barbarous'. Not least because the absentee 'nobility and affluent gentry ... spend much or all of their fortunes and time in England', leaving their places to be filled by a 'series of sub-landlords and tenants' each receiving a profit at the expense of the 'miserable tenantry'.[54] 'The tenure at will is indefinite oppression ... rents are not the *proportions* of, but nearly the *whole* produce, and in contrast to England where the law of public opinion, as well as the law of reason, terrifies a landlord from plundering of his own estate', the 'cultivator is seldom better paid than by scanty food, ragged raiment and a miry hovel ... and the peasant and the land are alike neglected, impoverished, and starved'.[55]

History was used to deceive rather than enlighten, and in this manner a 'great nation wastes its strength and reputation in antiquated follies and differences'.[56] The 'Protestant is not blameless with regard to the Catholic nor the Catholic with regard to the Protestant',[57] Catholics should be 'admitted to all the honours of their profession', but the 'barbarous customs and superstitions' of Irish Catholicism should not be 'confounded with one of the same name professed by the enlightened nations of Europe'. The Catholic poor 'are weapons wielded by the gentry at elections, and by demagogues against the gentry in rebellions', and the Catholic priests must 'co-operate in a generous system of national education' and 'advance learning – you SHALL not impede it!'[58] All 'nominal but degrading distinction should be abolished in a nation that fears the name degradation, more even than a reality', and the 'Catholic lawyer, soldier, sailor gentry, priest hood and nobility should all be admitted to all the honours of their professions and ranks'. 'Emancipate all our people; vivify your country ... not in extremities but within the heart.'[59]

As Joseph Spence has argued, Croker 'hoped his reading of Irish history could unite Irishmen and encourage Englishmen to redress their grievances', and his pamphlet probably represented the first to patriotically define 'the parameters of Irish Tory nationality and ecumenism for the post 1832 generation of biographers'.[60] Of greater significance for this study, and as we will see, Croker would also use essentially the same ideas and arguments in the early 1830s for good government to promote the conciliatory reform of proven abuses and defence of customary institutions, when representing the 'Conservative party' as the unitary *via media* for moderate Whigs and moderate Tories.

In the middle of his *State of Ireland*, Croker identified William Molyneux's *Case of Ireland* (1698) as 'the dawn of political discussion' that 'shook the presumption of one [the English] parliament and fortified the confidence of the other [the Irish]; hence a more modern policy'.[61] Burke, Grattan and Pitt were also praised, and Swift featured as an early proponent of patriotic Irish conciliation and moderation:

> Personal resentment was perhaps the first motive of the patriotism of Swift, but it assumed in its progress a higher port, and directed itself by nobler considerations: The jealousy of a partisan soon expanded into the generous devotion of a patriot ... His wisdom was at once practical and prophetic; remedial for the present, warning for the future: he first taught Ireland that she might become a nation, and England that she might cease to be a despot, ... and the foundations of whatever prosperity we have since erected are laid in the disinterested and magnanimous patriotism of Swift.[62]

Thomas Casey, a college friend, wrote that 'no better or finer discussion has appeared' since the days of Burke, 'whose character it is on all sides admitted you have drawn – as he deserves, and for which Ireland stands your debtor'.[63] James Prior, an Ulsterman who published a popular early study of Burke, dedicated it to Croker: Burke's 'eminent countryman who is himself connected to that part of Ireland where Mr Burke spent his earlier years', modelling much of his life on his predecessor, possessing 'much of his taste, much of his love for the Fine Arts, much of his literary talents, and no ordinary share of his devotion to public business'.[64] Comparisons Croker would have found highly flattering, and his early pamphlet echoed Burke's own advice to his son Richard when appointed to advise the Catholic committee in Dublin twenty-five years before. 'It is not about Popes but potatoes that the unhappy people are agitated', and not 'frantick zeal' to overthrow the state or the Anglican Church that they should be 'unwilling, after paying three pounds rent to one gentleman in a brown coat, to pay fourteen shillings to one in a black coat ... to desire some modification of charge'.[65] The same pragmatic principles would be central to Croker's ambitions for Ireland, and underwrite his fear that if government failed to address reform, others who did have a 'frantic zeal' to overthrow the Church and state would exploit popular concerns to do so.

Within months Wellesley appointed Croker his spokesman on Irish affairs during the first year of his Peninsular campaign, and Spencer Perceval, the attorney general, asked him to help organise the defence of the Duke of York over a scandal involving the latter's mistress who had been selling military commissions. The Whigs hoped to bring down the ministry on the issue, but as Canning said in the Commons when praising Croker's forensic attention to detail when presenting the defence, his 'laborious particularity and with convincing clearness by my honourable young friend ... was so completely satisfactory as to make it worse than useless to follow him'. This was an exaggeration, but the ministry survived and when Perceval became prime minister in October 1809 he appointed Croker first secretary of the Admiralty. This was a demanding post at any time, and during wartime a hugely responsible one. He would hold it until November 1830, but the formal proprieties it placed on him participating in some Commons debates, together with the time consumed in effectively managing the Royal Navy, placed substantial restraints on Croker's ability to build a parliamentary career. Within days of taking office he was 'thoroughly and completely in office, and up to my eyes in business, the extent of which is quite terrific'.[66] As he complained to Thomas Moore two years later, he could call on him any time for he was always at his desk. The *Dublin University Magazine* later summarised, his 'zeal, integrity [and] power of simplifying details of complicated machinery' would make him 'almost too useful for his own advancement',[67] and Perceval's other 'young bloods', Henry Goulburn, Frederick Robinson and Robert Peel, would soon move ahead of him.

Croker was a Commons veteran of two years when he first met the new arrival Peel. They socialised together within a fraternity of young politicians in the 'Alfred club' where they shared the same 'political sentiments and literary tastes' and eager ambitions to improve society. They were 'mocked for their earnestness and for their addiction to political gossip, but in their own minds they were merely taking their duties seriously'.[68] Apart from a short interruption during the split of 1827, Croker and Peel would remain close friends for the next forty years, and as the first editor of Peel's private correspondence remarks, Peel, 'normally none too lavish in his effusiveness', made a notable exception for Croker, signing his letters 'yours affectionately from the start'.[69] Norman Gash, Peel's celebrated biographer, describes Goulburn and Croker as his 'two greatest intimates', with Goulburn, 'quiet, solid, completely honest and unswervingly loyal', the 'perfect foil to his more nervous and brilliant companion: John Wilson Croker'.[70]

Croker's relationship with Peel has been the subject of one specific study,[71] but no extensive assessment of his influence has been produced from an examination of Croker's unpublished correspondence held in the North American archives. As we will see, it is clear that Peel placed great value not only upon Croker's friendship – and regularly sought his opinions on art and literature – but more importantly on political affairs and tactics. They would have few differences on Ireland in their early years, and remain close friends, but Croker would perhaps have a little more in common with George Canning, in that he also supported Emancipation, and as the son of a disowned member of the Irish gentry and an Irish actress, he had also made his way in politics with little more than his natural talents and his pen. Furthermore, as James Sack has argued, they were both early promoters of Burke's ideas during a period when a substantial section of Tories 'at best ignored Burke, at worst denounced him and nearly always compared him unfavourably with its *chevalier sans peur et sans reproche*, William Pitt'.[72] While Peel would find much to agree with in Burke, following his appointment as Irish chief secretary in 1812, he would align himself with the opponents of Emancipation and within a few years win the 'blue ribband' seat for Oxford University from Canning, as the young 'Protestant Champion' of the Pitt Clubs; institutions that Croker and Canning despised for misrepresenting Pitt's authentic legacy.[73]

Croker had presciently remarked in his *State of Ireland* that Emancipation must not be left to fester because such a 'nominal but degrading distinction should be abolished in a nation that fears the name of degradation more than the reality itself',[74] and Daniel O'Connell would become the 'Catholic Champion' by campaigning against the Emancipation bill of 1812–13 on the grounds that the Crown having the same right to veto Catholic episcopal appointments that it had with Anglican was a 'degradation'. Given that it also had the provisional support of the Vatican, was approved by bishops in Catholic Quebec and common practice in Europe, Croker and his circle of 'conciliatory Emancipationists' argued that this was a calculatedly cynical tactic to enable him to usurp control of the Catholic movement. Thomas Moore in his

Letter to the Roman Catholics of Dublin, angrily argued that religious 'bigots of both sects are equally detestable', and denounced the O'Connellite faction as exploiting 'anile prejudices'. Despite most Irish Catholics being in favour of mutual concessions, the 'factious would not hesitate to sacrifice the freedom of Ireland and the harmony of the whole empire'.[75] Other contemporary Catholic leaders like Richard Sheil described the anti-veto campaign at this time as swinging British parliamentary opinion against Emancipation and causing it to be 'indefinitely postponed', but unlike Croker and most of his peers, few scholars have seen much significance in O'Connell's campaign, and it has been largely ignored or treated as a curiosity.[76] In the latest biography, for example, the author reflects that 'it is difficult to see why the veto was so controversial', for it was 'perfectly compatible with the doctrines of the Catholic Church', and the affair is passed over in a few sentences.[77] Perhaps, as S.J. Connolly pointed out, the common assumption that the veto had to be opposed better reflects 'the extent to which it was the anti-vetoists who won the contemporary debate',[78] for almost all of O'Connell's contemporary critics of every political and religious persuasion agreed that his motives were self-serving rather than principled. Croker and his allies later believed that O'Connell's ambitions had a formative significance in destroying their ambitions for conciliation by establishing sectarianism at the centre of nineteenth-century Irish politics, and if their views and the influence this would have on their political campaigns are to be properly understood then we will have to spend a little time examining the 'veto controversy'.

On 6 May 1812, Henry Grattan, the parliamentary spokesman for the Catholic Board, proposed a motion to discuss the 'Catholic claims', and a few weeks later Canning moved for a debate upon what securities would be acceptable to protect the Established Church as a preliminary to an Emancipation bill. Castlereagh, the government leader in the Commons, supported the measure if securities such as the veto could be agreed, and despite having been a declared opponent, it was even believed that Spencer Perceval was willing to reach a settlement with Irish Catholic lay leaders. Peel commented that he was 'struck by the lack of feeling on the Protestant side',[79] and Daniel O'Connell privately expressed his own disquiet at what he called the 'insidious' development that Perceval might support the bill.[80] Five days later a crazed bankrupt shot Perceval dead. Lord Liverpool attempted to re-shuffle the cabinet and asked Canning, who had resigned from the ministry following a feud with Castlereagh three years before, to return to office.

Canning refused because 'of your unaltered opinions as to the policy of resisting all consideration of the state of the laws affecting his Majesty's Roman Catholics'.[81] Liverpool replied that he was not inflexible on the matter, and that the main stumbling block would be the Catholic opponents of compromise: 'I will fairly own that in the present state of opinions and feelings of the Roman Catholics, I do not believe a project to be practicable' or capable of 'really satisfying the Roman Catholics and of affording an adequate security to the Established Church and Constitution'.[82]

Canning's primary reason for refusing office was probably frustration that his own personal ambitions had been stalled when Castlereagh had been placed above him, but he went ahead with the bill as an independent, arguing that 'the process of public opinion has mitigated the violence of religious dissension – surely these are favourable circumstances.'[83] Henry Grattan said he was entirely in agreement with him[84] and Castlereagh, that not to concur with the proposal would be contrary to 'a principle which he had always avowed'. Furthermore, the government would not seek any 'securities that were at variance with the Catholic religion … nor any that would degrade or dishonour Catholics or that were not proper to be conceded by them as [those] received by Protestants'.[85] As Canning's biographer describes, the motion was 'triumphantly carried by 235 votes to 106', and 'few of the Emancipationists – certainly not Canning – doubted they were on the threshold of final victory'.[86] This is perhaps a little too effusive, for regardless of agreed securities many ultra-Protestant peers would be sure to provide stiff opposition on successive readings, yet it is abundantly evident that the conciliationists had good grounds to believe they could succeed if the Irish Catholic bishops approved the 'veto'. As Castlereagh had implied, however, the main problem began to develop when O'Connell launched a series of well-publicised attacks on those Catholic leaders as well as ministers he believed would be willing to compromise and he denounced the veto as an 'insidious' 'degradation' of Catholics.[87] He specifically targeted one potential waverer, the prince regent, when he passed a resolution at a Dublin meeting of Catholics 'boldly and savagely' attacking him for his dissolute and immoral lifestyle with his reputed mistress, Lady Hertford, who he described as a sinister 'witch'. To give the formal right to this 'impure source' of spurned 'public and private virtue' spellbound by 'fatal witchery' to veto Catholic appointments would inevitably bring God's wrath upon the heads of Irish Catholics. This was widely publicised in the press,

and although the right of veto now had provisional papal approval, as
Oliver MacDonagh describes: to the 'fright and chagrin of the cautious
party in the [Catholic] Board', O'Connell's campaign as an 'absolute
intransigent' opponent would prove increasingly effective in raising
concerns among the more pious or militant Catholics.[88] He would continue with his campaign until he was confident enough to 'lay down
the law for the Irish Church on the Veto ... defining the spiritual and
temporal limits of the Pope's authority and jurisdiction in the Irish
Church', publicly insulting the Papal envoy, Quarantotti, as 'odious and
stupid' for advocating support and any Catholic bishop who did the
same, as 'vacillating, venal and without learning'. [89]

In March 1813, when the bill was raised for discussion, the opposition
mocked the cabinet for being divided between ministers who argued
that Emancipation would strengthen the state and those who believed
that it would destroy it.[90] Following Peel's appointment as Irish chief
secretary in 1812, O'Connell had ridiculed him as the 'ludicrous enemy
of ours ... Orange Peel, a raw youth squeezed out of the workings of a
factory in England'.[91] Peel did not, in fact, make a substantial statement
of opposition until 1813, when he specifically identified Catholic critics
of the veto as having provided a weapon for the ultra-Protestant
opponents. 'If I were among the wavering friends of the Catholics, I
would advise the postponement of this consideration' to give them time
to 'reflect on their past conduct, on the prejudice their cause has
received from the intemperance of some of their advocates'. 'When
they charge us with bigotry and intolerance' let them recollect that they
are 'not only unwilling to pay the same price for political privileges,
which is exacted from the other subjects of his majesty', but also refuse
'to submit to the same restrictions, which are imposed with their own
consent, and with that of the Pope, upon the Catholics of all other
countries, wherein the Government is not Catholic'. Not long ago 'the
veto was admitted by the Catholic Prelates themselves not to be
incompatible to the Catholic religion',[92] but now they adamantly
refuse, illustrating 'the impossibility of coming to any final and conciliatory adjustment of the Catholic claims at the present moment'.[93]

It was difficult for the conciliatory Emancipationists and anyone else
to refute these arguments, and on 27 May after numerous attempts to
amend the bill, a despondent Grattan formerly dropped it as hopeless
to continue. Two days later the Irish Catholic bishops finally published
their rumoured decision that any such securities were 'utterly incompatible with the discipline of the Roman Catholic Church and the free

exercise of our religion'.[94] As had been argued by Peel, this was clearly not the case: the same veto had papal approval in other European states, had been freely sworn by Irish Catholics in the past and the majority of the Irish 'Catholic' newspapers and leading lay Catholics had supported the measure.[95] Given that Croker and many others who knew O'Connell were aware that he was not an orthodox or 'superstitious' Catholic, and something of a chubby Lothario himself, they could not accept that his campaign was really designed to protect the Catholic people from 'degradation' or divine retribution. Croker was predisposed to see him, as he did most populist and radical politicians, as an opportunist demagogue, but most others such as Samuel Whitbread, the leader of the radical 'mountain' in the Commons, argued much the same. There was one key which might unlock the origins of part of the disapprobation' of the bill: 'some of the leaders might be aware that the bill once passed, their temporary consequence was gone.'[96] The Irish Whig campaigner Henry Plunkett also described the opponents of the veto as having destroyed their shared hopes of 'a reciprocal spirit of concession on the part of the Roman Catholics' by rekindling 'all the mischiefs arising from religious animosities'.[97] In December 1813, Grattan wrote to the chairman of the Catholic Board, and sent the same letter to the Dublin newspapers and London *Times*, lamenting 'exceedingly the disappointment' and criticised the Catholic Board for having failed in their 'duty to the Catholic cause; to their Protestant brethren and to the legislature'. Only when they 'have adopted a spirit of accommodation and conciliation then, and not till then, can the Board claim it has endeavoured to do its duty'.[98] O'Connell put forward a new petition for him to present before the Commons; one that was not only futile at that stage, but presumably designed to serve its true purpose by being written in a calculatedly 'offensive' manner. When he refused to present it, 'Mr O'Connell severely assailed Grattan' and successfully convinced the board to replace him.[99]

Croker would have agreed with Oliver MacDonagh's assessment that 'the official [Irish Catholic] church was led or manoeuvred into overt opposition to both papal and British governments by O'Connell and his group of inflexible supporters', and that their campaign 'more than any other forced the hierarchy into secular politics in Ireland, and determined the role it was to play' over the following decades.[100] Aware early on that an 'ultra' Catholic campaign would probably render any effort fruitless and encourage further division among his own parliamentary party, Croker took almost no part in the public debates, writing later that 'not withstanding some private jealousies and personal ambitions' the ministry was 'tolerably well united on all the great points of foreign and domestic policy, except the Catholic question', which had 'in vain made what was called an "Open question"'. Over the next few years the 'subject was incidentally introduced into every debate', and the

> ... Opposition, seeing the embarrassment it caused, took care to ring in one or two solemn hearings in every session; and then was exhibited the intolerable anomaly of a portion of the Cabinet speaking, with a degree of zeal that sometimes sounded like asperity, against the other, and voting in frequent divisions with the violent opposers of the general measures of their own administration.[101]

For Croker and most of his circle, the differences on the 'Catholic Question' could have been overcome if the prejudices and the factional political and personal ambitions of some Irish and British politicians could be subsumed in its favour. He would continue to campaign for it behind the scenes, but it would be another six years before he dramatically re-declared his support when he seconded Grattan's last Emancipation bill, and presented his first extensive parliamentary outline of Conservative political principles.

PARTY AND THE PRESS, POPULAR POLITICS AND LITERARY REVIEWING

Croker suffered two personal disappointments partly as a result of his support for Emancipation. The post of chief secretary to Ireland was the only one he appears to have openly solicited,[102] but even if Liverpool was willing to move him from the Admiralty, the lord lieutenant said he should not 'send me a timid man or a catholic'.[103] Croker was certainly not the former, but he had rendered himself ineligible on the latter, whereas Peel held moderate yet 'sound Protestant opinions'.[104] He may have consoled himself that he had acted according to his principles, responding to a letter of thanks from his Catholic constituents that he was 'happy to have deserved their approbation; I felt it my duty ... to give my decided vote for what appeared to me a measure of just and liberal policy and of national conciliation.'[105] One would assume this might have won him the Catholic vote, but two months before the 1812 election, a friend at Trinity portentously reminded him of the risks entailed in trying to seek a middle way in Irish politics, facetiously congratulating him on 'raising the Irish Catholic Party to an eminence that they now look down on you; while the low prized Irish loyalists afford you but little affection'.[106] In October he lost his seat at Down-patrick, ascribing his defeat mainly to the influence of the local 'Catholic Bishop and his Priests',[107] but fortunately for him, he was judged an asset worth saving, and Peel wrote to Lord Liverpool saying that the lord lieutenant had returned him for the borough of Athlone.[108]

When they returned to London, Liverpool's main concern was not the threat from the Whigs, but from the estranged faction led by Lord Richard Wellesley and Canning who 'will represent themselves as hold-ing the same opinions as we do on all popular topics [and] say they have as much right to be considered the successors of Mr Pitt's party as ourselves'.[109] Croker was also concerned that they would join with moderate Whigs to form a 'government on the principle of the Catholic concession',[110] but he placed much of the blame on 'folly in the conduct of the last negotiations'. He told Peel that Liverpool should have made greater efforts to recruit them, concluding with the melodramatic emphasis he liked to use to make a point: 'Be assured we shall every day [have] more cause to lament it ... push down Canning! Push down fire, restrain steam!'[111] Croker's associations with both groups naturally raised suspicions of his loyalty, and Frederick Robinson wrote to Peel that he was 'more mixed up in a Canning and Wellesley intrigue than we are aware of', but had the 'ingenuity enough to turn his own version of facts to whichever cause he may espouse'.[112] While the latter may have been true, Robinson's views were not taken too seriously by Peel or Croker (both teased him as 'the Duke of Fuss and Bustle' for ec-centricities such as spraying his post in vinegar to avoid infection)[113] and by this time, despite some misgivings, Croker had identified his 'little platoon' in politics as the one assembled under Liverpool's pre-miership.

Croker's 'ingenuity' to turn his version of facts into convincing argument was, of course, a vital asset for any accomplished 'spin doctor', and although his presswork and relationship with Canningites under-standably raised suspicions, he appears to have been mainly concerned with encouraging unity among his party. This belief that factional poli-tics was the bane of good government was another important feature of his political philosophy, and while the idea of party may have suffered a 'false dawn' between 1807 and 1812,[114] Croker did his best to keep it above the horizon. In 1824, when compiling material for a historical study of Horace Walpole, he responded to a query about Walpole from

Lord Liverpool that his subject's overtly biased memoirs were representative of how such works could 'poison the minds of posterity', and that his recent studies of the period had reinforced his fear of parliamentary factions:

> There never lived a more selfish man; a more factious politician; a more calumnious writer. It is because I think him so that I am conscious to prevent him as far as I can from poisoning the sources of history. His descent, his name, his station, the force and veracity of his style, his perpetual professions of disinterestedness ... have all contributed to give him considerable authority ... and will give a most false colour to the transactions and operations of his day; his partiality without some corrective will poison the minds of posterity.
>
> Nothing can be more different than the two modes of conducting government affairs in this country, which are often confounded: I mean party and faction. Godolphin, Hurley, Walpole and latterly Mr Pitt and his Tory successors and his Whig opponents all proceeded on the principles of party. Newcastle, the elder Pitt and fix, the Grenvillites, Lord Bute and all their underlings ... conducted their administration by a balance of factions and the alternate purchase and dismissal of little political coteries. The fate of the coalition was the death blow to that system, a long peace and great internal prosperity by not affording great rallying points on which parties may be formed will, perhaps, revive factions and whenever that happens we shall see played over again all the lamentable scenes of the last years of George II and the early years of George III.[115]

This was another belief he shared with Burke, who is seen as having first 'pointed the way' for political parties in his *Thoughts of the Present Discontents* (1770),[116] as assemblies of like-minded men 'united for promoting their joint endeavours in the national interest', being best able to 'inculcate some consanguity' against parliament being 'infected with every epidemical phrensy of the people'. The often parodied: 'when bad combine, the good must associate; else they will fall, one by one, an un-pitied sacrifice in a contemptible struggle', is preceded by the less well known: 'no man, who is not inflamed by vain glory into enthusiasm, can flatter himself that his single, desultory, unsystematic endeavours, are of a power to defeat the subtle design and united Cabals of ambitious citizens.'[117] Once again, these are essentially the same principles he would promote in his *Reflections* some twenty years later. And as with their adaption and promulgation by Croker and what he saw as the connected advocacy of conciliatory government and firm opposition to extremes, it would not perhaps be unreasonable to see this tradition as partly the product of a beleaguered Anglican-Irish sensitivity to the need for 'good men associating ... else they will fall one by one, an un-pitied sacrifice' to united 'Cabals of ambitious citizens'.

This could also be applied to the importance these Irish thinkers all placed in the press or polemical political pamphlets, and as Thomas Crofton Croker, who was awarded one of the much coveted Admiralty clerkships by his namesake in 1818,[118] noted in his *Portraits of Eminent Conservatives*, Croker's particular talents as a press writer and manager were put to early use by his leaders.[119] Peel had been familiar with Croker's skills since the early days of their friendship, and as soon as he arrived in Dublin solicited his advice on how to deal with the notoriously partisan Dublin press. 'It is easier to silence an enemy's batteries than establish an effective one of your own, at least in the contents of the Press, I should do anything for your turn of paragraph, it would be invaluable here.'[120] Croker sent Peel a regular supply of advice on this and other Irish affairs as well as London news and political gossip; making him by 1817, according to Peel, 'the only man in London who takes compassion on your friends in foreign parts and enlightens their darkness'.[121] This was an amiable exaggeration, but their extensive correspondence indicates that he probably placed most value on Croker's views.

Like most politicians, Croker took considerable care to conceal his connections with the press, and as he insisted in 1818 when sending an article to William Blackwood, the publisher of *Blackwood's Edinburgh Magazine*, he only did so 'in strictest secrecy'.[122] But from what few letters there are and the accounts of others who were less protective of his reputation, it is clear that by the middle of the decade Croker was managing the political content of the *Courier*, the most important 'Tory' daily newspaper in Britain, and keeping many others such as the *Morning Post* 'on the right track', as well as acting as the political advisor to the ministry's most respectable literary mouthpiece, the *Quarterly Review*. Samuel Taylor Coleridge, for example, wrote that Wellington 'could neither have been supplied by the Ministers, nor the

Ministers supported by the nation, but for the tone first given, and then constantly kept up' by the *Courier*'s 'plain un-ministerial, anti-Opposition, anti-Jacobin, anti-Napoleonic spirit'.[123] To Croker's annoyance, after the war the ministers 'dropped' the *Courier*, and as Coleridge concluded sarcastically but appropriately, its editor, Peter Street, 'might not have had Croker to dine with him, or received as many nods or shakes of the hand from This Lord or That' but he may have won greater respect by being less obliging.[124] Croker also influenced opposition and less committed newspapers such as *The Times*, the most successful national daily in Britain, when and where he could. Its owner, John Walter, wrote to him in 1811 asking 'whether there would be any impropriety' in seeking the assistance of the Admiralty in smuggling French newspapers into England in order to win a scoop on news. Croker almost certainly obliged, for a year later Walter wrote thanking him for 'the score of friendly communications' and 'many motives for personal esteem and respect, but I cannot, I fear, extend these much beyond yourself, or at least not to the general body of the [Liverpool] Administration'. He hoped the 'political separation will produce no breach on my part of personal esteem',[125] and although much closer to the Whigs until late 1834, according to the history of *The Times*, they would continue to dine together, and Walter 'possessed few intimates; only with John Wilson Croker, the editor of the *Quarterly*, among politicians was he friendly'.[126]

As Croker acknowledged, the political loyalties of all newspapermen were primarily governed by the need to sell their newspapers, and while he would often be frustrated by their pursuit of popular opinion, he pragmatically accepted that they were of necessity 'needy adventurers', and that any dealings with them 'ought to be done in the most profound secrecy'. His own secret dealings continued to raise occasional suspicions of his loyalties, and whereas he expected and rarely challenged the resentment of his political and literary rivals, he was clearly offended to hear in 1814 that even Wellington had believed a rumour that he had criticised him in a newspaper article. Croker wrote an indignant letter denying it, but also leaving us some further evidence of the extent of his presswork. 'You know all that I have done with regard to him. In the worst times before his great achievements had put down the clamours of envy and faction against him I took the most incessant pains as far as my small abilities went to keep the public mind right and my pen was constantly, and I hope not uselessly, employed.'[127]

It is abundantly evident however, that he enjoyed this kind of work.

In particular, perhaps the skulduggery involved, and as an avid collector of French Revolutionary pamphlets and other publications he was much more sensitive to the political power of the press than most of his peers during this era when there was an 'explosive growth' of popular publishing.[128] While he believed that the press could have a destructive influence when exploited by the radical agitators, he also saw it as an important element of the political estate and having a potentially enlightening and politically constructive role. In the *Quarterly* in 1816, he praised the 'admirable writer and excellent statesman', Chateaubriand, and the 'luminous and eloquent argument which he makes for the liberty of the free press'. 'Government is founded on, and enlightened by, public opinion', and parliament 'cannot be aware of that opinion if the opinion has no organ' and 'the public must be aware of debates and decisions made in the chamber … where the interests of the people are debated'.[129] Croker would have agreed with what John Cannon has described in his excellent study of another of Croker's heroes, Samuel Johnson, that the expansion of newspapers and periodicals in Britain represented a largely neglected '*process* of enlightenment'. This trickling popular diffusion, rather than the elite enterprise ascribed to the more famous French *philosophes*, makes 'room for popular as well as classical literature, for popularisers and hack writers as well as writers of outstanding talent … printers, teachers, editors'; but central to this process, and the 'most striking illustration of this intellectual revolution, was the establishment of the popular press and its emergence as a political force'.[130] Croker would always remain a promoter of the free press, frequently drawing attention to the fact that its most avid censors were usually revolutionaries and/or tyrants such as Bonaparte. He accepted that overtly seditious publications might have to be repressed in times of public crisis, but it was of much greater importance that government should exploit the medium in order to counter such threats and retain popular support.

A short study of Peel and Croker's frustrating dealings with the Irish newspapers at this time can provide a good example of the symbiotic but fraught relationship politicians had with the press as well as illustrate some more of Croker's influence and ideas on Irish affairs. Following his appointment as chief secretary, Peel was ambitious to win over as many Irish papers as possible,[131] and one well-established method was the selective distribution of £10,500 allocated for publishing proclamations.[132] The *Freeman's Journal* had remained a wavering 'Castle Catholic' in receipt of such funding since 1798 when its editor had secretly supplied evidence leading to the arrest of Lord Edward Fitzgerald.[133] The O'Connellite *Dublin Evening Post* was, according to Peel, a 'nefarious paper' that did 'great mischief' raising dissent among Catholics.[134] However, its incautious reiteration of some libels O'Connell had made at public meetings in 1813 gave Peel the opportunity to prosecute its owners, the Magee brothers. They had protected O'Connell and employed him to defend them, but their 'unqualified approval' of him rapidly waned when he used the immunity of the court to promote himself with 'a reiteration and amplification of the libels' and a 'savage attack on the Attorney General'.[135] James Magee was sentenced to two years in prison, and Peel exploited this by offering to suspend the sentence if his newspaper dropped O'Connell and became a 'Castle Catholic'. According to William Gregory, the Irish under-secretary, he agreed with alacrity, professing 'an inclination to efface his misdeeds by serving us to the best of his power'.[136] Yet despite the threat hanging over the Magees and the contempt they now had for O'Connell, the *Post* could only go so far to 'efface its misdeeds' without reducing its circulation among Catholics. Barely a year later Gregory was raging at the contents of the *Post*, describing James Magee to Peel as 'the most impudent filch' he ever knew; 'having betrayed his own party, and not true to ours'.[137]

This indignation was not confined to the Catholic press alone, and as Brian Inglis argued, it would be fair to say that Croker and Peel's main concern was to present the government case and to lessen the divisive religious rivalry. John Giffard, the ultra-Protestant editor of the *Dublin Journal*, was, according to Gregory, 'a most dangerous' newspaperman whose extremism more 'injured' the Tory and Protestant cause than assisted it.[138] As mentioned, Giffard was an old friend of Croker's father, and he sometimes sent Croker a package containing 'all the Irish newspapers' and family gossip, such as one in February 1811 describing the college activities of his youngest son, Stanley Lees Giffard, who, as we will see, would later found the London *Standard* and become one of the most influential members of the press circle.[139]The *Dublin Journal* was awarded £2,432 in proclamation subsidies; yet despite this, and Croker having got him reinstated to his old customs post worth £600 pa, Giffard still ignored their requests to moderate his politics.[140] In 1815 Peel finally lost all patience and used the threat of closure to induce the *Journal*'s owner to force him into retirement; but even this had to be lubricated with a £100 increment of his customs pension that Croker negotiated after he had received a sarcastic letter from Giffard in April 1816: 'if you think I deserve the favour – so shall you be rid of another opposer of popery.'[141]

That same month in the Commons Peel despaired at the effort and expense he had poured into the attempt to moderate the press, exclaiming that Irish newspapermen were the most 'vile and degraded beings'.[142] He was twenty-four years old when he took up his highly demanding Irish post, and although it is clear that he was hostile to 'ultras' on both sides, his dealings with O'Connell and the more militant elements of the Catholic movement appear to have had a significant influence in reinforcing his antipathy to them and his opposition to Emancipation. Croker was familiar with the religious cut and thrust of Irish politics and accepted that O'Connell's use of personal abuse and 'demagoguery' was mainly designed to enlist the limited and disadvantaged resources available to him. Although he viewed his politics as divisively destructive and many of his subalterns as bigots, having known him since their time together on the Munster circuit, he never believed the latter of O'Connell. They continued to look upon each other fraternally, and as Croker wrote much later, when they did occasionally meet it was 'on the most good humoured terms ... even in the four years in which we sat in the House of Commons' between 1829 and 1833, until just before O'Connell's death, 'we parted as we had lived', in 'personal goodwill, and I might say cordiality'.[143]

Peel was much more sensitive to insults and had higher expectations of personal behaviour. In May 1815 this led to a violent confrontation with O'Connell after Peel accurately used extracts published 'in newspapers most in the confidence of the Catholic body' to argue that they insulted the Protestant religion and were opposed to making any conciliatory concession to facilitate Emancipation.[144] O'Connell responded by publicly accusing him of cowardice for making these criticisms within Commons privilege.[145] Peel initially ignored what became repeated challenges, and in July went on holiday to Paris with Vesey Fitzgerald and Croker, who had been asked by Castlereagh to act as translator to help draft the allied agreement at the post-Waterloo peace conference.[146] When Peel returned he challenged O'Connell to a duel despite Croker's repeated warnings that the main contest was in the press and he was playing into his hands by raising his public status. O'Connell was arrested en route, and refused another contest purportedly from a belated regret at having killed John D'Esterre, a member of Dublin Corporation some months before, but Peel belligerently pursued the issue by challenging his second, a Protestant named Lidwell.[147] He continued to ignore Croker's advice to give up the affair and treat his opponent 'with that contempt which the rest of the world feels in the conduct of the affair',[148] and wrote an excited letter en route to the contest: 'I think I could prove to you I have acted for the best ... Do not let the *Courier* insert my name for the next fortnight. My father takes it in.'[149] The affair fizzled out following a negotiated apology from Lidwell, but some reports appeared in the Tory press, and once again Croker illustrated his growing press influence in arguing he had no idea how it 'came to be published, as it was only the day before yesterday that Street gave his promise to me not to mention a syllable of the matter'. The *Morning Herald* also published a report, and Croker concluded that it could only have happened because the editor 'was absent from an indisposition' and it was probably the work of his deputy, 'an Irishman, I believe a Kerryman and a Papist'.[150]

The dispute naturally polarised Irish public opinion on religious lines, and as Croker had warned, if O'Connell's main purpose had been to define himself as the 'Catholic Champion' and Peel as his 'Protestant' equivalent, he had largely succeeded. Given that together with Palmerston and Croker, Peel had also written a number of press articles ridiculing the Whig opposition that one literary historian describes as being of a 'rather violent and quite personal nature', he should, perhaps, have been a little less sensitive.[151] First published in the *Courier*, the best among them were later published in a book entitled *The New Whig Guide* (1819), and two weeks before Peel described Irish pressmen as 'vile degraded beings', Croker had written to him saying that the plan was that he would write '4 of the 7 remaining days till Parliament meets; and if you can contribute for three, we shall not have let a day pass without a shot, *nulla dies sine linea*'.[152] Peel wrote the greater part of one of its most celebrated political satires, 'The Trial of Henry Brougham MP', ridiculing the most talented young Whig debater in a mock trial presided over by his buffoonish Whig patrons. In another piece written by the trio, the opposition leaders were represented as defunct naval vessels: Ponsonby, an 'old Hulk fitted up for the occasion to plunder' the public purse; Brougham, a 'fire ship loaded with brimstone' to 'blow up Fort Regent'; Whitbread, the wealthy brewer and Whig radical, the 'Vulgaris', and the Irish Whig, Sir John Newport, HMS 'Spinosissimus'.[153]

Brougham, a parvenu lawyer and brilliant product of Edinburgh University, was more Croker's rival than Peel's, in that he was a leading Whig 'spin doctor' and political writer for the *Edinburgh Review*, the Whig rival to the Tory *Quarterly*. In August 1816 Croker wrote to Peel saying that he was preparing an article on Ireland for the *Quarterly*, reassuring him that he 'need not fear my taking a too Catholic line', and asking for his opinions.[154] Peel's reply illustrated his increasing hostility to the Catholic movement and what he believed was a concerted campaign to raise religious tensions and opposition to the Union through the press and various popular publications.

> The very moment I received your letter respecting the Irish article I sat down and wrote you a very long letter – about ten sheets of paper ... I remember that I expressed great delight at your intention, complete acquiescence in your opinion that papal superstition is the cause of one half of the evils of this country, and serious doubts whether Catholic Emancipation would alleviate the half.
>
> I now send you a collection of choice documents consisting first of 'Cox's Magazine'. Cox is of no religion, but would call himself a Protestant if he were compelled to profess any. His object in his magazine was to ferment a bitter hatred against England. His principal assistants in writing were R.C. priests ... The little volume called 'A Sketch of Irish History' is a more infamous work than 'Cox's Magazine' ... on the first page are these words printed at the bottom 'Intended chiefly for the young ladies educated at the Ursuline convents. By a member of the Ursuline Community at Ash.' This work is written with great care – most mischievous and inflammatory – and yet it is thought to be impossible to convict the printer for libel. I also send a *Dublin Chronicle*. You know its history: It was established by O'Connell when he and his colleagues had brought the editors of all other papers into Newgate for publishing speeches which they composed and corrected and afterwards disavowed ...
>
> Perhaps the most noteworthy and extraordinary document of all is the [threatening] letter which I send you. It is written by a Priest in Longford to one of his flock, whom he suspected of giving information, [it is] an admirable specimen for which the priests of Ireland exert their spiritual influence. If I collect anything more I will send it to you.[155]

The following week Peel sent Croker an account of an atrocity in Limerick he had found particularly disturbing. 'If you must give a specimen – one specimen – of the humanity of the poor suffering, oppressed natives of this country, who are trained up by the priests in the paths of religion and virtue' and only made to commit 'outrage by the tyranny of their landlords or the insulting triumphs of Orangemen, I believe I can furnish you with a more complete specimen'. He enclosed a harrowing account of a gang of thirteen men bludgeoning a farmer to death, and then, 'when all apprehension of danger was at an end, could kill a woman [his wife] with an infant in her arms'. The child fled to neighbours 'for protection' but was told 'that "she might go to the devil"'. All comment, he concluded, 'would but weaken the unparalleled atrocity of this transaction'.[156]

Croker fully accepted that there was a proactive 'bigoted' element among the Catholic community, including a growing proportion of the rural clergy who were actively involved in local politics, and he had opened his letter to Peel that 'Popery' probably offered the greatest threat to the peace and improvement of Ireland, but he also believed that most disturbances were the product of competition for land and local power groups preying on the peasantry. Although he could be critical of the entrenched practices of the Irish peasantry, he would remain an unsentimental promoter of their virtues and as he argued in his *State of Ireland*, given the harshness of their lives and extent of deprivation, much of the rural violence, if not excusable, was understandable.[157] He appears to have decided against using any of Peel's information, but he illustrated some more of his views on Irish affairs and political ideas in a review of a book by an Irish Whig MP, William Parnell (grandfather of Charles Stewart), and together with a short study of one other, they will provide us with an example of his style of literary reviewing and why some of his subjects became dedicated enemies.

Parnell had written a romantic and pedagogic Irish novel, *Maurice and Berghetta: or the Priest of Rahery*. A tale, seeking to reform the state of Ireland and criticising the failings of the Irish peasantry and primitivism of their customs and agriculture in comparison to their British counterpart. He placed the blame for this on decades of English misrule and the dispossession of their traditional aristocracy, as personified by the hero and heroine of his novel, 'lineally descended from King O'Neill', but who now possessed nothing more than 'a beautiful pedigree written in gold upon velum, a mud cabin and a score of acres of hungry land'.[158] As William Thomas says, for Croker 'where most of his literary reviews were concerned', it was 'not a question of politics versus literature, because both callings carried a social responsibility and were to be judged by the same criteria'.[159] He saw Parnell's novel as another example of European romanticism adapted to create a pseudo-Irish history for explicit, or in the case of Parnell, naively implicit political purposes, and essentially a drawing room plagiarisation of cruder chap books and other vernacular works sowing disaffection among the lower classes that Peel had complained of.

Croker accepted that entrenched agricultural practices and retro-gressive customs were difficult to change, but expressed his 'reluctance, not to say disgust' at having to repeat Parnell's 'observations which appear to us as grossly injurious to the Irish character'.[160] Parnell had dedicated his book 'in a strain of what we should have thought was very fulsome flattery to the Roman Catholic clergy'[161] because they dominated his Catholic freeholders; yet given that most Catholic priests discouraged modernisation and improvement, they 'will give him very little thanks for his pains'. Furthermore, given that Parnell called for English practices to be imported into Ireland and promoted the English peasantry as an ideal model, it was 'absurd to pretend, in the wretched cant of the day, that England and the English government of the day in Ireland are responsible' for the distressed state of Ireland:

> Mr Parnell, indeed, dilates on this theme with great fluency; but when we have seen that he has no more forcible method of expressing his disgust at the Irish character than but con-trasting it with the English. When he affirms that the Irish are as filthy and lazy as the English are cleanly and active … as thoughtless and extravagant as the English are prudent … as *drunken* as the English are temperate, how [can] any man with a grain of logic, or even common sense in his head attribute these abominable vices in one country to the example or influence of another, which he admits to be of all the nations on the earth the freest from them.[162]

As one of his agricultural reforms, Parnell had suggested that 'instead of potatoes, the day labourers of Ireland should eat wheaten bread and cold meat' for a midday meal because they were more nour-ishing and take less time to prepare. Croker easily mocked this: 'would to God that the food of the peasantry could be improved', but given that they rarely had paid employment, had no money to spend on meat, and a family could survive on an acre of potatoes, then Parnell's talent as a 'visionary' was typical of theorists and literary seers. 'In tracing upon paper his schemes of reformation he has no obstacles, no difficulties, no prejudices to contend with; in a political romance a legislator may do what he pleases, and as he pleases.'[163]

Croker was particularly hostile to representations of Irish Protestants as non-Irish and that any section of Irish society should be exonerated from responsibility for the state of Ireland, describing Parnell's argument as characteristic of a 'fact, which is wholly suppressed by such flimsy theory mongers': 'Ireland, for the last century, has, of everything that relates to morals, manners and domestic economy (the points in which she is most deficient) been governed by herself.' Apart from a viceroy, 'the real power and the whole of the internal legislation and economy of the country have been in the hands of the Irish themselves.' The English conquest of Ireland had been a 'lingering war, both lay and clerical of many melancholy ages, accompanied and followed by mutual injuries and mutual hatred'. However, almost all improvements, 'whether in forms or in essentials, have been imported from England'. From 'parliament and the pulpit down to the plough and the spinning wheel, are the produce of the English connection. Nay to descend to minor objects, even Mr Parnell himself' was a 'boon' from 'England to Ireland'. It would be a 'great blessing ... if discontent and disaffection, old prejudices and rankling feuds could be eradicated, and that a general respect for the present state of the laws, constitution and property could be generally diffused'.[164] But in an 'Irish spirit of *conciliation*', Parnell sows disaffection by exaggerating antagonisms, rubbing salt into old wounds and providing romanticised legitimacy for historic myths. He 'judiciously reminds all the peasants' that 'whether their names be O'Toole or O'Neale, or O'Sullivan', they are 'descended from a line of kings, and though despoiled and degraded, the real owners of the soil and the just inheritors of the wealth and power of the country in Ireland'. The best 'we can do for Mr Parnell is to hope he does not quite know what he is doing – he is a child playing with firearms, an innocent who, by way of giving light to his neighbours, sticks his farthing candle into a barrel of gunpowder'.[165]

Croker's style of literary review seldom changed. He was frequently cutting and sarcastic, repetitively reinforced an argument, seldom missed the chance to conflate a political point and sometimes appeared spitefully eager to press home any advantage. But he usually made a good case as well as entertained his readers by building an evidentially based assessment exposing the inaccuracies or inconsistencies of his subjects as well as lampooning them. Charles Phillips, a young Irish Catholic attorney, had been a member of the O'Connellite faction, but after the veto opposition stalemated Emancipation he moved to Britain to build his career as a Radical. In 1816 he published a collection of speeches, some of which directly contradicted earlier published works and provided Croker with the easy opportunity to apply his favoured method. 'Our readers must be aware, that we are generally inclined (though we do not shrink from giving our own honest opinion) to permit authors to speak for themselves ... and to quote from their own works such passages as may appear to us to justify our criticism.'[166] He began by quoting some of Phillips' proto-nationalist poetry: 'Brian Borua ... The dove was an eagle compared to his smile! – Liberty's beacon, religions bright star – Soul of the Seanacha – the shield of the Emerald Isle.' This was easily mocked: 'the darkness which envelops the history of old Brian may be pleaded in excuse of the above passage,' before Croker moved onto the more serious business of portraying Phillips as representative of self-promoting political 'demagogues' seeking to elevate themselves by exploiting popular disaffection. In a recent pamphlet Counsellor Phillips had attacked 'Mr Grattan because, as he elegantly puts it, an Irish native has lost its raciness in an English atmosphere', but Croker then quoted from an earlier one: 'When the screech owl of intolerance was yelling and the night of bigotry was brooding on the land [Grattan] came forth with the heart of a hero! – And the tongue of an angel, till at his bidding the spectre vanished.'

What had changed, Croker argued, was that Phillips had abandoned Grattan when the O'Connellites forced his resignation and with the Emancipation movement in the doldrums the 'Dublin Demosthenes' moved to England and enlisted with British radicalism. This demanded that he adapt his principles to what seemed most likely to inflate 'the tumid and empty bladders upon which the reputation of Mr Phillips is trying to become buoyant'. Such opportunism was a characteristic 'of the lawyers of the Catholic Board', but even they are not usually 'capable of such a union of ignorance and confidence, of inanity and pretension', and 'for the honour of Ireland' it should be noted that his works are printed in England and little 'heard of in the place of their supposed nativity'.[167] Croker devoted most of the next five pages to systematically reinforcing these arguments with similar comparisons of Phillips' other speeches. His earliest publication had been dedicated to the prince regent, described as 'Ireland's Hope and England's ornament', yet now he cannot think of him 'without indignation'. Wellington, who had been an 'Irish hero who strikes the harp to victory upon the summit of the Pyrenees', was now a tyrant who had waged a war to 'force France out of her right to choose her own monarch ... and declared tyranny eternal'. In 1812, 'Buonaparte was a "despot – bloody – impious – polluted";

an infidel "who trod the symbol of Christianity underfoot – plundered temples and murdered priests", but now he was a "dethroned monarch": "How grand was his rather march! How magnificent his destiny!" Phillips had written that the English had a "prejudice against his native land above every other feeling, inveterate as ignorance could generate, as monstrous as credulity could feed"', but in a recent speech in Liverpool 'what he had described as the "cold blooded *Sasanach*" was now "the high minded people of England ... the emporium of liberality and public spirit, the birth place of talent, the residence of integrity". William of Orange had 'been a "Draco, a gloomy murderer ... vandal, tyrant", but he is now applauded, and the "reformers of 1688" and the Williamite Settlement, "the most glorious of our national annals"'.[168]

Croker was able to complete his rather devastating deconstruction by concluding that Phillips was a political opportunist who had lent his 'labours and his lungs to the cause of Catholic Emancipation, and preached up the doctrine of eternal petitions while they afforded any prospect of celebrity or profit'. But the 'scent has now grown cold' on Catholic issues, and with the 'reform of parliament being the cry of the disaffected in England, he imports his parcel of talent and celebrity into Liverpool' where he will 'make a very acceptable addition to the society of Major Cartwright and Mr Gale Jones [English Radicals]'. That is, of course, until some 'new turn in the wheel of state, or in popular feeling, shall again convert him', and then we may presume he will once again be 'bespattering Grattan and Ponsonby with his praises'.[169]

It is not difficult to imagine the impact of these reviews, nor is it surprising that they aroused the enduring resentment of his political and literary victims. And while it is fair to say that there is an irritable intolerance indicative of an 'ingrained critical mentality' in much of Croker's writing,[170] and a preoccupation with facts that does not lend itself to sympathetic reviewing of 'creative' literature, it must also be borne in mind that he was writing for one of the two most successful periodicals of the period and his style was clearly popular with his readers and political allies. The editor of a modern academic index of the *Quarterly* articles introduces them by saying that 'some of the material published in the *Quarterly* was vituperative [and] William Gifford and J.W. Croker exercised Pitt-bull instincts' and a 'slashing tone'.[171] While this may be true, it is difficult to see their articles as any more 'vituperative' or politically aggressive than those written by rivals such as Hazlitt, Leigh Hunt, Francis Jeffries, Brougham and many others.[172] The celebrated Whig

Edinburgh Reviewers are usually seen as having initiated much of the 'slashing' style of review,[173] and when the *Quarterly* was established as its Tory rival seven years later, its early attempts at moderation restricted its circulation.[174] As Stefan Collini says, this 'slash and burn style of reviewing' was common practice at the time,[175] and the enduring enmity Croker attracted offers the best proof that he was an effective reviewer; the circulation figures of the *Quarterly* that he was a successful one, and any assessment must be made within its historical context if it is to be balanced and as accurate as possible.

Croker saw little difference between what he viewed as the 'embroidered sentimentalities' of radical or romantic writers like Phillips, Parnell, or his old Dublin antagonist, Lady Morgan, and populist chap book romantic literature, but he was more concerned to disparage what he saw as the political foolishness and neo-Platonist conceit of this new wave of self-appointed 'unacknowledged legislators' than the artistic merits of their novels or poetry. In the case of Lady Morgan, for example, although he must have taken some belated pleasure in ridiculing her book *France* in 1817 for its flamboyant contrivances and numerous errors, he made sure to emphasise that she foolishly criticised moderate constitutionalists but was 'desperately enamoured of Buonaparte [sic] and his generals', despite them being 'tyrants' responsible for more desolation than Europe had experienced in centuries.[176] Although few literary scholars appear to be aware of it, *France* was in fact the only one of her books that Croker ever reviewed, and the unfortunate Lady Morgan received much the same and even worse treatment from many others. Among them her more natural allies, the Whig *Edinburgh Reviewers*, who described her as the 'ci-divant' producer of monstrous literary abortions, a 'blunderer and reviler' and an 'Irish she wolf'; or in the *British Review*, as a writer who 'spewed out of her filthy maw a flood of poison, horrible and black'.[177] It is satisfying to note that she usually gave as good as she got, but in the case of Croker considerably more than she ever received. In *Florence Macarthy* alone she portrayed him as the evil 'toady' counsellor Conway Crawley whose 'inauspicious birth' entailed 'his bilious saturnine constitution' and his 'overweening ambition' produced 'the dark bile, which from his childhood sallowed his cheeks'. One 'formed by nature to betray the land that gave him birth' where he had 'first raised his hiss, shed his venom' and turned his 'ink to gall and his pen to a stiletto' in order to defame 'a frail woman'.[178]

Few other than dedicated literary partisans took all this too seriously at the time and Croker ignored it for most of his life. His reviews of imaginative literature were of secondary importance to him, but he did believe that it was part of his work to defend higher standards from 'half-lettered charlatans who were filling the bookshops with trash'. A view, which as William Thomas continues, is 'as remote from modern attitudes as it could possibly be', and when the editor of the *Quarterly* wrote: 'Do favour us with the flagellation of some literary quack',[179] Croker was usually willing to oblige. This was, however, more because it took relatively little time and research to produce an entertaining article using the authors' own words against them than anything else. To adapt an old adage, his single greatest sin was to be on the losing side of literary history, but given the part this played in concealing his more significant work it still comes as something of a surprise to discover that of the approximately 300 reviews he wrote between 1809 and 1854, less than fifty were of creative literature and probably a third of these were more complimentary than critical.[180] They will have to be the business of another study, but it is worth exploring his views on the arts just a little further at this point because they give us a little more insight into his political philosophy.

He had the same rather narrow classicist view held by most of his peers, believing that no wisdom or insight comes without a disciplined effort, and that this principle could be applied equally to good art as it could to all human endeavours:

> It is one of the eternal and general rules by which heaven warns us at every step and at every look, that this is a mere transitory life; that what costs no trouble soon perishes; that what grows freely dies early; and that nothing endures but in some degree of proportion with the time and labour it costs to create.[181]

Nevertheless, it would be wrong to think he did not appreciate creative genius; he just believed it much rarer than the growing wider public appetite for romantic novels and poetry that within a genera-tion would become highly receptive to melodramatic disparagements of those who ridiculed their developing sensibilities. Although Byron was a Radical, Croker admired his 'genius' in describing 'the workings of the mind, the agitation of the intellect ... and possessing a wild, daring and romantic imagination'.[182] Genuine talent usually superseded tem-poral politics, and when John Murray, the owner of the *Quarterly* as well as Byron's publisher, sought Croker's opinion on parts of *Don Juan* because they contained a number of radical political and personal attacks, Croker responded: 'what interest can Lord Byron have in being the poet of a party in politics, or a party of morals, or of party in religion?' Murray should try and convince him to omit them, for they were thrown in 'wantonly and *de gaiete de couer*', but if needs be, he should publish regardless. 'It is an old and highly absurd phrase to say that poetry deals in fiction; alas *history*, I fear, deals in fiction, but good poetry is concerned with *realities*, either of a visible or moral nature ... What has a poet who writes for immortality to do with the temporary passions of parties'. Two or three lines of political prose 'will make two or three thousand dissatisfied with his glorious poetry'.[183]

As Byron said of Thomas Moore, Croker was certainly more predisposed to 'love a Lord', literary or otherwise, rather than a 'cockney poet', and one of the most commonly reiterated criticisms of him is Byron and Shelley's charge that his review of Keats's *Endymion* in May 1818 sent the tubercular young poet to an early grave: 'Who killed John Keats / "I" says the *Quarterly* / So cruel and so Tarterly'.[184] But when the modern biographer of Keats, Robert Gittings, read Croker's review he was surprised to find that it was nothing like as bad as many others. *Blackwood's* was harsher, 'Hazlitt's misrepresentation of Coleridge' was worse, and 'Croker's opinions seemed intended as genuine criticism which would find an echo in a large audience.' Croker had argued that Keats had not succeeded in writing with the power of imagination and invention he had hoped to bring to his work, but as Gittings continues, Keats himself had acknowledged this in his own preface, and Croker had described Keats as having 'powers of language, rays of fancy, and gleams of genius', which at that time was 'a remarkable admission by a critic of any stamp when applied to a modern, young and unknown poet'.[185] It was politically easier for him to praise the likes of Wordsworth, Coleridge and Southey, but he defended their work when other Tory critics ridiculed them.[186] Any case for Croker being an admirer of 'imaginative' work should certainly not be overstated. He best illustrated his usually pedantic preferences in a review of his friend Sir Walter Scott, 'the ingenious and intelligent author of *Waverly*', when summarising that rather than writing 'mere romance and the gratuitous invention of facetious fancy unsettling of all accurate recollections of past transactions', Scott should better employ 'himself recording historically the character and transactions of his countrymen'.[187]

Croker was of course a capable manager and producer of political propaganda himself. His hagiographic epic poem of Wellington's victory, *Talavera* (1809), was a bestseller for Murray; but he was averse to falsifying any specific historical evidence. Twenty years after Waterloo, Peel wrote to him saying he must see David's famous painting of the French Revolutionary Marat, 'Although I dare say you have already mentally ejaculated that you would not give a farthing to see any picture by so bad a painter, and so great a scoundrel … it represents with horrible fidelity Marat dying in the bath.' Given David's political reputation, this was a rather naïve assessment, and Croker's reply encapsulated the importance he placed on preserving the historical record; what he believed was the fraud behind most claims of artistic licence and his incorrigible hostility to Radical or revolutionary propaganda:

> I have no prejudice against David's painting, scoundrel as he was, he had some merits as an artist, and I think I have said somewhere that his brutal and bloody villainy have given him great force and truth in painting scenes of blood … You are quite right such a picture is not my taste, I prefer an ounce of fact to a ton of imagination and had rather have a natural sketch of Marat than all the heriatic and curiatic that David and his followers ever fancied.[188]

Not surprisingly his preference for fact over imagination was reaffirmed when he finally saw David's 'pieta' of a youthful Marat with pure skin and chestnut curls beneath a cloth crown tragically posed as the sacrificed redeemer of mankind. As a meticulous scholar of the French Revolution Croker had more than an 'ounce of fact' at his fingertips to know that Marat was 'near sixty', suffered from a chronic skin complaint, and had been stabbed by the wife of one of his many victims when lounging in his bath casually signing another sheaf of death warrants.[189]

Croker considered his historical reviews and essays on the French Revolution and eighteenth-century political history his best literary work, and as has been mentioned, they have been praised by most of the few historians familiar with them.[190] His punctilious methodology and obsession with facts was probably the main reason he failed to produce the single canonical study of the Revolution that many anticipated. Yet as Richard Cobb said in a blunt assessment, his work was superior to the Victorian 'carpet slippered … dull dogs' who treated history 'as an amiable offshoot of *belles lettres* or a form of sermonising'.[191] In his long articles, Croker probably made the earliest significant challenge to what became the enduring French 'whiggish' interpretations of the French Revolution, but after 1850 there was little more popular appetite for them than for his challenges to British Whig political history until Alfred Cobban made much the same revisionist case a century later. In 1834 Croker told Murray that prior to 1830 he had never published 'one purely political article' in the *Quarterly*; at least 'not one, certainly in which *party politics* predominated'.[192] While this was at best a very legalistic truth, Croker's 'pedantic' concern to portray historical events accurately is worth bearing in mind when weighing his testimony on events during the 1820s and 30s, when together with his press circle, his political articles, activities and ideas would have a highly significant influence on party policy and popular opinion, and they will occupy the rest of this study.

THE PRESS CIRCLE AND ITS FIRST EARLY SUCCESS

In an attempt to allay some of the anticipated criticism of her new book, *Italy* (1821), Lady Morgan had a statement bound in its front pages denouncing the '*chefs de brigandes* of the *Quarterly*', 'the supposed literary organ of government', and its 'subaltern scribes' the 'cankers of the calm' at *Blackwood's*, the *Morning Post*, *Courier*, *Literary Gazette*, *Guardian*, *The Edinburgh Monthly Magazine*. She never included a 'Cr—er', on this occasion, but few in politics and the press by that time could have doubted that he was the 'creature' and the 'cankers' his press circle. Although mainly inspired by their ridicule of her books, another factor provoking her ire had been the leading part Croker and his pressmen had just played in destroying the Whigs' first real chance of taking office for fifteen years.

Liverpool's ministry would remain weak up until 1821–2 and Croker's criticism of Phillips part-reflected his growing concern at the rise of radicalism and popular dissent as the wartime economy declined after 1814. Distress became widespread, and many became justifiably receptive to the idea that most members of the political establishment, or 'Old Corruption', were only concerned to enrich themselves. There was a 'remarkable rise in the parliamentary reform movement',[193] and although some of the Whig leaders were in favour of limited franchise reform, the main thrust of their parliamentary challenge concentrated on forcing the ministry to make £18 million worth of tax cuts.

The loss of this government income, while relieving the burden of taxation on the middling classes and above, undermined the ability of the ministry to fund poor relief and public work projects to address the distress.[194] Croker and most of his press circle were opposed to the tax cuts on these grounds, with the *Quarterly* criticising the government for undermining its ability 'to come to the aid of the suffering classes' when anybody 'who is not either a madman or a villain, must see that there is but one course – to mitigate the evil by giving as much temporary relief as possible'. The Whigs and their 'batteries of political economy' had swayed 'the House of Commons' and the political leaders 'will be held up to detestation, as insensible to the distresses of their constituents'.[195] The *Quarterly's* main target was of course the Whig and Radical opposition, but as we will see, the defence of the poor and demand for reforms to protect and improve their living standards would be an enduring feature of the press circles' campaigns. This was because it was a unitary Christian justice and requirement of good government in itself, but also in order to disarm the 'ultras' and any revolutionary threat. 'Let the Ultra Whigs make the breach,' the *Quarterly* continued, 'and the Spenceans will level the wall; what the shavers began the scalpers will finish' with all the 'triumphant zeal' of a 'new army of fanatics'.[196]

Within the same number Croker had emphasised the importance of the free press, he warned that 'in these times, when the main force' of it was brought 'to bear like a battery' on the state and the 'head of government', then of 'all the engines of mischief which were ever employed for the destruction of mankind, the press is the most formidable when perverted in its uses as it was by the Revolutionists in France'. In such times agitators can 'appear giants, who in the clearer and purer atmosphere of a well ordered and free constitutional government dwindle to dwarfs'. This is a truth 'which the history of all times and ages, and above all the history of the last twenty-five years, affords most convincing proofs'.[197]

The ministry made little attempt to address their dwindling press and popular support with reforms, but by 1819 most of the public protest had begun to dissipate following 'Peterloo' when the Repressive Acts proscribed mass political assemblies and forced the closure of many radical and 'seditious' publications. At the end of the year, the Whig, Lord John Russell, later the main architect of the Great Reform Act, took the opportunity to propose a motion for the transfer of representation from some 'rotten' boroughs to industrial towns in order to counter the 'evils of itinerant demagogues who went about the country and sought only the overthrow of the constitution which they pretended to reform'.[198]

Croker would justifiably earn his reputation as the most determined opponent of the 1832 Reform Act, but it is an error to represent him as an opponent of parliamentary reform. Like Burke, who Croker described as the 'the patriarch of rational reform', he believed that 'a state without the means of some change is without the means of its conservation'. The application of 'the two principles of conservation and correction'[199] kept society healthy, and it was central to Croker's philosophy that good government should 'lead and control the Reform movement rather than be mastered by it'.[200] There 'never was a revolution which might not have been arrested by a proper policy on the part of government – by a sufficiently steady resistance or sufficiently liberal concession',[201] and at the same time Russell was proposing his moderate 1819 motion, Croker drew up a more extensive Reform plan to enfranchise thirty-three towns with a population of over 10,000 and the removal of representation from some rotten boroughs. At first he was confident the proposal would be accepted, noting that he discussed it with ministers and 'the then Cabinet had almost agreed', but Liverpool 'received the proposition with indifference' and it was dropped.[202]

He was also frustrated by the continued failure of ministers to try and win support through the press, and in November 1819 he decided to establish a Sunday newspaper. He solicited articles and assistance from friends such as Sir Walter Scott and his future son-in-law, John Gibson Lockhart, a young Edinburgh lawyer and a leading contributor to *Blackwood's*. Croker had never met Lockhart before, but wrote to him saying that 'common friends' had suggested he might assist 'some literary gentlemen [who] have determined to set up a weekly paper'. This was 'on principles diametrically opposite to the weekly journals, which are now in vogue: that is principles of morality, loyalty, respect for the constituted authorities etc. – that is <u>Toryism</u>'. If the '*Constitution* [the intended name] shall appear to you and Mr. Wilson [John, the editor of *Blackwood's*] to deserve your support, I cannot doubt that the Whigs and Reformers in Scotland will afford you an ample field and plenty of game'. He concluded conspiratorially that he had not mentioned the matter to William Blackwood or John Murray of the *Quarterly*, and emphasised that Lockhart could 'depend on the name of the contributors remaining unknown'.[203] Lockhart responded immediately that he would see Croker 'has something from this place in good time', and complimented him on recruiting as editor George Croly (a fellow student at Dublin with Croker), who 'sparkled so beautifully in the *Courier*'.[204] Scott sent three short essays under the title of 'The Vision' for the first number that December, by which time the

name had been changed to the *Guardian*. A title probably adopted to
cock a snook at Brougham, who two years before had tried to establish
a Whig newspaper of the same name with Tom Moore as editor, but
had 'given it up for lack of friends just prior to the first issue'.[205]

The *Guardian*'s first editorial declared that although it intended to
be popular it would not be sensationalist and 'seek a guilty profit or
guiltier popularity, by reviling our holy religion, by libelling established
authorities, by calumniating magistrates, by puffing every bad poet, and
by insulting public decency under the pretence of reporting the Court
of Justice'. Neither did it intend to be 'a mere polemical and party pamphlet'; it would publish articles on 'foreign, commercial and literary
intelligence ... works of science', but 'we are for one party' and 'under
the existing circumstances against another'. We will combat 'Whigs and
Democrats, Presbyterians and Papists, Borough Mongers and Radicals',
for together with 'the proudest of the aristocracy and the basest of the
populace' they were now united in a 'monstrous' coalition.[206]

Although dedicated to being the guardian of the constitution, in
its second number the *Guardian* advocated gradual borough reform as a
corrective 'and safe mode of Reform'.[207] Three weeks later, and again
using arguments similar to those Croker would use in the early 1830s to
define fundamental Conservative party principles, it argued that 'Reform,
as the case arises is not only wholesome, but indispensable', whereas
Reform as 'a concession to clamour' or as a 'principle of change appears
to us to be pregnant with danger'.[208] The *Guardian* had some limited early
success, but slowly declined before closing three years later. This was
partly because popular antipathy to the ministry remained high, and partly
because it remained less sensationalist than most other Sunday papers, but
these problems were exacerbated by the failure of Liverpool and some
other ministers to even support it with official advertisements, providing
Croker with yet another irritating example of their casual neglect of the
press. He had invested over £1,500 of his own money on Liverpool's
promise that he would be reimbursed, but it took four years 'despite
repeated requests, pleas of poverty, and justified anger, to receive the
money'.[209] By the same process, as he remarked sarcastically to Peel,
his tenacity also won him the bonus of a 'distinguished place' in Lord
Liverpool's 'disesteem or distaste or dislike'.[210]

Almost thirty years later Croker recorded that this period had been
distinguished by a series 'of seditious riots ... insane turbulence of the
people' when 'the factious violence of the parties' was greater than he
had known since first entering parliament in 1807.[211] By 1820, however,

most of this 'turbulence' was directed at a totemic target of 'Old Corruption', the highly unpopular prince regent, on behalf of his estranged wife, Caroline. She had been living a well-funded and equally dissolute life in Italy for many years, but the prince was seeking approval for a divorce, and as early as 1817 Croker had expressed his concern to Peel that with 'the public only waiting to see the Prince take a part, to take one against him', then should he receive permission it could stimulate extensive disturbances. George III died in January 1820, and as Rohan McWilliam has recently argued, despite the 'Caroline crisis' having been dismissed by some 1960s social historians as 'humbug', it is clear from the evidence that it stimulated probably the most extensive display of national popular protest against the political establishment that Britain had experienced in living memory.[212]

Hazlitt expressed the Radical's irritation that the 'love of liberty' had failed to raise the 'wretched, helpless, doting, credulous, meddlesome people', and the cause of a queen became 'the only question I have ever known that excited a thorough popular feeling … into the very heart of the nation; it took possession of every house or cottage in the kingdom'.[213] Over the following months 'fervid support' grew for 'a not very virtuous queen' in opposition to her 'still less virtuous husband',[214] and Croker would find abundant qualification for his theory that most ambitious agitators would rapidly tailor their principles to any mass movement regardless of its 'humbug'.[215]

On 17 February the king reluctantly agreed to the cabinet's request that he should not pursue his controversial divorce on the condition that should Caroline return to England to be crowned alongside him, she would be the subject of a formal investigation into her adulterous conduct. That same month, ever alert to the propagandist influence of such things, Croker convinced him to remove Caroline's title from the Anglican liturgy: for 'if she is fit to be introduced to the Almighty, she is fit to be received by men, and if we are to pray for her in Church, we must surely bow to her at Court.'[216] Henry Brougham had been Caroline's lawyer for many years, and to Croker's disdain, he secretly sought an official appointment by holding the threat of her return to Britain over Liverpool's head, who feared that the government 'would be unable to survive the storm should she arrive'.[217] Before any negotiation could be completed, however, she arrived in Dover with the radical ex-mayor of London, Alderman Wood in early June, and her carriage was pulled by relays of sailors through villages full of cheering crowds until it was met by a massive demonstration in London.[218] Throughout the summer

'the Queen gave the London radicals a cause', allowing 'them back on
the streets with a display of pro-queen, anti-king political theatre'[219] as
press 'propagandists created an image of a wronged woman bravely
standing up to the wicked king and corrupt ministers who had attacked
the people's liberties'.[220] Within weeks, the overwhelming majority of
newspapers, periodicals and the rich variety of unregistered publications, salacious cartoon prints and pamphlets supported Caroline's
cause, outnumbering the ministerial press by as much as ten to one.[221]

Croker's ability to respond was limited by the risk to his reputation.
As Charles Knight, another of his press protégés and the *Guardian's* last
editor, recalled, given that it was widely known that the ministry 'countenanced' it, to have taken an aggressive part in 'the fierce battle of journalism' would have resulted in a huge loss of respectability for those
concerned.[222] He did what he could by secretly writing articles and
organising others to do the same. As one news-paperman corroborated
when seeking employment from the queen's faction, 'I can also prove
that Mr Croker of the Admiralty, at this moment, pays £50 per week to
certain persons whose duty is confined to vilification of the Queen',[223]
and from the other perspective Gifford, the editor of the *Quarterly*,
recorded that 'Mr Croker is the only link that unites us at all with the
Ministry and the service he has done them by his various papers is in-
calculable; but he cannot do everything.'[224]

Throughout the summer Croker and the press allies had little success,
doing the best they could in the newspapers and producing a few pamphlets such as one written by his clerk, Thomas Crofton Croker, *The
Queens Question Queried: A Pedantless Phillipic Production by an Irish
Barrister*, ridiculing the sentimental 'bundles of blarney' written about
the over-rouged middle-aged queen. The 'most injured and desolate of
women ... innocent with the bloom of beauty on her brow, the daisy, the
dandelion or the daffodil that crowns the crimeless cranium'. Remember how, when 'with her bare breasts she brightened the buoyant ball at
Naples ... Oh may we witness our wives and daughters resembling thee
in womanly wisdom and may the delicacy devolve to our dimpled
daughters'. Concluding with an Irish keen: 'Oh Hone! Oh Hone! Pray
leave us alone.'[225]

The most successful ministerial response was the pamphlet *A Letter
From the King to His People* (1820). Issued in over twenty-eight
editions,[226] it was written by J.W. Croker after consultation with, and
under the name of, 'George IV', in order to present the king's case in a
pacific manner and criticise the extent of the attacks on him. The 'liberty

of the press, in itself a great abstract good', was 'capable alike of being converted into a bane or an antidote'; capable 'of promoting and effecting immortal benefits to mankind, or inflicting upon them irremediable ills', but circumstances have now arisen 'where a portion of the daily Press ... unrestrained by truth, and so devoid of principle have goaded public opinion into extremes'. He ended with a conciliatory appeal that the king accepted he had been an 'extravagant prince ... the nation most generously paid my debts, made provisions for my ménage' and suggesting that he would reform his behaviour, but it was unjust that the queen's 'misdemeanours and high crimes' have been ignored because she 'has become the tool of party'.[227]

The legal case against Caroline for treasonous adultery, in particular with her Italian manservant Bergami, concluded in the Lords that November when she was found guilty by a slim majority of nine. Given the disturbed state of the country, Liverpool decided not to prosecute [228] but the popular agitation and hostility to the ministry continued. Croker remained worried that it could only worsen when the coronation was held in a few months' time and appears to have resolved to take more drastic measures.

In one of his few accounts of his role in the press at this time, he later described himself and some of his press 'disciples ... who later eclipsed their master', as having played the single most important part in countering the dangerous threat to overthrow the ministry. Their success had been

> ... so complete that it turned the press – I mean the preponderating force of the press – right round ... and the Opposition (what had, I believe, never happened in the history of English parties) – the Opposition complained loudly of the <u>licentiousness</u> of the press; which only means that they were no longer able to wield it exclusively to their purposes.[229]

As Caroline's biographer Jane Robbins has argued, the mass support for the queen represented a real and dangerous political threat, and the most effective measures used to combat it were the anonymous pamphlets written in the name of the king and the new Sunday newspaper, *John Bull*.[230] Those in the king's name were, as we have seen, certainly Croker's work, and as we will see, a very good case could also be made that he was almost certainly the secret founder of the notorious *John Bull*.[231] A paper that Thomas Barnes the editor of *The Times*, and no paragon of journalistic respectability himself, described as 'set up for the express purpose of libelling the Queen and those who visit her'. Of its authors, 'we speak only with pity, or hardly speak at all' given our contempt for the 'obscenity and malignity of the publication'.[232] Given that *The Times* had substantially increased its circulation by supporting Caroline, then Barnes's enmity was probably aroused by more than just moral indignation, but he amply illustrated the view of *John Bull* held by even the less than polite members of polite society.

Theodore Hook, a witty polemicist and musical entertainer, has long been identified as its editor and founder, and his biographer has examined some of his connections with Croker.[233] Hook appears to have first introduced himself to Croker in the spring of 1820 by sending him the rough draft of a satirical pamphlet mocking the Whig and Radical support for Queen Caroline.[234] Within it Caroline's champion, Alderman Wood, was portrayed as a cunning opportunistic Dick Whittington, and Caroline his amoral and spellbinding cat. 'One that all men may stroke and pat, it likes rats, but is more glad at catching men', particularly the rat 'westministererienses', and providing the magic concoctions 'to steal away men's senses'.[235] Only a few items of Hook and Croker's correspondence survive, but Croker was clearly enthusiastic and apparently rewrote the role of the queen, for Hook responded: 'Your "Catte" is a master stroke and indeed the powerful touches given to my sketch have totally changed its standing ... I could send you the copy before it went to press or the proofs after.'[236] Croker and Hook would meet frequently in the months before the first number of *John Bull* was published; something noted in the diary of a Miss Godman following the death of Croker's only child that May at the age of three years and four months.

This was the greatest personal tragedy of his life, and in a moving letter to his friend Viscount Lowther he said it rendered him indifferent to any personal political ambition, and to Peel that he threw himself into his work as the only way of deadening the pain of his loss.[237] Rosamund, who had suffered a number of miscarriages and at least one infant death in the thirteen years of their marriage, was so distraught that she could not be left unattended and a Miss Godman was employed to be her companion. Three months before the first number of *John Bull* appeared, she accompanied the Crokers on a visit to France designed to facilitate Rosamund's recuperation and noted that Theodore Hook joined them. A week later, Hook and Croker returned to England, and the following week returned to Paris.[238] On 23 September they met Thomas Moore, who corroborated this in his own diary,[239] and on 3 October that 'Mr Croker and Mr C. Stuart [Charles, the British ambassador in Paris] and Mr Canning' joined them. Miss Godman continued to make a number of other entries referring to Hook's presence until the last week of October when they all returned to London, where 'Mr Hook, as usual, dined with us.' Something he continued to do in the company of some leading Tory politicians and friends of Croker until Miss Godman's diary ended on 30 November.[240]

Both Croker and Hook were clearly gathering information about Caroline and her political supporters throughout this period. One of Hook's letters to Croker said that a man by the name of 'Lesswick, a confectioner in Fleet Street, has or had' somebody in his service 'who was on board the [*Clarinda*] or *Leviathan*', the ship that the queen and her lover Bergami had travelled on, and had seen 'more than has yet said they have seen'. More significantly, Hook continued:

> The P's [proofs?] will be done tonight ... the printer tells me that 500 answers every purpose. A new number of the Magazine will be out this evening with the Chronological table, including the fat old buck's reception at Brandyburg House [Brandenberg House, Caroline's London residence]. I shall take the opportunity of being here to put my case in order for your brief which you were so kind to offer to hold for me.[241]

Croker was also gathering information from other sources, among them Charles Stuart, who informed him in one letter that 'Le Fitte' had good evidence that Bergami had been paid £7,000 in the last ten days, implying that it had been provided by leading members of the Whig opposition.[242]

The first number of *John Bull* appeared on 17 December 1820, and both the expressions of frustration with the government's neglect of the press in its editorial as well as its style suggest that Croker was its author. *Bull* belligerently declared that it intended to speak 'the plain truth' about the queen and her supporters:

> The shameful licentiousness of a prostituted Press, the infamous tendency of the caricatures which issue from every sink of vice and infamy in and near the Metropolis ... are banes to our constitution and call for an antidote ... We waited long and patiently in the hopes that some of those commanding talents by which the machine of government is moved might have been directed to the humbler,

but no less useful, task of checking and correcting the evils which surround and threaten us; but finding silence (which in some cases is said to give consent) reigns amongst those who could ably have met and crushed the malign efforts of faction and sedition, we have ventured to espouse the cause of our KING AND CONSTITUTION ... The test by which we shall try everything is TRUTH. Truth is the sole corrector of the mischiefs which stare us in the face, and truth will eventually triumph.

This no holds barred declaration was put into immediate effect with detailed accounts of Caroline's rumoured sexual activities; but what most raised the appetite of the wider public and the alarm and fury of the Whigs was that *Bull* proceeded to name, satirise and recount similar gossip about the peccadilloes of Whig aristocrats, politicians and their allies. Behind the thinnest veil of innuendo it dedicated an extensive centre-page feature to retelling rumours about the Whig ladies under the title 'The Queen's Female Visitors who had signed the Queen's visitors-book at Brandenburgh House', concluding menacingly, 'to be continued regularly'.[243]

Not surprisingly, over the following weeks many readers at every social level eagerly awaited its titillating accounts with pleasure or trepidation, and as Lowther was pleased to report, *John Bull* was soon to be found in 'every public house in the country'.[244] He had also been gathering information for Croker in France and, although the son of one of the wealthiest Tory borough-mongers, apparently acting as a distributor for some of his publications. In one letter Croker mentions that Hook was bringing him news and that 'someone has reported today that she has been <u>surps'd</u> at Knightsbridge on Saturday – but I can hardly [believe] she is ripe for plucking yet ... I send you more of the Queen's magazines – if I were to send you 25 of each could you distribute them'.[245]

The Whigs and their ladies rapidly became more cautious about promoting Caroline's cause, and according to another contemporary pressman:

> After *Bull's* lampoons began to raise a general laugh those who were most severely handled by them ... the great Whig families, who had supported the Queen as a party manoeuvre only, rapidly moved away. The 'unprotected female' cry could not get a hearing – the 'injured wife'

appeal only excited unpleasant retorts – and any reference to the 'wronged Queen' elicited a burst of mirth ... the Queen had been overthrown by puns; threatened rebellion had been put down by a discharge of squibs.[246]

Henry Brougham later described *John Bull*'s 'practice of attacking every woman of rank' who accepted an invitation to visit the Queen, as having alarmed enough Whigs 'so as to my certain knowledge, to influence their votes in both the Houses'.[247] Its popularity rapidly outstripped most of the Whig competition, and despite receiving neither government money nor assistance, its service to the ministry was 'probably without parallel in the history of periodical literature'.[248]

On 19 July the queen noisily attempted to force an entry to Westminster Abbey during the coronation but her way was barred. Croker had remained at his Admiralty office to assist in directing any response to public disorder, and he wrote to Peel that this final act 'calculated to try her strength only proved her weakness' when she and Alderman Wood were 'hooted by the spectators' and she 'went off in a rage of disappointment'.[249] Within a fortnight her personal tragedy reached a poignant and unexpected climax when she died on 6 August from what appears to have been chronic congestion of the bowel. Her funeral stimulated a short-lived wave of parades and demonstrations, but by that time 'public opinion' had become largely settled after what may have been a highly theatrical, yet for Croker a nevertheless highly dangerous political catharsis.

Not surprisingly the Whigs were furious at *John Bull*'s success, and in May 1821 Henry Fox Cooper, another Irish pressman employed for three guineas a week to read proofs and manage publication, was summoned before the Commons to answer a technical charge of abuse of parliamentary privilege. Sir Robert Wilson, an ex-soldier of fortune and duellist, captured the extent of the Whigs' anger by violently denouncing the *Bull*'s producers as 'base and dastardly assassins' and threatening to publicly horsewhip Hook when he had the evidence to prove his involvement.[250] Rumours of Croker's connections were also circulating, and John Murray, who had known him since he first arrived in London, wrote to him on 16 May asking if he was familiar with a harsh satirical attack on Byron that had appeared in *Bull*. Croker replied 'that some persons have had the impudence and the falsehood to insinuate that I was, in some way or other, a supporter of the *John Bull* newspaper, of which I am as innocent as Mr Bennett or Mr Brougham can be'.[251] Murray clearly remained unconvinced, and responded with a teasing if rather un-subtle interrogation:

As to *Bull* – convinced as I am of the palpable good it has been the means of effecting, I have allowed my mind to conceive, though never my tongue to utter – that the happiest things were probably contributed by you; and, thinks I to myself, if Croker did not write that incomparable article, admired by all parties for its talent, on Sunday last – the <u>Devil did</u>. And now I can give you an equal proof of faith: I ... I believe!!! You did not – there!![252]

Croker angrily replied: 'I assure you on my honour, that I neither wrote that article you allude to, nor any other in *John Bull* ...and positively I neither know nor care about any of the thousand and one Bulls that are bellowing.'[253]

As Byron's publisher, Murray was annoyed he had been harshly ridiculed and that the 'Letter from John Bull to Lord Byron' had been issued as a pamphlet. Its author was John Gibson Lockhart, and Croker sent him a rather disingenuous letter on 21 May saying that rumours were circulating in London attributing the 'Letter' to Lockhart and querying whether there was any truth in it. Lockhart replied that he could 'not for my life divine' how it had been discovered; 'I would pay a tremendous fine rather than bear the blame of it for a week',[254] and he appealed to Croker 'to do everything in your power to stop the report ... I cannot say how much I am disturbed by this thing – not on my account, but Scott's.' Lockhart had recently married Scott's daughter, and prior to giving his approval, he had expressed concern at some of the aggressive and disparaging articles written by Lockhart, John Wilson and others for *Blackwood's*.[255] Scott knew nothing, Lockhart continued, please 'do so whatever is strongest and most effectual to save me from a great pain ... I am a most impractical fellow. No I have not written to Murray, I trust everything <u>to you</u>.'[256] Croker replied that he would 'contradict the report' but he feared that the printer of the pamphlet, a Mr Wright, 'a babbling sort of man', had guessed its author.[257] 'Mr Wright' was in fact a publisher Croker had secretly used for years, having printed *The New Whig Guide*, the 'Whittington' pamphlet, and Crofton Croker's *Pedantless Phillipic* against Caroline.[258]

As has been seen, Croker had only met Lockhart through correspondence the year before and they had no close relationship, but he nevertheless wrote a letter to Murray that same day flagrantly lying on his behalf:

> I had mentioned to Mr Lockhart that I had heard that <u>he</u> was the author of 'John Bull'; he answered me in utter ignorance and astonishment. He had never heard of the letter and knows nothing about it. Therefore we must look elsewhere for the author … Do you remember my writing to you some years ago that I thought Lord Byron's genius essentially dramatic and tragic. Mr Bull it seems supports the same opinion, but it happens to be the only one on which I concur with him.[259]

The controversy declined as public interest waned, and it is not unreasonable to assume that Croker's lies convinced Murray and his literary circle in London of Lockhart's innocence. Murray appears never to have discovered who wrote the 'Letter from John Bull', and in 1825 gave Lockhart the prestigious and well-paid post of editor of the *Quarterly Review*. John Wilson would edit and write for *Blackwood's* for most of the next three decades, and in June 1820 Croker successfully interceded with Lord Melville, the head of the Dundas political network, to win the appointment for him as lecturer in Moral Philosophy at Edinburgh University.[260] A year later Croker's connections with *Blackwood's* were further strengthened when he did the same to help William Blackwood obtain the office of Royal Bookseller for Scotland.[261]

In May 1821 Fox-Cooper and a printer named Arrowsmith were fined and imprisoned for three months.[262] Hook continued to publish elaborate denials of his own involvement with *Bull*,[263] but the Whigs wisely believed none of it, and in late 1822 they had him imprisoned in a spunging house for the defalcation of funds from an official post he had held in Mauritius some years before. A subordinate had probably taken the money, but Hook was legally responsible, and *John Bull* indignantly protested that the 'false implications' he 'belonged to this paper' were the cause of his persecution. By then few would have accepted these denials, and perhaps even fewer those made the previous week that it was 'utterly false' 'that we are connected somehow or other with somebody in the Admiralty'.[264]

Hook was released on temporary appeal, but in August 1823 he was imprisoned once again in what Lockhart described as 'a vile, squalid place, noisy and noxious, swarming with a population of thief takers, gin-sellers and worse'. While he was there he was visited almost daily by William Maginn, 'a man hardly – if at all – less remarkable than himself in natural talents and infinitely superior in the knowledge that can be acquired from books', who undertook 'some share in the affair of the *John Bull*'.[265] Maginn was another graduate of Dublin University, a child prodigy who had entered at the age of eleven, and probably the most gifted member of the press circle. He had been sending articles to *Blackwood's* and the *Literary Gazette* from his home in Cork, where he had been a local literary controversialist and schoolmaster since 1818. They had won him substantial acclaim, and in a letter to William Blackwood written in June 1823, Maginn said that Croker had recently sought his help on the *Quarterly*, and had 'whispered' to him: 'think thirty guineas a sheet ... As for *Bull*, I have *carte blanche* to do as I like.' Later in the same letter, and in what appears as an afterthought designed to counter earlier loose talk, he added: 'Croker does not write for "John Bull", depend on that'; it was all the work of himself, Hook and a clergyman – although Canning, they all believed, secretly wrote a 'famous article about Lambton's reform motion'.[266] Lockhart would become a close friend of both Hook and Maginn, and he wrote that Maginn moved permanently from Cork to London at this time, and for a wage of 'twenty pounds a month' visited 'Theodore [Hook in prison] and helped him with the writing of *John Bull*'.[267] He also told John Wilson that 'he has come over by Croker's advice to assist Theodore in *Bull*' and that given Croker's influence, 'of course M. looks forward to being snugly set somewhere'.[268]

Hook remained 'snugly' incarcerated, and in December 1823 he sought Lord Liverpool's help by reminding him of the service he had given to the ministry. He received the cool response: 'It is an invariable rule with me never to enter into private or personal correspondence on any official business ... the proper channel for all communications with it is through the secretary and I shall accordingly transmit your letter to him.'[269] Hook would remain locked up for most of the next eighteen months, and despite the threat to his own reputation, Croker visited him in prison with provisions and campaigned for his release by lobbying members of government and the opposition.[270]

He had little success until March 1825, when in an angry letter to the chancellor of the exchequer, Frederick Robinson, he denounced the ministers for their failure to help:

> If he be a criminal show me another in his class who has been more punished! ... Have you any expectation that by breaking his spirit and destroying his health by protracted confinement, he will become better able to discharge his debt.

Look at other defaulters; think of the sums they have abused! Have they pined in prison? Have they been deprived of the necessities of life, even down to a razor case, and why this savage virtue against Mr Hook alone? I can tell you; like a blockhead (which many a man of talent is), he mixed himself with politics, and what between the low people on our side, wishing to curry favour with Opposition, and high people on our side, not wishing to be attacked for favouring a person politically odious to their antagonists, he is visited a severity which, if he had not been suspected of being a Tory writer, would never have dreamt of, and which if he had been an avowed Whig, would not have been tolerated.[271]

Hook was finally released early that summer, and a few weeks later Lockhart arrived in London to take up his post as editor of the *Quarterly Review*, followed by a letter from Sir Walter Scott: 'Take devilish good care of your start in society in London' and make sure not to mix 'with funny easy companions' like 'Theodore Hook and Maginn'.[272] Mixing with what was assembling to become probably the most influential press circle in Britain over the next decade, however, would be something Lockhart would find as irresistible as their *chef de brigand*.

NOTES

1. Clements MS, uncatalogued 'Family Records', mainly compiled by Thomas Crofton–Croker.
2. *Croker Papers*, Croker to Justice Jackson, 4 December 1856, I, p.5.
3. Ibid., Sheridan Knowles to Croker, November 1856, I, p.6.
4. Ibid., Jackson to Croker, November 1856, I, p.5.
5. John Wilson Croker, *Essays on the Early Period of the French Revolution* (London, 1857), p.v.
6. See the 'Minute Books and Records of the Historical Society', 1797–1800, numbers 12 and 13 h, special manuscript collection, Trinity College Dublin.
7. Jonah Barrington, *Jonah Barrington: Personal Sketches of his Own Times* (New York, 1857), p.174.
8. J.W. Croker, 'A Sketch of the State of Ireland: Past and Present (Dublin, 1808), as published in Croker Papers, I pp.442–3.
9. *Irish Harmonic and Glee Club*, held by British Library MR. 280-a-80.5.
10. Brightfield, *Croker*, p.2.
11. *Croker Papers*, Croker to Jackson, 4 December 1856, I, pp.5–6.
12. *The Drennan–McTier Letters: 1802–1819*, ed. Jean Agnew, 3 vols (Dublin, 2006), II, 824 and 895.
13. *Croker Papers*, Croker to Charles Phillips, 3 January 1854, II, p.307.
14. J.W. Croker, *The Opinions of an Impartial Observer on the Late Transactions in Ireland* (Dublin, 1803), pp.4–13.
15. J.W. Croker [Anon] *Historical Epistles* (Dublin, 1803 or 1806), pp.30–1; there is some confusion here, with some of the same material published in collections of pamphlets containing similar arguments. See also *The Opinions of an Impartial Observer on the Late Transactions in Ireland*, pp.4–13.

16. See, in particular, Marianne Elliot, *Robert Emmet: The Making of the Legend* (London, 2003), pp.18–20, 100–20 and *passim*.

17. Clements MS, Lb. 26, Croker to Lockhart, 17 August 1834, ff.43–4.

18. A.L. Rowse, *Jonathan Swift: Major Prophet* ((London, 1975), p.32.

19. For Jonathan Swift, see his 'Tale of a Tub' (1697), in particular, pp.330–5, in *Gulliver's Travels and Selected Writings*, ed. John Hayward (Edinburgh, 1934). See also Edmund Burke, *Vindication of a Natural Society* (1756); *Reflections on the Revolution in France* (1791); *Thoughts on French Affairs* (1791), *passim*. For Swift, Burke as well as some other Irish thinkers and their 'conservative' political philosophies see Thomas Duddy, *A History of Irish Thought* (London, 2002), pp.124–67, 188–202; C. Cruise O'Brien, *Edmund Burke*, abridged by J. McCue (Dublin, 1997), p.254.

20. Edmund Burke, *Reflections in the Revolution in France* (London, 1988 [1791]), ed. Conor Cruise O'Brien; see in particular pp.211–15, 153 and 194–5.

21. See Joep Leerssen, *Remembrance and Imagination: Patterns in the Historical and Literary Representation of Ireland in the Nineteenth Century* (Cork, 1996) and *Hidden Ireland, Public Sphere* (Dublin, 2002)

22. Croker, *Historical Epistles*, pp.77–9.

23. J.W. Croker, [Anon] *Familiar Epistles to Frederick E. Jones on the Present State of the Irish Stage* (Dublin, 1804), pp.12–39, reprinted in *Poetical Satires* [anon] (Dublin, 1818), held by the TCD library.

24. Clements MS, box 1, folder 1, Horatio Smith to Croker, April 1804.

25. *Drennan Letters*, Drennan to McTier, 12 April 1804, III, 1129.

26. Croker mentions that the manager of the Theatre Royal in Crow Street earned £5,000 p.a., 'twice the income of two judges'. He may have underestimated the figure; according to the *Dictionary of National Biography* (Oxford, 1917 edn), Jones was earning between £6,000 and £7,000 p.a. during this period. See entry on Croker, p.124.

27. *Freeman's Journal*, 2 March 1805.

28. *Dublin Journal*, 3 April 1804. See also 16 March and 5 April, 1804.

29. Sydney Owenson [Anon], *A Few Reflections Occasioned by the Perusal of a Work Entitled Familiar Epistles to Frederick J——s Esq. on the Present State of the Irish Stage* (Dublin, 1804); and see Brightfield, *Croker*, pp.20–4 for a fuller account.

30. Brightfield, *Croker*, pp.22–4. Brightfield is perhaps overly hostile to Owenson, but none of the many scholars of 'Lady Morgan' appear to be familiar with the Croker archives, and my own research largely corroborates his account.

31. Sydney Owenson [Anon], *Cutchacutchoo, or the Jostling of the Innocents* (Dublin, 1805), pp.A1–13 bound in a volume of other pamphlets entitled *Poetical Sketches* (Dublin, 1818), National Library of Ireland, Dublin. See also Croker's response: *History of Cutchacutchoo* (1805).

32. Owenson, *A Few Reflections*, p.21.

33. *Anti-Jacobin or Weekly Examiner*, 20 November 1797, and see 27 November for one of the earliest satirical attacks made upon the political sentiments of what became the 'Lake Poets', in particular 'The Friend of Humanity and the Knife Grinder'.

34. *The Times*, 6 April 1801.

35. Clements MS, uncatalogued, box 1, folder 1.

36. Horatio Smith, 'A Greybeard's Gossip about his Literary Acquaintances', *New Monthly Magazine*, 1847, part 1, p.515.

37. See Brightfield, *Croker*, pp.9–11. In a remark correcting a comment made by Lord Russell that Croker hardly knew Moore in London at this time, Croker firmly refuted this saying he had letters to prove that they were friends, and that in fact he had even nursed Moore for some weeks when he suffered a severe 'bout of opthalmia', acting 'as an amanuensis, and one, or I rather think two, of Moore's prettiest songs first saw the light in my hand-writing'. *Correspondence between R. Hon. J.W. Croker and R. Hon. Lord John Russell*, p.22.

38. *Croker Papers*, I, p.9, and see also the *Quarterly Review*, July 1876, p.91.

39. J.W. Croker, *An Intercepted Letter from J——T—, esq., Writer at Canton, to his Friend in Dublin, Ireland* (Dublin,1804), part cited in Brightfield, *Croker*, pp.18–20.

40. Ibid., pp.19–20.

41. *Drennan–McTier Letters*, 20 May 1806, III, no. 129.

42. Clements MS, box 1, folder 6, Denis Browne to Croker, 17 February 1807. See also Peter Jupp, *British and Irish Elections: 1784–1831* (Newton Abbott, 1973) for a short feature on Downpatrick, pp.152–85.

43. *Wellington New Despatches*, Wellington to Hawkesbury, 9 May 1807, V, p.46; and see also *Civil Correspondence and Memoirs: Ireland, of Field Marshal Arthur, Duke of Wellington, K.G.* (ed.) 2nd Duke of Wellington (London, 1860), p.42.
44. *Hansard*, IX, 26 June 1807, cols 651–2.
45. Ibid., col. 652.
46. James Grant, *Further Recollections of the House of Commons* (London, 1836), p.97.
47. *Croker Papers*, diary entry, June 1807, I, p.11.
48. *Wellington New Despatches*, V, p.444, and see Brightfield, *Croker*, p.28.
49. See British Library Add. MSS 38079, single folder with no folio number for the memorandum from Wellington. The only notice taken of it appears to be a transcription published in the appendix of M. Roberts, *The Whig Party* (London, 1939), p.407; but he does not connect it with Croker's *Sketch of the State of Ireland*. See also *Croker Papers*, Croker to Lonsdale, 4 September 1852, III, p.259, telling him he 'concocted' his pamphlet with Wellington, and whatever his later image, as Croker liked to remind Wellington, the first speech he had made in the Irish Commons had been in praise of a Catholic Relief proposal. 10 January 1793, *Irish Parliamentary Register*, XIII, p.5.
50. J.A.F. Spence, 'The Philosophy of Irish Toryism, 1832–52: A Study of Reactions to Liberal Reformism in Ireland in the Generation Between the First Reform Act and the Famine, with Especial Reference to the National Feeling Among the Protestant Ascendancy' (DPhil. thesis, Birkbeck College, University of London, 1991), pp.171–4. Most of Spence's excellent study concentrates on the later period, in particular those figures connected with the *Dublin University Magazine* after 1833, but see Chapters 3, 4, 5 and 6 for some account of the earlier tradition.
51. J.W. Croker, *A Sketch of the State of Ireland: Past and Present*, p.459.
52. Ibid., pp.435–85, quotations: pp.435, 450, 455–6.
53. Ibid., p.452.
54. Ibid., pp.448–52.
55. Ibid., pp.455.
56. Ibid., pp.453–6.
57. Ibid., p.465.
58. Ibid., p.454.
59. Ibid., p.452, 458, 462–3, and see also p.465.
60. Spence, 'The Philosophy of Irish Toryism', pp.171–4. See in particular Chapters 3, 4, 5 and 6.
61. Croker, *State of Ireland*, p.438. His reference is to Molyneux's *The Case of Ireland Being Bound by Acts of Parliament in England* (1698); proscribed as seditious, it was, according to Swift's praise in his 'Fourth' *Drapier's Letter*, the original declaration of Ireland's right to have a free legislature.
62. Ibid., p.439.
63. Clements MS, box 1, folder 7, Thomas Casey to Croker, 11 February 1808.
64. James Prior, *The Memoirs and Character of the Right Hon. Edmund Burke* (London, 1824), p.xv.
65. 'A Letter to Richard Burke on the Protestant Ascendancy in Ireland' (1792), in David Bromwich (ed.), *On Empire Liberty and Reform: Speeches and Letters of Edmund Burke* (Yale, 2000), pp.425–8.
66. *Croker Papers*, Croker to Rosamund, 12 October 1809, I, p.20.
67. *DUM*, June 1842, p.800.
68. Brian Jenkins, *Henry Goulburn, 1784–1856: A Political Biography* (Liverpool, 1996), pp.22–3.
69. *The Private Letters of Sir Robert Peel*, ed. George Peel (London, 1920), p.36.
70. Norman Gash, *Mr Secretary Peel* (London, 1985), p.80.
71 See C.N. Breiseith, 'John Wilson Croker's Influence on Sir Robert Peel', unpublished BLitt thesis (Lincoln College, Oxford, 1962); a very good short study, but compiled almost entirely from British archival and secondary sources.
72. James Sack, 'The Memory of Burke and Pitt: English Conservatism Confronts its Past, 1806–1829', Historical Journal, 30, 3 (1987), pp.623–40, at p.625.
73. See Eric J. Evans, *Sir Robert Peel: Statesmanship, Power and Party* (London, 1991), p.10, and my PhD thesis, Chapters 3 and 6. For a little-known source of evidence illustrating the part this played in winning Peel the 'Blue Ribband' seat for Oxford University from Canning with ultra-Tory 'Pitt Club' support, see the editorials and letters published in *The Times*, 29 May and 2 and 3 June 1817.

74. *Croker Papers*, 'State of Ireland', I, p.462.
75. Thomas Moore, *Letter to the Roman Catholics of Dublin* (Dublin, 1810), republished in Brendan Clifford's neglected study, *The Veto Controversy* (Belfast, 1985), pp.37–57; and see *passim* for Clifford, critical assessment of the divisive significance of O'Connell's opposition and the activities of what Croker called 'ultra-Catholics'. See also Oliver Mac-Donagh, 'The Politicisation of the Irish Catholic Bishops, 1810–1850', *Historical Journal*, XVII, I (1975), pp.37–8.
76. See Brian Girvin, 'Making Nations: O'Connell and Religion and the Making of Political Identity', in M. O'Connell (ed.), *Daniel O'Connell, Political Pioneer* (Dublin, 1991), p.30.
77. Patrick M. Geoghegan, *King Dan: The Rise of Daniel O'Connell, 1775–1829* (Dublin, 2008), p.123.
78. Ibid., quoting S.J. Connolly, in W.E. Vaughan (ed.), *A New History of Ireland* (Oxford, 1989), V, p 53.
79. Gash, *Mr Secretary Peel*, p.154.
80. Oliver MacDonagh, *The Hereditary Bondsman: Daniel O'Connell, 1775–1829* (London, 1988), pp.110–12.
81. C.S. Parker (ed.), *Sir Robert Peel from His Private Papers*, 3 vols (London, 1899), Peel to Liverpool, 18 May 1812, I, pp.67–8 [Henceforth *Peel Correspondence*].
82. Ibid., Liverpool to Canning, 19 May 1812, p.68.
83. *Hansard*, XXIII, 22 June 1812, col. 665.
84. Ibid., col. 690.
85. Ibid., cols 694–6.
86. Hinde, *Canning*, p.252.
87. MacDonagh, *The Hereditary Bondsman*, pp.110.
88. Ibid., p.111.
89. Emmet Larkin, *The Pastoral Role of the Roman Catholic Church in Pre-Famine Ireland* (Dublin, 2006), pp.90–1, and for the factional conflicts within the Irish Catholic Church during this time, pp.90–112. For two interesting arguments on the politics of the Catholic clergy see the *Quarterly Review*, 'Romanism in Ireland', December 1841, and 'New Reformation in Ireland', June 1852.
90. *Hansard*, XXIV, 1 March 1813, cols 896–901.
91. W. Cooke-Taylor, *Life and Times of Sir Robert Peel* (London, 1851), vol. I, p.69. Cooke-Taylor was a fellow of Trinity College Dublin. He was critical of Peel and O'Connell, and his study presents Peel's career from an interesting and moderate Irish Anglican perspective; see also MacDonagh, *The Hereditary Bondsman*, p.112.
92. *Hansard*, XXIV, 1 March 1813, cols 900–15.
93. Ibid., col. 915.
94. *Annual Register*, 26 May 1813 (London, 1814), p.349.
95. MacDonagh, *The Hereditary Bondsman*, p.113.
96. *The Times*, 26 May 1813.
97. *Hansard*, XXIV, 1 March 1813, cols 941–8.
98. *The Times*, 25 December 1813.
99. Cooke-Taylor, *Sir Robert Peel*, p.71.
100. Oliver MacDonagh, 'The Politicisation of the Catholic Bishops, 1810–1850', *The Historical Journal*, XVII, I (1975), pp.37–8.
101. *Quarterly Review*, 'Friendly Advice to Some Lords', July 1831, p.520.
102. Clements MS, collection of loose boxed items for 1809 (no file numbers). Croker wrote to Perceval in late April 1809 that he would even like, 'for the sake of learning business, to have been private secretary to the Chief Secretary to Ireland', despite it being unusual at that time for an MP to take such a position; see also Brightfield, *Croker*, p.34.
103. Gash, *Mr Secretary Peel*, p.89, and Richmond papers, National Library of Ireland, Duke of Richmond to Lord Bathurst, 12 June 1812, f.1580.
104. Ibid., pp.167–72.
105. *Croker Papers*, extract from undated letter, but almost certainly the spring of 1812, I, p.39.
106. Add. MSS 52467, J.S. Emerson to Croker, 13 August 1812, f.35.
107. Ibid., 40320, Croker to Peel, 6 March 1829, f.110.
108. Ibid., 40280, Peel to Liverpool, 19 October 1812, f.66.
109. Liverpool to Peel, 7 November 1812, cited in Gash, *Mr Secretary Peel*, pp.106–7.
110. *Quarterly Review*, July 1831, p.320.

111. Add. MSS 40183, Croker to Peel, 26 October 1812, ff.63–4.
112. Parker, *Peel Correspondence*, I, pp.61–2.
113. Clements MS, Lb. 27, f.156; *Croker Papers*, II, p.208; and Jenkins, *Goulburn*, pp.64–70.
114. Roberts, *The Whig Party*, p.330; and Frank O'Gorman, *The Emergence of the Two Party System, 1760–1832* (Oxford, 1982).
115. Add. MSS 38299 (Liverpool Manuscripts), Croker to Liverpool, 13 October 1824, ff.140–2.
116. Duncan Watts, *Tories, Conservatives and Unionists: 1815–1914* (London, 1994), p.13.
117. Edmund Burke, *Thoughts on the Present Discontent* (1770) ed. E.J. Payne (Oxford, 1904), pp.83–6.
118. Brightfield, *Croker*, p.260.
119. T. Crofton Croker, *Portraits of Eminent Conservatives* (London, 1840); see section on Croker, *passim*. This is a large and expensively ornamented book, two copies held by the British Library.
120. Add. MSS 40280, 1 October 1812, f.44.
121. *Croker Papers*, Peel to Croker, 17 November 1817, I, p.108.
122. National Library of Scotland, MS 4003, Croker to Blackwood, 19 June 1818, f.31.
123. Arthur Aspinall, *Politics and the Press: 1780–1850* (London, 1949), pp.2, 371; E.H. Coleridge (ed.), *The Letters of S.T. Coleridge*, II, p.660.
124. Ibid., p.371.
125. *Croker Papers*, Walter to Croker, 9 May 1811 and 20 May 1812, I, pp.36–8.
126. F.G. Stevens, *The History of 'The Times': 1785–1841*, 4 vols (London, 1936), I, p.86.
127. Duke MS, box 1, Croker to Shaw, 9 February 1814.
128. See Aled Jones, *Powers of the Press: Newspapers, Power and the Public in Nineteenth-Century England* (Aldershot, 1994), pp.32–4.
129. *Quarterly Review*, 'Chateaubriand's Monarchy', July 1816, pp.440, 424–5.
130. John Cannon, *Samuel Johnson and the Politics of Hanoverian England* (Oxford, 1994), pp.200–1.
131. Add. MSS 40280, 14 September 1812, f.30.
132. Parker, *Peel Correspondence*, I, p.113, and for what still remains the most extensive study of Irish newspapers of the period, see Brian Inglis, *The Freedom of the Press in Ireland, 1784–1841* (London, 1954), notably pp.134–66 for the period of Peel's office.
133. Aspinall, *Politics and the Press*, p.116; see also pp.107–25.
134. Add. MSS 40385, f.137; and see Inglis, *Freedom of the Press*, p.134.
135. Inglis, *Freedom of the Press*, p.140.
136. Add. MSS 40188, f.60.
137. Ibid., 40199, Gregory to Peel, 17 June 1814, f.85; Aspinall, *Politics and the Press*, p.122.
138. Inglis, *Freedom of the Press*, p.151.
139. Add. MSS 56367 [Halsbury Manuscripts], Giffard to Croker, 28 February 1811, f.73.
140. *Wellington Civil Correspondence Ireland*, 13 March 1808, p.361.
141. Add. MSS 53637, Giffard to Croker, 23 April 1816, f.4, 16 June 1816, ff.9 –10, and also 40196, f.196; 40286, f.240; 40288, f.187; 40290, f.177; 40202, f.297; and Inglis, *Freedom*, pp.151–2.
142. *Hansard*, XXXIV, 26 April, 1816, col. 36.
143. *Croker Papers*, Croker to Phillips, 3 January 1854, III, p.309.
144. *Hansard*, XXXI, 30 May 1815, cols 505–10.
145. See the *Dublin Correspondent*, 1 September 1815 and *The Times*, 6 September 1815.
146. *Croker Papers*, Croker to Rosamund, 12 to 26 July 1815, I, pp.61–76.
147. Ibid., undated journal entry, I, p.130.
148. Add. MSS 40183, Croker to Peel, November/early December 1815, ff.306–7.
149. Ibid., f.302.
150. Ibid., ff.304–5.
151. Brightfield, *Croker*, p.166.
152. Add. MSS 40184, no folio number, and part cited in Brightfield, p.167.
153. *The New Whig Guide* (London, 1819), p.89 and *passim*.
154. Add. MSS 40184, Croker to Peel, 12 August 1816, ff.25–6.
155. Ibid., 40291, ff.168–71, Peel to Croker, 18 September 1816, and *Croker Papers*, I, pp.91–2.
156. *Croker Papers*, Peel to Croker, 23 September 1816, I, p.91.
157. This was a view he reiterated in the *Guardian* on 28 October 1821, and will be examined below.

158. *Quarterly Review*, 'Maurice and Berghetta', November 1819, p.471. See also 'Tours in Ireland', September 1849 for a fuller account of Croker's ideas on the growth and influence of this sort of Irish fiction during the first half of the century.
159. Thomas, *Quarrel of Macaulay and Croker*, p.50.
160. *Quarterly Review*, November 1819, pp.480–1.
161. Ibid., pp.478–9.
162. Ibid., p.481.
163. Ibid., pp.483–5.
164. Ibid., pp.481–2.
165. Ibid., pp.485–7.
166. *Quarterly Review*, 'Counsellor Phillips Poems and Speeches', October 1816, p.23.
167. Ibid., pp.30–2.
168. Ibid., pp.34–6.
169. Ibid., p.37.
170. Thomas, *Quarrel of Macaulay and Croker*, p.189.
171. See University of Maryland, *Quarterly Review* project, editor Jonathan Cutmore, at: www.rc.umd.edu/reference/qr/founding/intro.html.
172. See Robert Gittings, *John Keats* (Aylesbury, 1971), and more extensively, Louis J. Jennings, *Croker Papers*, *passim*, and Brightfield, *Croker*. See also Christopher Neri Breiseith, 'British Conservatism and the French Revolution: John Wilson Croker's Attitudes to Reform and Revolution in Britain and France' (DPhil. thesis, Cornell, 1964), who broke some fresh ground in his study of Croker's ideas and on his relationship with Peel.
173. See John Clive, *The Scotch Reviewers: The Edinburgh Review, 1802–1815* (London, 1957), Chapters 1 and 2, and Derek Roper, *Reviewing Before the Edinburgh: 1780–1802* (London, 1978).
174. See Smiles, *John Murray*, I, Chapter 1, *passim*.
175. See Stefan Collini's review of the work of the modern conservative polemicist, Christopher Hitchens: 'He would have been entirely at home with the slash and burn style of the early quarterlies … in style two parts Hazlitt to one part Cobbett with a dash of Croker's venom', *London Review of Books*, vol. 25, 23 January 2003, online at www.lrb.co.uk/v25/n02stefan-collini/no-bullshit-bullshit.
176. See, for example, Croker, *Quarterly Review*, 'French Novels', April 1836, pp.66–71; 'France, by Lady Morgan', April 1817; 'Chateaubriand's Monarchy', July 1816, pp.440, 424–5; 'Causes of the French Revolution', April 1833, p.155; 'Fisher Ames Essays', April 1835, pp.554–5.
177. See Paul Johnson, *Birth of the Modern: World Society 1815–1830* (London, 1991), p.424.
178. See Brightfield, *Croker*, pp.378–9 for two pages of extracts.
179. Thomas, *Quarrel of Macaulay and Croker*, p.177.
180. See Hill and Helen Shine, *The Quarterly under Gifford: 1809–1829* (Chapel Hill, NC, 1949), *passim*; and see Brightfield's appendix of Croker's reviews up until 1854.
181. Croker to Murray, 26 March 1820, cited in Smiles, *John Murray*, pp.413–15.
182. *Quarterly Review*, 'The Poetic Mirror', July 1816, p.470.
183. *Croker Papers*, Croker to Murray, 18 September 1816, I, p.94. The reference was to the third canto of 'Childe Harold'. See also Brightfield, *Croker*, pp.275–7.
184. See Johnson, *Birth of the Modern*, p.423, for a short account of the affair.
185. Gittings, *John Keats*, p.370.
186. National Library of Scotland, MS 4003, Croker to William Blackwood, 2 February 1818, f.27.
187. *Quarterly Review*, 'Waverly', July 1814, pp.316–17.
188. Add. MSS 40321, Croker to Peel, 22 May 1835 and *Croker Papers*, Peel to Croker, II, p.279, no date, but probably 21 May 1835.
189. Add. MSS 40607, f.239, undated, and part cited in Thomas, *Quarrel of Macaulay and Croker*, p.187.
190. Herbert Butterfield, *George III and the Historians* (London, 1957), pp.119–20, and see his chapter entitled 'John Wilson Croker and the Tory View'.
191. *Times Literary Supplement*, 28 November 1968, pp.1–3, and see also Hedva Ben-Israel, *English Historians and the French Revolution* (London, 1968), *passim*. I am indebted to William Thomas for drawing my attention to the opinions of Ben-Israel and Richard Cobb.
192. *Croker Papers*, Croker to Murray, 17 August 1834, II, p.229.
193. See P. Harling, *The Waning of Old Corruption: The Politics of Economical Reform in Britain, 1779–1846* (Oxford, 1996) and M.J. Turner, *The Age of Unease: Government and Reform*

in Britain, 1782–1832 (Stroud, 2000), pp.132–3.

194. Jonathan Parry, *The Rise and Fall of Liberal Government in Victorian Britain* (Yale, 1996), p.33.

195. *Quarterly Review*, October 1816, 'Parliamentary Reform', pp.274–8; Robert Southey wrote most of this article.

196. Ibid., pp.271–5.

197. Ibid., pp.433–6.

198. *Hansard*, XLI, 14 December 1819, cols 1108–9.

199. Thomas, *Quarrel of Macaulay and Croker*, pp.42, 175. The Burke quotation is from *Reflections on the Revolution in France* (London, 1968 [Penguin edn]), p.106; see also Croker, *Quarterly Review*, 'Revolutions of 1640 and 1830', March 1832; 'The Essays of Fisher Ames', April 1835; and Croker, *Essays ... French Revolution* (1857), pp.310–12.

200. *Croker Papers*, comment by Jennings, II, p.54.

201. *Quarterly Review*, 'Causes of the French Revolution', April 1833, p.173.

202. *Croker Papers* (no date, but Croker would later refer to it as late 1819/early 1820), I, p.136.

203. Clements MS, Lb. 9, Croker to Lockhart, 18 November 1819, f.75, part in *Croker Papers*, I, p.138.

204. Alan Lang Strout, 'Some Unpublished Letters of J.G. Lockhart to John Wilson Croker', *Notes and Queries*, 185, 6 (11 September 1943), Lockhart to Croker, 21 November 1819, p.154.

205. Aspinall, *Politics and the Press*, pp.301–2.

206. *Guardian*, 12 December 1819.

207. Ibid., 19 December 1819.

208. Ibid., 2 January 1820.

209. Sack, *Jacobite to Conservative*, p.21 and Clements MS, Lb. 9, Croker to Arbuthnot, 23 September 1819 and Lb. 10, 15 October 1821.

210. Add. MSS 40319, Croker to Peel, 25 August 1822, f.62.

211. *Quarterly Review*, 'Life of Lord Sidmouth', March 1847, p.552.

212. See Rohan McWilliam, *Popular Politics in Nineteenth-Century England* (London, 1998), pp.1–9; he takes the 'humbug' quotation from E.P. Thompson, *The Making of the English Working Class* (London, 1968 [Penguin edn]).

213. William Hazlitt, 'Common-places', *The Literary Examiner*, 15 November 1823.

214. T.W. Laqueur, 'The Queen Caroline Affair: Politics as Art in the Reign of George IV', *The Journal of Modern History*, 54, 3 (September 1982), p.417. See also Flora Fraser, *The Unruly Queen: The Life of Queen Caroline* (London, 1996); and T. Holme, *Caroline* (Edinburgh, 1979). Both are sympathetic treatments of the queen, but justifiably keen to compare her fairly alongside the king.

215. For Croker's views on such movements see, in particular, *Quarterly Review*, 'Essays of Fisher Ames', April 1835; 'Sir Robert Peel's Address', February 1835; and 'Democracy', June 1847.

216. Clements MS, diary entries, 1820, 6 to 16 February 1820; and see *Croker Papers*, I, pp.159–61.

217. Arthur Aspinall, *Lord Brougham and the Whig Party* (Manchester, 1927), pp.106, 99–108; Robert Stewart, *Henry Brougham: His Public Career, 1798–1868* (London, 1986), pp.145–8; *Croker Papers*, I, p.172.

218. *Croker Papers*, Croker to Yarmouth, 6 June 1820, I, p.175.

219. Laqueur, 'Caroline Affair', p.421.

220. Turner, *The Age of Unease*, pp.165–6.

221. See *British Parliamentary Papers, Select Committee Reports on Newspaper Duties*, section for 1820–21. It is only possible to make an approximate assessment of the popularity of a publication from the amount of stamp duty or tax on advertising revenues. Most publications willing to risk avoiding taxes were Radical, and I have included some allowance for them, but not the huge number of highly entertaining cartoons and single-page prints, most of which were also anti-king and ministry.

222. Charles Knight, *Passages of a Working Life During Half a Century*, 2 vols (London, 1864), I, p.264.

223. A. Aspinall (ed.), *The Letters of George IV: 1812–1830* (Cambridge, 1938), Thomas Ashe to William Vizard, 20 September 1820, I, pp.364–5.

224. Samuel Smiles, *A Publisher and his Times: The Memoirs and Correspondence of the Late John Murray*, 2 vols (London, 1891), Gifford to Murray, January 1820, II, p.53.

225. Thomas Crofton Croker, *The Queen's Question Queried: A Pedantless Phillipic Production*

by an Irish Barrister (London, 1820), no page numbers, held by British Library.

226. This figure is Laqueur's, 'Caroline Affair', p.418; there are, to my knowledge, at least seven of these held by the British Library.

227. J.W. Croker [George IV], *A Letter from the King to His People* (London, 1820 [7thedn]), pp.1–9, 27.

228. Turner, *The Age of Unease*, pp.166–7.

229. Clements MS, Lb. 23, ff.274–80, Croker to Planta, 21 August 1829 and in *Croker Papers*, II, p.23.

230. Jane Robbins, *The Trial of Queen Caroline* (New York, 2006), pp.301–2.

231. Aspinall, *Politics and the Press*, p.313, citing Crabb Robinson MS diary entry, October 1820.

232. *The Times*, 15 May 1821.

233. Bill Newton-Dunn, in his entertaining biography of Hook, *The Man Who Was John Bull* (London, 1996), gives numerous examples of Croker's involvement with Hook and *John Bull* at this time; and James Sack, *From Jacobite to Conservative*, p.15: that although the 'exact state of affairs may always remain murky', Croker appears 'to have been chiefly responsible for the establishment of *John Bull*'.

234. Regenstein Library, University of Chicago, Hook MS 619, cat. 242, f.36 no. 104, ff.1–3, undated but pencilled '1820' [Henceforth Chicago MS].

235. Vicesimus Blinkinsop [Theodore Hook and J.W. Croker], *Tentamen, or an Essay Towards the History of Whittington, Sometime Lord Mayor of London, by Vicesimus Blinkinsop* (London, 1820), pp.27–43; a number of copies are available at the British Library.

236. Chicago MS, Hook cat. 242, ff.1–7, also in Newton-Dunn, *John Bull*, pp.108–9.

237. Carlisle MS, D. Lons 21/2/116, 7 September 1820, and to Peel, *Croker Papers*, I, p.180.

238. Duke MS, no catalogue detail other than 'Miss Godman's Diary', some extracts also quoted in Newton Dunn, *John Bull*, pp.112–13.

239. W.S. Dowden (ed.), *The Journal and Correspondence of Thomas Moore*, 6 vols (New Jersey, 1983). 23 September 1820: 'Met Croker at St Clones with Theodore Hook, who is his travelling companion (what favour these peculators are in with placemen)'. See also 14 October 1820, and on 17 October, II, pp.345, 351, 352.

240. Duke MS, 'Miss Godman's diary'.

241. Chicago MS 619, Croker to Hook, ff.4, 5; and Newton-Dunn, *John Bull*, p.130.

242. Duke MS, box 3, Stuart to Croker, December 1820 and see mixed folios box 2, 3, November 1820 to 26 May 1821. For some other letters see Clements MS, Lb. 10, ff.21–1, 41, 227, 341, 317.

243. *John Bull*, 17 December 1820.

244. Aspinall, *Politics and the Press*, p.29.

245. Carlisle, MS, D. Lons 21/2/116, Croker to Lowther, no date or folio. See also at the same reference for other letters referring to Stuart and other activities in Paris. There are approximately 300 letters from Croker to Lowther for the period between 1810 and 1939 held at Carlisle, but more from Lowther to Croker are held at Duke University, with some others at the Clements, Michigan.

246. Myron Brightfield, *Theodore Hook and His Novels* (Harvard, 1928), p.132, quoting from G.F. Berkeley, *Life and Recollections* (London, 1866).

247. Henry, Lord Brougham and Vaux, *The Life and Times of Henry Lord Brougham, Written by Himself*, 3 vols (Edinburgh, 1871), II, p.318. See also Aspinall, *The Letters of George IV*, III, p.65; Mrs Arbuthnot, in the spring of 1821, recorded that *John Bull* 'has done more towards putting down the Queen than anything', *The Journal of Mrs Arbuthnot 1820–32*, eds F. Bamford and the Duke of Wellington, 2 vols (London, 1950), I, p.26.

248. Newton-Dunn, *John Bull*, p.121.

249. *Croker Papers*, Croker to Peel, 24 July 1821, I, pp.196–7.

250. *Hansard*, 10 May 1821, V, col. 650.

251. Clements MS, Lb. 10, 17 May 1821, f.319.

252. Brightfield, *Croker*, p.175. Brightfield could not accept that Croker's extensive denials were lies, and on these grounds rejected the idea he was involved in founding *John Bull*, pp.175–8.

253. Ibid., quoting a letter now in the Murray Collection, NLS.

254. Lockhart to Croker, 21 May 1821; Alan Lang Strout, 'Lockhart on Don Juan', *The Times Literary Supplement* (hereafter TLS), 30 November 1940, 30 August 1941 and August 1841.

255. See Joanne Shattock, *Politics and the Reviewers: The Edinburgh and the Quarterly in the Early Victorian Age* (Leicester, 1989), pp.45–6 and Chapter 3, *passim*.

256. Strout, 'Lockhart on Don Juan', *TLS*. Most of the letters between Croker and Lockhart are held by the National Library of Scotland or at the Clements Library, but Dr Strout published some more of their correspondence for 1819–1837 in *Notes and Queries*, numbers 6, 7 and 8, September, October and November 1943.
257. Clements MS, Lb. 10, Croker to Lockhart, 24 May 1821, f.328.
258. Ibid., f.340.
259. Ibid., Croker to Murray, 24 May 1821, ff.327–8. See also ff.330–49 for other letters between Croker and Lockhart.
260. See Duke MS, box 2, John Wilson to Croker, June 1820, no folio numbers.
261. Clements, MS, Lb. 10, Croker to Blackwood, 28 June 1821, f.373.
262. See *The Times*, 8 May 1821.
263. *John Bull*, 21 January 1821. See also Newton-Dunn, *John Bull*, pp.133–8 for an entertaining account of some of Hook's other attempts to distract attention from his role in *Bull*.
264. Ibid., 17 November and 10 November 1822.
265. J.G. Lockhart, *Theodore Hook: A Sketch* (London, 1842), p.60.
266. Mrs Oliphant, *Annals of a Publishing House: William Blackwood and His Sons, Their Magazine and Their Friends*, 2 vols (Edinburgh 1897); Maginn to Blackwood, 25 June 1823, I, pp.396–400.
267. Lockhart, *Theodore Hook*, p.60.
268. Mary Gordon, *Memoir of John Wilson* (New York, 1963), p.289; Thrall, *Rebellious Fraser's*, p.179.
269. Add. MSS 58578 (Liverpool Manuscripts), Liverpool to Hook, 19 December 1823, f.31.
270. *Croker Papers*, I, pp.269, 261 and Chicago MS, cat. no. 242 marked August 1824, letter number 14; see also 12 and 13 and see Newton-Dunn, *John Bull*, pp.183–206.
271. Ibid., 26 March 1825, I, p.286.
272. Andrew Lang, *The Life and Letters of John Gibson Lockhart*, 2 vols (London, 1898), I, p.373.

CHAPTER TWO

The Eclipse of Irish Conciliation and Fall of the Tories: 1821–30

*It costs us something to give up our prejudices and partiali-
ties ... Historical events and characters are disfigured and,
we are sorry to be obliged to say, traduced with all the
malignity of political party [and by] the suppression of
circumstances which ought in candour to have been given ...
By these means, and by the use of disparaging or contume-
lious epithets, he disfigures, and sometimes totally alters, the
complexion of facts.*

*In the elegant expression of Junius ... 'trifles float and
are preserved; while what is solid and valuable sinks to
the bottom and is lost for ever.'* (J.W. Croker, 'Walpole's
Memoirs', *Quarterly Review*, April 1822, and 'Nathaniel
Wraxall's Historical Memoirs of My Own Time', April
1815, p.215).

In March 1820 Peel asked Croker whether he thought 'that the tone of
England ... is more liberal – to use an odious but intelligible phrase –
than the policy of Government' and 'can we resist for seven years
Reform in Parliament?'[1] Like *The Times*, Croker clearly believed that all
the accumulated factors in favour of Reform should have acted like 'a
dose of wormwood on Ministers'.[2] In February 1822, shortly after Peel
was appointed head of the Home Office, he wrote to him: 'The cause of
Reform ... has made great progress – public opinion is made by the press
or by public meetings, and by the number and weight of the
advocates of the cause', and now 'almost the whole press, and all
public meetings are loud for Reform'. The 'address of abuse granted spontaneously, or at least naturally ... sometimes appeases the public mind
without giving it any higher idea of its own public power', whereas any
government that would 'be so absurd as to take up the defence of such a
case with a high hand would lose itself, its object, and the country'.[3]

Peel broadly agreed, but as with Emancipation, the ministry would continue to neglect the issue until it reached a crisis. Croker made few speeches in the Commons other than on Admiralty business in these years, but rather than being a fervent opponent of all reform and modernisation, as he has been portrayed, over half of his interventions were for 'liberal' measures. Among them the funding of public galleries and museums; legal aid in capital trials; state support for the preservation of historical buildings and historical documents and for extensive Irish Church tithe reform as early as 1809. He also solicited support for artists and scientists such as Babbage to develop his early 'computer', as well as for early steam navigation and gas lighting, and with Croker, Ireland may even be able to claim the first parliamentary proposal for the adoption of metrication and decimalisation. Not surprisingly, he won scant support for it from a rather chauvinist Commons in the year after Waterloo,[4] but the evidence qualifies the indignant argument he later made in one of his few attempts to defend his reputation, that he had been an early reformer and an 'emancipator when Emancipation would have done some good instead of mischief'. In '1820 and again in 1829, far ahead of Huskisson, Palmerston and Melbourne in my opinions of the expediency of some parliamentary reform', and paraphrasing Burke, that 'on the whole I belong to the class of *rational reformers*, my aversion is to touch the roots – to meddle with the foundations, but I have no objection to prune the tree to improve the fruit – not to enlarge the house as our family wants increase.'[5]

In 1817 he compiled a bill to give Roman Catholics access to high positions in the army and Royal Navy. Enacted on 10 July, it represented the first major concession to Catholics for almost twenty years and *The Times* praised it as a 'wise, temperate and conciliatory' measure heralding the right for Catholics to sit in parliament.[6] Peel had not opposed it, but he had spoken against Grattan's Emancipation bill, which as Eric Evans says, 'irrefutably established him on the Protestant wing of the Tory party, and as the most effective champion of their cause'.[7] When Grattan presented another on 3 May 1819, Croker dramatically re-declared his own support for full Emancipation by seconding it with a far more extensive series of legal and political arguments.[8] Grattan's speech was mainly concerned with reassuring the members that the Roman Catholics had good intentions, and that the old power of the pope and 'the Roman Catholic combination of Europe has ceased, the race of the Pretender is extinct'. Far from undermining the Union, Emancipation 'will give strength to the Protestant Church, to the Act of Settlement' and 'preserve tranquillity at home'.[9]

Croker began his case by attempting to prove by using carefully researched evidence from historical documents that denying Catholics full civil rights was contrary to 'the state of the laws by which oaths or declarations are to be taken'. He placed copies on the division table for members to examine, and then argued that, like the law, the constitution was not a fixed entity but an organic evolved one.[10]

> In tracing, as I have lately had occasion to do, the stream of pains and penalties from its source in the rugged times of our ancestors down to the present day it is impossible not to be struck with the gradual character of mildness and mitigation which it has assumed. The law raged in the higher periods of our history with the penal fury of a torrent; but ... so much indeed has been done by gradual concession, and by silent conciliatory operation of time, that a great portion of what the Catholic asks, and what the Protestant hesitates to grant, has been already virtually conceded; and by complying with the request of our Roman Catholic fellow subjects ... [we would be] only perfecting the course in which our ancestors have led the way.[11]

He then made his earliest substantial parliamentary declarations of a Conservative political philosophy by mocking doctrinaire notions held by opponents of Catholic Relief who talked of the 'good old days' and 'stand on the immutable forms of the constitution'. The constitution was in a 'continual course of partial destruction, and partial renovation'. [12]

> I would ask those gentlemen ... to what days do they allude; before the latter end of the reign of Charles II, Catholics sat in Parliament. In the reign of William III, popery was an offence punishable by a variety of strange and monstrous afflictions, which do not now exist, and which no one, I presume, would wish to see re-enacted ... These, therefore, cannot be the good old days to which the zealous Protestant of the present days refers. No sir, our constitution, like our physical natures, is in a continual course of partial destruction, and partial renovation. It is an edifice, built at various times, by various hands, and fitted, in the course of successive alterations, to the increased necessities or advanced conveniences of civilized

life ... I therefore challenge those hon. Gentlemen who wish to stop the stream of experience and the course of nature, to open our history and put a finger upon that very year of our annals, and that very state of our constitution, to which they would have us return. If they cannot do that, let us hear no more of adhering to the wisdom of our ancestors, and resolving to stand on the immutable forms of the constitution.[13]

Drawing to a close, he confessed that he felt 'the most poignant regret at differing on this first and, I hope, last and only occasion from the opinions of so many of those with whom I have the honour of concurring on all other subjects, and above all, at differing from my right honourable friend'. This was a reference to Peel, for whom he felt 'the liveliest and most unalterable affection', and these 'considerations have kept me long silent upon the subject; for ten years I have avoided it', but now 'I feel that I should be guilty of cowardice, and treachery to my personal honour and to the public interest' by continuing to do so.[14]

In concluding, he quoted Blackstone, Burke and Montesquieu to reinforce his arguments that good government should not meddle with the foundations, but they should adapt the constitution and implement prudent corrective reforms. 'Our whole being, [whether] physical, moral and political is a system of expediency and compensations; and what are called the natural rights of man must always be merged with the paramount claims of society at large.' Both the few and the many must be 'curbed and restricted in the use of any portion of that natural force which they should appear disposed to abuse, and which might endanger the general happiness and security of a social and political state'. But Catholic Emancipation would be a healing and improving measure, for if the system under which Catholics had 'suffered had produced uneasiness and dissatisfaction', then why should we 'suppose that it would revive with irresistible malignity under a system of conciliation'.[15]

The motion was lost by 241 to 243 votes, but this was closer than any since the 1812–13 debacle, and the opposition and the Irish Catholic press praised Croker for his efforts.[16] Thomas Spring Rice, who would soon sit in the Commons as Whig MP for Limerick, wrote to their mutual friend Thomas Casey in Dublin:

I have just heard your friend Croker, and you could not wish him or any favourite of yours to have made a stronger or more favourable impression upon the House. His speech was one which was calculated to conciliate at this side of the Channel and to gratify the other. It was replete with ingenuity and yet free from fanciful refinement. It was characterized by an acuteness of legal deduction, and yet exempt from the sophistry or the pedantry of profession. It treated a worn out subject and made it appear a new one. But its principal merit in my eyes lay in its frankness, warmth and sincerity. It redeemed the pledge and fulfilled the promise of his 'Historical Sketch'. It showed him to be an honest Irishman no less than an able statesman. It showed him to be disinterested and ready to quit the road of fortune under the auspices of his personal friend Peel ...[17]

Croker would not 'quit' his party or Peel, but in Ireland religious tensions had been markedly rising in the latter years of the second decade and he had to reassure some of his friends and supporters at Trinity College, who were becoming concerned that the ultra-Catholic element was becoming increasingly influential and proactive. He reminded them that he had supported Emancipation for twenty years, but not from any sympathy with 'Popery'; his first and greatest object was to protect 'the Protestant Church', and he lamented 'from the bottom of my heart, this unhappy question which divides not only Catholic from Protestant, but the Protestants themselves'.[18]

Terms such as 'Popery' are naturally unappealing today, but almost all Europeans who considered themselves enlightened saw the Roman Catholic Church as a regressive institution. The Whig Thomas Moore was a Catholic, but not, as he argued, a 'Papist', in that like Croker and all the old conciliatory circle he differentiated between 'Papist in Conscience and Papist in faction';[19] almost no Emancipationist in Britain, Whig, Tory or Radical, 'wanted a seemingly superstitious, bigoted Catholic religion to play too great a role in Irish society'.[20] Grattan's efforts to emphasise that the 'old power of the Pope' was now extinct and Emancipation would give 'strength to the Protestant Church' was almost certainly designed to dispel growing concerns that the Catholic clergy in Ireland were increasingly directing popular dissension against the Anglican Church and community. Irish Protestant concerns were often exaggerated by their own beleaguered desire to preserve their privileges, and of course what can appear as just plain bigotry, but if Croker and his circle's part in the later success of the Conservative party are to be properly understood, then their view of developments in Ireland must be examined a little further and assessed in its own historical context.

In his review of Parnell's novel in 1819, Croker had expressed concern on whether 'Catholic Emancipation and religious toleration [were] mere pretences? And is revolution in rank and property the real object of the Catholic claims?'[21] Over the next few years, like all his circle, he would become convinced that many Catholic clerics and lay local agitators were secretly working to raise and dominate a mass movement by exploiting religious antipathy. He accepted that this was partly the product of frustration at their failure to achieve equal privileges; yet partly in order to restore their own diminishing authority and part of a local and nationally orchestrated conspiracy connected with wider European religious politics. As one historian of the papacy describes, after 1814, with Bonaparte contained, there was a notable growth of Vatican militancy, and despite protests from more conciliatory Catholic lay powers, the pope restored both the Inquisition and the Jesuit order.[22] This was partly in response to a growth of evangelical Protestant organisations, when from the Catholic authority's perspective, 'the Pope, as it were, woke to discover' that the Protestant Bible societies were 'marching all over the globe, distributing bibles in the vernacular and assisting modernizing rulers with the organization of schools and the provision of educational material'.[23] As Alan Acheson says, 'much ink has been spilled on the so called second Reformation' in Ireland, but it appears untenable to even rudimentary research that the activities of fervent Protestants was primarily responsible for destroying the chance of ecumenical harmony.[24] Most accounts continue to identify the ultra-Protestant Bishop Magee's speech against the Catholic Church in late 1822 as having initiated the 'Bible war', and Croker would denounce Magee as an 'Orange bigot', but like all his press circle, he believed that ultra-Catholic militants played an earlier and more significant part. Most of this had been considerably more secretive and/or at the social level of the kind Peel had drawn attention to until it broke the surface in January 1820 when the young lecturer and 'rising star' at Maynooth, Fr John MacHale (later the famously belligerent bishop of Tuam) launched a public campaign against the Anglicans with his *Hierophilos* letters to the Dublin press denouncing Scripture being read in schools.[25]

The circle believed that O'Connell became an early ally, moving noticeably closer to the ultra-Catholics after a papal bull was issued in 1818 stating that reading Scripture, 'even without note or comment', must be prohibited in any school teaching Catholics.[26] Thomas Lefroy, the MP for Trinity College, later insisted on reminding the Commons that it was from this time on that Daniel O'Connell, in 'obedience to the Court of Rome ... mounted upon his Bull and rode to the Catholic Clergy, and stirred them up to the most active and effective hostility to the system of education then established'.[27] Lefroy was an ally of Magee, and as we will see, denounced by Croker as an ultra-'Protestant Jesuit', but he expressed the shared opinion that this was when O'Connell first fully realised that if he were to win national power in Ireland, he would have to affiliate his ambitions with the increasingly more militant group of Catholic clerics. The early targets of their growing campaign were the non-denominational, successful Kildare Place Society (KPS) schools.[28] Designed to educate poor Catholics and Protestants together, while there may have been some illicit proselytising, it was fairly strictly forbidden, and the society 'strove to avoid confessional controversy' and placed a heavy emphasis on 'useful knowledge'.[29] It did, however, have Scripture reading on its daily syllabus, albeit 'without note or comment', and had a number of leading Catholic figures such as O'Connell on its board for some years.[30] But in 1818 or early 1819 O'Connell resigned and denounced his ex-colleagues as some of the 'bitterest enemies of Catholics' rights and religious liberties'. Shortly after this, the long-established Protestant Bible Societies 'were surprised to find O'Connell, Sheil and other Catholic orators assuming now the role of lay apologists, by invading their meetings and challenging them to public debate'.[31] According to Thomas Wyse, the liberal Catholic Association leader, these 'interventions' became increasingly common as 'O'Connell led the Roman Catholic objection to the Society and used the education issue on which to bind the Clergy to his organisation.'[32]

When Plunkett proposed another cross-party Emancipation bill in 1821[33] Croker supported it, but when moving an amendment to make state provision for the Catholic clergy expressed his own concern by emphasising the urgency of winning their support. Castlereagh concurred, but asked him to leave it in 'amicable repose' for fear it may antagonise some of them and disrupt attempts to pass the bill. Croker agreed, but on the condition that 'his object is, in great measure, gained by the admission of the principle'.[34] He would continue to support Emancipation, but most of his press circle would become dedicated opponents, and O'Connell would denounce them as 'Orange bigots', and their writing has been dismissed in similar terms ever since. They certainly became fervent opponents of the Catholic movement, and some of them had been hostile before this, but contrary to common assumptions much of the Tory and most of the ministerial press was not opposed to Emancipation prior to when O'Connell 'mounted his

Bull'. As James Sack has pointed out, the *Sun* had supported the measure until 1819; the *New Times* until 1825; the *Courier* and *Morning Post* under the editorship of the Dubliner Nicholas Byrne had done so with some reservations since before 1812, but 'both opposed the idea completely by 1825'. *Blackwood's* was 'pro-Catholic in the early 1820s, yet switched in the mid-1820s' to become an outspoken opponent. Croker would stop writing for the *Quarterly* after a mainly personal disagreement with Murray in late 1825, and in 1828, 'with Southey in the ascendant' it 'dutifully joined its Tory confreres in strict opposition'. The *British Critic* did the same the year before, as did George Croly, ex-editor of the *Guardian*, who abandoned Emancipation and made the *Monthly Magazine* 'the most furious anti-Catholic magazine in Britain'.[35]

The normative interpretation is that in 1824 the proposal for the 'penny rent' would finally bring the energy of the disaffected Catholic masses under the direction of the association's local 'lieutenants'. By this time O'Connell's most influential subalterns were the Catholic priests, and while some of Croker's circle would become obsessed with the idea of a papal and Jesuit as well a local clerical conspiracy, it was not, perhaps, too paranoid to see a connection between the pre-1820 growth of militancy and the fact that large numbers of priests first began joining the new Catholic Association in 1823 when Leo XII was elected pope. As Richard McBrien describes in his history of the papacy, Leo's pontificate was even more 'extremely conservative' and proactive. He stepped up the campaign against Protestantism, 'condemned religious toleration, reinforced the Index of Forbidden Books and the Holy office (formerly the Inquisition), re-established the feudal aristocracy of the Papal States, and confined the Jews to ghettos'.[36] O'Connell's biographer, Oliver MacDonagh, argues that when founding the association, he knew that Irish peasantry 'would not remain passive under Orange oppression' for much longer, and that they would not be won by concentrating the campaign on Emancipation alone, but 'by raising the consciousness of the Catholic masses by ranging over the entire body of their grievances and then using their rising and compacted anger as a lever'.[37] Croker would have vigorously contested the idea that the Catholic masses had their 'consciousness' raised in any appealingly positivist sense, arguing that few among the peasantry had much contact with what could accurately be described as 'Orange oppressors', and that their 'rising and compacted anger' was almost entirely the product of material grievances. He had expressed his fear that religio-political issues such as Emancipation and tithe reform could be made a 'panaceatic' for all the grievances of the peasantry since 1808, and by the early 1820s he believed that O'Connell and his local lieutenants were doing just this, and calculatedly diverting attention from practical reforms onto the Protestant Church and community. 'O'Connell's object is to bring the Catholics into direct collision with the [Anglican] Church,' he wrote to Peel in March 1824, and if the government should fail to defend it, 'the Church of Ireland will be swept away like a damn in a torrent.'[38]

As has been seen, Croker was critical of ultras on both religious sides, but also with the government's failure to take a lead with effective practical reforms and leaving Emancipation to fester. Developments such as the 'unfortunate system of middlemen' had 'reduced the last wretched occupier of the overloaded land – the real cultivator of the soil to the most abject penury and wretchedness',[39] and according to his theory, whatever their stated justifications, the real contest was almost always one for political power between local 'social superiors', who would seek to elevate themselves, or preserve their own privileges by exploiting popular disaffection. In an Irish scenario, the most influential element of this 'class' were the Catholic priests, who were, of course, almost all the offspring and politico/religious affiliates of local petty elites. As Kevin Whelan has recently described in not dissimilar terms, this class 'donned the middleman mantle and with it acquired an ancestry, an ideological pedigree and a rhetoric',[40] and for Croker and the circle, they naturally exploited whatever mixture of local animosities or resentments were available to move the masses in the direction of their ambitions.

It should never be forgotten that the formal political and economic structures were under the control of the Protestant minority and that Catholics were largely excluded, but as Croker wrote, this did not mean they were passive, and as Irishmen of his and his circle's background knew very well, the Catholic clergy had always been active in local politics.[41]

> Partial relaxation of the penal laws, which conferred the elective franchise on Roman Catholic electors, but left neglected and stigmatised the Roman Catholic Clergy, peerage and gentry was a great mistake. Thence grew the Catholic Question; a question not originally raised by the Catholics themselves, but by rival Protestant parties at contested elections – those who found themselves weakest in the elections throwing themselves into the arms of the new interest.[42]

He acknowledged that many priests sought to improve the condition of the poor, but believed that, 'in a most important degree', social and material improvements were most hampered in Ireland because of 'the adverse influence of the Roman Catholic priests, who have always been jealous of any improvements or instruction, even in the ordinary arts of life [as] likely to diminish their own influence'.[43] He wrote later that because of this he had always expressed 'approbation of paying a due respect to that priesthood' and 'urged with whatever power of reasoning or persuasion we may possess, that no measure of improvement – not even agricultural instruction – will or can be successful until that body is made independent in pecuniary circumstances and brought into harmony and closer contact with the state'.[44]

> These Priests from temporal as well as spiritual motives, which we may lament but cannot wonder at, could never do otherwise than execrate the Reformation; they alike abhorred the *heretic* and hated what they called the *usurper*: and with the same term of obloquy – *Sasanach*, denounced – to an enmity as evergreen as their native shamrock – the *Englishman and the Protestant* ... They adopted the device of embarking all their co-religionists in the same cause; and in this view made it their business – an easy pleasant and popular one – to keep alive in the minds of the people a strong animosity against the tithe paying, combined with all their old clannish notions and all the claims (by the lapse of time become quite imaginary) to forfeited estates.[45]

Such arguments were easily accepted by 'a poor and ignorant population whose only learning was such legends and traditions', and they 'very naturally adopted suggestions which flattered vanity, favoured indolence, and gratified and stimulated their aversion for the stranger and the heretic' when promoted by 'those whom they believe to be the guardians of their temporal rights, as well as the guides and even arbiters of eternal salvation.'[46]

Amalgamated with this were Catholic hedge schoolmasters, balladmongers and chap book historians Peel had railed against, who, together with parish priests, composed similar lessons and were, in effect, the 'disaffected men of letters' Croker would collectively describe as 'Ultra-Catholic parties of adverse agitators'.[47] The moderate Catholic bishop, James Doyle, was, of course, naturally more sympathetic to Catholic interpretations, but he continued to support KPS schools up until 1823, and as his biographer noted, his 'view of the hedge school and its master was not characterised by any of the romance which later generations would retrospectively attribute'. They were men, Doyle wrote, who usually 'have no fixed abode, no settled maintenance ... and their manner of teaching as rude and as absurd as you can well imagine'. Dependent on the community for their sustenance, in return for partaking in the 'well spread table of potatoes of the hospitality':

> He counts over the traditions of the country, tells of battles which were won and lost ... prodigies of valour performed by Irish heroes – of cruelty and perfidy of the English, especially Cromwell and his followers ... of the ghosts who had frequently appeared, and with whom he had conversed, of the prophecies of Columbkille [sic] the originals of which he had perused, the politics of the present day and all that would shortly happen or was to occur in the future. He retires with the younger branches of the family and inflames their minds anew, and before the rising sun has summoned them to labour, they are perhaps all bound to some mysterious compact by an unlawful oath.[48]

It was the naive adoption of this sort of material by novelists such as Parnell that Croker and the circle found most politically annoying and irresponsible, initially underestimating the appetite for it in its more vernacular forms that existed among the Catholic masses and the influence it had upon their local leaders. Circumstances varied in different parts of Ireland and, as with its European neighbours, there had long been a religious and ethno-cultural aspect to popular politics. But as most modern research agrees, prior to the 1820s, agrarian and material issues were by far the main concerns of the poorer classes.[49] Furthermore, the Irish peasantry had a long tradition of not remaining passive under the oppression of a Protestant or Catholic superior,[50] and prior to this time the local Catholic clergy often had a fragile authority over the Catholic masses.[51] Another of Croker's circle, William Phelan, a native Irish speaker and son of a Catholic wool-comber from Clonmel,[52] made this same point in a pamphlet published in 1817. He agued that the influence of local priests was 'notoriously in decline', and that the growing militancy of some of them during and since the veto crisis was connected with their ambition to re-establish their authority. Phelan had converted to Anglicanism, but he was not a proselytiser, and also criticised the

Protestant Bible societies for encouraging what he was beginning to fear was a growing sectarian conflict.[53] Maginn was another Irish speaker, and together with Crofton Croker, as a collector of Irish folk stories between 1815 and 1823 he regularly socialised among the Munster peasantry. He became firmly convinced that the single greatest blow to the peace and prosperity of Ireland had been the funding of Maynooth College. While he complimented the old continental-trained clergy, the 'Priest of modern days, entering Maynooth as he does with all the rudeness of his class' had no enlightening education to soften his prejudices and 'produce allowance and conciliation that regard the interest and feelings of others which constitute civilisation'. Maginn's close friend and fellow pressman, the Jesuit priest and former lecturer at Clongowes, Francis Sylvester Mahony ('Fr Prout'), agreed with most of this assessment, and that, as Maginn continued, most young rural priests of this class naturally came away with their rural prejudices embellished and 'deeply imbued with the importance of promoting, by every means in his power, the interests, not of religion, but of the church to whose service he is devoted'.[54]

Whatever the merits of this assessment, and although Mahony remained a priest, he had been sacked from Clongowes and was hostile to the Irish Catholic establishment, all of the circle, and Croker in particular, would have appreciated the French Revolutionary inferences of a recent conjecture that the Catholic clergy could be seen as the proponents of an Irish form of a wider 'bourgeois revolution'. As they would, with what Dror Wahrman says of similar socio-political developments in Britain and Europe: that the growing political consciousness and ambitions of this group demanded that they make their own interests the cause of 'public opinion'.[55] For Croker and the circle however, most of the ideological comparisons would stop there, and they would have agreed with Tom Dunne that for the most part it was the ideology of the Catholic *Vendee* that triumphed in Ireland in 1798, and the 'politicisation of the Catholic masses was to continue to have a strong sectarian orientation during the next critical half century'.[56] *Amhráin na nDaoine* [Songs of the People], ballads, poems and chap books were adapted according to contemporary events and concerns, but a fairly constant feature were: 'Foul descendants of Calvin,' 'Luther's Breed', 'damned heretical clan' accompanied by the general de-humanisation of Protestants as 'wild dogs' etc. who deserved violent destruction at the hands of 'St Peter's Flock' or the 'brave Romans'.[57] By the early 1820s, there had been a huge rise in the circulation of overtly sectarian Catholic publications such as 'Pastorini's Prophecies' chiliasticly describing the grim apocalyptic fate awaiting Irish Protestants when God took his predicted vengeance upon them in 1825. As Irene Whelan describes in her own accomplished study, 'there is much contemporary evidence in literature and journalism to suggest that the 1820s and 1830s were years in which Irish Catholicism at the popular level assumed the jealous, exclusive and self-righteous tone that was to characterise it for the remainder of the century and beyond.'[58]

It was not, therefore, too surprising that the circle became increasingly alarmed by the reports they read of these developments in the local press or heard from friends and family in Ireland, and this naturally hardened their views of the Catholic movement. A typical example was a package containing a copy of 'Pastorini's Prophecies', sent to Croker in May 1823 by William Ellis, a college friend and lawyer on the Connacht circuit, and 'circulated in its hundreds of thousands'. Its 'success is incredible', he continued, 'in the last year alone almost two hundred poorer Protestant families' in 'Sligo, Leitrim and Roscommon ... have been driven, with their principles, their property and their industry to colonise strange lands, by terror, by disgust, by indignation and by persecution ... We are indeed fearfully fulfilling the prophecies of Pastorini.'[59] In early 1824 Phelan dispiritedly reported to the Parliamentary Commission on Ireland that his prophesy of 1817 had been largely fulfilled, and that now most of the Catholic 'laity are tools in the hands of the priesthood'.[60] By January 1825, according to another letter from Ellis, the Catholic Association had now established 'such a general body of lay and clerical officials and familiars as no Govt. before perhaps ever had'. It was now common for even Catholic children, some 'not more than eight years old ... to chant sectarian slogans' at Protestants, mocking them all as 'Orangemen'. Even 'in the near vicinity of Dublin [many] stayed away from Church on Christmas day for fear of assault.' 'I go to Ballinrobe to try – if they let me – a Priest for beating a schoolmaster in the discharge of his spiritual supremacy', but there was now little chance any jury would have the courage to find him guilty.[61]

In 1825 a series of long letters that had first appeared in the London *Courier* were published in a bound edition entitled 'The State of Ireland'. Almost certainly the work of Croker, one of them argued that the 'various elements of combustion' had now amalgamated to form a powerful national Catholic movement. This was not only the result of agitation and religious ambitions, however, it been partly facilitated by the ministry's failure to address reforms. If talented Catholics like

O'Connell had been given equal access to office, instead of 'every term seeing youngsters passing him on their [bar] career ... it is no violent supposition to enfer that his energies would have taken another turn.' Whereas now, after twenty years of political agitation, he had firmly established himself as 'the alpha and omega of the Association':

> Whatever the defects of his public character everyone must allow him the three great requisites for business – boldness, activity, perseverance – Without him the Association never would have been formed ... There are various elements of combustion he draws upon. There are the gloomy and ferocious bigots of the Church, zealots in their religion, holding heretics as outlaws, whom it is acceptable to God to persecute and destroy. There are the heirs to the original estates, no very considerable sect, burning under a desire for revenge ... There is the Priesthood partaking in no small degree of these sentiments and embodying these feelings. There is the peasantry more immediately under their influence and mere puppets of their will [and] goaded on to acts of violence and bloodshed. Previous efforts to marshal these materials of power into an effective array had from various causes proved unavailing ... the want of unanimity and want of means were the chief impediments [but] these impediments are now removed.[62]

The Catholic leaders might have 'taken another turn' had the ministry addressed issues like Emancipation. It may also have stemmed the divisive influence it had in cabinet and neutralised the continual service it provided in rallying the parliamentary opposition.

Through little effort of its own, however, by late 1822 Liverpool's government had never been stronger. The economy was recovering, most public demonstrations had dissipated, and with Peel, Canning, Plunkett and other talents in the cabinet, there had never been a better opportunity for dealing with both parliamentary reform and Catholic Relief. The Whig leader, 'a despondent Earl Grey ... was again expressing his wish to retire from politics', and barely bothered to attend any Parliamentary sessions,[63] and as Theodore Hook gloated in *John Bull*, Emancipation now remained 'the great sheet anchor of the Whigs – the only subject upon which they could venture to count noses'.[64] The more resolute Whig leader in the Commons, Viscount Althorp, wrote to Brougham: 'I assume we are to make Ireland the great object of our attack',[65] and the parliamentary opposition directed most of their energy onto Emancipation and associated Irish issues. The most controversial of these was Irish Church tithe reform, and in March 1823 Joseph Hume proposed a motion for Church property in Ireland to be appropriated for the benefit of the whole community, arguing that if the problems of Ireland were to be solved then the 'real remedy for the evil was to break up the Church establishment'. Presumably aware that he would receive little support from most property owners or rentiers of any persuasion for much more practical proposals of land or rent reform, he took care to emphasise that this did not apply to 'private property, because it was inherited by individuals in Ireland'.[66]

Indicative of polarising tensions in Ireland, and although at least partly under provocation from the ultra-Protestants, even the moderate Catholic Bishop Doyle published a pamphlet in 1823 declaring that the Irish Anglican Church was illegitimate and, 'should not be suffered to exist in a civilised country and that peace and concord' would not be re-established so long as tithes existed.[67] Liverpool sought to dissipate some of this combined assault from Ireland and the opposition with a commission of enquiry into the state of Ireland. One of its recommendations was for a less controversial method of fixed tithe payment, and he rounded on Churchmen who objected that he was separating the Church from the standards applicable to private property, that if not done it would be imposed upon them by the landowners 'from self-interest' and 'in the most disadvantageous terms'.[68] According to Croker's circle, this eagerness for campaigning against tithe payments and Church property was a traditional one for many Irish landowners. Partly to divert attention from their own exactions, and as Bartholomew Lloyd, Croker's former tutor at Trinity College, argued angrily in a pamphlet, if tithes were oppressive, then rents were far worse, so why are they not to be commuted? The reason being that rather than improve the state of Ireland or address the concerns of the poorer classes, the main aim of 'those who declaimed most vehemently against the tithe proctors ... was in reality to wrest from the Clergy their property'.[69]

The outbreak of 'Rockite' disturbances following the bad harvests of 1820–1 had been dramatically featured in the British press and also played a major part in the discussions of the parliamentary commission. But while the diffuse demands of 'Rockites' were mainly economic and property related, with the development of religious tensions and allied ultra-Catholic propaganda, many of these agrarian secret societies were increasingly using anti-Protestant motifs.[70] The parliamentary opposition took up these disturbances to support their campaign for tithe reform, and in April 1824 one of the Whigs' main press writers, Thomas Moore, rushed into print his hugely successful *Memoirs of Captain Rock*. As Moore's biographer Ronan Kelly describes, within it 'the muscular Catholicism of Captain Rock comes to the fore', and in the second part the 'sectarian element is particularly noticeable' as he 'deliberately shied away from the underlying issues of land and property – so sacred, of course to his friends the Whigs', in order to represent tithes as central to Catholic grievances.[71] Mortimer O'Sullivan, another member of Croker's circle who would become a leading Irish Conservative pressman, responded with *'Captain Rock Detected … by Munster farmer'*. Lady Jersey mentioned to Moore that she suspected Croker was the author,[72] and although they had an amicable pact not to review each other's work,[73] he was almost certainly involved.

O'Sullivan's response has normatively been dismissed as 'anti-Catholic bugbear-baiting' by a 'celebrated Catholic renegade and Protestant bigot',[74] but Charles Gavan Duffy described him as being an opponent of 'furious bigotry' who 'sympathized with the wrongs of the Celts' and 'embraced the whole volume of their hopes'.[75] This is perhaps a little over-generous, and in the later 1830s O'Sullivan would become a 'furious' opponent of 'Popery', but it is evident that his main concern was that Moore was naively playing into the hands of the ultra-Catholics and diverting attention away from practical reforms onto religious issues. O'Sullivan accepted that tithes added to the heavy pressure upon the peasantry; yet their main predators were the landlords and sub-rentiers who 'would think it just as unnatural to let a tenant save and hoard as they would to leave their sheep for two years go unshorn'.[76] Emancipation and tithe reform would do nothing to improve the lives of the Irish poor who were 'daily sinking into wretchedness'. A more ominous concern, however, was that leaders of the Catholic Association, who had 'confined themselves to intemperate harangues and violent abuse of their opponents', had now *'effected a union with the Roman Catholic Clergy'*.[77] He denounced the ultra-Catholics, especially the priests among them, but perhaps held Moore in greater contempt as a flippant 'hanger on upon bloated aristocrats', who in foolishly 'flinging fire-brands' had 'collected within a portable compass all the topics that can stir the blood of the uninstructed Irish'. In contrast to his compatriots, and *'with a perfect safety to himself'*, he will continue to perform in the Whig salons of England undisturbed 'by shouts and shots, and the more terrific sounds of battered doors' that bring terror in Ireland.[78]

Moore clearly drew on popular Irish chap book histories as well as
sectarian 'Prophecies', but as with Croker's mockery of Parnell's
romantic Irish novel, all of the press circle saw such works as potentially
dangerous propaganda, synthesising snd legitimating emotive sentimental tropes common to divisive vernacular works in circulation in
both Britain and Ireland. Maginn would regularly entertain his readers
with satires evocative of modern mockeries of 'pseudery', such as in
this case Lady Morgan, his victim in 'The Green, Green Powldoodies
of the Burren':

> His eyes were like the flaming coal fire, or a star shining
> clearly in the middle of a dark heaven at night ... Like a
> morning stag – or even skimmed milk ... When he first
> deserted me I thought my heart was plucked away, I did
> not sleep till peep of day; kicking off all these blankets, the
> sheets and the counterpane ... till I stirred a little – and
> managed to dine on fried tripe and brandy.[79]

He admired some of Moore's ballads, but the more sentimental or
political ones received similar treatment:

> Tis the last lamp of the alley burning alone,
> All its brilliant companions are shivered and gone.
> Then I will stagger, as well as I may,
> By the light of my nose sure, I'll find my way,
> Tis the last glass of Claret, left sparkling alone, etc.[80]

Together with his Catholic friend Mahony, Maginn would lampoon
Moore for plagiarising classical texts, Irish ballads and other popular
works, sometimes publishing closely similar originals (and invented others) alongside them to further discredit him, and was genuinely indignant at the 'imagined' Irishness under construction by 'bestial cockney'
authors and songwriters 'who ... put into our mouths what they think
fit to write as Irish': if he should ever meet an inventor of 'Larry
O'Lasham, Looney Mactwolter or Judy Finnegan ... I should kick him
down the stairs'.[81] There was, however, a more serious concern with the
developing influence of the projection of chapbook proto-nationalist
Catholic historiography into English consciousness. In March 1825 an
indignant editorial in the *Dublin Correspondent* drew attention to the
tendency even in government publications 'to speak of the Irish as if
synonymous with Roman Catholics – a piece of craft which can offer no
imaginable purpose of advantage to those who employ it'.[82] For Croker

and the circle this was becoming an associated and more sinister consequence of the Whig parliamentary and the wider literary campaign playing into the hands of the ultra-Catholic movement by helping to define its mission against the Anglican connection, Church and community as synonymous with all 'Irish' grievances and ills of the Catholic masses.

Mortimer O'Sullivan's brother Samuel, a writer for *Blackwood's*, published an article in the July 1824 number succinctly representing the circle's views. 'Castle *Rackrent* is the only and undoubted birthplace of Captain Rock', and 'in giving the go-by to every subject in which the real grievances of Ireland are concerned' parliament was obscuring the fact that 'rackrent' was 'the great question – the *one* question'.[83] In March 1825 the *Quarterly Review* published a much longer statement in a forty-page review of Mortimer's *Captain Rock Detected* and a pamphlet by the liberal Anglican bishop of Limerick, John Jebb. Written mainly by William Phelan, with help from a number of the circle under the supervision of Croker,[84] the first section acknowledged that the Irish Church 'stood in need of a most extensive reformation and retrenchment'. There were, however, no practices sufficiently detrimental 'to justify its overthrow and confiscation of its revenues'. Tithes were far less oppressive than rent, usually less than a third of the official 10 per cent tithe entitlement and few cottiers paid any at all. If 'nearly all the evils with which Ireland is afflicted' can be attributed to tithes and 'the country never can be at peace till this grievance shall have been entirely done away with', then they should be, but if most of 'the miseries of the Irish population are to be traced essentially to the landlords or to the system which usually prevails in the management of their property' then their income should also be the 'proper subject for the interference of Parliament'.[85]

During the recent disturbances 'the first demand [was] an abatement of rent',[86] and in comparison to most landlords, most Anglican clergymen 'stand honourably aloof from all the vexatious jobbery unhappily so prevalent' in Ireland, spending 'their money in the country from which they receive it, and their time and talents in ministering to wants of the distressed'. This had been long acknowledged by the Irish poor, as during the outrages in Munster, when 'the clergyman could travel the country uninterrupted and suffer not the least violence' whereas local gentlemen 'could not so much walk into their shrubberies without armed protection'.

> The great and overwhelming curse of the country, as the authentic testimony, as all rational and judicial observers

demonstrate, is the degradation, the abject condition, of the lower classes. A finer race of men than the Irish peasantry, more nobly gifted and more generously disposed, is not to be found upon the habitable globe [but] they are absolutely ground to powder: there is too frequently no sympathy between the landlord and his tenants; and rents are enormous. It cannot be otherwise, because the proprietors are wandering to more inviting places of residence and leave their wretched dependents to the tender mercies of middlemen and agents ...

Now in what way can the extermination of the Clergy, and the sale or confiscation of Church property, diminish these acknowledged and overwhelming evils? Will the subtraction of that wealth from Ireland, which now according to the reformers enables twelve or thirteen hundred clergymen to wallow in luxury ... be the most successful mode of curtailing the cupidity of the landlords, or raising the character or comforts of the poor. Is this the panacea for the deeply seated maladies of a sensitive and despairing people! A most original method of diffusing comfort and contentment by exasperating sufferings already so difficult to endure, and from the Pandora's box of Irish affliction expelling even the last refuge of hope ... Let the landed proprietors, who vote for plundering the Church, look well to the consequences.[87]

As Croker knew and drew attention to in his *State of Ireland*, tithe charges had in fact long been a target of agrarian societies, but as modern studies have shown, it was rarely levied on poor cottiers or on small potato crops other than in parts of Munster. When crops were liable, the actual charge to smaller farmers was often as low as 2.5 per cent of the officially permitted 10 per cent, and although we may be confident that some parsons and proctors tried to charge more, it was certainly a much commoner venal practice for the middlemen to overcharge their sub-tenants and blame it on the tithe.[88] While there would have been resentment to paying for an alien Church, there does not appear to have been any strong hostility to the Anglican pastoral clergy in most parts of Ireland prior to this period. Perhaps not least because one positive offshoot of the growth of evangelism was the mission to care for the poor, and while many may have had ulterior motives, it would be equally fair to assume that many of their religious rivals also had less appealing reasons for raising communal antipathy against them.[89]

What is beyond dispute was Samuel O'Sullivan's accusation that O'Connell 'has never attempted to regulate rents or obtain for the poor farmer permanency of possession [and] he has invariably opposed enactment of the Poor-Law'.[90] As Peter Gray shows in his extensive study of the Irish Poor Law, O'Connell opposed these measures almost all of his political life on rather convoluted moral grounds that are difficult to see as sincere given that liberal Catholics likes Bishop Doyle often tried to convince him they were unwarranted.[91] Croker and the press circle barely feature in any study of the Poor Law campaigns, despite almost certainly being the earliest and most active group of press promoters of compassionate Poor Laws for Ireland, but they argued that O'Connell's opposition to it and other practical reforms was mainly because neither he nor most of the Catholic petty elites dominating the Catholic movement saw any benefit for themselves in doing so. While this might be overly cynical, Catholic society was no more homogenous than any other. The 'Hereditary Bondsman' was in fact a holder of far more land and rental income than most of his Protestant peers. As Oliver MacDonagh describes, O'Connell was a 'traditional Irish landlord, negligent and un-improving',[92] and in 'general the Catholic proprietors were proverbially as exacting as Protestants'. They successfully concentrated on 'readily perceptible religious and political issues [and] exploited economic grievances merely for their propaganda value'. On land reform, agricultural improvement and Poor Laws, they 'adopted no constructive purpose'. Emancipation was to be the 'panaceatic' for all these ills, although this was hardly surprising, James Reynolds continues, because 'in the 1820s few men appreciated the basic nature of the land problem in relation to the misery of the Irish peasant. At least no one offered a serious solution.'[93]

But this was clearly not the case, and if more scholars of Irish history looked beyond Whig and/or Catholic publications they would discover, as James Sack's research illustrates, that 'there was a remarkably uniform viewpoint' on many of these issues in the Tory press. Its writers called for Poor Laws, poor rates, campaigned against 'economic oppression', 'absentee Irish (usually Protestant) landlords and their obnoxious middlemen', and even anticipated 'Parnell's demands to stop evictions ... and Gladstone's Land Acts to lower exorbitant rents'.[94] In his famous social history published over fifty years ago, Harold Perkin described the publications of the press circle as the firmest defenders of the poor and radical advocates of extensive reforms. The *Quarterly Review* 'rallied to the defence of the Poor Laws as early as 1823', he continues, and *Blackwood's* 'anticipated the spirit of the Bismarckian, if not the British, Welfare State'. They were, however, 'signally defeated' and their legacy 'dissipated into the romantic feudalism of Disraeli, Lord Manners and Young England', and has 'suffered the neglect and misunderstanding of most lost causes'.[95]

Perkin identified a few of the circle by name – Samuel O'Sullivan's *Blackwood's* articles and those of another more elusive Irish press writer, W. Johnston, as well as the brilliant economic essays of David Robinson. Croker and G.R. Gleig had in fact written the 1823 *Quarterly* article in defence of the Poor Laws,[96] but eleven years before this the *Quarterly* had argued that there was 'something rotten in our internal policy' that permitted 'great profits to be made from neglecting the poor'. It also criticised Malthusians, political economists and other promoters of 'brute materialism' who 'deprave the morals and harden the heart' while the 'rich are to be called upon for no sacrifice' and defended the old Poor Law, calling upon government to reform rental agreements and implement public work projects to relieve distress.[97] In 1816 it argued for a property tax to fund poor relief, describing it as 'villainous' for anyone to suggest it should be withheld from the able bodied,[98] and in July 1819 Croker argued in the Commons that any laws applicable in Britain should be equally applicable in Ireland.[99]

During the Irish harvest crisis and subsequent local famine of the early 1820s, *John Bull* listed the food exported from Ireland since January 1821 and launched a typical *Bull* tirade against the landlords, larger farmers, merchants, traders and speculators who 'would not send provisions across the stream to save their fellow countrymen'. A Poor Law should be established to force them to maintain the victims, 'lower their rents, increase their wages, do all in their power to stop the land-jobbing', and in March of that same year, *Bull* called for a 20 per cent tax to be imposed on absentee landlords.[100] In 1821 Croker's *Guardian* defended the old Poor Laws in Britain as the only 'humane' method of relief,[101] and argued that in Ireland, 'the present causes of the outrages are ... unquestionably connected with the great causes upon which the unhappy state of the lower classes of Ireland is built – ignorance, poverty and oppression.' So numerous are the 'degradations of the Irish poor ... that it is almost impossible to know how to class them', but the 'prevalence of the Popish religion', the non-residence of the 'landed proprietors and the oppression of the middle-men' were major obstructions to reform. If the government wanted 'to lessen the power and authority of the parish priest' they 'must evince to the Catholics the purity of our intentions':

> There was an utter heartlessness in the conduct of the professed absentee ... society should have some badge of shame to set upon such men. The late evil which calls so loudly for redress is the system of tyranny pursued by the middle-men ... If the poor tenant found the cultivation of his farm answer to himself [sic], he would always be ready to pay the price stipulated for its possession; but when the management of the estate devolves upon the middle-men, they uniformly turn it to their advantage ... Thus the middle-man believes he has the right to act as a tyrant and treat his inferiors as slaves. The remedy in this, as in the preceding instance [is] a better system of morals in the rich themselves. The residence of the rich would dispense with the middle-men.[102]

George Croly probably wrote this article, and Croker was, and would be, more moderate on such reforms than most of his circle, but as Peter Gray pointed out, with the possible exception of Lord Anglesey, he was the only leading Tory parliamentarian who campaigned for Irish Poor Laws.[103]

The members of the press circle would be dedicated enemies of the Catholic movement, or 'Popery', and quite understandably this can be simplistically construed as 'bigotry', but they would be equally passionate in their demands for radical reforms and defence of the poor, and as we will see, this would be a much commoner feature of their writing and closely connected with their contempt for the O'Connellites and ultra Catholics. On 26 February 1825 the social reformer Henry Drummond wrote to Croker: 'what madness to think that the miseries of the Irish people will be alleviated by emancipation.' 'Carry over there the English Poor Laws, they would give more happiness to the many than all the toleration' but 'this is a truth that well conditioned people like you dare not utter.'[104] Croker agreed, but replied that Emancipation must also be passed or it would continue to be exploited and distract attention from effective reforms.

> Alas poor Ireland, but I think we shall carry the Catholic question, which I look upon as the best chance for her. While that question affords a furnace to heat the people, and to light the firebrands of demagogues, there will be no

peace; but I look upon the measure only as a sedative under the influence of which other more effective machines may have opportunity of operating.[105]

Three days later, when the Radical Sir Francis Burdett introduced another Catholic Relief bill, Croker seconded it and designed one of the accompanying 'wings'.[106] Described as probably the single most important parliamentary battle for Emancipation,[107] Croker would later believe it represented the last opportunity for conciliatory Emancipation. The single most important reason being that Daniel O'Connell was now willing to support securities and was in London throwing his energetic talents behind the campaign. On 2 March he sent an excited note to his wife Mary saying that it was rumoured that Lord Liverpool would support the measure: 'We are to be emancipated! The tide has turned in our favour.'[108] Peel wrote that 'there is little feeling, I think, upon the question. People are tired of it, and tired of the trouble of opposing it, or thinking about it', but he saw this 'general apathy as no reason for abandoning his own principles', however, and continued to oppose the measure.[109]

Wellington did not believe Emancipation would satisfy Irish Catholic claims, but like Croker he was essentially a political pragmatist, considering it a 'political and not at all a religious question'.[110] As Croker reminded him on a number of occasions, his first speech to the Irish Commons had been in support of the proposed Catholic Bill of 1793,[111] and by 1825 he privately acknowledged the urgency of the measure now that a 'sort of' Roman Catholic 'Theocracy in Ireland' had 'acquired the knowledge of the means of organising the mass'.[112] When seconding the motion Croker told the Commons that although the measure 'ought no longer be deferred', he would no longer 'consent to any arrangement which did not include the Roman Catholic Clergy and embrace a provision for them', because 'no measure ... could be efficacious which should not include an adequate provision for them'.[113] In private he was blunter: if 'not adopted a rebellion and massacre will go near to pull the *establishment* about our ears', yet optimistic and 'delighted Plunkett and Brougham both considered the plan as practicable, and likely to be accepted by the priests'. Although the 'Catholic Associators and others look upon it with great jealousy – to be sure it would spoil their trade'.[114]

The bill would have two accompanying clauses, or 'wings', and O'Connell would support both as concessions to ease Protestant concerns. One was for the payment of the Catholic clergy, the other to disfranchise the forty-shilling freeholders, and it is clear from his correspondence that Croker designed the former and was highly active behind the scenes with George Canning and other cross-party figures to pass the whole package.[115] On 12 March he wrote to Plunkett saying he was 'getting my proposition relative to a provision for the Roman Catholic clergy into an ostensible shape immediately'.[116] Four days later Canning sent Croker a short note: 'I shall be very glad to see you at the hour, which you should propose. I have written to Mr Plunkett in order to [obtain] a report from him.'[117] Huskisson wrote the same day saying he would be unable to attend Croker's planned meeting to discuss the Catholic bill, but he supported the 'repeal of all disabilities and disqualifying clauses and a pension for a Catholic Clergy be secured ... Make my excuses to Mr Plunkett and Sir Francis Burdett'.[118] Croker scribbled on the back of this letter: 'Present at the settling of the Catholic bill, 19 March: Sir Francis Burdett, Mr Tierney, [undecipherable], Wynn, Plunkett, Newport, H. Parnell, [undecipherable] Charles Grant, Rice, Lord Palmerston, Abercromby, Croker'.[119]

O'Connell noted on 4 March that he had spent the previous day discussing the bill with Burdett and Plunkett, and that they were willing to 'emancipate the Catholics in the most conciliatory manner possible ... a provision will be made for our Clergy ... so much better for the Friars as it will leave almost all the individual donations free'.[120] For him to be finally supporting concessions represented a substantial public change of heart, and his more militant Irish colleagues violently attacked him for it.[121] British radicals such as Cobbett also fulminated that he was 'bartering' the civil liberties of the 40/- freeholders and expecting Protestants to fund Catholic priests;[122] as did some of the press circle such as George Croly for having represented himself as the saviour of the oppressed but now proposing to 'sacrifice the elective franchise of three fourths of the population'.[123]

Bishop Doyle publicly vowed that Emancipation would lead to the end of religious conflict in Ireland, and won Protestant support by publicly rebutting the papacy's right to politically dictate to the Irish Catholic Church: 'We should oppose him by every means in our power, even by the exercise of spiritual authority.'[124] Charles Brownlow, whom Peel accurately mocked as having previously 'gloried in being an Orangeman', told the Commons that he had been won over by the conciliatory testimony of Catholic bishops like Doyle,[125] and it was left to George Dawson, Peel's Irish brother-in-law, to make the strongest speech against the bill. It was a political fraud, he argued, and if it were not for

O'Connell telling the Irish masses that 'they were the most oppressed people in the World because he could not be a Member of Parliament or a judge, they would not trouble their heads with Catholic Emancipation'.[126] Peel made his main statement of opposition on 21 April, criticising Canning for describing opposition arguments as 'absurd apprehensions of danger' when it was clear to everybody that the Catholic clergy were 'manipulating the minds of ignorant and credulous peasantry'. Unlike his fellow cabinet member, he would 'never consent to any measure which diminished the security of the Protestant Establishment'.[127]

The bill passed by a majority of twenty-seven. The 'wings' followed, with the provision for the clergy passing by 205 to 162; Croker having arranged for Francis Leveson-Gower to propose it with the additional authority of being seconded by Wellington's brother-in-law, Hercules Pakenham.[128] O'Connell wrote home: 'the bill will actually pass this session. Recollect I tell you so!'[129] and *The Times* celebrated that all the 'enlightened men' were for it save 'Mr Peel ... the single man above mediocrity in the House of Commons who persists in his hostility to the measure of Catholic Relief'.[130] Wellington tried to convince him to drop his opposition 'pointing out that statesmen should not act on personal feelings', but Peel responded that he 'had made up his mind'.[131] As Norman Gash describes, the 'key to the position was in Peel's hands', and when he threatened to resign Liverpool became increasingly concerned with the difficulties this would create and it bolstered his waning opposition.[132] On 17 May he made an emotional speech against the bill in the Lords, saying he 'detested' the issue 'from the bottom of his heart' and was thoroughly sick of the divisiveness it had created. The two Irish communities were not 'united and knit together' primarily because of the 'bigoted and intolerant conduct' of the Catholic clergy. A 'great and powerful engine was at work to effect the object of re-establishing the Catholic religion', and if it succeeded, the Protestant ascendancy would 'not be worth a farthing'. The Lords rejected the bill by forty-seven votes; a majority that surprised Liverpool, for although he had been 'unyielding in his denunciation', he had believed he was making a final protest against the inevitable.[133]

Not surprisingly, O'Connell was furious and 'immediately announced his intention of renewing agitation' in Ireland, and that the ministry could now 'abide any evil consequences that may ensue'.[134] For the first time since the veto crisis, he could honestly refute accusations that he was unwilling to support substantive conciliatory concessions and argue that the responsibility for the failure rested entirely with a few ministers and the ultra-Protestant peers. His unilateral decision to support the 'wings' continued to attract what might have seemed a hubristic barrage of attacks from ultra-Catholics and Radicals, and he had to agree that in 'the future they should demand unqualified emancipation'.[135] Canning, Croker and other ministerial supporters of the bill had to defend themselves from the jeers of not only some of Croker's increasingly estranged press circle, but an enervated Whig opposition led by Brougham who mocked them and demanded to know why they remained with colleagues who continued to oppose Catholic rights.[136]

Peel's own hubris was three years away, but in the meantime he continued to enhance his reputation as a man of strong principles enjoying the toasts of the Pitt clubs and his Oxford University electors as their Protestant champion.[137] If Croker recorded any criticism of him at this time it does not appear to have survived, but some years after Peel's forced 'apostasy' of 1829, he expressed some more of his views on politicians who refuse to accept that 'when time passes – circumstances vary – men disappear – the *Constitution itself is altered* – storm succeeds calm – clouds to sunshine'. It was 'foolhardy' to believe 'his opinion itself must be immutable' or that '*Hansard's* inexorable register [be] consulted as if it were a book of fate' and adopt

> ... a high and intelligent principle of consistency in a constitution, which like ours must be worked by the machinery of Party ... Can we without a smile of wonder see the most distinguished members of the *Pitt* Club, and the loudest professors of the *Pitt* principles, resting their claims on an opposition to Mr Pitt's policy and pledges.[138]

Whatever disappointment Croker may have felt at the failure of Emancipation and increasing signs of division in his party, the practical demands of realpolitik continued, and in September Wellington told him that he was 'aware that a Protestant Government could not be formed, nor could a Catholic one'. He 'would not raise the No-Popery cry', but in order to strengthen the ministry's position in what was once again a growing economic crisis, he would advise Liverpool to 'seize the propitious moment and dissolve parliament' in the chance of gaining a stronger 'protestant' ministry.[139] In the polarising political climate of the elections in Ireland the following year, the Catholic priests and factions would also display their political power as a national force for the first time. After which Croker would retain little hope that Emancipation could serve as a conciliating measure, taking little satisfaction from Plunkett's report from Dublin following their extensive election interventions: 'had your advice been taken this could not have been – but what is to be done, *regredi? Impossibili*'.[140]

CANNING'S SHORT-LIVED VICTORY, 'THE FOOLS, THE FOOLS, THE FOOLS', AND EMANCIPATION AS A 'SORDID NECESSITY'

On 17 February 1827 Lord Liverpool suffered a stroke, and over the following weeks the ministry publicly ruptured when Peel and Wellington refused to serve under Canning or any other 'Catholic' as head of government. The commonest view of events has been that their decision was probably principled if misguided,[141] but Boyd Hilton has argued that 'it is more likely Peel refused to serve under Canning for the same reason he offered to resign from Liverpool's ministry in 1825, that is to facilitate emancipation' being carried while he was out of office.[142] Croker elected to support Canning and played a leading part in helping him in the difficult task of assembling a ministry, and his account broadly supports the argument that Peel's decision may have been more opportunistic than principled.

Having been a 'Catholic' all his life Croker had few political qualms about supporting Canning, but once again his initial concern seems to have been to hold the party together, and although he knew there would be the usual contest for places among his political colleagues, he did not anticipate the extent of the division. Under a diary entry marked 18 February, he recorded that he 'called on the Duke of Wellington, whom I found at breakfast ... He said that he wanted to keep the Government together, not merely for their own sakes but for that of the country for that "after them comes chaos".' Croker agreed, but thought that 'the only way of keeping us together was to make Canning the [Prime] Minister.' This would require the least change and 'answer all the expectations, provided Mr Canning should engage to take the Government on the same terms and in the same spirit in which Liverpool had held it'. Wellington 'seemed to assent to what I said about Mr Canning', and then asked Croker if he thought Peel would 'assent to that arrangement? I said I did not know, but that I thought he ought; that I was sure it was the course which would ensure him becoming [Prime] Minister in time'.[143] Later that same day:

> Peel called on me at the Admiralty to ask me to take a walk.
> I had told him all along of what I had said to the Duke
> of Wellington ... and though he never made any direct

declaration, I had no reason to doubt that he would acquiesce, if the Duke did, in Canning's promotion. This was strongly confirmed during this walk. Huskisson, who was Canning's alter ego, had been ill and confined to his house, and Peel proposed that we should begin by paying him a visit at Somerset House, which we did, and nothing could be more cordial; and to those who know Peel's very peculiar manners, this volunteered visit and cordiality at that moment will be conclusive that he had no idea of separating himself from Canning ... We were then opposite to Lord Eldon's [the leading anti-Emancipationist in the Lords] and pointing to his house, I said 'would he stay', upon which Peel squeezed my arm tightly under his, and said, 'he will if I do'. I had no doubt that Peel had no disinclination to such an arrangement.[144]

A few days later the Commons was occupied with another of Burdett's motions on the Catholic question rumoured to have been compiled in 'consultation with Canning'.[145] In the elections the year before there had been a growth in militant 'Protestant' support in Britain.[146]Most of this was probably in response to press reports about the rising religious tensions in Ireland and the character of the Catholic movement, but the Catholic clergy's interventions were having the opposite effect on many Irish members according to Brougham, who commented sarcastically during the debate that now 'a notorious majority' of them 'are all by necessity voting for Emancipation' from fear of losing their seats or worse should they oppose it.[147] Another member called upon Burdett to change the title of his bill to the more appropriate and 'honest' term 'expediency', and he concurred, adapting it to 'This House is Deeply Impressed with the *Expediency* [*Hansard's* italics] in Taking into Consideration the Laws imposing Civil Disabilities ... on Roman Catholics.'[148]

George Dawson remained one of the most scornful opponents and, not surprisingly given his relationship with Peel, many believed that his views were a more forthright expression of their faction. Peel left his contribution to the end of the debates, and argued that Emancipation had almost no practical purpose other than as a political tool for the 'Catholic religion', which had something 'engrafted upon it' 'for the purpose of establishing the power of the mind over the hearts of men'. Canning publicly ridiculed him for his concerns,[149] but the 'Protestants' won the day and the bill was rejected in an unusually crowded

Commons by 276 votes to 272. *The Times* dispiritedly reporting that 'the Catholic Question' now had 'little chance of being decided on any ground of right or reasoning, of justice or wisdom, but on necessity alone, on imminent sordid necessity'.[150]

This growth of opposition to the measure and Canning's mockery of his arguments may have helped sway Peel, for when Croker dined with him a few days later he noted for the first time: 'I fear that he is quite indisposed to serving under, not Canning, he says, but a Catholic Premier. He would like the Duke or Lord Bathurst, or even Lord Melville.' To which Croker responded with what appears to have been a wry comment in his diary: 'I observed to him that Lord Melville was a Catholic.'[151] On 28 March the king sent for Canning, Wellington and Peel. Canning refused to give a pledge that he would not promote Catholic Relief and that his honour demanded that he must either have the substantive power of first minister or resign. Peel said he could not serve under a 'Catholic' and the meeting ended in deadlock.[152] Croker had fully committed himself by early April, and wrote to Canning warning that, given his dwindling allies, he must make greater efforts to win aristocratic support and ignore advisors who 'talk slightingly of Blue Ribbonds'. He also gave Canning his main reasons for standing by him despite his 'regard for the Duke of Wellington, who first brought me into politics – my private love for Peel', he was, above all, 'most anxious that you should all hold together':

> Neither political gratitude, nor private friendship blind me to the fact that in such a union, your present and relative station entitles you to expect the lead, and that such an arrangement would afford the best chance of holding the Government together. At least so I think; and these have long been my opinions.[153]

This would prove futile, and on 10 April the king finally and angrily accepted that the breach would not be healed and directed Canning to assemble a ministry. Peel and Wellington formally resigned, followed by Goulburn, Westmorland, Bathurst, Eldon, Londonderry and approximately forty-one other Tories in lesser positions. Croker tried to remain on good terms with Peel, writing that he had only discussed him with Canning on one occasion and the 'impression this conversation left in my mind was that you were likely to stay in office'. His hopes that he would stay had been 'excited' by what 'he had heard from Mr Canning himself', concluding 'I know that friendship in this country is impaired too often by party, but we are not yet, I hope, in opposite parties.'[154] Peel responded with a formal note breaking off their twenty-year friendship.[155] Croker had almost certainly acted honourably in these dealings, but in fairness to Peel, his propensity for 'meddling' understandably made him suspicious, and although Croker's defence of himself appears to be in accord with what evidence is available, he had spoken against Canning the year before and had been keeping Wellington informed of some of his connections with the opposition.[156] Either way, Croker 'never heard, and Canning told me he never knew, what changed Peel's disposition – for change he, like me, thought it was. Peel never again spoke to me on the subject.'[157]

Unable to recruit many Tories, Canning was forced to appoint a substantial number of Whigs. Something made more difficult because the king stipulated that Emancipation must remain an 'open issue'. As the ultra-Protestant Duke of Rutland recounted with satisfaction, having alienated the Tories because of his support for Emancipation, Canning had the 'galling appendage' of a 'Protestant tin kettle tied to his tail'.[158] Lyndhurst, the lord chancellor, later recorded that Croker was probably Canning's most important advisor during this crisis, and that when the three of them were discussing the final cabinet arrangements over dinner, Canning said, 'in a tone of pleasantry, "and now Croker, that you have settled almost all the offices of the State, what do you mean to take for yourself?"'. Croker had replied: 'sincerely circumstanced as I was, I could not change my position' and that he would remain secretary to the Admiralty.[159] Other than his declared lack of ambition for political promotion since the death of their only child, Croker appears to have refused a ministry partly because of his role with the press, saying he preferred to remain 'where I was master of my own business, and not unacceptable to the public'. Eligible for a three-quarter pension, he even offered to resign his Admiralty post if Canning should need it to win another supporter.[160] All of which appears to have been sincere, for he said much the same to Lowther and to his old college friend Thomas Casey in Dublin when thanking him for finding him volumes of the *Irish Parliamentary Debates*. 'It is a shame for an Irish Member – nay an Irish Historian not to possess them', joking that if 'two Irish proprietors in the Imperial Home Department shocks some of our English Tory friends', and that he liked Spring-Rice 'so well, I would willingly have seen him Sec. of the Admiralty, where he would have offended no prejudices'.[161]

Croker was able to fulfil one long-held personal ambition however, when Canning elevated Plunkett to the peerage, and finally freed him from a promise to Liverpool not to run against him at Dublin University. Canning considered Croker's absence at such a time to be an unnecessary loss given that he had a borough seat from Lord Hertford, but he finally conceded saying he would also offer John Henry North, a fellow 'Catholic' rival at the college, 'a seat without contest or expense, what can I say more?' Ending grumpily that 'it is a little too much to leave us aground; and then to make our not calling for other help the condition of coming back to us ... Ever Yours, G.C'.[162] With the rise of religious tensions even some of Croker's closest friends at the college were now hesitant about backing him,[163] and he wrote trying to reassure them that he held few illusions that Emancipation would herald any 'great breach being made in Irish Popery by the force of reason ... Look what I said in my "State of Ireland" twenty years ago', but he still believed the measure was best for 'the safety and the honour of the Establishment'. 'I have not changed, but reasserted my principles ... I support the Catholic claims and boldly say that I could not alter a line ... I implore you, for your sake as well as mine, but most for yours, to throw off these nervous feelings.'[164] When he finally arrived in Dublin he was surprised at the extent of the political and religious antipathy, and wrote asking Canning to seek the assistance of the lord lieutenant 'against Mr Lefroy, the Orange (or so they tell me George Dawson's) candidate'.[165] Two days later he solicited the support of Irish Whigs in order to 'assist the liberal cause in the college' and defeat Lefroy 'who has no chance with me if the Protestant Jesuits do not succeed in absolving my young friends from their promises'.[166]

The most significant borough-holding Tory aristocrats, the Lowthers, had followed Wellington and Peel, and as young Lowther's close friend,[167] Croker was asked to intervene. He rejected his attempts, but praised Croker for his 'friendship and kindness on all occasions' and that it was 'with grief that I believe this is the only occasion that I have not been so ready to accept your suggestions'.[168] Unlike Peel he remained on close terms, sending Croker news from the Commons, and on 14 May reported that 'Dawson has taken his seat on the opposition benches, and appears as if he was to be leader.' Peel remained on the cross-benches, but he would not be 'surprised to see him follow his *beau frère*' and firmly commit himself.[169] Peel's position may have appeared more moderate in public than Dawson's, but the fervently ultra-Protestant Duke of Newcastle visited him at this time and noted in his diary that 'all the principal people of our side were there',[170] and Croker wrote to Canning saying that he was now sure that Dawson, 'who had been referring to me as one of the corrupters of the press', was the '*primum mobile* of the Orange opposition', and that he could hardly 'doubt that Peel is using his weight to defeat me'.[171] He was franker to Lowther: 'Dawson is at the bottom of Orange opposition to me here and I have proof, of which I can not doubt, that Peel himself has exerted influence against me.'[172] According to a recent history of Trinity College, Thomas Lefroy, an 'erudite lawyer and stern unbending Tory', was supported by Peel,[173] and when Bartholomew Lloyd officially announced Croker's candidature, 'pandemonium never sent forth such a yell'.[174] An 'Orange mob of Collegians' burst open the doors of the Examination Hall where the election addresses were to be delivered and 'created a deafening scene of tumult … yells, blowing of horns, hammering of sticks and other discordant sounds'. Croker was unable to speak, and when his supporters attempted to, 'a desperate attempt was made to tear down the barricades', windows were smashed, 'the Horse Police were sent for and cut scalps and bruised shins were the consequence'. After the tally, however, the Catholic *Freeman's Journal* was delighted to report that despite the 'indecent abuse poured upon Mr Croker' for being a 'staunch supporter of civil and religious liberty' he won the final 'triumph of liberality' over the 'flag of Orange bigotry'.[175]

In Britain, although the *Courier* continued to support Canning, most of Croker's press circle, notably the *Morning Post*, *Morning Herald*, *John Bull* and *Blackwood's* were becoming increasingly hostile. He still exercised some moderating control over Hook, but the Duke of Newcastle took it upon himself to intervene and noted in his diary:

> Called on Mr Hook in Putney … He gave that he was in the habits of the greatest intimacy with Mr Croker who had persuaded him in the first instance … that Mr Canning deserved all praise for the honourable manner in which he stepped forward to take responsibility on himself and support King and Country – this wretched intriguer and political jackal [Croker] took the editor in. [Hook] assured me that his eyes were [now] completely opened and that in future (without pay) he should be as strong as ever in favour of the good cause.[176]

The newly established *Standard* newspaper was Canning's most aggressive press critic, describing him as the 'most ardent, angry and intolerant of all the English zealots of the popish question'.[177] Emancipation was a conspiracy to serve the 'Romish priests' and keep the Irish poor the 'slaves of degrading superstitions'. Those who foolishly believed that it would be 'another step in the "March of the Mind" – another example of the Enlightenment – another precedent in favour of liberal opinions' were disregarding all the 'instructions of all history' and all the 'immortal intolerance of Popery given at Carlow, Carrick, Cork and twenty other meetings in Ireland' of the inevitable consequences of 'Roman Catholics armed with despotic power over Ireland'.[178] The *Standard* would rapidly become one of the most successful Tory dailies in Britain (the forerunner of the famous *Evening Standard*), and almost every number raged against the Catholic movement, publishing graphic reports gleaned from Irish newspapers of fiery Catholic speeches or attacks against Irish Protestants, and if these were in short supply, reminding its readers that 'the menace of St. Bartholomew, the fires of Smithfield, the holocaust of Scullabogue, the bridge at Wexford' all provided abundant evidence of the murderous ambitions of 'Popery'.[179]

The editor was Stanley Lees Giffard, the son of John Giffard of the *Dublin Journal*, who had moved to England in 1811 as a twenty-three-year-old lawyer, but like Croker began writing for the press as soon as he arrived and by 1819 was the editor of the thrice-weekly *St James's Chronicle*. First established in 1761, Goldsmith, Burke, Sheridan and Boswell had all written for it, but by the time Giffard took control it was already 'bitterly opposed to Emancipation' and promoting the view that 'the Roman Church was simply a political conspiracy carried on under the name of religion.' One of Stanley's brothers, Ambrose, was married to Rosamund Croker's sister; another, seventeen-year-old William, had been pulled from the Dublin Mail on the plains of Kildare and hacked to death by rebels in 1798. This certainly exacerbated John Giffard's antipathy to the Catholic movement, and presumably Stanley's, but as with most of the circle he had Irish Catholic friends. Among the closest, and perhaps most incongruous, was Charles Phillips, the Catholic Board lawyer and Radical whose pamphlets Croker had reviewed so devastatingly in the *Quarterly*, and with whom Stanley Lees remained 'intimate' all his life.[180]

The *Standard*'s assistant editor was the ubiquitous William Maginn, brought over from Cork by Croker to help Hook edit *John Bull* in 1823, and many believed he was responsible for 'much of the abuse poured out in prose and verse' against Canning in the Tory papers at this time.[181] The *Standard*'s motto, fixed beneath its title every day, would become synonymous with the enduring clarion call of beleaguered Irish Protestantism: 'Plant here the Standard: Here we shall best remain.' This was probably at Maginn's suggestion, *Perge, Signifier*, taken from Livy, being the nickname used by the co-writers of *Blackwood's* satirical literary serials to describe Maginn's character, Sir Morgan O'Doherty, the 'Ensign' or 'Standard Bearer'.[182] The Duke of Newcastle almost certainly part financed the *Standard*, and Croker later wrote that George Dawson 'had a chief hand in setting it up'[183] and that 'Wellington and Peel countenanced that paper.'[184]

Although Croker was also attacked in it by his old allies, somebody sent a note to Canning pointing out his connections with them, and Canning wrote to Croker saying that 'he was not in the habit of putting faith in anonymous letters, but do you happen to know of a man of the name of Maginn?'[185] He enclosed the letter:

> Dear Sir,
> As it is only right that you should know your friends and enemies, I beg leave to inform you that much of the slander in prose and verse against your administration which fills the *Standard* and other London newspapers is written by an unprincipled Irishman named MAGINN, who styles himself Doctor, who is the protégé and friend of Mr John Wilson Croker. Dr Maginn is also at the bottom of all the abuse poured against you in *Blackwood's*.[186]

Croker replied promptly:

> I have never seen the *Standard*, but I hear that nobody is more abused in it than I myself am, and I have also understood that the editor and author of the abuse is Mr Lees Giffard. As to the doctor (who is a regular graduated doctor as I believe), I have already told you all that I know of him. He may call my acquaintance 'friendship and protection', but if he does, I think he would hardly contribute to a paper which is so abusive of me and of those to whom I am connected ... I went as far as I could in what I threw at him about three months ago, but I have no kind of hold, or even claim, upon him; indeed he may perhaps be offended at the reserve and distance with which I have treated him. But I am obliged to do so; for having begun life by being a kind of author myself, I have been haunted by everything

that has pretensions to authorship and particularly by all that Ireland sends hither to be a success. This obliges me to know a little, but at the same time warns me to know as little as may be of several persons of this description. Tho' I know my reserve offends them and makes enemies who take their revenge in newspaper libels.[187]

Croker's denial of any personal association with Maginn and Giffard since late 1825 was probably true, and his final remarks were a suggestion that Canning should be more sympathetic given the press service he had provided to him and the party. It was, however, disingenuous of him to surmise that its editor was Stanley Lees Giffard, given that he had known him since his childhood.[188] Furthermore, and by a morbid coincidence, Croker had received a letter from Rosamund's sister that very day containing the news that her husband had died of dysentery en-route from Ceylon and the legal post Croker had solicited for him fifteen years before. The responsibility had fallen on Croker to write to Stanley breaking the news that the 'excellent man' his brother Ambrose 'is no more', and that 'you, Mr Richard Pennell [Rosamund's brother] and myself were named executor'.[189] This letter was prefixed 'Dear Sir', however, indicating that they did not have any close relationship at this time, but they would handle Ambrose's meagre estate together and the Crokers provided a home for Mrs Giffard in Molesley and virtually adopted three of her many children.[190]

Canning would make no mark as prime minister. At the end of July Croker wrote to Hertford saying he was concerned at his declining health; not least because he had recently employed a doctor who had spent 'all his life as a naval surgeon, and the majority of his cases required mercury ... and he gave Mr C. so much he actually salivated him'.[191] On 7 August: 'Mr Canning is no more – and that is all I can tell you; though the event must have consequences that will be felt all through England.' Whatever new ministry is formed, 'an exclusive Protestant Government cannot, I am satisfied, stand; there would be an opposition of 250, which would stop all public business.'[192]

In anticipation of a royal summons, Wellington remained at Stratfield Saye while Henry Hardinge sent him the political news, and they appear to have been particularly interested in Croker's views:

[9th of August] ... Croker remarked that in the Commons some of the Whigs ought to be obtained ... but thought Lord Lansdown and his two or three friends would remain, and he should consider him more manageable than Grey ... and that both parties must be mixed whatever might be the extent or quality of the mixture.

[11th of August]: Croker told me this morning that the King's confidence in Canning was to an extent unlimited ... Croker repeated his conviction that you ought to form the new Government ... and having accomplished it see you retiring from the Premiership into your natural pro- fessional position of army and ordnance ...With his usual confidence, [Croker's] Govt. was as follows: Lord Goderich, First Lord of the Treasury; Peel, Chancellor of the Exchequer and leader of the Commons; Lord Lans- down or Melville, Home dept. or the Colonies, as could best be managed; Lord Grey, Foreign Office ... Croker talked of retiring having earned his pension of £1,500 a year.

[13th of August] Croker told me yesterday the King and Lord Goderich were serious in going forward ...[193]

The king remained angry with Wellington and Peel for refusing to serve under Canning, and he dashed their ambitions by asking Goderich, formerly Croker and Peel's old friend, Robinson, the 'Duke of Fuss and Bustle', to try and form an administration. On 11 August Goderich also sought Croker's advice, who repeated to him that if Wellington, Peel and Lord 'Grey could be introduced into the present Cabinet it would make one of the most powerful and, as far as I could foresee, the most popular Governments that could be formed'. Goderich, a 'Catholic', doubted Peel would join his ministry, 'having stated that his sole reason for not serving under Canning was ... because he could not act under any person voting for Catholics'. But Croker responded that Peel had not gone out 'on the mere question that the head of government should be a Protestant'. The implication being that Peel's main concern was his public image, and that now that a resignation stood between him and the charge of inconsistency, then he would not feel 'any insurmountable difficulty in having a moderate Catholic head to the Government'.[194]

Peel would not join, and as Croker wrote at the end of December, ever 'firm as a bulrush', all the jostling for places, intrigue and resent- ments 'quite bewildered poor Goderich'.[195] The prospects 'of a pure Whig Administration (if anything Whig can be called pure) becomes more distinct'; 'Brougham boils the pot'; rumours have it that 'Hol- land is to come in ... Palmerston and Charles Grant are to profess to be Whigs, and what's more, I regret, Huskisson! ... What fools! fools! fools! our Tory friends have been.'[196] A week later, and by then 'in a most pitiful state', Goderich broke down in tears and the king offered his 'blubbering' first minister a handkerchief wearily acknowledging that his government was 'defunct'.[197] Having little practical choice, he reluctantly asked Wellington to form a ministry on two conditions: that the Catholic question remain an open one and the king's personal 'bugaboo' Lord Grey be excluded.[198] Wellington's first act was to 'immediately send an express' to Peel requesting that he return to the Home Department and become leader of the Commons; and in little more than a week they had put together essentially the same ministry they had obstructed Canning from assembling.[199] Croker believed that this was the best option, but in expressing his frustration to Hertford, he 'lamented' that 'Canning had been driven to coalesce' with the likes of Lansdowne and other more 'unruly' Whigs, and on the irony that Wellington and Peel had now 'thrown overboard' old ultra-Protestant allies such as Lord Eldon.[200]

Sir John Barrow, the under-secretary at the Admiralty, recorded his own disdain that with the exception of Croker, all of Canning's political 'friends' deserted him in the days when he was dying.[201] Following his return from the funeral, Croker composed a memorial poem and wrote to Lowther expressing his disappointment that Peel had not seen fit to attend, 'even though he of the late Ministers would have been alone'.[202] Not surprisingly, Mrs Canning was deeply offended by the behaviour of her husband's other old colleagues, especially with Huskisson, with whom she waged a 'vicious' public row.[203] When Wellington met Croker in mid-January he bullishly defended his 'Canningite' ministry, saying he had been so 'beset with importunities and remonstrances' that he was forced to assuage 'what gentlemen call their feelings' and quoted the arguments Peel had used to convince him that 'those who are for forming an exclusive [Protestant] Ministry expect that I am to go into the House of Commons with half a party to fight a party and a half'.[204] Suppressing his irritation, Croker 'clothed himself in Cicero's toga' once more, and confined his views to his diary and a letter to Hertford saying he felt free of any obligation to his leaders other than a slight one to Wellington for first helping to bring him into parliament. Since the death of Perceval, he had never received any substantial display of gratitude for his efforts; 'on the contrary, all my political friends seemed inclined to leave me where they found me, and they neither did me, nor offered me any kind of political favour.' He was tempted to resign, but refrained from doing so out of loyalty to the Crown and 'the Catholic question, which (altho' I will never consent to press it upon the King's conscience, if he declare against it) I must always support of principle, tho I may postpone it as to the time; and thirdly my pecuniary affairs'.[205] On the latter, however, 'I have consulted my wife ... and she is ready to join me in such sacrifices as will render the loss bearable.' 'I have no ambition of honour or higher office, and if I had, I know that service is not the way to obtain them.'[206]

Two months later, his anger had subsided and he offered Peel an olive branch: 'The interruption of our intercourse has been so exceedingly painful to me that I can no longer refrain from making an effort to terminate it ... Do make me happy by a return to our former intercourse; you know how little politics has to do with it.'[207] Peel's response was positive if lukewarm, but he corroborated the value that both he and Canning had placed on Croker as an ally and advisor:

> The suspension of my intercourse with you was caused by the part which I had reason to believe you were taking in those arrangements ... Mr Canning declared to more than one person that there was no one to whom he was so much indebted for suggestions as to the course which he should pursue as he was to you. Such an avowal ... was sufficient reason for my declining to hold any intercourse with you on matters of a public nature. I am perfectly ready to bury in complete oblivion the causes of our misunderstanding and alienation.[208]

Croker replied that Peel's letter had given him the 'sincerest pleasure', but he still criticised him for not joining Canning. If he had done so 'he would be in the same position today that Mr Canning had been to Lord Liverpool' and probably the prime minister, but he would not 'damp a pleasure which I hope is mutual by retrospections'.[209] Peel and Croker never discussed the Canning issue again, and Croker 'never mentioned the subject to the Duke', because although 'his kindness to me continued not only unaltered' during the period of Canning's ministry, 'I did not think he had treated me with confidence in not telling me his change of opinion.'[210]

When parliament assembled for the 1828 session the issues of parliamentary reform and Catholic Emancipation predictably re-surfaced once again. In May 1827, when the Whigs had proposed a motion to enfranchise two great industrial towns, Croker had sent Canning a copy of the reform plan he had compiled in 1820.[211] 'Allow me to suggest to you a suggestion I made under less favourable circumstances on the subject of Grampound to Lord Liverpool', and he recommended the redistribution of some of the seats from probably corrupt boroughs to three Yorkshire districts: York, Cleveland and 'Holdness'. This would increase the urban representation without overly offending the county opponents and thereby enable Canning to 'put off for a little the question of enfranchising the great towns'.[212] Canning had opposed the measure, but when Reform came up again in the 1828 session Croker wrote to Peel saying that he 'would be glad to see both Retford and Penryn transferred to Birmingham and Manchester; but I fear that would be thought too reforming'. He proposed a compromise whereby an industrial town would achieve greater representation while technically remaining a country seat.[213] Either way, if some measure of moderate Reform was not conceded,

> ... we shall have a great, and I think not unfounded, outcry. The crowd in and out of the House will exclaim that the popular side has no longer any hope of gradual reform, and will renew the cry for radical reform with more effect; and those who look deeper will say that in order to evade a proper reform, you are in truth making a real innovation on the constitution ... Having, luckily, now two boroughs to dispose of, you may, if not satisfy, at least conciliate both parties, and which is still more important you will keep open the future power of Parliament to adopt one or other course on a view of the individual circumstances of each respective case.[214]

This was essentially the proposal put forward by Peel in the Commons, but confusion arose leading to the resignation of Huskisson, Palmerston, Lamb [later Melbourne] and some other 'Canningites'. Wellington told Croker that 'he would not invite Huskisson to remain' and took the opportunity to bring in Tories who were loyal to him such as Henry Hardinge and George Murray, ex-officers from his old military campaigns, and thereby fuelling a growing press and parliamentary outcry on the illiberal intransigence of 'old corruption'.[215] This was exacerbated by his attempt to retain the post of commander-in-chief of the army, and Croker criticised the unconstitutionality of what was a politically foolish rather than sinister act, but his greatest concern was the continued failure of the ministry to address their leaching popular support. 'Look at *The Times* today, that paper is worth notice because it endeavours to follow, not to lead the public opinion, and it generally forms its opinion from what it sees likely to prevail in the world.'[216]

On 26 February 1828 Russell moved for the abolition of the Test and Corporations Act. It passed with little controversy, having, as Croker said, demanded 'a declaration which means nothing'.[217] Catholic Emancipation, however, remained an ominously stalemated issue, and when another bill was proposed that May, Croker's description caught the mood:

> Peel made a good statement on the treaty of Limerick, but really one might as well, at this time of the day, talk of Noah's flood as of the treaty of Limerick. Lord William Paget [Anglesey's son] said a few words to explain his conversion ... Lamb made a short and fine burst for conciliation and harmony; after which the House would hear no more and Lord Sandon moved an adjournment on which every one got up and walked away.[218]

This complacency was about to be dramatically ruptured when Vesey-Fitzgerald was appointed to the Board of Trade in the reshuffle, and the rules demanded he had to stand for re-election to his family seat in County Clare.

The events of the Ennis election have long been identified as a watershed of Irish history, but for Croker and his circle they represented the fruition of the tactics used by the Catholic movement since the early 1820s, culminating in the success of the Catholic priests and violent factions in some of the 1826 elections.[219] The only significant difference on this occasion was that the forty-shilling freeholders would be marshalled to vote for a Catholic, Daniel O'Connell, rather than a pro-Emancipation Protestant. The plan being that he would refuse to take the MP's oath of allegiance (containing the offensive declaration that 'the sacrifice of the Mass and the invocation of the blessed Virgin Mary and other Saints as now practised in the Church of Rome are impious and idolatrous'), stimulating a political crisis accompanied by the threat of mass popular disturbances, or even civil war.

Vesey-Fitzgerald and his family had been popular progressive landlords, actively pro-Emancipation and the promoters of Catholic appointments, and Croker wrote on 21 June reassuring him that having been such 'an old and steady friend of the Catholic claims' he doubted O'Connell would defeat 'you just because you support the Duke'.[220]

O'Connell's advisors, however, in particular his talented financial and general manager, P.V. Fitzpatrick, convinced him he would raise all the funds needed to win as well as plan their tactics, and immediately struck 'out on a strong sectarian line' when writing his election address.[221] Fitzgerald was denounced as 'the sworn libeller of the Catholic faith' and 'ally of ... the most bitter persevering and unmitigated enemies of Catholics'.[222] There was little need for anyone in Britain to read the press circle's shrill accounts; even *The Times*, a supporter of O'Connell, expressed its concerns at the overtly sectarian nature of the Catholic campaign and the barely restrained threats of sectarian violence. Fitzgerald and his supporters were intimidated off the streets, particularly after the house where he and his organising committee were meeting was stormed and they were only saved from serious injury, or even being murdered, when the 'timely appearance of a party of constabulary under arms prevented the outrage'. The 'degradation' of Catholics was 'inconsistent with the spirit of the Constitution', *The Times* continued, but the reports of 'the wild and ferocious character which has lately distinguished the Catholic Association and studied prominence which has been awarded by the leaders ... to the power and claims of their Church ... can end no otherwise than in the precipitation of a bodily and bloody conflict between the two "united" nations'.[223]

Lay and clerical agitators hastened to Ennis, among them ultra-Catholic firebrands such as Fr John Murphy of Corofin, and the leading association member, Richard Sheil, caught the mood when he recorded his own discomfiture after seeing Fr Murphy celebrate Mass and call upon the people 'to sacrifice themselves for O'Connell, their faith and Fatherland':

> Eyes blazing with all the fire of genius ... he laid one hand on the altar, and shook the other in the spirit of almost prophetic admonition, and as his eyes blazed and seemed to start from his forehead, thick drops fell down from his face and his voice rolled through lips livid with passion and covered with foam ... the multitude burst into shouts of acclamation, and would have been ready to mount a battery roaring with cannon at his command.[224]

Fr Thomas Maguire, an accomplished theologian and scholar, adapted his interpretations for more blood-stirring accounts, describing Fitzgerald as the latest in a line of confederates who 'have through all the ages joined the descendants of the Dane, the Norman and the Saxon in burning your churches, levelling your altars, in slaughtering your priests and in stamping out your religion'.[225] By the time the candidates were officially proposed there were, reputedly, 150 Catholic priests in town,[226] and John Leslie Foster reported to Croker that 'the efforts of the priests and the enthusiasm of the people are increasing every hour. When the priest has abjured them from the altar the people think that they are sworn ... Intimidation is one of their chief instruments.' Croker rapidly lost any hope that Fitzgerald could resist this sort of opposition,[227] and by the end of the contest *The Times* was even more concerned that 'no calumny too foul for factious purpose of inflaming the multitude' was left unused. Catholic priests had 'spouted forth the terrors of eternal damnation against any peasant freeholders ... such a perversion ... of spiritual power is as abominable as the success of it.'[228] O'Connell won 2,057 votes to Fitzgerald's 982, and given that his rival could still win almost a third of the poll, it was not unreasonable to assume that this provided him with another example of the importance of retaining the support of 'lieutenants' like Fathers Murphy and Maguire.

Croker certainly believed so, and in an assessment of the Catholic movement written later he described O'Connell as having elected to lead a 'distinctively Roman Catholic party' and target all Catholics who criticised him as 'apostates or renegades' and any Protestant as an 'Orange bigot' and 'bloodhound'. Considering the part Croker believed O'Connell would play in destroying his hopes for uniting Ireland, he was fairly pacific in his later assessments, continuing that 'under a swaggering air of rough rash and reckless audacity', O'Connell was a man of 'not only great ability, good sense and prudence, but of natural humanity, personally kind hearted and good natured, and sincerely averse to the shedding of blood'. But as in all such situations, and like the agitators of the French Revolution, he too became caught in the 'whirl of revolutionary movement: he that stops must fall', and 'over-confident in his own and his priesthood's power over the multitude', his pursuit of power demanded that he pursue his course regardless of the risk of 'a national calamity'.[229] 'The Priests are, in a like manner, though not in an equal degree obliged to agitate for theirs ... the two species of agitation are connected by this common principle.'[231] Croker employed the same principles to assess all popular political or religious agitators, believing that however much they adorned their arguments with enlightened ideals of liberty, emancipation or rationalist social theories, 'unprincipled men of talent, if they cannot rise to distinction through the institutions of their county, will always attempt to subvert the institutions.' During the French Revolution, its promoters never 'advised such horrors, and agitated the people with only such fair words as toleration, liberty and universal peace, but the truth is that human passions, when once roused, pursue their fearful course with little reference to the cause that roused them'. The guiding principle for good government in dealing with them and the antidote to their demagoguery was corrective reform, he argued in 1833, expressing the Burkeian Conservative view that 'there never was a revolution which might not have been arrested ... by a sufficiently steady resistance or a sufficiently liberal concession'. The common 'misfortune is that weak monarchs or weak ministers are bold when they should be cautious, or shrink when they should strike'.[231]

Within hours of receiving the result from Ennis, Croker presented Peel with the draft of a motion to prevent O'Connell from taking his seat, arguing that in the face of such extensive threats of further public disorder, Peel must not take 'a timid or temporising course'.[232] When he met Wellington he reiterated this saying that despite supporting the measure for many years he 'would not vote Catholic on account of the Association ... Unless we can put down the Catholic Association, I am against Emancipation.' It will 'only give them the triumphant face of victory and enable them the better to attack the Protestant establishment and the English connection. These are the new lead objects of the contest', and the 'reign of terror will be carried on with a higher hand – the Protestant gentry will emigrate and the Protestant poor will fly to be converted, the Protestant Church will be despoiled.'[233] By that time, however, having secretly agreed with Wellington that Emancipation was now a necessity, Peel was on the verge of compiling an Emancipation proposal for the next session. As early as 17 August 1828 the ultra-Tory *New Times* published rumours of his 'apostasy', whereas the *Standard* indignantly dismissed any suggestion that its champion was 'in favour of removing any disabilities on Roman Catholics', and that it had the 'AUTHORITY TO STATE THAT NO SUCH LETTER HAS BEEN WRITTEN'.[234]

In Ireland by this time, as Tom Bartlett has described, 'general disaffection characterised the Catholic nation'. Tensions rose through the summer as Catholic parades and demonstrations continued, and reports of 'Irish crime had an enormous impact on English perceptions of Ireland'.[235] The members of the press circle continued to dedicate themselves to making sure that these events had an impact on 'English' perceptions, but also, of course, their Scottish, Welsh and Irish readers. Not least among them the pro-Emancipation Dissenters, who over the next few years would also become increasingly concerned at the character of the Catholic movement and its ambitions.[236] By now Croker had little influence upon his old press allies, and while most of them continued to refute the rumours of Peel's approaching 'apostasy', all of them ridiculed ministerial efforts to play down the rising threat in Ireland, such as Lord Lieutenant Anglesey's pronouncement after a massive Catholic demonstration in Borrisoleigh that he 'felt encircled by friends on whose honour, loyalty and patriotism he could rely'.[237] This was foolish and fraudulent, argued *John Bull*; Borrisoleigh being representative of much of Ireland at this time, where violence and intimidation were 'so flagrant, that any person who is, or has recently been resident there, actually laughs at the suggestion that Protestants were "encircled by friends"'. The Catholic peasantry 'are regularly organised – there are captains in every village ready to lead them' and the 'provincial Irish papers' will 'provide a mass of evidence against the fallacy of Irish tranquillity'. Although the press circle were keen to raise alarm in Britain by dramatising such events, the 'provincial press' and many contemporary accounts largely corroborate their reports. The Catholic *Dublin Evening Post*, for example, reported that, unlike Anglesey's assesment of Borrisoleigh, Richard Sheil was fearful the peasantry 'might by a single spark be ignited into an explosion'.[238]

Little attention has been paid to local Irish newspapers, and as Gary Owens argues, despite most scholars having long treated demonstrations and allied incidents 'as ephemeral curiosities', they were more than just political self-assertion.[239] Led by green-uniformed local leaders, with many of the largest taking place in counties most disturbed by Rockite activities,[240] they were naturally dominated by local agrarian gangs and factions as well as Catholic priests, who sustained low-key threats such as 'playing anti-Orange tunes outside Protestant Churches during divine services', and even Catholic children, according one foreign observer, were describing 'the green uniformed marchers as the warriors "who would kill the Protestants"'.[241] While O'Connell publicly declared his opposition to any violence, he clearly played an excitable part in keeping tensions high, denouncing any Protestant who did not support him an 'Orange bigot' or 'bloodhound' and any Catholic as a traitor and apostate. As Fergus O'Ferral has described, on one occasion he 'almost triggered a sectarian bloodbath' by encouraging the mass incursion of roughly 40 to 60,000 Catholic marchers into the Protestant Ballybay area of Monaghan in an attempt to intimidate the local communities into funding his campaigns.[242]

'The Irish masses', as another historian describes, now 'organised in an unprecedented movement of national solidarity, had pushed the British Government to the edge of the cliff: concession or resort to force'.[243] However, for Croker and many other Irishmen who saw their long-held ambitions for conciliation turning to ashes, the events of the past few years represented the very opposite of 'national solidarity'. It would be difficult to describe Thomas Romney Robinson, professor of Astronomy at Armagh, one Ireland's most famous scientists and another college friend of Croker's, as a bigot prior to this period, but he expressed the increasingly consensual Anglican point of view that a 'gang of needy lawyers and intriguing priests' had now established a 'system of persecution against all, of whatever persuasion, who refuse to submit to their guidance'. Fire 'murder, robbery are busy at their command; and with all this they have the matchless impudence to call themselves the pacifiers of Ireland'.[244]

This may be an exaggerated perception, but all of the Irish members of the press circle received regular reports from family and friends and scoured the provincial Irish news-papers for reports of Catholic depredations. The poorer classes suffered the worst, particularly any convert to Protestantism, and while the circle certainly had a propagandist agenda and sensationalised incidents, such as combining in one column a number of more chilling incidents reported in the Mayo–Sligo press, as Giffard and Maginn did in the *Standard* that October, it is not difficult to imagine their influence on readers:

> Two Brothers named Hart near Tobbercurry had from the study of scripture in their native language ... become converts of the Established Church. They suffered various insults and persecutions from their neighbours ... until they were ordered to attend Mass or they would meet with a sudden or un-provided death ... A widow by the name of Ruane from Rousskey was ordered that she attend Mass or be put to death [All three obeyed] ...
>
> Another man named Dunleavy from Cloonacool in the Parish of Achonry ignored the threats and had his house demolished ...
>
> Martin Culkin [A Catholic convert to Protestantism] of the parish of Achoura, a barger at the fishery at Ballina was murdered in the most shocking manner; his head was severed from his body; his legs, thighs, arms and back were broken to pieces, his body was ripped open, his bowels were torn out and part of them wrapped round his legs.[245]

My own still limited research into such incidents in this district suggests that although there appears never to have been any attempt to study or assess them, many of them can be corroborated by other sources. As Irene Whelan argued after her own more extensive studies, Protestant converts were denounced by priests from altars, forced to recant or move, and together with Bible teachers and readers 'continually beaten and persecuted, and on occasion murdered'.[246] Many middle- and lower-class Protestants in the three southern provinces lived under daily threat in some areas, and although Croker seldom used such material in his own articles, a few examples of the personal experiences of his friends and family perhaps partly illustrate why so many of the circle became so hostile to the Catholic movement. His nephew Walter and his two nieces had a common rural experience when their house near Clonmel was robbed by '20 well armed and well appointed ruffians' who stole three guns, £34 and various other items.[247] His mother's family lived in and around the Galway market town of Gort, and in July 1828 the Anglican rector sent a plaintive letter dramatically capturing the collapse of their hopes for conciliation and national unity. The local priests had recently led a large Catholic demonstration into town:

> They swore that the time had come when they would have blood for blood, that they would recover what was lost at Aughrim [and] massacre every Protestant in the Town ... My curate and myself are insulted in the discharge of our spiritual duties so that I dread to attend a funeral ... I sleep with a blunderbuss and a case of pistols double loaded; This is very disagreeable to a man of peace; and strange when I was in the best of terms with every one, and have rendered them many acts of services ... many Protestants have been frightened into going to America.[248]

The market town of Foxford, County Mayo, was also on William Ellis's circuit and not far from where Croker spent his early childhood. It had a substantial Anglican minority, most of whom were weavers in the declining linen industry, and that summer, Fr John McHugh, the parish priest, using 'the most insulting language against Protestants of the town', and by 'threatening severe punishment of them', hustled them to the front of his Sunday parades compelling them to dance 'from fear of being assaulted' and having their homes burned.[249]

It should, of course, always be borne in mind that Catholics suffered similar abuse when circumstances allowed. Another Croker, the law agent for the Catholic Association in Monaghan, represented a Catholic who had been accosted on his way home by three Orangemen and after being badly beaten he only narrowly escaped being murdered when their gun misfired.[250] In Limerick there were numerous attacks on vulnerable Catholics,[251] and following a meeting of the Dublin Brunswick Club 'two persons recognised as Catholics were attacked by a mob, all of whom were armed with bludgeons, the greater number with dirks and spring daggers.' These were, reputedly, a mob of students from Trinity College, and if so probably the same 'well dressed rabble' which later 'battered in the windows of Mr Sheils' house' and O'Connell's home in Merrion square, terrifying Mary who was alone in the house with their children.[252] Further representative of this polarisation, the Protestant Brunswick Constitution Clubs were established at this time along the same lines as the Catholic Association.[253] Croker criticised them on the same grounds for attempting to intimidate the 'legislature or executive in the exercise of their respective function' and that together with the predicted 'resurrection of the Orange societies', this would certainly bring into 'conflict the two great bodies into which the population is divided'.[254] On 11 January, when he met Wellington, he had never seen him 'so moved as he seemed to be on this occasion, or talk with so little confidence of his power of managing affairs'. He offered the duke little consolation on this occasion however, telling him that 'during the twenty-five years that I had been advocating the question, I had been all my life anxious to see [Emancipation] settled on the grounds of policy', but the 'late proceedings of O'Connell and the Catholics had now brought it to the point of intimidation, and that I for one was ready to vote against any concession to intimidation'.[255]

During the autumn, *John Bull* reported that Peel continued to attend ultra-Protestant public meetings and dinners. At one in Manchester in late October, he 'was hailed with rapture' and toasted together with Lord Eldon and the 'Protestant Ascendancy', with the 'loudest cheers and drunk nine times nine'. 'We can securely affirm,' *Bull* assured its readers, 'that no man more cordially or sincerely participated in the feeling than the Right Hon. Gentleman, whose principles and practice have done so much in its support.'[256] Peel had, of course, been planning to support Emancipation for some time, and just after Croker's January meeting with Wellington the cabinet was informed he would manage a bill through the Commons. Most of the leading Tories who had opposed the measure agreed to support it,[257] but most of Peel's electors at Oxford University were shocked and angry, and he resigned his seat. This inspired a critical missive from Croker echoing Burke's famous principle that first duty of a member of the Commons was to serve the national interest according to his own judgement, not as a delegate under his electors' instructions.[258] Peel would not change his mind and, concerned that his resignation could be 'liable to a suspicion of insincerity', he 'begged' Croker to 'insert in the *Courier*, as from myself, his letter to the Vice-Chancellor'. Croker obliged, sending it with 'a few complimentary words, but in the character of the editor'.[259]

Not surprisingly, when the news of his 'apostasy' broke Peel suffered enduring and extensive abuse from his old press supporters, and Croker could not resist commenting to Hertford on the irony that the *Standard*, the newspaper 'Dawson had a chief hand in setting up' and used 'to libel me', has now 'turned like Phalom's bull against its inventor'.[260] He tried to mollify his old circle where he could, meeting Hook on 13 February but failing 'to induce him to moderate his Protestant politics'.[261] Peel lost the Oxford election, and Croker wrote to Hertford in St Petersburg asking him to give Peel a seat, but there was no time to wait for a response if he were to manage the bill in the Commons, and he was forced to accept the offer of the closed borough of Westbury in Wiltshire controlled by Sir Manasseh Lopes. A man the *Standard* described with contempt and accuracy as 'a dealer in political corruption and during several months an in-mate of Newgate'. Peel 'won', but even in such a 'sleepy country town, Protestant feeling was raised to such a pitch of violence' that both his agent and Lopes were pelted.[262]

Lord Lowther was offended by the secret dealing, and Wellington wrote to Croker, 'for God's sake advise your friend not to resign.' He agreed, and in doing so again emphasised his belief in the importance of party loyalty and of politicians adapting empirically to contingencies.

> In the first place, however a party may be blamed for deserting an opinion, an individual is always more blamed for deserting a party … Moral duties are always clear and always reformable upon one's own conscience – but legal and political duties are so debatable in nature, and influenced by such a variety of circumstances over which no individual can have any control, that the common sense of mankind allows individuals to be influenced by the crowd without any imputation on his personal honour … Life is a chain of events and if you break one link now, how are you to connect your past and your future conduct; when

you have left the friends of your youth where are you to
look for others, and how can you tell but you will be forced
into measures as foreign to all your wishes and principles
as that which you now wish to avoid ...[263]

Lowther voted against the bill, but remained in office. A mission of
Irish bishops represented one last attempt at resistance, and Croker wrote
to warn Wellington that 'Ferns, an old friend of mine, is come over on
their invitation, and [although] he is not disposed to go to the lengths of
that Protestant Jesuit, the Archbishop [Magee] of Dublin', the delegates
were, 'for the most part, his tools and should be rebuffed'.[264] They had
little influence, and the bill passed through the Commons on 30 March
accompanied by clauses to disfranchise the forty-shilling freeholders and
disband the Catholic Association. But not with the provision for the
Catholic clergy Croker wanted, because Peel and most of the cabinet were
opposed, and in later years Wellington, like Croker, 'would often lament
what seemed to him a lost opportunity for stabilising the country through
salaried Clergy and a modified concordat with the Vatican'.[265]

Croker made almost no contribution to the debates, only rising to
refute an assertion that the fellows and students at Dublin University
were opposed to Emancipation, and noting in his diary that 'from want
of practice' he had 'lost a good deal of my power of public speaking'
having 'remained too long in subordinate office to think of Parliamentary eminence'.[266] Confined by illness the night of the vote, he told Peel
that he would have to 'submit to the mortification of not giving my
assistance to the final days of the great and ... happy measures which
must be passed tonight, I shall, however, endeavour to pair off'.[267]
Rather than illness, this may have been a private protest, for as he complained in a letter just prior to the final count, what has long been
'denied to reason is surrendered to intimidation'. I had been 'all my
life friendly to Emancipation till this moment, when I fear it is too late
to conciliate Catholics, and is sure to alienate Protestants'.[268]

His contribution was little needed. The bill passed by 320 to 142.
'The greatest majority' the ministry had ever had, he wrote to Hertford,[269] but this was only achieved with the support of the opposition,
and Croker was concerned that more Tories than ever before had also
voted against the ministry or abstained.[270] The final tally of noes was
202 in the Commons and 118 in the Lords, of which 173 of the
former and 109 of the latter were Tories.[271] While the final success of
the bill perhaps provided evidence that Emancipation could have been
successful years before if it had received concerted ministerial support,

the anger of many of the ministry's British and Irish supporters would be slow to subside and 'the Ultra-Tories subordinated all other considerations to the goal of punishing the government for emancipation.'[272]

THE LAST TORY MINISTRY

A few weeks after the final passage of the bill, Croker attended a function where the Duchess of Richmond had a 'number of stuffed rats under glass cases on her drawing room table, to which her grace affixed the names of all the apostates', and somebody 'equally wise and witty' released a live one in the Lords.[273] This portrayal of Peel and Wellington as cowardly rats abandoning the Protestant ship of state and/or grovelling before the pope would be tirelessly reiterated in the Tory press over the following months. The *Standard* published the most vituperative denunciations of its old champion and his brother-in-law 'Iscariot' Dawson for having submitted to 'the shirtless, shoeless un-lettered savages of a barbarous province' who were herded by those who do not 'care a feather for Catholic Emancipation', and whose true purpose was to 'prepare the way for popery, bigotry and bloodshed'.[274] In contrast to this, the Whig press and politicians heaped praise upon Peel and Wellington for having performed 'the most complete *bouleversement* of politics and personality' in living memory. This was not entirely the disinterested celebration of their shared 'liberality', for given the divided state of the Tories, many leading Whigs were now confident that Wellington would be forced to recruit them in order to bolster his fragmenting support.[275]

Croker initially believed that the ultra-Tory anger would soon dissipate, and he wrote optimistically on 16 April that 'Lord Chandos and the more reputable of the Ultra-Tories seem to have kissed and are friends with us again.'[276] He would be disappointed in this, but the extent of disaffection over Emancipation should not be overstated. Captain Swing, Captain Rock's English cousin, would torch plenty of barns and hayricks and Luddites smashed plenty of looms, but as Linda Colley has pointed out, there were no anti-Catholic riots; 'no one was killed and no Catholic chapels burnt to the ground.'[277] After 1829 a more important issue would be the mixture of popular demands for social and fiscal reforms that would coalesce with resentment that a religious and constitutional tradition had been 'most vilely betrayed' helping to energise a mass national campaign for parliamentary reform to make the Commons representative of frustrated public opinion.[278]

In April 1829, following a minor Whig parliamentary reform proposal, Croker wrote that 'we were very much afraid of a vote on East Retford last night, which could have accumulated the Whigs, the Liberals and the angry Tories against us.'[279] A few weeks later at a public meeting comprised of concerned artisan and middling classes in Birmingham, Thomas Attwood, destined to become a leading figure of the National Associations for Reform, called for an 'array not more formidable than that legally exhibited in Ireland' in order to 'compel' the government to reform its economic policies.[280] A petition was presented for Peel to repeal features of what was seen as his finance act of 1819, because it had 'defeated all the calculations of prudence, and rendered all industry and enterprise ruinous'. He responded by accepting that in some regions 'industry and enterprise' as well as some groups of workers were experiencing acute distress, but 'it was impossible to restore this country to a sound and healthy state without producing a great deal of suffering'.[281] This further enraged the *Standard*: 'The orange sucked we fling the Peel away', and it vilified him as the 'principal partisan of Free Trade that had led to the misery and moral disorganisation of the manufacturing districts … the starving of whole classes' because he worshipped economic theories 'as barbarians did' their 'preposterous idols'.[282] From this period on until the fall of the last Tory ministry, the *Standard* would call for more extensive reforms than the Whigs and even some Radicals. Among its fluctuating demands: a vote for every man paying tax; annual parliaments; secret ballots and numerous measures to relieve working people 'at present starving under means so miserably inadequate' or 'starving wages', and 'compulsory provision for the poor of Ireland'.[283]

Peel made some attempts to address popular concerns, notably with a proposal to introduce a form of income and property tax, but Wellington blocked it for fear of antagonising landed and mercantile interests.[284] For the most part, however, Peel was a believer in *laissez faire* economics, and later described the Reform campaign as mainly 'an Attwood-ite plot to subvert the gold standard'.[285] A bemused Croker recorded that as late as 1833, Peel told him 'there would be an entirely new combination' for which 'currency questions would be the basis',[286] and Peel's predisposition to be either unwilling 'or unable to adjust a theory to fit recalcitrant facts' has been examined elsewhere.[287] This susceptibility to the 'plausibilities of theorists', rather than any 'liberal' or pragmatic adaptability, was central to understanding his political career, according to Croker when he later assessed Peel's second great 'apostasy' on the Corn Laws in 1846.[288]

The 'Union of the Middle and Lower Classes for the Attainment of Parliamentary Reform' was established in late January 1830,[289] and this rapidly developed into a mass national organisation of similar unions in other parts of the country. In February 1830, some ultra-Tories introduced a parliamentary reform motion calling for seats to be transferred to large towns from rotten boroughs and for a substantial number of new categories of voters to be enfranchised. The House rejected it by 160 to 57, and five days later John Russell presented a more moderate Whig bill seeking representation for Manchester, Birmingham and Leeds, which lost by 140 to 188.[290] That same month Croker wrote to Peel warning that they should not be seen as inflexible on Reform, and he recommended the distribution of some seats from 'corrupt boroughs' to industrial towns. The great difficulty was 'the landed interest, which would then get nothing ... but above all they must see that they will not be able to prevent a torrent if they refuse to pacify us by the admission of two drops'.[291] Following this letter there is another gap in their correspondence, but Louis Jennings, who had access to the archives before the disappearance of some of Peel's letters, recorded that despite Croker's recommendations 'Mr. Peel was opposed to any extension of the suffrage.'[292] In June 1829 Peel spoke against Reform in the Commons, and during the debate on Russell's February motion, argued that although as 'general principle popular representation was necessary, Manchester and other towns had not suffered by the absence of it'.[293] On 28 May 1830 he told the House that he 'had to consider whether there was not on the whole a general representation of the people in the House; and whether the popular voice was not heard. For himself he thought it was.'[294] This remark was little different to the famous statement of trenchant opposition Wellington would make six months later, and although he was almost certainly in favour of moderate Reform, it meant that Peel became widely seen as opposed. What may be said with greater certainty is that contrary to Croker's later reputation, and as John Cannon pointed out, 'John Wilson Croker urged his leaders to take Reform into their own hands', but neither Peel nor Wellington 'showed much desire to come to terms with Reform'.[295]

Any hope of the ministry addressing growing dissension through the press was further hampered by the increasing alienation of the Whig and more moderate ministerial publications as the crisis deepened. Only the *Morning Post*, the *Courier*, the *Quarterly Review* and *John Bull* remained critically supportive, and Croker tried to convince Wellington in September 1828 that much more had to be done.[296] In March

1829 Wellington asked Croker to explore the prospects of establishing a newspaper. Croker raised it with Lockhart, by then the editor of the *Quarterly*, but Lockhart wrote to Walter Scott saying he rejected Croker's attempt to connect him with 'the Reptile Press':

> I will not, even to serve the Duke, mix myself up with the newspapers. That work it is which has damned Croker … As for Croker's hints about the advantages of being constantly among the rulers of the land … the great rulers I should see would be, I take it, mostly the Plantas, Croker, *et hoc genus*. Their illustrious society does not flatter me …[297]

As we have seen, Lockhart had been, and continued to be, secretly involved with the 'reptile press'; Croker was 'constantly among the rulers of the land', and his emphatic remarks were perhaps more to reassure his father-in-law than defame Croker. There was justice in saying that by this time Croker's activities with the press had 'damned him' in the eyes of some of his political leaders and the more respectable elements of informed public opinion, but another factor raising Scott and Lockhart's concern was that by this time Croker and John Murray, having been estranged since late 1825, were re-establishing their old relationship.

Lockhart had been appointed editor of the *Quarterly* in 1825 at the same time as the twenty-one-year-old Benjamin Disraeli had convinced Murray to set up a national daily to rival *The Times*. Croker warned Murray it would fail, but Disraeli, 'already gifted with the powers of convincing others … eloquent, persuasive and ingenious', convinced Murray to persevere.[298] This is perhaps a little unfair; Murray was an experienced publisher and eager for the venture, but within months the *Representative* proved the spectacular flop Croker predicted and almost bankrupted Murray. The following year Disraeli caricatured Murray as a befuddled heavy drinker in *Vivian Grey* (1826). He did take to his cups, and his embarrassment at the failure probably did the most to perpetuate the rift with Croker. In later life Disraeli would famously portray Croker in his novel *Coningsby* as the political intriguer and toady 'Rigby' (1844), but as a young man he admired and sought to emulate him. In fact he described him in *Vivian Grey* as 'Vivida Vis', 'one of the two sublimest men in the United Kingdom'.[299] Furthermore, and although once again it will have to be the business of another study, preliminary research suggests that Disraeli not only drew upon Croker and the circle's writing for his ideas of a territorial constitution and one-nation Conservatism – and in particular upon Maginn for his flirtations with Radical Toryism and Young England – but even directly plagiarised some sections of their writing.

In November 1827 Murray finally broke the ice and sent Croker a flattering letter asking if he would review Lady Morgan's latest novel. Croker said he was not interested, but he might review a historical study of the French General Foy, concluding with a slight reprimand: 'Have I seen you more than once these two years?'[300] A few months later an agitated Murray, and perhaps with a drink or two taken, wrote saying he had heard a rumour that Croker was to become the 'future editor of the *Edinburgh Review* ... which would, inevitably, prove so fearfully injurious to my property, and so overpoweringly painful to my feelings, that I hope you will pardon me asking if there is any foundation for the report'. Croker responded: 'Dear Murray, You are either mad or you must think Messrs. Longman and I are in that unhappy condition ... I advise you to instantly send for Dr Matin. I hope to hear tomorrow that you are better.'[301] While not eager to return to general literary reviewing, it is important to note at this stage that Croker was certainly back on friendly terms with Murray by early January 1829, something reinforced when he offered to finance and facilitate Croker's long-held ambition to compile an annotated edition of Boswell's *Life of Johnson*.[302]

Over the following two years Croker would devote much of his free time to the task; writing letters seeking opinions, information and corroborating anecdotes on Boswell, Johnson and their contemporaries. Despite his earlier remarks, Scott better illustrated their twenty-year friendship and his own good nature when he replied to Croker on 30 January 1829: 'Your continued friendship and assistance on many occasions in life entitle you not to solicit, but to command anything in my power to aid your wishes.'[303] Isaac D'Israeli, Benjamin's father, a friend of Croker's since they were both involved in the foundation of the *Quarterly*, responded that 'it is with pleasure I recognise your handwriting ... Your correspondence is too agreeable an incident for me ever to wilfully occasion its extinction ... I imagine I could "Boswellise" with you through a long summer's day. Whenever you consult me I shall rejoice to aid you.'[304] The first of five volumes, approximately one-fifth comprised of Croker's 'copious notes' and 'Johnsonia', would appear in the early summer of 1831; by which time Croker was completely reconciled with Murray and fully in control of the political contents of the *Quarterly Review*, the new Conservative party's most authoritative publication.[305]

Back in August 1829, however, he was still battling to get the party leaders to address their still leaching newspaper support. In a long letter to Joseph Planta MP, officially delegated to deal with their press, he described some of his own work in the past and the growing importance of modern politicians properly managing this increasingly important element of the political estate. 'It is not everybody that can write for the newspapers: the latter is an art, perhaps I should better say a knack', and what today might be called the 'sound bite': a 'short epigrammatic style, both of thought and expression, is what produces most effect'. But how is a political pressman to know what line to take?

> For instance if I, an old, and some of the gentlemen of the press used to think, a good hand, pretty high in office, not inattentive to the state of Europe, had been obliged to answer the article in the *Morning Journal* which you sent me, I should not have known what to say ... No one but a Cabinet Minister could do this safely and completely – not that if a Cabinet Minister were to hold the pen, he need tell state secrets, but he alone would thoroughly understand the case, and know what to avoid, what to hint, what to deny, when to leave folks in their errors, and when to open the real views of the Government. I have heretofore conveyed to the public articles written by Prime and Cabinet Ministers, and sometimes have composed such articles under their eye – they supplied the *fact* and I supplied the *tact*, and between us we used to produce a considerable effect. In a Cabinet like ours, surely there might be one person who could find leisure for this sort of supervision, if not for some more co-operation ...
>
> The times are gone when statesmen might safely despise the journals, or only treat them as inferior engines, which might be left to themselves, or be committed to the guidance of persons wholly unacquainted with the views of the Ministry. There is a prodigious change now in progress all throughout Europe, in this particular the French Journals are edited by Peers, Privy Councillors, and the Deputies, and see the result – they are undoubtedly the best written and the most effective body of literature that ever existed ... The example of France will be contagious, and we shall see men of high hopes and attainments conducting Journals, and obtaining, at last, through their literary character a seat

in the House of Commons. Depend upon it all this is coming; and the day is not far distant when you will (not see, nor hear), but know that there is some one in the Cabinet entrusted with what will be thought one of the most important duties of the State, the regulation of public opinion.[306]

He concluded with the instructive example of his part in saving the ministry during the Queen Caroline crisis when, together with some of his protégés, who later 'eclipsed their master', their success 'was so complete that it turned the Press – I mean the preponderating force of the press – right round'.[307] His letter was clearly designed as a memorandum for wider circulation, and Planta forwarded it to Wellington, who appears to have made no response before formally returning it in December.[308] A few weeks later Croker commented privately: 'the Duke is resolved there shall be no distress anywhere – "there is no distress – there can be no distress – there shall be no distress" – I hope that he may be able to bring the country gentlemen to his opinion.'[309]

By this time the rising public hostility was also affecting the loyalty of the more moderate Tory newspapers. Croker described the *Courier* as 'a most insidious enemy ... I will give it up and assuredly never send it another article',[310] and as the *Standard* sneered, what support there was in *John Bull* was only due to the influence of 'Mr Canning's intriguer with heart and soul'.[311] Croker's ability to induce Hook to moderate its criticisms was becoming limited however, noting that he had a foolish 'idea that the Duke of Newcastle might bring him into Parliament'.[312] Of perhaps greater influence, *Bull* had been losing circulation for some time, and by the early 1830s there was little chance of reviving it by supporting the ailing Tory ministry.[313]

The Times had continued to give Peel and Wellington some critical support for having given 'a fatal blow to the intolerance',[314] but as Croker remarked, it served as a political barometer in that it endeavoured above all else 'to follow, not lead public opinion',[315] and it was markedly more hostile when the new session opened. One factor restraining the Whigs from making any serious challenge was that George IV was unlikely to summon his old 'bugaboos' to form a government. But he died during the night of 5 June 1830, and Croker wrote that Brougham, who now had little hope Wellington would recruit him, 'gave us some intimation what we might expect' with a 'short but pithy lecture ... that without a certain and zealous majority in the House of Commons, no Government could get on'.[316] In preparation for the election required for the elevation of William IV, Brougham wrote a declaration of intent in an 'anonymous' pamphlet entitled '*The Country Without Government*'. He reviewed it himself in the *Edinburgh*, accurately arguing that the Whigs had not launched any serious 'barrage' upon Wellington to date; but should 'Mr Stanley, Mr Graham, Lord Althorp' and 'above all, if Mr Brougham, *in himself a mighty host* [Brougham's own emphasis], unmask the battery ... how could so baseless a fabric continue to exist for even a short period.'[317] The following month during Brougham's Yorkshire election campaign, his 'battery' would illuminate the path for the Whigs to finally rise to office during what is acknowledged today as the 'emblematic contest' of parliamentary reform.[318]

A year later, Croker published an account of the process leading to the Whig leaders adopting an extensive programme of Reform, and most of his arguments are impressively consistent with modern academic challenges to the interpretations promoted by 'Whig' historians.[319] 'Many persons think that the concession of the Catholic Question by affording an example of an inroad on the constitution has mainly contributed to the triumph of Reform', but although 'there is much truth in this proposition, it is much exaggerated'. It was only one of a number of problems the Tory ministry faced. They were 'already weakened by the retirement of those who called themselves Liberal Tories', when they were 'irreparably mutilated by those who were denominated Ultra-Tories ... indignant at being abandoned by their leaders in whom they had so long and so implicitly confided':

> And here it is important to observe, that in all this period of intrigue and manoeuvring, and during all this discussion about Manchester and Penryn and East Retford and Birmingham, not a single Reform petition was presented, nor was the question of Reform sufficiently popular, either in the House or in the country, to be selected as the field for the great battle which the new coalition was desirous of fighting; ... Not a year ago, Reform was anything but the formidable engine it has been made ... It was the state of the parties which waked the spirit of Reform, and not Reform which created the state of the parties. This point, so important both for the present consideration and for future history, has been so much misunderstood, and so constantly mis-represented, that we are desirous of developing and explaining the reasons for our opinion.[320]

Croker was, of course, keen to present his party leaders in a positive light, but between 1823 and 1829 there were almost no petitions calling specifically for parliamentary reform. Financial and material concerns, or as Croker emphasised, 'the simplification of the public accounts and the economy of the public money – and *not parliamentary Reform*, were the popular topics of that so recent period.' It was only during the election of August, he continued, that 'Reform, as a popular electioneering topic ... was advocated by some of the Whigs, and more particularly by Mr Brougham ... clever beyond any identified opposition and triumphantly aware of the fact'.[321]

In July the proprietor and editor of *Leeds Mercury*, the Congregationalist Edward Baines, and a circle of wealthy manufacturers decided to promote Brougham as a candidate. They were not Radicals in pursuit of any major social reforms any more than Brougham was, and as Michael Brock describes, 'the "factory Question" tended to keep masters and men apart in Leeds'; 'the mill owners were suspicious of their operatives' distinctive type of Tory radicalism, and willing to accept a Whig as their champion.'[322] Yorkshire was in many ways the centre of popular Reform, but it was a constituency where two rival groups placed different priorities on different reforms. Michael Sadler and Richard Oastler, normally described as Tory Radical, protectionist and Anglican social reformers, would dominate one, and most of the press circle, in particular Giffard and Maginn, were keen supporters of Sadler. Brougham would be elected by the other, perhaps best described simplistically as Whig, capitalist and Dissenter, and as *The Times* reported, it was during his Yorkshire campaign that he declared 'from this moment on he "would leave in no other man's hands the cause of Parliamentary reform" and 'stand forward as champion of the cause'.[323] This was to the initial 'horror of some of the older Whigs', who had been planning to renew Russell's moderate proposal,[324] but they soon began to appreciate the potential of an extensive measure, and 'when the session opened on 2 November, Reform immediately became their major preoccupation.'[325]

As we have seen, all of Croker's press circle had been demanding a number of radical economic and social reforms for many years, and during the elections *Blackwood's* criticised the Whig and Tory leaders for being addicted to theories of 'Free Trade and currency ... the ultras of one party go quite as far as the other'. On 'Parliamentary reform', it continued, 'the Wellington party has annihilated every valid plea on which it could be resisted.' 'Public feeling is in favour of reform – we mean such reform as would be cautious, gradual and practical; and it would be equal idle to prove it is in error.' It also called for 'Protectionist' measures to stimulate the economy and address the suffering of the poorer classes in Britain and Ireland, who were driven to seek relief and work in England because of the 'enduring great misery of inadequate wages' and no system to relieve or maintain the poor.[326] The *Standard* advocated extensive parliamentary reform, describing Peel and Wellington as 'odious to the great body of the people' and called upon voters and constituents to use 'every faculty of body and mind to an improvement of the House of Commons by which we shall be rescued from the most despotic; the most incapable and the most dishonest administration that ever cursed a country pretending to be free'.[327] Throughout that summer Giffard and Maginn re-published extensive sections of Michael Sadler's speeches demanding radical reforms, Poor Laws in Ireland, and as usual, assailing the 'quackery of political economists', 'stockjobbers' and 'the absentees of England and Ireland [for] depriving thousands of their daily labour and bread, and deeply injuring hundreds of thousands more'. Sadler would not stand for Yorkshire that year (he had been given a safe seat by Newcastle), so the *Standard* called upon electors to support Brougham and the Whigs as best representing the growing 'union of un-disgraced members' dedicated to reform and rallying 'our lately conflicting divisions into one country party'.[328]

Six months earlier, William Maginn, who is described in an early *Cambridge History of English Literature* as 'a brilliant *improvisatore*; the compound constituting a perfectly ideal magazinist', founded what would rapidly become one of the most popular publications of the period, *Fraser's Magazine for Town and Country*.[329] Seen as the forerunner of satirical magazines such as *Punch*, it would provide the perfect vehicle to carry Maginn's capricious talent for witty invective and political polemics.[330] Like the rest of the circle, every month *Fraser's* demanded reforms and denounced the Tory leadership for their betrayal on Emancipation, but most often for their failure to relieve the misery of the poorer classes when the tables of both Houses had 'literally groaned under the weight of petitions from the people'.[331] The 'agricultural labourer was reduced to rags and pauperism', and 'thousands of weavers, miners and spinners whom the currency bill of Sir Robert Peel had reduced to live-like slaves' were working long hours to barely survive or starving.[332]

During the election many candidates were put under pressure from disaffected constituents and even a quarter of the normally safe ministerial county seats changed hands.[333] Croker wrote to Peel during his own Dublin contest: 'you can have no idea of the Protestant zeal here.'[334] He publicly ridiculed Lefroy as an 'evangelical bigot ... parading in a newly washed surplice ... backed by the Orange faction',[335] and Lefroy him as 'an obsequious instrument of Government'.[336] But what *The Times* called Lefroy's 'curious and apocryphal twaddle' had greater appeal to increasingly siege-minded Protestants leaving a disappointed Croker dependent on Hertford for a nomination seat in Suffolk.[337] When he arrived back in London he found 'Sir Robert Peel and the Duke ... both equally surprised and vexed at the result of our election.'[338] The 'Whigs and Ultra Tories and Radicals and Reformers and economists were everywhere successful against those who stood in the Government interest', and he saw in the result 'the seeds of the most troublesome and unmanageable Parliament since that of 1640'. In this same letter to Lowther, he again outlined his belief in the need for corrective Reform and for 'the representation of the three or four great towns, which alone could pretend representatives'. But he was adamant that if any greater measure was conceded, especially under duress from mass public agitation, it would make parliament 'more democratical than it is now [and] you and I will live to see the English throne and peerages swept away as early as those of France'.[339]

In one of his last efforts to influence the press, he tried to intervene with *Blackwood's* again in late October, [340] but the following week it vilified Wellington as the 'old withered pantaloon' and his 'subalterns' as 'even more deficient than their miserable leaders'. The neglect of 'this apostate government' was allowing a revolutionary situation to develop in Britain and in Ireland, where despite the ambitions of the deluded that Emancipation would appease the Catholics, 'the most memorable period of disorder is now impending'. The distress 'from the total want of Poor Laws, is ... marked by scenes that in other countries would be a scandal to Christianity and civilization'. No longer 'protected by their political value as voters', the poor 'are everywhere expelled without mercy – as mere nuisances and vermin' and forced to starve or emigrate and 'scramble' 'for a pittance from the impoverished peasantry of England and Scotland'. Concluding prophetically: 'and upon all this widespread domestic misery' 'does Mr O'Connell descend like some incarnation of evil principle to vex and plague the wretched land', and 'never was Ireland in a situation to give such dreadful effect to his inflammatory doctrine.'[341]

Croker would have privately agreed with most of this, and by now he accepted that the ministry had little chance of surviving much of the first session. In one of his last efforts to recruit some crossbenchers and moderate Whigs, Wellington sent him to ask Palmerston, who was now affiliated with the Whigs, 'are you resolved, or are you not to vote for parliamentary reform?' He replied that he was, and Croker responded: 'Well then, there is no use talking to you any more on the subject.'[342] On 2 November Wellington instigated their fall with his famous declaration in the Lords that he 'was not prepared to bring forward any measures' of Reform and that he 'should always feel it his duty to resist such measures when proposed by others'.[343] On 15 November the Irish Whig spokesman for the Catholic Board, Henry Parnell, brother of William the novelist, called for a vote against the Civil List, and Whigs, Liberal Tories, ultra-Tories and Radicals combined to bring down the last Tory ministry.

Blackwood's, while not overly keen to see the Whigs in power given their even greater preoccupation with 'delusions' promoted under the banner of the 'Spirit of the Age', still celebrated the defeat of the Tory leaders. They had subscribed to many of the same callous economic theories, and those 'who blindly oppose all reform ... will do well to reflect, that while they are doing it the present system is hourly making a radical reform'. For many years the Tory ministers had 'not only arrayed the people against the institutions and laws, but incited every interest and class to seek the ruin of the others'. They 'taught the masters to seek wealth in the starvation of their workmen'; the 'workmen to look for abundance in their masters' loss of capital'; 'manufacturers and trade' to seek 'prosperity in the sacrifice of agriculture', and the 'divisions, fury and strife this generated ... fed the general hostility to the constitution and the laws'.[344]

The *Standard* said much the same, and in *Fraser's*, Maginn summarised that Wellington had left the country in a state of something 'approaching to a *jaquerie*, with funds sinking, revenue declining and a population divided and disaffected. He had promised to bind Ireland closer to the English Crown', yet the final days of his administration were 'marked by a proposition for the first time brought forward in a tangible shape for the repeal of the Union'. All connection to him and Peel 'must be avoided as if it conveyed the plague', and another victory 'scarcely less important, is the smoking out of the vermin ... flinging forth of Twiss, Croker, Planta, Holmes ... and all the other scent animals who thought themselves fix-tures in the offices they held'. The country 'is no longer considered to be in the hands of a mere club of boroughmongers and parasitical clerks. In this point of view we rejoice at the promotion of Brougham.'[345]

Peel was barely less pleased to be out of office, Mrs Arbuthnot writing that 'when the opposition cheered at the division ... it was with difficulty he refrained, he was so delighted at having so good an opportunity for resigning.'[346] Croker was relieved, but his characteristic pessimism was tinged with much greater concern than usual for what lay ahead:

> I am appalled at the prospect before us. I am not afraid of the mob violence or insurrectionary movements, yet I am afraid of the more plausible and smoother road to ruin called Parliamentary Reform. Would to God that the advice I have given them these last ten years past for transferring the franchise of the convicted boroughs to the great towns had been carried ... It would have satisfied public opinion, wiped off a real blot and given the existing constitution a real lease. Now I am sadly convinced that any change, any reform, however right or rational in itself would open a floodgate, which in the present temper of the world never could be closed.[347]

NOTES

1. *Croker Papers*, Peel to Croker, 23 March 1820, I, p.170.
2. *The Times*, 6 and 8 April 1821.
3. Ibid., Croker to Peel, 1 February 1822, II, pp.52–3.
4. See *Hansard*, X, March 1824, cols 626, 636 and 1474; VIII, 1127, April 1823; XII, 785, 1266 and 1348–9, February and March 1825. For metrication, *Hansard*, XXXIV, 1025–267, June 1816 and for Irish tithe reform, XIV, 643–5, 19 May 1809.
5. See Thomas, *Quarrel of Macaulay and Croker*, pp.45–6, citing Brougham MS, August 1842 and February 1851 and *Croker Papers*, II, pp.228 and 244–5.
6. See *Parliamentary Acts*, 7, 57, George III, cap. 92 (1817), and *The Times*, 11 July 1817, for an account.
7. Eric J. Evans, *Sir Robert Peel: Statesmanship, Power and Party* (Suffolk, 1991), p.141.
8. *Hansard*, XL, 3 May 1819, col. 8.
9. Ibid., cols 6–10.
10. Ibid., col. 23.
11. Ibid., cols 26–32.
12. Ibid., cols 30–50.
13. Ibid., cols 49–50, and remark apologising to Peel, col. 52.
14. Ibid., cols 52–3.
15. bid., cols 55–6.
16. *Freeman's Journal*, 11 May 1819.
17. Duke MS, box 2, T. Spring Rice to Thomas Casey, 3 May 1819, and part cited in *Croker Papers*, I, pp.131–2.
18. Ibid., p.135.
19. See his *Letter to the Roman Catholics of Dublin* (Dublin, 1810), in Clifford, *Veto Controversy*, p.42, and Ronan Kelly, *Bard of Erin: The Life of Thomas Moore* (Dublin, 2008), pp.15, 31–3, 71, 231, 431 and 495–503.
20. Parry, *The Rise and Fall of Liberal Government*, pp.15–16.
21. *Quarterly Review*, November 1819, p.485.

22. Richard P. McBrien, *The Lives of the Popes* (San Francisco, 2000), p.332.
23. Irene Whelan, *Bible War in Ireland: The Second Reformation in Ireland and the Polarisation of Protestant–Catholic Relations, 1800–1840* (Dublin, 2006), pp.133–4.
24. A. Acheson, *A History of the Church of Ireland; 1691–1996* (Dublin, 2002), pp.160–7.
25. See Brendan Clifford, *The Veto Controversy* (Belfast, 1985) for a good study of ultra-Catholics, pp.110–142; Portsmouth, 'Croker', PhD thesis, Chapter 5, Section 3; The Most Rev. John MacHale, *The Letters of the Most Rev. John MacHale, Archbishop of Tuam* (Dublin, 1888), 'Hierophilos', January–March 1820; U.L.C. Bourke, *Life and Times of the Most Rev. John MacHale* (Dublin, 1882), pp.62–5.
26. McGrath, *Bishop Doyle*, p.157.
27. *Hansard*, VI, 9 September 1831, cols 1272–4, see also cols 2195–98 and 1302.
28. Antonia McManus, *The Irish Hedge Schools and Their Books: 1615–1831* (Dublin, 2002), pp.52–3; D.H. Akenson, *The Irish Education Experiment: The National System of Education in the Nineteenth Century* (London, 1970), pp.88–91 and 142.
29. Niall Ó Ciosáin, *Print and Popular Culture, 1750–1850* (London, 1997), p.142.
30. See Akenson, *The Irish Education Experiment*, p.90 and Whelan, *Bible Wars*, p.135.
31. J.A. Reynolds, *The Catholic Emancipation Crises in Ireland, 1823–1829* (Yale, 1954), pp.66–9; Bowen, *The Protestant Crusade*, pp.84, 96–7 and 83–123; Thomas McGrath, *Politics, Interdenominational Relations and Education in the Public Memory of Bishop Kanes Doyle of Kildare and Leighlin* (Dublin, 1999), pp.157–8.
32. Wyse, *Historical Sketch*, I, p.231, and Akenson, *Irish Education Experiment*, p.87; Bowen, *Protestant Crusade*, p.96 and his *Souperism: Myth or Reality* (Cork, 1970), *passim*, for the campaign against the Bible societies.
33. *Hansard*, IV, 2 April 1821, cols 1540–8.
34. Ibid., 29 March, cols 1499 and 1500.
35. Sack, *Jacobite to Conservative*, p.236; for *Blackwood's* see 15 March 1824, p.287.
36. McBrien, *Lives of the Popes*, p.333.
37. MacDonagh, *The Hereditary Bondsman*, p.206. See also Thomas Bartlett, *The Fall and Rise of the Irish Nation: The Catholic Question 1690–1830* (Dublin, 1992), for a short account of the involvement of the Catholic clergy, pp.330–2.
38. Add. MSS 40319, ff.116–7, Croker to Peel, 4 March 1824.
39. *Quarterly Review*, December 1847, p.281.
40. Kevin Whelan, *The Tree of Liberty, Radicalism, Catholicism and the Construction of Irish Identity: 1760–1830* (Cork, 1996), p.38. See Chapter 1 for a description of the growth and the nature and influence of this Catholic 'middlemen' class.
41. *Quarterly Review*, 'Ministerial Measures', December 1847, pp.269–70 and see also 'Essays of Fisher Ames', for a more extensive expression of Croker's ideas, April 1835, p.555.
42. Ibid., 'Policy of Ministers', September 1843, p.575.
43. Ibid., 'Tours in Ireland', June 1849, p.497.
44. Ibid., p.549.
45. Ibid., 'Ministerial Measures', December 1847, pp.269–71.
46. Ibid., pp.270–1.
47. Ibid., 'Ireland', June 1845; see in particular pp.277–82.
48. See Thomas McGrath's excellent study, *Politics, Interdenominational Relations and Education in the Public Memory of Bishop Kames Doyle of Kildare and Leighlin, 1796–1834* (Dublin, 1999), p.165.
49. Samuel Clarke, *Social Origins of the Irish Land War* (Princeton, 1979), remains one of the best-researched studies. Up until this period most disturbances were 'considered to be agrarian': faction fights and power struggles in contrast to the unrest of the early 1820s and later period when a growing proportion could be 'characterized by particularly vicious sectarianism'; see pp.74–9, 352–4, Chapter 3 and Conclusion.
50. See Joseph Lee, 'The Ribbonmen', in T.D. Williams (ed.), *Secret Societies in Ireland* (Dublin, 1973); various essays in C.H.E. Philpin (ed.), *Nationalism and Popular Protest in Ireland* (Cambridge, 1987), in particular those by M.R. Beames on the Ribbon Societies, T. Garvin on the economic profile of the leadership of the Defenders, Ribbonmen and others and M.J. Bric, 'Priests, Parsons and Politics'. See also Thomas N. Brown who seems to have blazed a trail for so many others with his 'Nationalism and the Irish Peasants: 1800–1848', in *The Review of Politics*, vol. 15 (October 1953), pp.403–45, and Paul E.W. Roberts, 'Caravats and Shanavests', in S. Clark and S.J. Donnelly (eds), *Irish Peasants, Violence and Political Unrest,*

1780–1914 (Manchester, 1983), pp.80, 82 and 90; Seán Connolly, *Priests and People in Pre-Famine Ireland* (Dublin, 2001 [revised edn), for the role and status of the Catholic clergy.

51. Emmet Larkin, *The Pastoral Role of the Roman Catholic Church in Pre-Famine Ireland* (Dublin, 2006), p.64.

52. See Margaret Phelan, *The Remains of William Phelan, with a Biographical Memoir*, 2 vols (Dublin, 1832), I, pp.1–13.

53. William Phelan, *The Bible, Not the Bible Society* (Dublin, 1817), pp.47–51 and 168–71; Desmond Bowen, *Protestant Crusade in Ireland: A study of Protestant–Catholic Relations Between the Act of Union and the Disestablishment* (Dublin, 1978), pp.59–60; and Irene Whelan, *Bible Wars in Ireland* (Dublin, 2005), p.131.

54. *Fraser's Magazine for Town and Country* [henceforth *Fraser's*], 'Ireland and the Priests', March 1833, pp.255–7; F.S. Mahony, *The Reliques of Father Prout*, ed. C. Kent (London, 1873), pp.xii–xv. In 1826, 172 new priests were the sons of farmers, 11 of graziers, 21 in trade, 17 in manufacture, 8 others: Patrick J. Corish, *Maynooth College: 1795–1995* (Dublin, 1995), p.39.

55. Emmet Larkin, *Historical Dimension of Irish Catholicism* (Dublin, 1997), p.9; and Dror Wahrman, *Imagining the Middle Class: The Political Representation of Class in Britain, c. 1780–1840* (Cambridge, 1995), pp.65–74.

56. Tom Dunne, 'Ballads, Rhetoric and Politicisation', in H. Gough and D. Dickson (eds), *Ireland and the French Revolution* (Dublin, 1990). It should be noted that some scholars disagree, believing political motives were paramount, notably Kevin Whelan, 'Politicisation in County Wexford and the Origins of the 1798 Rebellion' in the same collection, pp.156–78, and see his and L.M. Cullen's essays in D. Keogh and N. Furlong (eds), *The Mighty Wave: The 1798 Rebellion in Wexford* (Dublin, 1996).

57. Tom Dunne, '*Tá Gaedhil Bhocht Craidhte*: Memory, Tradition and the Politics of the Poor', in L.M. Geary (ed.), *Rebellion and Remembrance in Modern Ireland* (Dublin, 2001), pp.97–8 and *passim*; James S. Donnelly, 'Sectarianism in 1798 and in Catholic Nationalist Memory', pp.15–37. See also Maura Cronin, 'Memory, Story and Balladry', pp.112–134, both in the same collection; Ó Ciosain, *Print and Popular Culture*, Chapters 5, 6 and 10, and Gearóid Ó Tuathaigh, 'Gaelic Ireland, Popular Politics and Daniel O'Connell', *Journal of the Galway Archaeological and Historical Society*, vol. 35 (1975), pp.21–34. For the most extensive history and collection, although only available in Irish, see Brendán Ó Buachalla, *Aisling Ghéar* (Dublin, 1996), *passim*.

58. Whelan, *Bible Wars*, pp.156–7; see also Chapter 5, pp.153–87.

59. Add. MSS 52466, Ellis to Croker, 4 May 1823, ff.1–6.

60. *Parliamentary Papers*, 1825, VIII, (129) p.494, and part cited in Bowen, *Protestant Crusade*, p.60.

61. Add MSS 40319, Ellis to Croker, 2 January 1825, ff.138–40.

62. *State of Ireland: Letters from Ireland on the Present Political, Religious and Moral State of that Country, republished from the 'Courier' Newspaper* (London, 1825), pp.11–14.

63. Turner, *Age of Unease*, p.191.

64. *John Bull*, 14 August 1825.

65. Mitchell, *Whigs in Opposition*, p.178, citing an Althorp MS; see also pp.139–93 for the Whigs' policies and tactics at the time.

66. *Hansard*, VIII, 4 and 9 March 1823, cols 368–70 and 859.

67. J.K.L. Doyle, *A Vindication of the Religious and Civil Principles of the Irish Catholics* (Dublin, 1823), pp.28–40. See also *Letters on the State of Ireland Addressed by J.K.L. to a Friend in England* (Dublin, 1825) and Whelan, *Bible Wars*, pp.196–9, for a good account of Doyle at this time.

68. McDowell, *Public Opinion*, p.73, and *Hansard*, IX, cols 602 and 1434.

69. Bartholomew Lloyd, *An Inquiry Whether the Disturbances in Ireland have Originated in Tithes* (Dublin, 1823), pp.vii–xi and p.70. See also his *Miscellaneous Observations on J.K.L.'s Letter to Marquis Wellesley* (Dublin, 1824), p.25.

70. See Shunsuke Katsuta, 'The Rockite Movement in County Cork in the Early 1820s', *Irish Historical Studies*, XXXIII, 131 (May 2003), pp.278–96; T. Garvin 'Defenders, Ribbonmen and Others: Underground Political Networks in Pre-Famine Ireland', and M.R. Beames, 'The Ribbon Societies: Lower Class Protest in Pre-Famine Ireland', both in C.H.E. Philpin (ed.), *Nationalism and Popular Protest in Ireland* (Cambridge, 1987); J.S. Donnelly, 'Pastorini and Captain Rock: Millenarianism and Sectarianism in the Rockite Movement of 1821–4', in *Irish Peasants: Violence and Political Unrest* pp.102–42. The nearest thing to a major study of such letters is S.R. Gibbons (ed.), *Captain Rock, Night Errant: The Threatening Letters of Pre-Famine Ireland, 1801–45* (Dublin, 2004).

71. Ronan Kelly, *Bard of Erin*, pp.401–3.
72. Thomas Moore, *Journal*, 22 December 1827, III, p.777.
73. Ibid., II, pp.617–18. On 23 January 1823, when Moore asked him to review one of his works, Croker reminded Moore that 'we both agreed that no friend should ever review the work of a friend.'
74. Quoted in Kelly, *Bard of Erin*, p.402, who draws attention to the validity of O'Sullivan's criticism that Moore turns 'actual Rockite bloodshed and murder into an amusing sideshow'.
75. Bowen, *The Protestant Crusade*, pp.117–19.
76. Mortimer O'Sullivan, *Captain Rock Detected, or the Origins and Character of Recent Disturbances, by a Munster Farmer* (London, 1824), pp.7–9 and 148–9.
77. Ibid., pp.404–5 and 413.
78. Ibid., pp.127 and 199–201.
79. William Maginn, *Miscellaneous Verse and Prose* (London, 1885), pp.62–3.
80. Ibid., p.335.
81. Ibid., pp.310–12.
82. *Dublin Correspondent*, 1 March 1825.
83. *Blackwood's*, 'Captain Rock Detected', July 1824, p.109.
84. Duke MS, box 3, Goulburn to Croker, 4 October and 8 November 1824.
85. *Quarterly Review*, 'The Church in Ireland', March 1825, pp.492–99.
86. Ibid., p.514.
87. Ibid., pp.521–7.
88. See J.S. Donnelly, 'The Rightboy Movement', *Studia Hibernica*, no. 18 (1978), pp.120–202, notably pages 15, 130, 150, and 153–62.
89. Bowen, *Protestant Crusade*, p.135. See also his *Souperism: Myth or Reality*, *passim*.
90. *Blackwood's*, 'Ireland', December 1834, pp.753–4.
91. Peter Gray, *The Making of the Irish Poor Law, 1815–43* (Manchester, 2009), pp.86–91.
92. MacDonagh, *Hereditary Bondsman*, p.189.
93. James A. Reynolds, *The Catholic Emancipation Crisis in Ireland, 1823–1829* (Yale, 1954), pp.73–4.
94. Sack, *Jacobite to Conservative*, pp.166–70.
95. Harold Perkin, *The Origin of Modern English Society, 1780–1880* (London, 1969), pp.243–5 and 251; see also Anna Gambles' excellent *Protection and Politics: Conservative Economic Discourse, 1815–1852* (Suffolk, 1999), parts I and 2; Elizabeth Thrall, *Rebellious Fraser's* (New York, 1934), pp.147–93; and R.L. Hill, *Toryism and the People, 1832–1846* (London, 1927), pp.71–102.
96. *Quarterly Review*, 'Poor Law', January 1823.
97. Ibid., 'Inquiry into the Poor Laws', December 1812, pp.321–8 and 332.
98. Ibid., 'Parliamentary Reform', October 1816, pp.272–7.
99. *The Times*, 17 June 1819.
100. *John Bull*, 11 August 1822, 30 January 1822 and 3 March 1822. See also Croker, *Sketch of State of Ireland* (1822), pp.47–9.
101. *Guardian*, 21 May 1821 and 21 October 1821.
102. Ibid., 28 October 1821.
103. Gray, *Poor Laws*, p.64.
104. *Croker Papers*, Henry Drummond to Croker, 26 February 1825, I, pp.283–4.
105. Ibid., Croker to Drummond, 4 March 1825, I, p.284.
106. *Hansard*, XII, 28 February 1825, col. 785.
107. G.I.T. Machin, 'The Catholic Emancipation Crises of 1825', *English Historical Review*, vol. LXXVIII (1963), pp.458–81.
108. *O'Connell Correspondence*, O'Connell to J. Sugrue, 2 March 1825, III, no. 1179.
109. Add. MSS 40334, Peel to Gregory 21 March 1825, f.118; see also 40334, ff.119–20 and Gash, *Mr Secretary Peel*, p.413.
110. R.W. Davis, 'The Tories, the Whigs and Catholic Emancipation, 1827–9', *English Historical Review*, no. 382 (1982), p.99.
111. See *Quarterly Review*, June 1845, p.244, quoting from the *Irish Parliamentary Debates*, 10 January 1793.
112. *Wellington New Dispatches*, II, undated, but 1825, p.597.
113. *Hansard*, XII, 28 February 1825, col. 785.
114. *Croker Papers*, 2 March 1825, I, pp.279–80.

115. Ibid., I, p.279.
116. Ibid., 12 March 1825, I, p.280; see also Duke MS, box 3, 27 April 1824.
117. Clements MS (Canning–Croker correspondence), vol. I, 16 March 1825, f.82.
118. Ibid. (Huskisson–Croker correspondence), vol. I, 16 March 1825, f.18.
119. Ibid.
120. *O'Connell Correspondence*, 4 March 1925, III, p.128.
121. Ibid., O'Connell to Dwyer, 15 March 1825, no. 1189; see also the *Morning Herald*, 15 March 1825 for the Lawless letter.
122. *Political Register*, 12 and 19 March, also 19 July 1825; see also G.I.T. Machin, 'The Catholic Emancipation Crises of 1825', p.473.
123. George Croly, *Popery and the Irish Question: Being an Exposition of the Political and Doctrinal Opinions of Messrs. O'Connell, Keogh, Dromgoule, Gandolphe etc.* [sic] (London, 1825), p.101.
124. McGrath, *Bishop Doyle*, pp.33–4.
125. *Hansard*, XIII, 19 April 1825, cols 20–1. Peel's description, April 21, col. 110.
126. Ibid., cols 36–7.
127. Ibid., cols 107–21. For Canning see cols 84–106.
128. *Quarterly Review*, June 1845, pp.279–80.
129. *O'Connell Correspondence*, 25 April 1825, III, no. 1209.
130. *The Times*, 10 May 1825.
131. Gash, *Mr Secretary Peel*, p.419, and see pp.411–23 for a fuller account of Peel's actions and views during this period.
132. Ibid., p.418; see also Boyd Hilton on Peel's forebodings, 'The Ripening of Sir Robert Peel', in Michael Bentley (ed.), *Public and Private Doctrine: Essays in British History presented to Maurice Cowling* (Cambridge, 1993), pp.68–9.
133. *Hansard*, XIII, 17 May 1825, cols 740–52; see also Fergus O'Ferrall, *Catholic Emancipation: Daniel O'Connell and the Birth of Irish Democracy, 1820–1835* (Dublin, 1985), p.101, and Norman Gash, *Lord Liverpool* (London, 1985), pp.232–5.
134. MacDonagh, *The Hereditary Bondsman*, p.219. *O'Connell Correspondence*, III, no. 1219.
135. Reynolds, *The Catholic Emancipation Crises in Ireland*, p.40, and MacDonagh, *The Hereditary Bondsman*, pp.217–23; McDowell, *Public Opinion*, p.100.
136. Dixon, *Canning*, p.263.
137. *The Times*, 28 May 1825, p.6 and 31 May 1825, p.3.
138. *Quarterly Review*, June 1845, pp.250–4.
139. *Croker Papers*, Croker to Lord Hertford, 22 September 1825, I, pp.281–2.
140. Duke MS, box 3, Plunkett to Croker, 15 September 1826.
141. See Arthur Aspinall, *The Formation of Canning's Ministry*, Camden Third Series (London, 1937), Introduction, and *Croker Papers*, I, pp.362–94 for Croker's account.
142. Hilton, 'The Ripening of Sir Robert Peel', p.66.
143. Clements MS, Croker Diary marked '1827', 18 February 1827, part cited in *Croker Papers*, I, p.364.
144. Ibid., 18–22 February 1827 and *Croker Papers*, I, p.364–5.
145. Ibid., box 10, folder 13, Lowther to Croker, 27 February 1827.
146. See G.I.T. Machin, *The Catholic Question in English Politics* (Oxford, 1964), p.85 and D.G.S. Simes, 'Ultra-Tories in British Politics: 1824–1834', unpublished DPhil. thesis (Oxford, 1974).
147. *Hansard*, XVII, 1 May 1927, col. 426.
148. Ibid., XVI, 6 March 1827, cols 1007–8.
149. Ibid., cols 959, 964, 965, 973, 1007–8.
150. *The Times*, 8 March 1827.
151. Clements MS, diary marked '1827', and part cited in *Croker Papers*, I, p.365.
152. See Dixon, *Canning*, p.278 and Hinde, *Canning*, p.438; Knighton, *George IV*, pp.285–92 for a similar account of events from the Court perspective.
153. Clements MS, Lb. 19, 3 April 1827, f.209.
154. Add. MSS 40319, 18 April 1827, ff.239–50 and Clements MS, Lb. 19, ff.251–6.
155. Ibid., Croker to Peel, 18 and 20 April 1827, ff.250 and 251; see also Parker, *Peel Correspondence*, I, Peel to Croker, 18 and 20 April, pp.470–2.
156. *Wellington New Despatches*, March 1826, III, p.109; *Croker Papers*, I, pp.314–15.
157. Clements MS, diary marked '1827', and part quoted in *Croker Papers*, I, p.365.

158. Aspinall, *The Formation*, Rutland to Mrs Arbuthnot, 20 April 1827, p.136; see also Mitchell, *Whigs in Opposition*, for an account from Whig sources, pp.194–215.
159. *Croker Papers*, 27 November and 3 December 1856, III, pp.369–70.
160. Ibid., unreferenced comment and citation by Jennings, I, p.376.
161. See Carlisle MS, D. Lons. L1/2/116, May 1827, to Lowther, and to Casey, Clements MS, Lb. 20, 21 July 1827, f.127. The original of this and sixty-eight others to Casey are held at the Smithers Library, University of Florida, MS Group 20, box 2, folder 57. For Spring–Rice and Croker correspondence see Duke MS, box 3, marked 1827.
162. *Croker Papers*, Canning to Croker, 18 April 1827, I, p.372.
163. Clements MS, Lb. 19, 18 March 1827, ff.196–8, 318–19 and random folios 203 to 342.
164. Ibid., Croker to Charles Elrington, 30 April 1827, f.331.
165. Ibid., Croker to Canning, 2 May 1827, f.345.
166. Ibid., Croker to Sir John Newport, 4 May 1827, f.351.
167. Clements MS, box 10, folder 14, Lowther to Croker, 16 April 1827. Lowther's correspondence with Croker forms an extensive part of the loose letter Clements collection for this period.
168. Ibid., box 10, Lowther to Croker, folder 14, April 1827, and Clements MS, Lb. 19, ff.230 and 243–4, both part cited in *Croker Papers*, I, pp.372–4.
169. Ibid., box 10, folder 15, Lowther to Croker, 14 May 1827.
170. Lord Newcastle, *Unrepentant Tory: Political Selections from the Diary of the 4th Duke of Newcastle-under-Lyme, 1827–1838*, ed. R.S. Grant (Suffolk, 2006), diary entry 3 May 1827, diary entry 13 May 1827, p.27.
171. Clements MS, Lb 19, Croker to Canning, 7 May 1827, ff.356–7.
172. Carlisle MS, D. Lons L1/2/116, Croker to Lowther, 8 May 1827.
173. R.B. McDowell, 'Trinity College Dublin and Politics', in *Historical Essays 1938–2001* (Dublin, 2002), p.76.
174. *The Times*, 18 May 1827.
175. *Freeman's Journal*, 14, 15 and 16 May, and on 'the heat and fury at this election', unsurpassed 'in intemperance and all sorts of violence', Croker to Lowther, 15 May 1827, Carlisle MS, D. Lons, L1/2/116.
176. Newcastle, *Unrepentant Tory*, p.25.
177. *Standard*, 21 May 1827.
178. Ibid., 22 and 28 May 1827.
179. Ibid., 6 July 1827.
180. Dennis Griffiths, *Plant Here the Standard* (London, 1996), pp.17, 40–1 and 51.
181. Aspinall, *Politics and the Press*, p.327.
182. See David E. Latane Jr. 'Perge, Signifer – or Where did William Maginn Stand', in James H. Murphy (ed.), *Evangelicals and Catholics in Nineteenth-Century Ireland* (Dublin, 2005), p.62. Latane's fine essay is, I believe, the only study of Maginn, apart from Thrall's *Rebellious Fraser's*, to make any serious attempt to analyse Maginn's political ideas, career and influence.
183. Clements MS, Lb. 22, Croker to Hertford, 14 February 1829. f.407. See also Add. MS 56368, Newcastle to Lees-Giffard, 15 May 1827, f.146 and Griffiths, *Plant the Standard*, p.44.
184. *Croker Papers*, 1 and 2 January 1828, I, p.396.
185. Clements MS (Canning–Croker Collection), 22 July 1827, f.105; also in Aspinall, *The Formation*, p.268.
186. Ibid., also marked f.105.
187. Ibid., Lb. 20, Croker to Canning, 23 July 1828, ff.135–6.
188. Apart from the connections between the Croker family and the Giffards illustrated in Chapters 1 and 2 above, there are some references among the Halsbury Manuscripts held by T.L. Giffard of Great Bromley, Essex, in file box 100/6B/28 May 1808, ff.1–3, and Grey file box 1811, no number. I am indebted to Professor Jacqueline Hill of NUI Maynooth for these references and obtaining the permission of T.L. Giffard to use them, to whom I am most grateful.
189. Clements MS, Lb. 20, Croker to Stanley Lees-Giffard, 23 July 1827, f.134.
190. Ibid., Lb. 20, letters of 12 November 1827, f.390 and Lb. 21, 24 and 28 July 1828, ff.3–8.
191. *Croker Papers*, Croker to Hertford, 7 August 1827, I, pp.380–2.
192. Ibid., 8 August 1827, I, pp.382–3.
193. *Wellington New Despatches*, Hardinge to Wellington, 9 to 13 August 1827, IV, pp.75–90.

194. *Croker Papers*, 'Memorandum of a Conversation with Lord Goderich', I, pp.384–90, and see also Croker letter to Goderich in Clements MS, Lb. 20, 11 August 1827, ff.220–1.
195. Clements MS, Lb. 20, 3 September 1827, ff.275–8.
196. *Croker Papers*, Croker to Hertford, 31 December 1827, I, pp.392–3.
197. Clements MS, Lb 21 ff.5–8; see also folios 8 to 38, part cited in *Croker Papers*, I, p.400. See also Hibbert, *George VI*, p.301 for an account of the crises from the Court perspective.
198. Longford, *Wellington*, p.147.
199. See Philip Ziegler, *Melbourne: A Biography of William Lamb, 2nd Lord Melbourne* (London, 1978), pp.97 and 85–99 and *The Chronicles of Holland House*, vol. II, p.94 for a Whig view of events.
200. Clements MS, Lb. 21, Croker to Hertford, 21 January 1828, f.76.
201. Sir John Barrow, *An Autobiographical Memoir of Sir John Barrow, Bart.* (London, 1847), p.351.
202. *Croker Papers*, Croker to Lowther, 16 August 1827, I, p.383.
203. Dixon, *Canning*, p.283.
204. Clements MS, Lb. 21, Croker to Hertford, 19 to 21 January 1828, ff.68–76 and *Croker Papers*, 2 to 4 January, I, p.404.
205. Ibid., Lb. 21, Croker to Hertford, 2 January 1828, ff.5–7.
206. Ibid., Lb. 21, f.8.
207. Ibid., Lb. 20, Croker to Peel, 1 October 1827, ff.252–3.
208. Add. MSS 40319, ff.254–6, and in *Croker Papers*, I, p.375.
209. Ibid., ff.256–7.
210. *Croker Papers*, I, pp.364–5; see also diary entries, Clements MS, diary '1827', dated between 16 February and 16 March 1827 but evidently added to at a later date by Croker.
211. Clements MS, Lb. 20, 28 May 1827, f.5.
212. Ibid., Lb. 20, 30 May 1827, f.10.
213. Add. MSS 40320, Croker to Peel, 14 March 1828, ff.7–11, and part cited in *Croker Papers*, I, p.410.
214. Ibid., ff.10–11; see also 24 March 1828, ff.14–19.
215. *Croker Papers*, diary entry, 7 June 1828, I, p.423; Longford, *Wellington*, pp.158–62; and Turner, *The Age of Unease*, pp.203–5.
216. Clements MS, Lb. 21, Croker to Hardinge, 28 May 1828, f.305 (The numbering appears to be in error on this folio for it is placed between 359 and 360).
217. *Croker Papers*, diary entry, 14 March 1828, I, p.413.
218. Clements MS, '1828' diary entry, 9 May 1828, and *Croker Papers*, I, p.418.
219. See Bartlett, *Fall and Rise*, pp.336–42, defining the importance of the 1826 elections.
220. Clements MS, Lb. 21 Croker to Fitzgerald, 21 June 1828, f.416.
221. Ibid; MacDonagh, *The Hereditary Bondsman*, p.250.
222. *Freeman's Journal*, 28 June 1828, and part cited in MacDonagh, *Hereditary Bondsman*, p.250.
223. *The Times*, 2 July 1828, reporting events of 28 June 1828.
224. MacDonagh, *The Hereditary Bondsman*, pp.251–3 and for the original see R.L. Sheil, *Sketches, Legal and Political*, ed. M.W. Savage, 2 vols (London, 1855), vol. II, pp.117–18.
225. Charles Chenivix Trench, *The Great Dan* (London, 1984), p.153; see also MacDonagh, 'The Politicisation of the Irish Catholic Bishops', p.43; *The Hereditary Bondsman*, p.251; and Sheil, *Sketches*, p.136.
226. O'Ferrall, *Catholic Emancipation*, pp.196–7.
227. Duke MS, box 3, Foster to Croker, 1 July 1828.
228. *The Times*, 10 July 1828.
229. *Quarterly Review*, December 1844, 'Repeal Agitation', pp.224–7.
230. Ibid., p.283.
231. Ibid., 'Lord Russell on the Causes of the French Revolution', April 1833, written with Lord Mahon pp.162–9.
232. Clements MS, Lb. 21, 9 July 1828, f.454; Add. MSS 40320, ff.54–6; *Croker Papers*, I, pp.427–8. For the letter from Wellington to the king, see *Wellington New Dispatches*, vol. IV, p.514.
233. Clements MS, Lb. 22, Croker to Wellington, 11 September 1828, ff.100–4.
234. *Mrs Arbuthnot's Journal*, II, p.202; *The Standard*, 22 August 1828 also contains the citation from *The New Times*.
235. Bartlett, *The Fall and Rise*, pp.345–6.

236. John Bew, *The Glory of Being Britons: Civic Unionsim in Nineteenth-Century Belfast* (Dublin, 2009); see in particular pp.52–140.
237. *John Bull*, 1 September 1828.
238. Ibid., 1 September 1828; *Dublin Evening Post*, 2 September 1828; and see Gary Owens, 'A Moral Insurrection: Faction Fighters, Public Demonstrations and the O'Connellite Campaign, 1828', *Irish Historical Studies*, XIX, 120 (November 1997).
239. Owens, 'A Moral Insurrection', p.514.
240. Ibid., pp.515–17.
241. Ibid., pp.519 and 532–7.
242. O'Ferrall, *Catholic Emancipation*, pp.210–13; see also *The Times*, 29 September 1828.
243. Palmer, *Police and Protest*, p.275.
244. *Dublin Evening Mail*, 15 October 1828.
245. *Standard*, 30 October 1828.
246. Whelan, *Bible Wars*, pp.180–1; see also pp.181–8.
247. *Clonmel Herald*, 17 March 1827, part republished in *The Times*, 21 March 1827.
248. Add. MSS 40397 (Peel Manuscripts), 10 July 1828, ff.46–8.
249. *Ballina Impartial*, 21 July 1828 and the *Mayo Constitution*, 24 July 1828.
250. *The Times*, 8 January 1828.
251. Ibid., 22 October 1828.
252. Ibid., 23 February 1829.
253. O'Ferrall, *Catholic Emancipation*, p.208; Suzanne T. Kingon, 'Ulster Opposition to Catholic Emancipation: 1828–9', *Irish Historical Studies*, XXXIV, 134 (November 2004), pp.137–55.
254. Duke MS, box 3, Wallace to Croker, 4 September 1828. Wallace was repeating the contents of an earlier discussion when Croker had expressed these opinions.
255. 'Memorandum' written by Croker on 11 January 1829, *Croker Papers*, II, pp.5–6.
256. *John Bull*, 28 October 1828.
257. See Longford, *Wellington*, p.176 and Gash, *Mr Secretary Peel*, pp.546–7.
258. Add. MSS 40320, Croker to Peel, 7 February 1829, ff.104–7; see also 40321, Croker to Peel, 30 July 1835, ff.156–7 for a fuller account of Croker's opinion on this subject.
259. *Croker Papers*, diary entry, 9 February 1829, II, p.9.
260. Clements MS, Lb. 22, Croker to Hertford, 14 February 1828, f.407.
261. Ibid., diary entry, 13 February 1829.
262. *Standard*, 23 February 1829; see also Gash, *Sir Robert Peel*, p.565.
263. Carlisle MS, D. Lons. L1/2/116, Croker to Lowther, 10 February 1829, no folio no. See also White, *The Conservative Tradition*, p.35, for Burke's views on contingency and political combination.
264. Clements MS, Lb. 22, Peel to Croker, 19 March 1829, and *Wellington New Despatches*, V, Croker to Wellington, 19 March 1829, p.532.
265. Longford, *Wellington*, p.192.
266. Clements MS, diary entry, 13 March 1829.
267. Add. MSS 40320, Croker to Peel, no date, March 1829, f.115.
268. Clements MS, Lb. 22, Croker to Hertford, 18 March 1829, f.484; and *Croker Papers*, II, p.16.
269. *Croker Papers*, Croker to Hertford, 30 March 1929, I, p.12.
270. Ibid., 9 April 1829, I, p.14.
271. Turner, *Age of Unease*, p.207.
272. Ibid., p.207.
273. *Croker Papers*, letter to Lord Hertford, 7 May 1929, II, p.15.
274. *Standard*, 9 and 13 February 1829.
275. Michael Bentley, *Politics Without Democracy: 1815–1914* (Oxford, 1996 [2nd edn]), p.41; Parry, *The Rise and Fall of Liberal Government*, p.56.
276. Clements MS, Lb. 23, Croker to Hertford, 16 April 1829, f.65.
277. Linda Colley, *Britons: Forging the Nation: 1707–1837* (Reading, 2005 [new edn]), p.332.
278. See Eric Hobsbawm and George Rude, *Captain Swing* (London, 2001 [paperback edn]); George Kitson Clarke, *Peel and the Conservative Party* (London, 1964 [revised edn]). For Tory and ultra-Protestant Reform agitators see D.C. Moore, 'The Other Face of Reform', *Victorian Studies*, vol. 5 (1961), pp.17–34, and John Wolfe, *The Protestant Crusade in Britain: 1829–1869* (Oxford, 1991), pp.22 and 65–72.
279. Clements MS, Lb. 23, Croker to Hertford, 7 April 1829, f.46.
280. *The Distressed State of the Country* (1829), a report of the meeting in Birmingham, May

1829, and part cited in Brock, *The Great Reform Act*, p.57.

281. *Hansard*, XXI, 4 June 1829, col. 1713, and XXI, col. 1714.
282. *Standard*, 15 and 23 July; see also 15 and 16 September 1829.
283. Ibid., 16 and 18 July 1829. For more extensive declarations on the need for economic and radical social reforms at this time, for Poor Laws for Ireland, see 15 September, also 19, 26 and 30 October.
284. Parry, *The Rise and Fall of Liberal Government*, p.66.
285. Hilton, 'Peel: A Reappraisal', p.591.
286. *Croker Papers*, Croker to Hertford, 25 March 1833, II, p.205.
287. See Boyd Hilton, *Corn, Cash and Commerce: The Economic Policies of the Tory Government, 1815–1830* (Oxford, 1977), pp.233–9 and *passim*.
288. *Quarterly Review*, 'Close of Sir Robert Peel's Administration', September 1846, p.552.
289. *The Times*, 27 January 1830, reporting the meeting of 25 January. See Nancy LoPatin: *Political Unions, Popular Politics and the Great Reform Act* (New York, 1999) and Elie Halévy, *Liberal Awakening*, II, pp.283–285, for a description of the more conservative nature of the demands.
290. John Cannon, *Parliamentary Reform: 1640–1832* (Cambridge, 1973), p.195.
291. Add MSS 40320, ff.152–3, 24 February 1830, and part cited in *Croker Papers*, II, pp.54–5.
292. *Croker Papers*, II, p.54.
293. *Hansard*, XXI, 8 June 1829, col. 1685 and XXII, 23 February 1830, cols 897–906.
294. Ibid., XXIV, 28 May 1830, col. 1243.
295. Cannon, *Parliamentary Reform*, p.195.
296. *Wellington New Despatches*, Croker to Wellington, 14 September 1828, V, pp.53–4.
297. Lang, *Lockhart Letters*, 30 March 1829, II, pp.50–1.
298. Smiles, *John Murray*, II, p.182. See also Shattock, *Politics and the Reviewers*, pp.49–55.
299. See my PhD thesis, 'The Intellectual and Political World of John Wilson Croker ...', Chapter 6 for a full account; also Brightfield, *Croker*, pp.234–8, 383 and *Croker Papers*, III, p.306.
300. Clements MS, Lb. 20, Croker to Murray, 4 November 1827, f.360.
301. Brightfield, *Croker*, p.197, citing Murray correspondence now held at the NLS.
302. *Croker Papers*, Croker to Murray, 9 January 1829, II, pp.25–6, and 10 January, p.27.
303. Ibid., Scott to Croker, 30 January 1829, II, pp.27–46. For other letters assisting Croker in his research see also Duke MS, misc. files for 1829–30 and Clements MS, Lb. 23, ff.280–400.
304. Ibid., II, pp.40–3.
305. *The Life of Samuel Johnson, LLD, Including a Journal of a Tour of the Hebrides by James Boswell, Esq: A New Edition with Numerous Additions and Notes, By John Wilson Croker, LLD, FRS*, 5 vols (London, 1831). A ten-volume edition was published in 1835 including two separate volumes of notes.
306. Clements MS, Lb. 23, Croker to Planta, 21 August 1829, ff.274–7, part cited in *Croker Papers*, II, pp.21–4.
307. Ibid., f.276.
308. Aspinall, *Politics and the Press*, p.233, citing Wellington MSS.
309. *Croker Papers*, 12 January 1830, II, p.55.
310. Clements MS, Lb. 24, Croker to Hertford, 5 January 1830, ff.26–30.
311. *Standard*, 23 February 1829; see also Croker to Hook, August 1829, Clements MS, Lb. 23, ff.296 and 405.
312. Clements MS, diary entry 13 February 1829, no cat. no., marked '1929'. See also Chicago MS 619, Hook Manuscripts, February 1830 to March 1831, ff.29–53. Hook's diaries have disappeared, but Hammersmith and Fulham libraries, ref. DD/763, hold a partial transcript recording of meetings with Croker, Holmes and/or Lowther. Bill Newton-Dunn, *John Bull*, also identifies these connections and sources, pp.261–80.
313. See *Parliamentary Sessional Papers*, 'Accounts and Papers', vol. XXV, 1830 and XXXIV, 1832, pp.350, 357, 128 and 119. Duty payments for *John Bull* for 1827: £1,679, 1828: £1,333 and 1829: £1,278. The *Standard*, after a rapid rise in circulation during 1828, had an annual sale of 1,367,000 copies in 1829 and 1,281,000 in 1830. In 1829, the *Courier*: 995,200, falling to 831,000 until it dropped its support for the Tories and its circulation rose to 1, 237, 000.
314. *The Times*, 23 July 1829.
315. Clements MS, Lb. 21, 28 May 1828, f.306. There is a sequential error to the folio numbers at this point in this letterbook.

316. Ibid., Croker to Vesey-Fitzgerald, 28 June 1830, II, p.68.
317. Aspinall, *Brougham*, p.174, citing the *Edinburgh Review*, July 1830, and Brougham's pamphlet, p.8.
318. Edward Pearce, *Reform! The Fight For the 1832 Reform Act* (London, 2004), p.57.
319. See Turner, *The Age of Unease*, pp.210–26, for a selection of some of the more recent historiography. See also Michael Bentley, *Politics Without Democracy: 1815–1914* (Oxford, 1984), pp.45–60; Cannon, *Parliamentary Reform*; F. O'Gorman, *Voters, Patrons and Parties* (Oxford, 1989); Parry, *The Rise and Fall of Liberal Government*.
320. *Quarterly Review*, 'Friendly Advice to the Lords', July 1831, pp.518, 525 and 529–30.
321. Ibid., November 1831, p.530.
322. Brock, *Reform Act*, p.96. See also Stewart, *Brougham*, pp.241–7 for a good account of the election.
323. *The Times*, 1 October 1830, and part cited in Brock, *Reform Act*, p.104 and *Leeds Mercury* of 2 October 1830. For Brougham's own account of events see Brougham, *Life and Times*, III, pp.38–44.
324. Mitchell, *Whigs in Opposition*, pp.242–4.
325. Ibid., p.244; see also Parry, *The Rise and Fall of Liberal Government*, pp.68–9.
326. *Blackwood's*, 'Parties', July 1830, pp.88–9 and 94.
327. *Standard*, 5 July 1830.
328. Ibid., 16 July, 30 July and 14 August 1830. Similar comments appeared throughout the year increasing in hostility and critical support for an alternative government. See also *Standard*, 28 July 1830 for praise of Brougham's election speech and 15, 16, 19 and 26 September 1829 on Sadler and poor reforms.
329. A.W. Ward and A.R. Waller (eds), *Cambridge History of English and American Literature*, vol. XII (Cambridge, 1907–21), p.40.
330. *Fraser's*, February 1830, p.1.
331. See Miriam Thrall, *Rebellious Fraser's* (New York, 1937), pp.149–52.
332. Ibid., p.150; see also *Fraser's*, June 1830, p.591.
333. Cannon, *Parliamentary Reform*, pp.198–202.
334. Add. MSS 40320, Croker to Peel, 22 July 1830, f.166; see also Add. MSS 40321, ff.165–7 and forwarded by Peel to Croker.
335. R.B. McDowell, *Historical Essays: 1938–2001* (Dublin, 2003), p.70.
336. *Dublin Evening Post*, 6 August 1830.
337. *The Times*, 27 July and 9 August 1830. In his *Historical Essays*, pp.76–86, McDowell argues that it was only following the Reform Act that the college became consistently 'protestant' in its politics.
338. Clements MS, Lb. 24, Croker to Archdeacon Singleton, 10 August 1830. f.383.
339. Carlisle MS, D. Lons. L1/2/116, Croker to Lowther, 13 August 1830.
340. Clements MS, Lb. 25, 25 October 1830, f.25; *Croker Papers*, II, p.72.
341. *Blackwood's*, 'Political Anticipation', November 1830, pp.720–1 and 734–5. This article was written by Thomas De Quincey; see also 'Expiation' by John Wilson, October 1830, pp.628–43 and 690–4.
342. Cannon, *Parliamentary Reform*, p.200.
343. *The Times*, 3 November 1830, p.224.
344. *Blackwood's*, December 1830, 'Letter on the Spirit of the Age', pp.909, 913–16; 'The Late Cabinet', pp.970–80.
345. *Fraser's*, December 1831, pp.600–5.
346. *Mrs Arbuthnot's Journal*, II, p.402; see also Norman Gash, *Peel* (London, 1990 [paperback edn]), pp.68 and 138–9.
347. Clements MS, Lb. 25, 8 November 1829, f.153.

CHAPTER THREE

The Battle Against the Reform Act and the 'Invention' of the Conservative Party: 1831–2

The Temple of history is not the floor for a morris-dance [and] we protest against this species of carnival history ... We are ready to admit a hundred times over Mr Macaulay's literary powers – brilliant even under affectation with which he so frequently disfigures them. He is a great painter, but a suspicious narrator; a grand proficient of the picturesque, but a very poor professor of the historic. These volumes have been, and his future volumes will be, devoured with the same eagerness that Oliver Twist or Vanity Fair excite ... but its pages will seldom ... find a permanent place on the historic shelf [and] be quoted as authority on any question or point of the History of England. (J.W. Croker, 'Macaulay's History of England' in the *Quarterly Review*, March 1849, p. 630)

THE CONSERVATIVE PARTY AND THE GREAT REFORM ACT

On 17 November 1830 there was a meeting 'at Peel's of forty official members of the House of Commons – he announced first that we were out, and secondly that he meant to retire to private life – to give no opposition and not to lead the party.' When the duke heard of it, Croker continued, 'he announced he intends to keep the party together; not to oppose – nay, to support – the King's Government in all that may tend to public safety' and this, I hope, 'will warm the cold caution [of Peel] into some degree of party heat; but if he won't lead us there are others who will at least make the attempt.'[1]

Peel would not offer consistent leadership for some years, but he had 'warmed' to the idea a week later when parliament re-assembled, and what Croker described as 'the Conservative party of observation under General the Duke of Wellington and Lieut. General Sir Robert Peel' were entertained by an old rival:

> Our whole party took the Opposition seats and as O'Connell, Hume and Co. have not gone over with the Whigs, it was very difficult to get a place ... O'Connell having made an observation on the number of retired Chancellors now existing (four) there was a general *movement de hilarite*. ... There is a great deal of turmoil in the country – audacity in the common people, and the most lamentable apathy and cowardice in the Gentry.[2]

The term 'Conservative party' was first used in the January 1830 number of the *Quarterly Review* to differentiate between Tory supporters of moderate Reform and those 'opposed to all change whatever':

> We despise and abominate the details of partisan warfare, but we now are, as we always have been, decidedly and conscientiously attached to what is called the Conservative party ... Some of this party object to all change whatever; and, by the obstinacy they have displayed on this point, and the coolness and distance which have often marked their demeanour, they have, in our judgement done essential injury to the side to which they belong. But these are neither considerable in numbers, in rank, or in influence. We have no hesitation in stating it to be our conviction, that an immense majority of the *tories* are as anxious to promote prudent and practicable amelioration of the state, as any of their fellow subjects.[3]

This article, entitled 'Internal Policy', was an important one for the *Quarterly*, because Murray had suffered from a lack of accurate political information since losing Croker in 1825, and after Southey's anti-Emancipation article of October 1828 in particular,[4] he had been seeking to convince readers that he still had a privileged conduit to ministers. Lockhart later described the events to Croker:

> Southey began to put in his wedge, and I let him drive it home because I had taken a wrong view of what was to be done ... your secession left me to my own poor lights. I did not then understand the nature of official men at all ...

and had you been by us at the decisive moment to interpret the talk of Downing Street in the details of Albermarle Street [Murray's offices], neither Murray nor I would have allowed Southey to overrule us ... I never had the least inclination on the anti-Catholic side.[5]

For over a century Croker had been accredited with the invention of the name 'Conservative party', but in 1940 Myron Brightfield argued that he had not written any article for the *Quarterly* between December 1825 and January 1831, and therefore the 'Internal Policy' was probably written by John Fullarton or John Miller.[6] *The Wellesley Index to Victorian Periodicals*, a directory established to identify the authors of review articles, suggests Miller, a young lawyer at Lincolns Inn,[7] and in his popular history of the Conservative party Robert Blake writes that 'one of those persons who would be stigmatised by Sir Winston Churchill as a "tiresome researcher" has discovered that Croker was not writing for the *Quarterly* at that particular time. So the god-father of the Conservative party remains anonymous.'[8]

However, a little more research could also be used to qualify an argument that if not the author of the article, Croker was almost certainly responsible for the introduction of the term. His contemporaries appear to have never refuted it; he was back on close terms with Murray a year before the 'Internal Policy' article, and Murray was very keen for Croker to write political reviews, or at least guide those who were.[9] Perhaps most significantly, as *The Wellesley Index* also identifies, in his private register of the *Quarterly*'s contributors Murray attributed the 'Internal Policy' article to Croker.[10] Wellington certainly believed he was responsible for the political contents of that number, for as Lockhart wrote on 30 January 1830, he 'sent for' Murray, 'Croker and Barrow and rowed them out' for some remarks in the latest *Quarterly* which 'had produced panic' and 'caused a 2% fall in stocks'.[11]

It is useful to bear in mind that as with all reviews of the period, the *Quarterly*'s articles were anonymous not only because this protected the author, but also because this preserved a politically and theoretically consistent image. As Hill and Helen Shine, the compilers of the first index of its early writers, describe, articles were 'considered entirely the property of the periodical' and often pulled apart and entirely 're-jigged' by the editor or a political advisor like Croker.[12] Authors were expected to accept this practice and write in accord with the *Quarterly*'s past arguments and tone.[13] Almost all of them did, and only highly prized contributors such as Southey the Laureate, who saw himself as creating the 'prophetic brought forth with pain', were occasionally able to over-rule this.[14]

It is unlikely that Fullarton would have been fully entrusted with a political review in January 1830, and in April 1831 when he wrote most of the important 'Parliamentary Reform' article, it was almost certainly compiled under Croker's supervision.[15] Later that year Lockhart wrote to Croker that another was being prepared and Fullarton had asked for Croker to assist, and 'very desirous' that he should.[16] John Miller had written two articles for the *Quarterly* prior to 1830, both of them in 1825 when Croker was acting as editor during John Gifford's demise. The first presented the *Quarterly*'s political views following the failure of the Emancipation bill that year, making it highly unlikely that it would have been entrusted to a novice other than under Croker's supervision. The second, in October just after Croker became estranged from Murray, was co-written with J.T.Coleridge (nephew of the poet), by then the temporary editor, following which Miller appears to have written nothing else until 1830,[17] suggesting he may have been another of Croker's *protégés*.

All of the article's main arguments are very similar to those Croker had made throughout his career, and are worth exploring in a little more detail because of their relevance to the development of Conservative political ideas at this time. As an avid collector of French political pamphlets, Croker was probably more familiar with terms such as 'conservative' and its continental political applications than all of his party peers. It was not entirely alien to Britain before 1830, however, Burke remarked in his *Reflections on the Revolution in France* that 'the state without the means of some change is without the means of its conservation ... it might even risk the loss of that part of the constitution which it wished the most religiously to preserve.'[18] Little more needs to be said to illustrate the influence the French Revolution and Burke's canonical work had on Croker's ideas, and James Sack has illustrated some other early uses of the term; and Croker had close associations with them all:

> The first edition of Samuel Johnson's Dictionary defined conservative (from the Latin *conservo*) as 'having the power of opposing diminution or injury'. Edmund Burke in the *Reflections* nudged the word towards a slightly political connotation when he discussed the necessity of preserving a 'rational and manly freedom ... for the great conservatories and magazines of our rights and privileges'.

Quite possibly the earliest English usage of the word in a starkly political sense occurred in June 1816 in the *Anti-Jacobin Review*, where a contributor lauded the Pitt clubs as supporting those 'conservative principles which all good men ought not passively to foster and cherish, but actually to promote, and sedulously by combining, to perpetuate'. In Western Europe the *annus mirabilis* of the word was 1818, when a Conservative Association was formed at Gloucester. In January 1818, in the *Quarterly Review*, Robert Southey, the poet laureate, was juxtaposing the 'struggle between the destructive and the conservative principles of society, the evil, the good, the profligate against the respectable'. And, perhaps more important, in October 1818, in Paris, Chateaubriand launched a glittering, if short lived, magazine, *The Conservateur*, ... Yet somehow, as an ordinary method of conveying a political message, the word languished in England until suddenly, in January 1830, in one of the most famous *Quarterly Review* essays of the nineteenth century ... it achieved apotheosis.[19]

Twenty years earlier, Canning, Croker and the editor of the *Anti-Jacobin Review* were among the few who had refuted Whig jeers by boldly acknowledging the appellation 'Tory' and arguing that their 'Tory party' was in the tradition of Pitt's followers.[20] Furthermore, in a highly important *Quarterly* policy article in July 1831, Croker specifically described Pitt's coalition of moderate Whigs, who like Burke joined like-minded Tories at the time of the French Revolution, as having first 'formed the conservative party' when they combined 'to act on the principles of enlightened Toryism':

> We are aware that many distinguished persons, such as the Duke of Portland, Lord Spencer, Mr Windham etc, who joined Mr Pitt on the breaking out of the French revolution, nay that Mr Pitt and Lord Grenville themselves, were not professed Tories, but as they all opposed the Whigs, and formed the conservative party, we talk of them in common parlance as Tories; and in fact they did unite and act on the principles of enlightened Toryism.[21]

Any irrefutable authority for the invention of the term is unlikely to be found, but of greater political significance, and as the remainder of this study will illustrate, rather than the *Tamworth Manifesto* being when 'Conservatism was, to all intents and purposes invented by Sir Robert Peel.'[22] Croker would be most responsible for the 'invention' and the promotion of these principles some years before his leaders publicly acknowledged them. Between 1831 and 1834, from the floor of the Commons, and much more significantly through his *Quarterly Review* articles, he would represent the new Conservative party as the *via media* of British parliamentary politics where moderates could unite to defend Church and constitution against extremes, and conciliate popular concerns with corrective reforms. This would not be a single-handed campaign, however, any more than there can really ever be any one seminal document or individual responsible for the apotheosis of modern conservatism. By 1832 his disaffected circle would recombine to face 'the revolutionary threat', moderate their more radical demands, and acknowledge the *Quarterly* as the 'flagship' of their initially small beleaguered Conservative press flotilla.

THE FIRST BATTLES OF THE REFORM BILL

On 30 November Croker 'left the office and the house, in which I have spent the last twenty-two years ... with the kind of regret that one feels at hearing of the death of a very old acquaintance whom one was not very fond of'. They all felt much the same: 'we wished to get out', believing it 'safer for the country that we should go on a question of form (that is, of confidence), than on so vital a question of Reform'.[23] It was suggested to Croker that he could have had a place in the Whig ministry with some of the other Canningites, but he rejected the proposal as contrary to his beliefs on loyalty to and the importance of party:

> I am one of those who have always thought that party attachments and consistency are in the first class of a States-man's duties, because without them he must be incapable of performing any useful service to his country. I think more over that in part of our well understood tho' unwritten constitution that a party which aspires to govern this country ought to have within itself the means to fill all its offices, and I therefore disapprove of making a subscription Ministry to which everyman may belong without reference to understood principles or practices.[24]

He looked forward to spending more time on his historical studies and 'glad of a good excuse for retiring'. Although 'the loss of income will be an inconvenience ... My wife and girl [Nony, his adopted daughter] are happy that I am out of office, and are quite contented with the more economical course of life which we must adopt.'[25] But any respite would be largely forgotten that winter in the face of the growing unrest and agitation evocative of revolutionary France: 'I had hoped to have quitted public life with office, and so I should have done, but that this tremendous question of Reform called upon me as an honest man to offer whatever resistance I might to what I believe to be the overthrow of all the existing institutions.'[26]

The Reform bill proposals were being kept secret, with one of the Whigs' problems being, according to Croker, that their magnates wanted a minor measure, and their 'Ultras' an extensive one.[27] He evidently had a source leaking details of cabinet discussions, and Lord Grey wrote to William IV's secretary complaining that recent articles in *John Bull* 'could not have been obtained except from persons who had accurate information', and he suspected 'Mr Croker' had some part in it.[28] One insider was tipping off Lowther, who confirmed Grey's suspicions in a letter to Croker: 'I have just seen a friend, who was a guest at a large Whig or Ministry dinner. They did you the honour to fix upon you as the person who was likely to give them the most trouble and vexation – I have not heard from Hook, I shall call this afternoon.'[29]

On 11 January Croker sent Hertford the latest rumours. The Whigs proposed to enfranchise 'half a dozen great towns' and extend some of the franchise, to which he would 'have no objection at other times and in other circumstances', but now the 'question is not reform but in fact revolution'. In the face of threats and popular disturbances Croker was now opposed to any Reform concession, believing that like Emancipation it too had been made a 'panaceatic' empowering agitators.[30] At the end of January, most leading members of the party assembled at Wellington's country home to plan tactics for the new session, and Croker dramatically rejected any suggestion that they support 'Moderate Reform! = Moderate Gunpowder!'[31] Wellington shared his sentiments and was 'in very low spirits about politics', fearing that the 'King, from pique or fright or folly will consent to some sweeping measures of reform and when the crown joins the mob all hope is lost'.[32] Croker's concerns were exacerbated by Peel's failure to attend. As Ellenborough noted, when Wellington left the room Croker 'complained bitterly of Peel, and of his wish to remain alone and unconnected with others, of his selfishness etc. He exaggerated a good deal, but Peel does think chiefly of himself and has not the manner or the character to become a popular leader of a Party.'[33]

By 20 February Peel had become more actively involved with the others once more, and at a meeting at his house in Whitehall Gardens it was agreed that given public pressure on MPs, they let the bill appear and, as Croker argued, gradually win support from those 'not ready to shut the door in its face' but 'will concur to turn it out' at a later date and help in 'exhibiting the Government to be as weak as it really is'.[34] They saved the government from defeat on a West Indies bill, and Croker was pleased that 'all agree that the Government holds its seat at the mercy of Sir Robert Peel'. But 'until Reform is disposed of', and some proper plan for replacing them 'matured, or at least feasible, it would be madness to dislodge the present Ministry'. By the morning of 1 March when the bill was due to be introduced however, Croker was much less comfortable with this tactic: for 'when I see some of the steadiest old country gentlemen ratting over Reform, I am alarmed.'[35]

He had good reason to be; Lord John Russell astutely pulled the rug from under their plan by proposing a bill 'so far from being a half-measure I had anticipated', it was 'so extensive and so violent as to have astounded [even the Radicals] Hunt and Hume'. 'Every existing thing is changed,' Croker continued, 'every constituency, every right of voting throughout the whole Kingdom is altered, and a pretended system of uniformity and simplicity substituted.'[36] Some 168 seats were to be abolished; boroughs with less than 2,000 electors lose their two representatives, and those with less than 4,000, one seat. Twenty-seven new boroughs would be created, and although it would be decided upon a little later, a £10 franchise qualification would increase the electorate by an estimated half million. There was a huge uproar in the Commons, and rather than being the product of any great desire among the Whigs to extend the franchise, most scholars now see Russell's proposal as a political tactic. 'Reform was essentially a move in the party game', but 'the old system was fundamentally indefensible' and it could not 'have been postponed much longer without an explosion. The party that successfully invested in the movement for reform was bound to secure great dividends.'[37]

The crucial moment came when Russell finished speaking and expected Peel to respond immediately, then press for a vote and foil the plan. But 'Peel sat shaking with rage, aware no doubt that because of the government's unexpectedly aggressive attacks on the rotten boroughs he had been left with no alternative but to make up with the despised Ultras.' He decided not to speak until the third night, Boyd Hilton continues, whereas 'the shrewd Croker believed that if only Peel had divided the House as soon as Russell sat down, reform would have been scotched there and then.' By the time he did speak two days later, 'the argument had begun to slip away from the anti-reformers'[38] and as Russell later wrote in his memoirs, he was 'much pleased when he found that the leaders of the Opposition did not intend to dispute the introduction of the Bill'. The 'nine nights of debate' provided time 'to hold public meetings' and for constituents to communicate 'to their members the popular, and what turned out to be the almost universal opinion in favour of the proposed measures'.[39]

Peel would give an impressive speech on 3 March, describing Russell's bill as a reckless 'attempt to substitute ... a different constitution' and having 'raised the storm waves of the multitude ... when all prudent consideration ought to have forbidden it'. But it was largely rhetorical, and concentrated on defending the constitution, 'the most perfect in the World', and warning that 'the late revolution in France is coming to this country.'[40] The following day, Croker made a much more substantial challenge based upon detailed research into the bill's features in order to discredit both it and its authors to the House and the country via the parliamentary reporters as guilty of bias, incompetence and cynical opportunism.

Such an extensive measure was neither a necessary nor a safe response to popular concerns, he argued, and having researched the petitions sent to parliament in the last ten years, although most had been organised by the Whigs and their supporters as a 'political lever to move the previous Government from its place', few had in fact been for Reform. 'The first object of the petitioners is, generally, reduction of taxes, the second the suppression of tithes, and Reform occupies most frequently the third place in the prayers of the petitioners.'

> I find that in the year 1821, 19 petitions only were presented in favour of reform. In the year 1822 the number was reduced to twelve. In the year 1823 the number was 29. In the year 1824 there was no petition; in the year 1825, no petition; in the year, 1826, no petition; in the year 1827, no petition; in the year 1828, no petition; in the year 1929, no petition; and even in the session of 1830, only 14 petitions presented in favour of reform. Such then was the state of the public mind on this subject, up to that date.
>
> Then came the late dissolution of Parliament. The noble Lord [Grey] and his political friends ... looked about for a political lever to move the government of the day from its

place, and then from hustings and windows, and their
different places of canvass, they instigated the clamours of
the people in favour of reform ... 650 petitions have been
the result of that appeal ...[41]

The bill had been introduced 'under the name of restoration of
usurped rights', but it was 'a complete substitution of new modes and
principles in every part of our system'. Many poorer voters – freemen,
burgage tenants and scot and lot – would lose their rights, and 'one
single class of voter, the £10 or £15 householder', would gain a
disproportionate representation at the expense of the lower and upper
classes. He then turned to specific anomalies in the bill's proposals and
mocked any abstract or idealistic theories used to qualify them. As with
all such 'dry numerical details of that mass of figures that our tyro
legislator looks to for the seeds of a new social and political constitution', their innovations would undermine rather than improve. Wiser
statesmen, the 'Pitts and Foxes, Burkes and Cannings – who looked at
the constituent classes not merely numerically; who saw in the body of
people various interests, various localities, various pursuits and various
conditions of persons and property', had wisely rejected projections to
'model all the institutions of Empire by the four rules of arithmetic'.
They usually concealed less appealing ambitions, such as with the con-
ferral of 'the most indecent patronage on a small number of – I do not
say favoured – but certainly fortunate boroughs'. For example, the
town of Malton, along with Richmond and Thirsk would send four
members to parliament, whereas the industrial towns of Huddersfield,
Halifax and Wakefield, with three times the population, would send
one less. There appeared to be a calculated design to preserve Whig-
controlled boroughs and abolish Tory ones, and 'I warn the noble Lord
[Russell] that I am now making a charge against him of the gravest
description ... a charge of negligence and temerity – a charge of not
having duly, nor according to any principle of justice, considered the
great and momentous operation of the measure he has proposed.'[42]

Croker also drew attention to the Whig patronage appointments as
equally less representative of 'Old Corruption', and implicitly questioned
the competence of an old rival in print, Francis Jeffrey, the ex-editor of
the *Edinburgh Review*, recently appointed lord advocate after twenty-five
years' press service to the Foxite Whigs. Another new Whig MP, and the
Edinburgh Review's most talented young writer, Thomas Babbington
Macaulay, would provide a 'rational for ministers, who had a policy
but needed a philosophy'[43] by defining the bill as the 'march of

progress' and inevitable product of 'the struggle between the young energy of one class and the ancient privileges of another'.[44] Having challenged Whig pretensions at 'arithmetical' politics and history already, Croker pointedly referred to Macaulay's seat by its full title, 'Calne and the liberty of Bowood', Lord Lansdowne's palatial country home, implying that Macaulay had received a 'rotten' borough in order to perform the same service for the Whigs in parliament that he had in the press:

> There is a certain borough in the south of England which certainly never stood higher in this House than it does at this moment, in consequence of the able and eloquent speech made by its representative the other night. I mean the borough of Calne ... Well sir this borough of Calne contains 4,612 inhabitants [and when combined with] Tavistock, Knareborough and Bedford they contain altogether about 20,000 inhabitants, and those 20,000 inhabitants are allowed ... as I have already stated eight members to this house ... while Tynemouth and Brighthelmstone with each above 22,000 are to be put off with one [thereby] throwing such enormous, undivided and unbalanced patronage into the hands of half a dozen selected individuals.[45]

Croker's attention to detail and determination to discredit the motives of the Whigs would be the main tactics of what would effectively become the filibustering campaign he would lead against successive Reform bills over the next sixteen months. During this early (earliest?) example of a later Irish parliamentary speciality, he would come into conflict with Macaulay on a number of occasions, and according to William Thomas, his rival 'was a great hater, and his hatreds, far from being part of the hearty give and take of political life as his nephew [G.O. Trevelyan] claimed, were matured in private and often reflect the passionate vindictiveness of an introverted child'. Rather than accept Croker's criticisms as part of the cut and thrust of politics, Macaulay came away from these encounters nurturing a deep resentment, recording angrily in his diary: 'see whether I do not dust that varlet's jacket for him in the next number of the Blue and Yellow [the *Edinburgh Review*]. I detest him more than cold boiled veal.'[46] The first published expression of this came later that year in what John Cannon has recently described as his 'spiteful, petty and unfair' review of Croker's edition of Boswell's *Life of Johnson*.[47] Croker would respond twenty years later with an equally coruscating but much more scholarly review of Macaulay's *History of England* (1849). By which time, however, together with the more determined efforts of other literary and political enemies, Croker's reputation was well on the way to being subsumed well before Macaulay's nephew G.O. Trevelyan censored his correspondence to portray what Hugh Trevor-Roper called his 'almost pathological hatred' as 'a rational political and intellectual disapproval'.[48]

Of greater academic importance at this stage, Croker ended his first speech by appealing to the moderates on both sides by cautiously suggesting that the Tory leaders acknowledged their past errors, arguing that the threat to order, property and constitution was too high a price to pay for any past failings. Although he would not at this stage publicly concede any need for parliamentary reform, he would tentatively imply that government should be sensitive to popular concerns by arguing that the Commons must be a calming institution and able to deliberate on reform free from duress, 'however popular clamour may be excited ...Government could not exist if it were otherwise, and all history attests to the fact.'[49] In this first speech he basically defined what would be the main features of his party's campaign, and Wellington wrote to him: 'I read the report of your speech in the newspapers; and I read it again last night with great satisfaction. It is a most able view of the plan of Reform.'[50] Lord Melville recorded that it was not only 'the best one of the Reform Bill, but the only very good one that was uttered'.[51] These would be the first of many public and private compliments he would receive over the following months, with Brougham later noting in his memoirs: 'Croker was the most important person in opposition. Nothing could exceed his ability and his thorough knowledge of the subject ... Althorp's knowledge of the Reform Bill and Croker's were the two wonders of the day; but Croker debated far better.'[52]

On 23 March the bill just passed its second reading by 302 to 301, and in anticipation of defeat pro-Reformers organised mass demonstrations, burnt effigies of Reform opponents and sent a tide of petitions to parliament supporting the bill. Croker became increasingly fearful that although they may win the arguments in the Commons, influences out of doors were being 'resolved into one – Terror', making many members increasingly fearful of rejecting the bill.[53] He could understand the demagoguery of the likes of 'Hume, Hunt and O'Connell', who are 'nothing without the populace', but 'cannot express to you the indignation at seeing the destinies of this great empire become the playthings' of ultra-Whigs such as 'yellow Lambton and Johnny Russell'.[54] On 10 April his doctor confined him to bed, but he wrote encouraging Peel to rally the most effective opposition possible; and in this letter he made an astute prediction on the significance of these events on the development of two-party politics. 'This was a crucial time' for both the constitution and Peel's future political career, for 'two parties are now being generated which never will die – you never could be more than the tail of one; you are, I hope, destined to be the victorious and, as to fame, the immortal head of the other.'[55]

Aware that they would probably lose the final vote that April, the Whigs sent Brougham to convince the king to dissolve parliament and appeal to the country with an election.[56] Croker was even more alarmed at what he saw as a flagrant attempt to risk revolution by raising 'the mob' to intimidate parliament. 'We had here tonight such scenes as I, in 26 years of political life, never [saw] before' and with the predictable public agitation and violence that would follow, 'not one man in England will venture to gainsay the principle of some Reform.'[57] During the elections that followed many candidates were subjected to intense popular pressure and intimidation. There were riots in London and other cities, rural arson and machine breaking were renewed, Wellington had the windows of his London house completely smashed, forcing his servants to defend themselves with blunderbusses, and the catch-cry of 'the Bill, the whole Bill and nothing but the Bill', reputedly the invention of Brougham for *The Times*, became the chant of crowds nationally.[58] Of the eighty contested English county constituencies, the Whigs took all bar five; even Lowther's family seats in Cumberland were swept aside, and as he wrote to Croker, 'no-one would have believed the degree of opposition had the election not put it to the test.'[59] Despite having been pro-Reform, one ultra-Tory arrived in his constituency of Liverpool and within minutes 'his face, his hair and his clothes were covered in gobs of spittle ... not from a mob of the lowest sort, but from men his own equals.' Only 187 'Conservatives' and Tories won a seat in England and Wales; many of which were for uncontested constituencies marked for abolition by the Reform bill.[60] Whatever merits there may have been in Croker's earlier arguments that parliamentary reform had been a 'panaceatic', or as recently argued, 'attributable to bad government and that bad government the result of the unreformed House of Commons', it was now an indisputably popular national issue.[61]

In a long assessment of the 'Progress of Misgovernment' Croker would write for the *Quarterly* at the end of that first year, he argued that, rather than being moved by any great desire for Reform, the Whigs risked the destruction of the state when they found 'the ground slipping from under them'. An early concession might have been justifiable, and 'in an ordinary case, may sometimes save the dignity of a government, but since society first existed it never was the means of preventing a fresh demand' and the constitution was 'too dear a price to pay for even the short-lived gratification of personal malice, party revenge and long hopeless ambitions'.[62] In this article, published at the height of the Reform contest, Croker would promote the 'Conservative party' as firm defenders of the constitution, but that good government should reform proven abuses when public peace prevailed.

> It has never been denied by any person professing to belong to the Conservative party, and certainly not by us, that on this, as on all other subjects of moment, public opinion (by which we mean the prevailing opinion of persons competent to form sound judgment on such matters) must, in the present state of society, sooner or later overcome all obstacles that may be set against it. And it has been justly described as one of the most important branches of the conservative duties of the Peers, to take care that due time be afforded in all cases for the opinion being deliberately formed and clearly ascertained ... at least until it should have been put beyond all doubt, that such is really the well considered and deliberate opinion ... to take care, in brief, that under the pretext of yielding to public opinion the nation be not sacrificed to public clamour.[63]

As will become evident, essentially the same arguments, albeit tentatively at first, would be made within some other *Quarterly* articles during 1831, and Croker would continue to do so up until the summer of 1832, and more explicitly after the Reform Act was passed.

After their dramatic election defeats of May 1831 Croker was acutely aware that if any plan to win support for the Conservatives and represent the ministry as dangerously irresponsible was to succeed, then their arguments would have to be communicated to the public. However, by the spring of 1831 even the *Courier*, the moderate Tory mainstay, had abandoned them for the Whigs when the proprietor 'shamelessly ... offered Grey as obsequious support as he had given to Wellington' and even handed the Whigs 'all the correspondence he had received from Tory administrations'.[64] The ministerial and pro-Reform press would remain overwhelmingly dominant, with *The Times* at the forefront, having first acquired its nickname as the 'Thunderer' calling on 'the people everywhere to come forward and petition and thunder for Reform'.[65]

Herries complained that he failed to interest Peel on the subject of the press,[66] but a committee was formed to address the problem and belatedly accepted Croker's advice by including three former cabinet ministers: Arbuthnot, Herries and Ellenborough. A list of the newspapers was compiled with comments alongside their titles: In 'politics' the *Courier* was a 'prostitute'; the *Morning Herald* and *Times* 'hostile'; the *Morning Chronicle* 'extremely hostile'; the *Sun* 'moderately hostile'; the *Age* 'hostile to ins and outs', with only the *Morning Post* and the *Albion* 'conservative' and the now repentant *John Bull* rated as 'exemplary'.[67] Ellenborough and Herries would 'assist the *Morning Post* and *Star*'; Croker was 'to secure a morning and evening newspaper and *John Bull*', and given that William Blackwood had just written to him saying he would be 'gratified should you be tempted at any time ... to send me communications on anything', probably *Blackwood's* as well.[68] Like all the papers of the press circle, *Blackwood's* had remained pro-Reform, arguing that 'to say that Reform must necessarily be revolutionary ... is not only groundless but ridiculous.'[69] However, it qualified support for reform on the Burkeian grounds that 'we must have no change on principle', but in order to 'repair dilapidations, defects and remove abuses' have a Commons where 'each interest and class must be duly represented'.[70] It had little affection for the Whig ministry; its message to 'Tory opponents of Reform' was that they 'have the deepest interest in reform ... we strongly urge you for your own sake to change'.[71] The *Standard* and the *Monthly Magazine* took roughly the same line, with *Fraser's* remaining the most belligerent supporter of the Whig ministry in anticipation of extensive practical social and economic as well as parliamentary reform.

Apart from his work with *John Bull* and the *Quarterly*, Croker left most of the press management to the others, remaining the '*èminence grise*' and letting them consult him on issues such as their attempt to get the *Morning Post*, a daily paper edited by the Dubliner Nicholas Byrne, to report their Commons speeches in greater detail. The *Post* had a substantial circulation, and Byrne was sympathetic yet cautious of losing readers for the 'prospect of making his paper a more political one'.[72] Indicative of their problems with even their few press supporters, Lowther reported to Croker that he tried to get him to report the debates 'more fully and that a larger sheet should be launched and that we should have a superintending editor', but he would only agree to 'insert anything we will give him … a scrambling way of going on, but there is nothing else to be done'.[73] Ellenborough tried to raise funds for their campaign, and praised the work of 'Theodore Hook who is very active indeed',[74] but 'a sign of the times that none of our old literary Tory supporters will risk any of their capital in a morning newspaper', and even some leaders 'run away directly a subscription is proposed'.[75] Croker knew any process of improvement would be a slow one, and that furthermore they would have to be cautious whose support they enlisted. The ultra-Protestant Duke of Newcastle, having described Croker as a 'wretched intriguer and political jackal' for supporting Canning three years before, introduced himself in a letter by praising his role in the Commons and seeking advice on establishing a daily newspaper. He was thanked for his compliments, but Croker said he would never again have any 'connexion with a newspaper' and advised him against establishing one. 'A good and zealous morning newspaper would be a great advantage no doubt, but no paper can be made effective by mere patronage, or even money' if it did not have 'in the country at large friends and supporters sufficiently zealous and numerous'.[76]

Croker would concentrate his own efforts in the *Quarterly Review*, and although he certainly retained his 'connexion' with the newspapers, his main contribution would be in presenting principles and arguments in the *Quarterly* for their friends and supporters nationally and in the press. The first complete review we can be entirely confident he wrote was a historical one in January 1831, appropriately entitled 'Military Events of the French Revolution',[77] but he was clearly advising on others at this time. The following month he returned the rough draft of a political article to Murray, describing it as 'admirable', although it was 'somewhat like vanity to say so because the view the author takes is that which I have taken, and if I had read the sheets before you left them yesterday, I should, to arrest any future charge of plagiarism, have shown you on paper my own opinions'.[78]

This was almost certainly 'Reform in Parliament' published in the April number of the *Quarterly*, and it was perhaps more than just a coincidental 'plagiarism' of his own views. As Maginn remarked conspiratorially when reviewing it in *Fraser's*: it was composed by 'Fullarton' but almost certainly 'touched up by a superior hand'.[79] The article examined the history of Whig support for Reform and discrepancies contained in their bill, as 'brought to the notice of the House of Commons by Mr Croker', with the ministers portrayed as not having considered Reform of any greater importance than most Tories until it offered them the chance to gain and retain public office.[80] They had no more claim to be reformers than many of the Tories; in fact the recent Reform issue had 'been first sounded from a quarter from where it was least apprehended – from a small band of High Tories ... deeply offended' by the Catholic Relief Act, and in 'response to the reluctance, perhaps somewhat indiscreetly manifested by Ministers, to submit to the distresses of the country'. It was an injustice to depict Wellington and Peel 'as hard hearted unfeeling theorists' because it had been too dangerous to accede any measure; for a 'revolutionary flame thus kindled, thus spread, as was to be expected, in all directions'. 'Burnings and machine breakings began to spread in Kent – a clamour was got up in London ... and a most alarming agitation set on foot in Ireland for the repeal of the Union.'[81] It would have been a dangerous error to dignify excitements 'of so ephemeral a character – generated, or at least fomented by, such violent and extraneous causes with the name of public opinion'.[82] Much of this may have been 'spin' designed to portray Wellington and Peel as willing to address popular concerns, but more importantly, there is the distinct suggestion that if public peace was restored any ministry they managed would be no more hostile to corrective reform than the Whigs.

Croker would finally take full responsibility for the *Quarterly*'s political policy and content after the major defeats of the election that spring.[83] Murray was delighted, and Lockhart wrote a magnanimous letter accepting the diminution of his own role as editor. 'It is a great comfort to me to hear you mean to render regular assistance in the Q.R. Your hand will be the salvation of the review.'[84] In the next number of the *Quarterly*, Croker made the same case for his party being sympathetic to corrective reform within an article entitled 'Friendly advice to some Lords on the Reform Bill' responding to the promotion of the ministerial case organised by Brougham for the *Edinburgh Review*. 'Why Reform at this time?', Croker asked, for the Whigs had presented no plausible reason 'other than the vociferations of the mob'. Russell argued that it was intended 'to restore our constitution to some former state of purity' and 'with elaborate absurdity' placed the foundations of the bill in the days of the 'Henries and Edwards', whereas his rationalist ally, Francis Jeffrey, 'laughed at such antiquarian nonsense' and described Reform as 'made in the "spirit of the Times"' and commensurate with

the 'experience of America and France'.[85] Both theories were 'egre-
giously facile', for as William Shakespeare, the 'greatest observer of
human nature, warns us of the uncertain and disputable value of opinion: "A plague on opinion I may wear it on both sides like a leather
jerkin".' Producers of political blueprints are 'fond of repeating that all
Governments have been the patrons of abuses and are the enemies of
improvement', but they ignore 'one important political truth':

> *Governments* were originally constituted for the express
> purpose of preventing and resisting change – it is essential
> that they should have a strong tenacity to things as they are
> – that while on the one hand, such resistance and tenacity
> should not be so obstinate as to neglect manifest public
> expediency, or to disregard matured and undisputed
> public opinion, they should, on the other, be strong enough
> to restrain *sudden and epidemic violence* – to afford the
> public time either to recover from *delusion*, if delusion
> there be, or to ascertain and consolidate the wishes and
> opinions of the majority in the cases where there may be a
> rational desire and real necessity for alteration.
>
> The proper action of Government may be assimilated to
> that of the pendulum of a clock. It should check and regu-
> late the action of the great popular weight, which, without
> the constant, but elastic – the gentle, yet steady resistance
> of such a regulator, would hurry the works into a whirl of
> unchecked motion, dislocating the parts, and ultimately
> destroying the machine. A Ministry, which like that of Lord
> Grey, not only removes the pendulum, but adds weight to
> the already unbalanced preponderance of the moving
> power and grossly *miscalculates* the *theoretical*, and fatally
> *misapplies the practical power* of GOVERNMENT.[86]

The evolved constitution must be defended against '*sudden and epi-
demic*' demands; good government should have a 'tenacity to things as
they are'; yet not so as to not 'disregard matured and undisputed public
opinion' if society and the state were to remain functionally healthy.
These are Burkeian arguments for a political philosophy of custom, and
essentially the same Croker had made in his early writing and in trying
to convince his political leaders to take the lead with Reform before it
reached a crisis, as well as in his Commons speech of 1819 seconding
Grattan's Emancipation bill. Although they only made up a small part

of this July 1831 article, they are a fairly clear statement that a Conservative ministry would not ignore appeals for reform where, as he said, 'there may be a rational desire and real necessity for alteration'. Furthermore, given that this article was in response to the ministry's case made in the *Edinburgh*, and as knowledge of Croker's control over the *Quarterly*'s politics became widespread, it is not unreasonable to assume that they would be seen as the principles of what by that time was increasingly being described as the 'Conservative party'.

By the early summer most of his old press circle were beginning to express disappointment with the ministry. The earliest shared sign of this was their hostility to the commission then discussing a proposed New Poor Law. The January number of the *Quarterly* had supported Michael Sadler's radical proposals for extensive social reforms and denounced Nassau Senior, the Whig Poor Law theorist and his allies, predicting that their anticipated reports would justify the starvation of the poor so as not to disturb 'the superfluity of the rich'. That February, in an article entitled 'Poor Law for Ireland', it called for compassionate Poor Laws and that landlords and middlemen be forced to fund poor relief and facilitate employment to improve the state of Ireland rather than exporting the 'mass' of food 'for want of which her own population are dying by inches'.[87] As we have seen, the *Standard* had supported the Whig ministry in the hope it would create a unitary and reforming 'country party', but it denounced Nassau Senior as a 'humbug' and a 'quack'; a product of that 'effete' school of economics advocating the 'sacrifice of human life and human happiness to the accumulation of capital'.[88] The following month in defence of Sadler's appeal for extensive publicly funded poor relief in both kingdoms, *Blackwood's* described the commissioners as the 'worst of bigots and fanatics' and praised the 'enlightened Christian philosopher' who had written 'in *Quarterly Review*' and the 'great editors of the *Standard*'.[89] Many of the same arguments appeared in *John Bull*, and as Miriam Thrall argued in her neglected study of *Fraser's*, from its first number Maginn 'declared an early war on Malthusian theory and remained the most vehement defender of' the 'common people steeped in wretchedness to the very lips' and the 'white slaves' of the manufacturers.[90]

Maginn would be the most reluctant to return to the fold, and in April he vilified Peel and others who had turned Liverpool's cabinet into a 'sort of bear garden'. But this was largely because their 'paltry paradoxes in commerce founded on political economy were enforced with the solid perseverance of a community of hairdressers commissioned to overturn the Newtonian philosophy'. Their 'matchless folly' and 'revolting injustice, opened the eyes of the common people' and together with the 'Popish concession bill ... broke the chains that bound [what] had always been the conservative party'.[91] Maginn welcomed the Reform bill as 'a magnificent measure, a bold, a fearless and just invasion of the strong-holds of corruption'; but he was becoming noticeably worried that 'the manufacturing and mercantile interests have been obtaining an ascendancy over the landowners and the cultivators of the soil'.[92] Concern for the poor, the state of Ireland, and what may be collectively described as 'protectionism' would be, as Anna Gambles has argued in her study of Conservative economic discourse, the 'crucial component in the electoral and intellectual revival of the party'.[93] And by the late summer of 1831, all of Croker's old pressmen would have lost most hope that the Reform ministry would address their ambitions and concerns.

In that same number, Maginn abused Croker in a satirical account of his clash with the *Edinburgh*'s Francis Jeffrey, but it would be one of his last attacks on his old patron and Jeffrey got a little more lash. So dull and ineffectual had been the 'thin and petty gurgling' of the Scotsman's oratory that it was only stilled by his 'feeble incapacity' to stand any longer:

> It was very proper that Croker should have answered him: The Flower of Auld Reekie and the Poddle [a polluted Dublin stream] are fit antagonists for one another. Hack *Quarterly* versus hack *Edinburgh* are fairly matched ... The first was all *feelosophy*, he dealt in *abstark* principles; the Irishman, who never pretended to any acquaintance with principles, bothered about blots in the detail [and] upon the enormity of Malton, only having five inhabitants above 4,000, having two Members ... Do like a good fellow and an honest man, and clever argumenter, drop the dirty [Admiralty] pension – do the decent thing ... there's a good fellow.[94]

Some of this was almost certainly the product of personal rather than political resentment. In 1825 Maginn had asked Croker to get him an official post on the Commission for Publishing State Papers, and Croker praised his talents to Peel 'as one of the cleverest men I ever knew in my life'. He was a 'fellow of extraordinary talent ... and acquirements in all the branches of literature and a very powerful writer', but given his unpredictability and 'ill-mannered' behaviour 'I think it right to keep him at arm's length.'[95]

This was a fair judgement, for apart from his heavy drinking and public roistering, Maginn anarchically ridiculed almost every successful literary and political figure, declaring that public office ruined the character of even the best of men. Swift and Michael Sadler were among the few spared, and anyone who detracted 'from the intellectual merits of Burke' deserved to be called 'a blockhead of the first class', but as 'his friend Goldsmith' had said, he wasted much of 'what was meant for mankind' on behalf of parliamentary pay and party.[96] Maginn's talents certainly lay outside formal politics, and *Fraser's* style of lampoonery and wit together with his intelligent if frequently abusive literary reviews and political commentary meant it rapidly won a circulation of nearly 10,000. This meant an actual readership in clubs, reading rooms and coffee houses of probably ten times that figure, making *Fraser's* at times more popular than any magazine in its class during much of the 1830s.[97] It remains almost entirely neglected by scholars, however, presumably because of its ridicule of many celebrated theorists and writers as well as its denunciations of 'Popery', despite having been 'conspicuous among the magazines' in its early publication of 'unsparing records and sufferings and degradation ... setting forth the shocking cruelties perpetuated upon workers and injustices accorded to criminals'. This view of Miriam Thrall's perhaps neglects the other publications of the press circle and some Radicals, but *Fraser's* was certainly at the forefront of the campaign to represent the suffering of the poor in harrowing dramatic articles before the famous efforts of the likes of Dickens, who acknowledged Maginn's contribution and talents by inviting him to write the first editorial of his *Bentley's Miscellany* in 1836.[98]

The *Standard* would be the first to declare its disappointment with the bill. Describing it that March as 'not Reform, but *revolution*, nothing in the whole constitution of the House of Commons is to be left untouched'. It also predicted that, if defeated, the Whigs would stimulate a 'treasonable insurrection in their favour' and 'by dissolving Parliament they would gain the advantage of a House of Commons elected under the influence of terror.' Giffard's hopes for unitary reform had been shattered by a 'Jacobin Revolution Bill' designed to empower 'the very dregs of the class of householders', the middle classes and manufacturers, leading to the 'dissolution of the ordinary obligations of Society'.[99] Peel would make a similar point to Croker a few weeks later, writing that the 'fatal error' of the bill would be as 'Orator Hunt' had described, the empowerment of the '£10 householder class … the vulgar *Pedlary*', thereby antagonising the Radical reformers and uniting 'the aristocracy and the disenfranchised population'.[100]

As the *Standard* moved closer to the Conservatives, it would not drop its demands for reforms, but further alarmed by the April election coup, Giffard appealed to his Tory readers to heal their differences, and even praised his old champion Peel as 'the hope and head of the Conservative party who stood by the constitution'.[101] *Blackwood's*, while remaining a 'friend to reform' as a means 'to repair dilapidation, defect and remove abuse', also quoted from the *Quarterly's* April article on Reform, suggesting that it was the work of Croker, and praised his 'admirable speech in which he tore that of the Lord Advocate to rags'.[102] It had always been a 'Friend of the People' and 'advocated its vital interests', but now 'the Whig party' was 'attempting to intimidate a House of Commons' and 'strike a fatal blow against the constitution'.[103]

By May Maginn was concerned that nobody 'apprehends any harm from a smirking and smiling Whig philosopher' like Russell, yet 'who can persuade us that a grim and bloody Jacobin is not whetting his knife in the rear'.[104] He had supported the ministry because it had been elevated on 'the pledge to maintain *peace*; … the pledge to enforce *retrenchment*; and thirdly, the pledge to introduce a *moderate* measure of reform' when the tables of parliament had 'literally groaned with the weight of petitions of the people complaining of distress':

> They came from the agricultural labourer reduced to rags and pauperism – from the fathers and brothers of those whom long suffering and despair had driven to crime and spoliation, to rioting, pillaging and burning. They came from the slaving artisan; from the thousands of weavers, whose utmost exertions could not earn more than five shillings per week; from miners and spinners whom the currency bill of Sir Robert Peel had reduced to live like slaves upon truck … from every description of labourers and operatives, and from retailers and middle classes generally, [that] it had pleased the Wellington ministry to turn a deaf ear and treat with the utmost arrogance and disdain …

But had the Whig ministers attempted 'to relieve those sufferings which they, while in opposition only a few moons previously, had so hypocritically deplored? Not they – honest, consistent, patriotic statesmen!' Parliament 'should be reformed – in fact reform is not only necessary, but unavoidable.' However, 'this particular measure of reform is, at the best, but a party measure, a cabinet test, an impotent but dangerous *coup d'état* ... to sustain in power a declining power of an incapable administration.'[105]

In the previous number he made one of his last attacks on 'Croker, who now so pathetically laments over the measures of the Whig ministers' for having 'helped forward reform in all its branches, while he only fancied he was striking a blow at Protestant bigotry'. For Maginn 'Reform is continually needful and a free government exists in no small degree to make it. Abuse and defect, like weeds, spring spontaneously, and thrive from neglect ... There may sometimes be destruction in reform, but without it there can be no conservation: those who wish to preserve must at least repair.'[106] These are the same Burkeian arguments Croker would have made, and despite still retaining his resentment over Emancipation, Maginn could also argue with much justice in May that it was now clear to everybody that 'nothing can be more true than the peace of Ireland and the integrity of the empire are in the hands of whatever factious demagogue the priesthood of that happy island support.'[107] While he would never be an uncritical ally, Maginn's disappointment with the ministry's failure to address practical reforms, and as importantly, his concern for the state of Ireland and fear for the future of the Irish Anglican Church and community would eventually make him and many others the keenest advocates of building a strong and united new Conservative party.

THE SECOND DRAFT OF THE REFORM BILL AND ORGANISING THE NEW PARTY

Prior to the new session Peel wrote to Croker complaining about the more radical and reformist elements among the 'Conservatives':

> I apprehend that there are two parties among those who call themselves Conservatives – one which views the state of the country with great alarm ... which is ready to support monarchy, property and public faith [and the other] by far the most numerous, which has the most presumptious confidence in its own fitness for administering public affairs ... which sees great advantage in a [fiscal] deficit of

many millions and thinks the imposition of a property tax on
Ireland and the aristocracy a Conservative measure ....
Now to this later section I do not, and will not, belong ... A
Radical and Republican avowed are dangerous characters;
but there is nothing half so dangerous as the man who
pretends to be a Conservative ...[108]

By mid-summer the press circle were foremost among the most
'Radical' but far from 'Republican' reformers calling themselves
Conservatives, and although Peel may have been unhappy with their
activities, they would play a much more active part than him in
campaigning for and attempting to unite its 'two parties' into a single
successful one.

In June 1831 Henry Goulburn tried to convince him to support the
plans for Conservatives and ultra-Tories to meet and organise shared
tactics, but the suggestion was 'subjected to withering ridicule',[109] and
it was perhaps sufficient that Peel 'supplied an executive ethic around
which others ... might assemble a party structure. Temperament, outlook and doctrinal belief isolated the un-clubbable Peel from such
activity.'[110] As Robert Stewart has argued, despite the 'misleading
emphasis which has been placed on Peel's contribution to the Conservative recovery after 1832 – briefly that he united a new party behind
the reformist policy – the original impulse to organise the party came
from other men.'[111] At Croker's suggestion a party planning committee
met regularly at the Athenauem (the now famous club he had founded
with Sir Humphry Davy in 1824),[112] and plans were put in place to establish a party headquarters at Planta's old house in Charles Street
where Conservative MPs could meet and tactics could be planned and
supervised.[113] In early May 1831 a proposal was made to purchase the
Standard. The money was never raised, but by the time parliament
reassembled there was little need to; for by then the harshest critic of
Canning, and then Wellington and Peel, had become the Conservatives'
most important daily newspaper. [114]

Joseph Planta wrote to Croker before the Reform debates that July,
saying Peel had returned to London and 'requests a meeting of us 4
officials at his house, he is in high health and very good force'.[115] Given
the extent of their election defeat, Croker knew that there was little
chance of defeating the bill, but argued that it should still be vigorously
opposed as part of their tactic to use the Commons as an arena to
improve their public image and discredit the ministers.[116] This policy of
fighting the bill at every step has been ascribed to Peel, normally by

quoting from a letter he wrote in February 1832. 'Why have we been struggling against the Reform Bill? ... Not in the hope of resisting its final success in that House, but because we look beyond the bill' and we 'want to make the *"descensus"* as *"difficilis"* as we can'.[117]

But Croker's records suggest that Peel was not initially committed to this policy, and that he organised it some months before Peel's *'descensus'* letter. On 8 July 1831, four days before the new Reform bill debates, he wrote to Peel saying that he disagreed with his proposal to challenge only its major sections, and argued instead that

> ... at every great step of this affair [the government] should be brought to a division no matter what the result. We cannot be worse than we are but we owe it to the Lords and posterity to mark every stage of rational opposition by a division. We are not to attend bowing and complimenting the robbers, and helping then to pack their booty ...[118]

This is very similar to language Peel would later use, and Croker concluded with what appears to have been more of a directive than a request: 'pray arrange something of this sort and settle also and moreover in what way we had better try our strength on the disfranchisement clause.' Ellenborough corroborated Croker's account in his diary on 23 July 1831:

> Met the Duke, Peel and others at dinner at Croker's. The Duke and Peel seem very low about publick [sic] affairs. Peel thinks they would have done better in the Commons to have made the discussions shorter and taken only the great points. It was Croker who got up the debates about the several places disfranchised.[119]

The week before this he recorded that Peel sat out the greatest part of the debate and then 'went away without speaking or voting'. He 'has made the party very indignant, it disheartens and disgusts', and 'Peel certainly has none of the qualities which are required in the leader of a party, although he has most of those which make an admirable Secretary of State.'[120] The backbencher Charles Forbes made similar complaints, and Ellenborough wrote to Henry Hardinge 'begging him, if he could, to get Peel to say something to tranquilise the party'. Hardinge did so, and Wellington acknowledged the problem, but responded that little could be done and that 'the party could neither do with him, nor without him'.[121]

Peel would warm to the contest once again, and his leading part in the campaign should not be understated; yet despite occasional absences due to illness, Croker made at least ninety-one speeches and interventions during the Reform debates between 26 July and 13 August, followed by Peel's seventy-seven.[122] Croker would challenge every feature of the bill he could that summer, and these tactics, as Michael Brock argues, 'brought the opposition onto far better debating ground. They demanded to know how the reformed House would improve on the unreformed one in composition and the policies it would adopt. This question naturally embarrassed the Government and they did not give a convincing reply.'[123]

In describing Croker's role, James Grant, a young press reporter, wrote that 'few constitutions could have stood the amount of physical labour, while the several clauses of schedules "A" and "B" were being discussed, for some weeks he spoke every consecutive evening against particular clauses of the Reform Bill, upwards on an average of three hours.'[124] Representative of this was an intervention on 12 July, when, according to *Hansard's*, his attempt to speak was again met with 'loud expressions of impatience' and theatrical groans in anticipation of what would be a long detailed challenge. Croker's Irish 'brogue' and the way he pronounced the letter 'r' were mocked, and when the clamour subsided he commented that 'personal observations' were 'one mode of shortening the debate', and another 'was that the Ministers did not or would not answer' because they were unable to respond to the 'powerful arguments' of its critics.[125] He then moved on to outline another series of 'glaring deficiencies', such as Stockport, with a population of 44,000, designated to receive just one member, while Malton with an estimated population of 4,005 would retain two. The ministry's figures, he continued, had been compiled either ineptly or with a marked prejudice in favour of the Whigs, but if the 'noble Lord' Althorp, the Whig leader of the Commons, would provide the House with an explanation, he 'would not press the amendment'.[126]

Althorp was well thought of on both sides of the House. Appealingly amiable, often dishevelled with detailed notes sticking from his pockets, he was closely familiar with his brief, but a poor speaker, and according to Brougham he had 'muzzled his party colleagues on finding that they, being unacquainted with the details, were perpetually getting him into scrapes', leaving 'Croker watching the sight of the Whig officials unable to explain their own bill.'[127] Given the large ministerial majority, Althorp was under little pressure to win support, and in one famous incident he responded to a 'most able and argumentative speech of Croker', 'that he had made some calculations which he considered as entirely conclusive in refutation'. Unfortunately, he 'had mislaid them, so that he could only say that if the House would be guided by his advice they would reject the amendment'. He still won a substantial majority, and as Hardinge concluded wryly in his account, 'there was no standing against such influence as this.'[128]

While Croker's interventions may have achieved little short-term success, he was consistently presenting arguments via the press to the public and, or so he hoped, denigrating the architects of the bill as inept and dangerously irresponsible in contrast to the dedicated conservers of the constitution. While it is difficult to accurately assess his influence, as a number of historians have argued, the parliamentary debates were keenly followed, and 'public opinion in the crisis' was the 'factor perhaps above all others, to which the ministers constantly referred, and not merely in their public utterances'.[129] No other political event was more keenly followed out of doors, and it would infuse 'elections with a new sense of principle and the electorate responded with a new degree of inter-election partisan loyalty'.[130]

The bill's chief architect and its most earnest promoter, Lord John Russell, later recalled that 'while Sir Robert Peel was the most eminent both in weight of argument and oratorical ability of opponents of the Bill, Mr Croker, by his profusion of words, by his warmth of declaration, and his elaborate working out of details was perhaps a still more formidable adversary.' He tempered this by saying that Croker's 'own statements of details were singularly inaccurate', and even when 'he was not mistaken, his exaggeration of its importance was repulsive to the House of Commons'.[131] The latter may have been true, but it is clear from the amendments the Whigs were obliged to make that many of his details were accurate, and although his interventions were clearly 'repulsive' to his rivals, as many party supporters like Lord Elgin believed, he was providing them with a 'standard to rally around' and 'from no speeches during the progress of the Reform Bill ... has more satisfaction been felt by those who are well-wishers to their country and the Constitution than from yours'.[132] In an unrecorded Common's interjection, even Daniel O'Connell complimented him and averted to their early Irish connections, with Croker responding with equal amity: 'I was anxious to have stated last night how much I was personally gratified by your allusion to our previous acquaintance and your expression ... of your early feelings towards me, but you saw I could not obtain a hearing and I am therefore obliged to content myself for the present by talking to you in this way.'[133]

By this time the *Standard* was paying him increasingly lavish compliments. 'Though the numbers were all on one side the reasoning was on the other, Mr Croker's speech ... was the best of the night.' Was there ever 'an example of Greek, Roman or English eloquence' delivered with 'more neatness and dexterity'; even *The Times* 'reported the cheers and laughter Mr Croker received ... he has drawn to him the hope of all who love their country.'[134] That June *Fraser's* argued that parliamentary reform was 'indispensable' in order to correct 'the abuses of the system', but ridiculed 'squealing whigling' Macaulay and the 'metaphysical intertwistings' of Whig theorists[135] as well as the popular 'mania' to support 'not a moderate measure', but what could be the 'most sweeping measure of revolution'.[136] In September Maginn also dedicated a page of praise to Croker (save for one barb identifying him with *John Bull*) and claimed him as a compatriot:

> There is not a cleverer fellow in the dominions of King William the Fourth ... The same spirit which gave causticity to the *Familiar Epistles*, ... assailed the Whigs and Whiggery in the satiric articles, grave and gay, of the *New Whig Guide*, *John Bull*, the *Quarterly Review*, and fifty other vehicles of minor renown ... Ireland boasts the birth of Mr Croker he is a Galway man ... In Parliament he is assuming his station, from which he has too long suffered himself to be shouldered by plausible mediocrity, [who were] supported by hypocritical candour, and the low underling tactics of St Stephens and Whitehall ... We start him for Secretary of State in the next ministry.[137]

One of the most eagerly awaited serials of the period was a *Blackwood's* feature entitled *Noctes Ambrosianae* [Nights at Ambrose's Tavern]. It took the form of a conversation between a number of politically minded and literary inclined drinking friends, most of whom were members of an extended gathering of the press circle. Largely the contrivance of Maginn some twelve years earlier, he played the character 'Sir Morgan O'Doherty'; F.S. Mahony was 'Fr Prout'; John Wilson was 'Christopher North'; Lockhart, 'Pierce Pungent'; Thomas Crofton Croker, 'Ensign Cornelius O'Donoghue'; and W.M. Thackeray and a number of others wrote under silly pseudonyms such as 'Timothy Tickler':

Tickler: Even Pitt had his Fox to grapple with, and Canning had his Brougham; but now there's no competition – not even the semblance of rivalry. Neither need I be talking about Croker to *you* – you well know that nothing but his position in the government, and yet *out* of Cabinet, could have prevented him from being the best speaker of his time, ere this time of day ... The effect was such that after ten minutes, the Whigs could not *bear it*. They trooped out file after file, black grim scowling, grinding their teeth, in sheer imbecile desperation.

North: I have heard Croker in days past, and can easily conceive what he must be now that the fetters of office no longer cramp him ... What a blasted disgrace to the party that they kept him out of the cabinet, and set over his head, among others, so many, comparatively speaking, sheer blockheads – some of whom moreover have deserted us.[138]

Croker may never have been in cabinet, but he appears to have been organising his parliamentary party. In September Hardinge wrote to Peel asking him to join a group planning tactics: 'A meeting will take place at Charles Street tomorrow – Croker has engaged the D. of Wellington to attend for the purpose of ascertaining the most convenient day for the bill going up to the Lords.'[139] They decided not to delay the vote on the bill any longer, and Baring 'threw out the advantage of Peel's saying something as if he was not opposed to all Reform – this he resolutely refused for he did not see his way – and he would pledge himself to nothing which he did not see and understand.'[140] On 22 September the bill passed in the Commons by 345 votes to 236, but the Lords rejected it. Pro-Reform newspapers were published with black-fringed borders; huge demonstrations were held in industrial centres; riots erupted in Bristol, Derby, Nottingham and other large towns; public buildings were ransacked and destroyed,[141] and the startled ministers suspended parliament until they could introduce another bill in December.[142]

The Whigs and Radicals blamed 'the anti-Reform Junta' in parliament,[143] and fears of revolution rose when political unions called for a National Guard to 'protect property', workmen's groups for a 'Popular Guard' to protect them from the former,[144] and *The Times*, having deprecated the adoption of 'Conservative' by the opposition, helped disseminate the term and concept of 'conservatives' as moderate reformers and defenders of property by calling for a 'Conservative Guard' to protect the 'whole mass of householders'.[145] On 1 November, under the facetious title 'The first year of Liberty', Croker wrote to Peel indicating that he had regained some influence with another old press ally. It was 'indispensable, that the *Courier* of tonight should give some account of our position ... I am willing to be the scribe, but you and the Duke must tell me what to say as to our position.'[146] Peel, however, understandably concerned for the safety of his home and family in the industrial Midlands, had hurried back to Drayton, and replied that 'it seems to me that counter-associations for the purpose of defence must be formed ... the only safety is in preparation for the defence.'[147] Croker shared his fears, but emphatically rejected this. 'When it becomes a matter of association, it is a mere affair of numbers, and eventually of physical force.' Their only option was to remain calm:

> I see no field for any exertion on our part but Parliament
> – our speeches there, as long as they permit us to speak,
> may have some effect and may perhaps bring round a few,
> and at last more and more of the country gentlemen and of
> the country ... Things of this kind, but even wilder and
> more absurd, happened in France from 1789 to 1793.[148]

Like *The Times*, many moderate reformers were frightened by the revolutionary implications of the disturbances, and a week later Croker sent Peel some more positive, if exaggerated news: 'In all the clubs – in the stage coaches – and in all such accidental meetings, I am told it is rare to meet a Reformer.'[149]

That November in another long *Quarterly* article, Croker described the violent disturbances as 'the predictable response to the call the government has made' by raising the 'mob' and the ministers were now being 'overtaken rather earlier than expected by their Frankenstein Monster'. He then argued that it was clear that the 'public were, on the Reform Bill, divided into three great classes of opinion'. Two of them took strong opposing views, leaving the majority of moderates in the middle. On the one extreme were 'the ultra-whigs, the dissenters, the republicans, and all that party which derives its origins from the reign of Charles 1, and on which every occasion that has since successively offered has shown itself hostile to the monarchical and ecclesiastical parts of the constitution'. On the other were the ardent 'Anti-Reformers', and although he treated them considerably more gently than the former, his own sympathies were with the third 'class of opinion', the 'moderate reformers':

The moderate reformers are composed of many subdivisions. As a body, they are friends to the existing constitution ... All were favourable to the enfranchisement of a few great towns; but some were also inclined to disfranchise some nomination boroughs, and the process by which it was to be operated. Though none of these would have originally supported anything like the revolutionary principles of the bill ...

At this stage of the contest he could hardly propose there was much merit in the Whig bill, but he argued that many of its opponents, though reluctant to enter into 'a *system* of change', would have been 'most anxious for representation of the great towns' in the past.[150] Once again this was a veiled acknowledgment of the need for government to address corrective reform combined with an appeal to moderate reformers; or those he would describe in the next number as 'conservative' Whigs when appealing for them to join with their natural allies the 'Conservatives' and resist the 'ultras'.

When the new session opened in early December he was pleased to be able to write to Hertford that it 'seems quite certain that there is a split in the Cabinet between the moderates and the Radicals'.[151] Four days later he had another confrontation with Macaulay, who had argued that the opposition's resistance to the Reform bill had stimulated the violent riots. The 'history of England' was one of government giving way, 'sometimes peaceably, sometimes after a violent struggle', but 'the great march of society proceeds, and must proceed'. Croker reacted predictably, and this clash was given some additional piquancy because Macaulay had just reviewed his edition of *Boswell's Johnson* in the *Edinburgh*, and as he told his sister, 'beaten' him 'black and blue': 'Croker was smashed.'[152] Although increasingly exhausted by his efforts, Croker was far from smashed, and once again he ridiculed his rival's interpretations. 'Had the learned gentleman', who 'scanned with the eye of a philosopher the probable progress of future events ... seen the termination of the course?' 'Not at all!' yet they 'were all to throw open the gates with safety, exposing their property to plunder and their persons to massacre'. The Whigs were neither heralds of progress nor the leaders of Reform, but puppets 'pressed forward by those who were behind with a dire and irresistible force'. Let the anarchy 'in Bristol speak for itself; let Derby, let Coventry, let Nottingham'.[153]

Macaulay had also argued that all great parliamentarians had been elected in contested constituencies, permitting Croker to mock him again, for as all who know the 'political history of their country' are aware, the greatest political figures had, in fact, entered parliament in the same manner that he had. 'Indeed the greatest of them all', Edmund Burke, had first gained public fame as the member of a nomination borough.[154] Burke had also made his name through the press, and Croker lightened his tone to parody parvenus who used this path; mocking himself, of course, but also Macaulay, Brougham and Jeffrey who aspired to greater respectability by embellishing their ambitions with appealing theoretical qualifications. 'There was a lawyer – bold, voluble, slippery, enterprising, universal, at everything in the ring. He spoke at the bar – he harangued in the House – wrote pamphlets – wrote in the Reviews – wrote in the newspapers.' Here, *Hansard's* records, 'there was considerable interruption from the Ministerial benches.' Croker responded that 'there might be those who despised reviews and newspapers', but he would rather be a 'writer honestly giving forth his sentiments to the people ... than be one of those who were incapable of composing their own election address'; and to 'loud and repeated cheers', that he would rather be a poor speaker than 'one of the mutes of despotic Government who could do nothing but to strangle a discussion of which their masters were afraid'. [155]

He followed this with the rhetorical ploy of returning to a serious topic by describing an incident in a melodramatic style he would have mocked in a review, whereby a respectable mother and daughter had been driven from their home by a mob and clung to each other in wet fields in terror till rescued the next day. The mother later died, and he reminded the members that these and recent violent disturbances had occurred in Revolutionary France, and 'the enormous mischief of democratic anarchy of the most unbridled kind' was at its most dangerous 'when it was asserted that reason had made such progress, and information and liberal opinions were so prevalent'.[156] Lord Edward Stanley, the Irish chief secretary, also raised cheers by answering Croker with a good speech, producing the response from Daniel O'Connell that his 'attempt to reply to Croker was at least daring', but 'he was rushing to his own destruction for as Croker had Burked Jeffrey and Bishoped Macaulay he would apply a tar plaster to the mouth of the Irish Secretary at the first opportunity.'[157] Croker thanked him again, but remarked to Hertford that 'O'Connell is such a Jesuit that there is no trusting him even when he promises mischief', and his compliment was probably because at 'the moment Stanley is the chief object of his attack'.[158] Croker's earlier allusion about 'a split in the Cabinet between the Moderates and the Radicals'[159] was a reference to a growing conflict on Irish issues between Stanley and the 'ultra Whigs'. One that would deepen over the next two years, eventually causing him and his 'conservative' Whig allies to resign and create the circumstances for Peel to take office.

Peel spoke after Stanley, commenting that there was little need 'to offer any additional observations, after the unanswerable and matchless speech of his right hon. friend (Mr Croker) beside him',[160] but, taunted that he might have a change of heart on Reform as on the Catholic question, Peel angrily responded that this was the fourth occasion Macaulay had 'returned bursting with all the sweltering venom which had been collecting during the days and nights that had passed since the last attack'.[161] He had long remained 'silent under these charges', and frankly told the members that he had not supported Emancipation under any illusion that 'it would produce satisfaction and harmony', but because there had been 'a certain and impending evil, which could only be averted by incurring the remoter hazards of concession'.[162] Although he was not 'opposed to well considered reform', in a statement that would have significant consequences in the next session he then declared that unlike the Catholic Relief Act, he would never support the Reform bill:

> I will continue my opposition to the last, believing, as I do, that this is the first step, not directly to revolution, but to a series of changes which will affect the property and totally change the character of the mixed constitution of this country. I will oppose it to the last ... I take my stand, not opposed to a well-considered reform of any of our institutions which need reform, but opposed to this reform in our constitution because it tends to root up the feelings of reverence and attachment, which are the only sure foundations of Government.[163]

Early that morning two weeks before Christmas, the bill passed its second reading by 324 votes to 162, and Croker wrote to Hertford, 'in its details it is a great triumph for me and our party ... for there is not one of my points on which we divided in the committee which is not conceded'.[164] The Pyrrhic irony being that these 'alterations blind many foolish people to the deformity of the principle'.[165] Next year, however, 'if our party can only be united' and 'show some fortitude and talent, we may still make a formidable appearance' and 'the moderates will be a great party ... I almost doubt whether we should despair of defeating it once again.'[166]

The bill passed its third reading by 355 votes to 239 on 23 March 1832 – seventy-eight more against than before – and together with 'moderate' Reformers on the Whig benches that Croker hoped would be future allies, it represented a growing pool of potential support. On 14 April it passed its second reading in the Lords, but only with the backing of a number of Tory/Conservative 'Waverers', and when Croker dined 'at the Duchess of Kent's with a large Conservative party' three days later, nobody believed it would succeed unless the king created 'a large batch of peers'.[167] Ellenborough consulted Croker on tactics for the Upper House in early April,[168] and then forwarded his 'most valuable brief' to Wellington.[169] This appears to have been a plan to facilitate the final passage of the bill with a plan of amendments designed to serve the post-Reform advantage of the Conservatives. On 24 April Wellington wrote to Croker: 'I have seen Lord Lyndhurst. He is very anxious to have some conversation with you. He is turning his mind to an alteration of the Reform Bill. Will you settle a time to see him?'[170]

Following this meeting Croker created what was, effectively, an alternative Conservative Reform bill. He sent a copy of it to Peel, explaining that although he still believed that 'democracy will be strengthened' and ultimately 'overthrow the constitution', he 'thought it was of great importance to get these gentlemen into the right way'. He would not make Peel 'any aspect a party to or responsible for my proceedings'; his wish was 'simply to have the benefit of your advice'.[171] Peel approved of 'the general principles of your letter. I see nothing left now that the House of Lords has approved of the Reform Bill, but a strenuous concerted effort … to mitigate the evil of it'; yet it would be better as 'the result of amendment to the present Bill [rather] than of a new scheme of Reform, proposed by Anti-Reformers'.[172]

Probably because he wanted to prepare party supporters and undermine support for the ministry, Croker suggested that he should write and publish a pamphlet outlining his proposals. Wellington firmly rejected the idea, saying that he was willing 'to try to improve the Bill in my sense', but would do so while publicly 'protesting against it and intending to vote against it upon the third reading'. He insisted that nobody 'connected with the late Government in particular, or connected with the Conservative party' should publicly declare their support for the plan because the 'whole world is ready to throw upon us the entire responsibility for what is going on; perverting every fact, and inventing lies of all descriptions to prove that we are the cause of the mischief'.[173] Ellenborough agreed, and wrote to Croker suggesting that for the final draft 'it might be both popular and safe to propose the substitution of a scot-and-lot franchise with three or two years' residency in the same town' by way of compensation for the raising of the franchise qualification above £10. 'I feel satisfied that if you exclude the lower class from direct representation we shall have a civil war and universal representation.'[174]

Further plans were delayed when Rosamund became seriously ill and Croker cancelled his meetings to remain with her at Molesey. Wellington wrote to him on 1 May, and once again it is worth quoting most of the letter because it not only illustrates Croker's status, but the degree of political intrigue they were all involved in:

> My Dear Croker,
> I will wait here till four this afternoon in case you should come to town. [If] you should come tomorrow morning, let it be by nine o'clock, and apprise me this day of your intentions in order that I may have Lord Lyndhurst and Lord Ellenborough here.
>
> I doubt our being able to go as far as you propose in the matter of franchises and large towns, however we can talk over the details hereafter ... We are very awkwardly situated in relation to the Waverers. They are the object of detestation and jealousy to our friends and supporters. They are with great reason ... our communications must be very guarded, and we must keep to ourselves anything of which it is desirable that our opponents should not have the knowledge ...
>
> I think the proper time for publishing the work will come. It is but fair and proper to you that it should be published. But I am convinced that it would be a very false step to publish at the present moment ... I wish just to refer you to the advantages derived by our opponents on the same subject by the secrecy in which they involved their measure [the Reform bill of March 1831] until the last moment at which it was opened in Parliament ... if we had known what the measure would be, we should have opposed it; and the Opposition would have been successful.[175]

Ellenborough sent Grey their alternative Reform plan containing proposals for the disfranchisement of small boroughs; the distribution of 113 seats to large towns and populous counties; a reduction in the number of boroughs to be abolished; clauses to exclude borough property from the county vote and to modify the £10 suffrage and retain the 'Scot-and-Lot' voters. Although at first not entirely hostile, Grey later became 'incensed by the Waverers' perfidy' in double dealing and 'categorically dismissed these proposals'.[176] According to Croker, he then asked the king to make 'fifty new peers ... the King offered the compromise of twenty, and the Ministers resigned.'[177]

Wellington and Peel were summoned to form a ministry on the grounds they would pass an 'extensive measure' of parliamentary reform.[178] Wellington agreed, because, he said, nothing would prevent him from doing his duty to the king and helping him 'shake off the trammels of his tyrannical Ministers'.[179] Croker, Lyndhurst and Peel visited Wellington to plan their tactics, and Lyndhurst proposed Peel should be prime minister. He responded 'that he could not, and would not, have anything to do with the settlement of the Reform question'. It should be settled now on the basis, as he understood, of the present bill, but he 'was peculiarly circumstanced – he had been obliged to arrange the Catholic question by a sacrifice of his own judgment, and he would not now perform the same painful abandonment of opinion on the Reform question'. Croker agreed with Peel, and suggested Lord Harrowby as a more 'natural person to undertake the Government on such a basis ... I walked away with Peel and he suggested the Speaker [Manners-Sutton] as Premier.'[180]

That same evening Croker returned to the Commons and when Ebrington moved a vote of confidence on the Whig Reform measures, he was impressed that although a similar vote had received a majority of 131 in October, on this occasion 'we made a good division, 219 to 288,' and the 'announcement of the numbers was received with cheers on both sides'. Later that night, on 'reconsidering the state of affairs' he changed his mind, believing that this offered proof of a good opportunity to mitigate the worst of the bill as well as rebuild their support, and if 'the Whigs were allowed to return triumphant over the King's scruples the revolution might be looked upon as consummated.'[181] He wrote to Peel urging him to lead the government and outlining the personal failings that might deter him. 'The more I think of the situation of affairs the less satisfied I am with the line which you seem inclined to adopt ... I think your feeling a little obscures your judgment.' 'Despite your personal position in reference to the unhappy Catholic question ... I still think it may be your positive duty as a man of honour to take office.'[182] The 'real consistency would be that you did all that was possible to avert the danger', rather than rigidly adhering to principles:

A man easily finds, or rather fancies, colourable reasons for not doing what he has a mind to [but] if the King and the Constitution sink under your eyes, without your having jumped in to attempt to save them your prudence and consistency will be called by less flattering titles in that black-edged page of history ...

Honour! Character! Yes the greatest, the only moral treasures of our nature; but they must be allied to courage and self-devotion! What but disgrace can result to the whole party, if after having committed the House of Lords and encouraged the King, to this violent rupture they are to be abandoned, and thrown upon the tender mercies of their exasperated enemies? If the Whigs are allowed to get back without a struggle on the part of the Tories, and you personally, *en dernier resort*, depend upon it, instead of honour and character; we shall have only degradation and contempt. We shall be despised as fellows who had not the courage to take advantage of the events they had prepared and to which they had instigated others ...

It is easy enough to say: 'I will have nothing to do with it!' but you must have something to do with it, for your refusal is a very important and responsible something. This requires no answer, only your serious thoughts, I shall see you tomorrow.[183]

The next day Croker called upon Wellington and told him he had 'written to urge Peel' and was now en-route to entreat him to lead the government. Wellington said to tell him 'he was ready to serve with him or under him' and then put Croker in an uncomfortable predicament. 'I am particularly pleased with the advice you give Peel, because it leads me to believe that you mean to act on the same principle yourself and to help me in this great emergency.' Croker replied that he had informed Wellington in 1830, both 'verbally and in writing', that he would never again hold government office. He had no personal political ambitions and 'nothing but my own personal character to hold by, and I would leave him to judge what would be thought of me if after the part I had taken I should be found supporting "schedule A", and accepting high office and salary as the price of that support'. Furthermore, given the extent of his role in the Commons and his well-known activities with the press, he would do the 'cause more harm than good; whereas out of office and independent, I should be at liberty to adapt

myself to the new circumstances of the case and my opinions might
have some weight in the House and in the country'. Wellington
'acquiesced in what I said', although 'rather, I thought, more readily
than I expected, but still with an air of pique and disappointment'.[184]

Croker met Peel later that day, and he told Croker that for him
'individually to take the conduct of such a bill – to assume the responsibility of the consequences which I have predicted as the inevitable
result of such a bill – would be in my opinion personal degradation to
myself'.[185] He quoted from a letter he had just prepared to send Croker
and a section of a published speech he had made to his Tamworth constituents, 'one of a hundred declarations to the same effect made by me',
firmly opposing Reform. He believed they should look 'beyond the exi-
gency and the peril of the present moment without diminishing the extent
of the danger, and I do believe that one of the greatest calamities that
could befall the country would be the utter want of confidence in the declarations of public men'.[186] Wellington tried to form a ministry, but few
others would commit without Peel, and after a few angry attempts he conceded defeat. On 17 May Croker wrote dejectedly to Hertford that he
now saw no better chance 'for [the] peace of the country than that those
who had raised the storm, should be allowed to direct it'.[187]

The opportunity of managing the Reform crisis with what Croker
had believed would become an increasingly stronger government col-
lapsed into what Norman Gash describes as a 'comedy'. Peel had 'saved
Wellington from an immense blunder [that] would have meant not only
failure but ignominy'.[188] This is a reasonable assessment, but would it
have been an immense blunder? It may well have strengthened the Conservative cause, and many of Peel's colleagues did not see his decision
in such a positive light. He was seen as passing 'sentence of death upon'
their May Ministry, 'it was remembered against him', and Wellington's
resentment soured relations between them for the next two years.[189]
Ellenborough did not accept Peel's 'reasons as creditable … He is afraid
of being again taunted with inconsistency and so he exposes the country
to peril' and the Whig Brougham wrote later that although it would
have been a 'very difficult task' for Peel and Wellington to have managed the country for the first few weeks, 'I have always considered that
it would have had a fair chance of success.' There would have been 'no
small number of men in the House of Commons disposed to join a
strong Government' and 'by degrees, the Reform fever, as it was called,
would have been allayed … The real obstacle was Peel, who would not
undertake the Commons.'[190]

Peel might well have made the best decision, but Gash's remark that Croker, although 'adamant against taking office himself in a reform ministry thought with peculiar illogic that Peel should',[191] perhaps fails to see that there was some justice in Croker's arguments. Unlike Peel, he had long vowed to resign, never held cabinet office, and given his leadership in the battle against Reform and his reputation for intriguing with the press, he probably could have better served them out of office rather than provide the Whigs with more ammunition to attack their ministry. Ellenborough accepted that Croker's 'reasons for not taking office ... were personal and had been known to the Duke and others long ago' and that 'he could be of more use to us out of office than in'.[192] Furthermore, with regards to managing the country, as Croker argued, many moderates, both in and out of doors, had clearly become more favourable to the Conservatives, and there was little reason to believe they would insist that an 'extensive measure of Reform' had to be carried by a Whig government. As recent scholarship has argued, the influence of popular agitation during the 'days of May' was greatly exaggerated by polemicists in the Whig and Radical press and successive historians who have paid too much attention to their arguments and too little to the wider evidence.[193] *The Times*, for example, may have continued to thunder denunciations of Wellington and demand the Whigs be reinstated, but it was unable to report any 'Great Meeting' in London until one in Blackheath on 22 May, and although it clearly attempted to puff the attendance: 'estimated by some at 15, by others at 20, and by others from 20 to 30,000', even the unlikely higher figure would hardly have been 'Great' enough to threaten revolution.[194]

The Whigs returned to office, and Wellington organised the passage of the Reform bill in a House of Lords almost empty of Conservative and Tory lords. On 7 June the Great Reform Act received the royal assent, and as Michael Turner argues, 'passing a measure of Parliamentary reform was an important success' for the Whigs, and 'they needed it, for on foreign policy and finance they had been seriously embarrassed.' The popular clamour dissipated and 'respectable opinion was satisfied with the settlement. Property remained essential to the political influence. The middle classes were brought behind the established order and the forces of radicalism frustrated. There was no democracy, no revolution.'[195]

Professor Gash concludes that 'Peel had been obliged to thread a narrow path between alternating dangers; to oppose reform without opposing in principle ... The reform crisis left him more unpopular and more estranged from his party than he had been in November 1830.' There was, however, a 'substantial consolation. He had come through the crisis with his character un-compromised, and his future policy un-committed.'[196] However, the last sentence also begs the question: if Peel was not committed to defining a 'future policy' for national supporters, who was? Lockhart knew that somebody had to address the *Quarterly*'s readers' concerns by producing principles, policies and arguments for what they saw as their party; and like all of the press circle, he did not believe their leaders were doing it. Two weeks after the Reform Act was finally passed, he wrote to Croker:

> There is an essential difference of views between those who have long breathed the atmosphere of St Stephens – still more Downing Street – and the Tory mass throughout the country. For the last we must have bold words, or they will not be pleased with us or do their duty to the real approaching crises of Reform, i.e. the elections ... They do not consider the battle to have been fought bravely in Parliament after all. They consider Peel with suspicion, and too many who have fancied themselves leaders, with utter contempt.[197]

In the election that winter, the opposition suffered the substantial defeat Croker had feared. They may have anyway, but perhaps if Peel had been willing 'to take advantage of events', 'Dish the Whigs' on Reform, and firmly acknowledge policies such as those later contained in the *Tamworth Manifesto*, and already introduced to the Conservative supporters through their press, they would have won over the moderate reformers in 1832 rather than 1835, and perhaps even won a Commons majority before 1841.

NOTES

1. Clements MS, Lb. 25, 1, 22 and 30 November 1830, ff.62–9.
2. Ibid., and see 77–8, part cited in *Croker Papers*, 30 November 1830, II, pp.77–80.
3. *Quarterly Review*, 'Internal Policy', January 1830, pp.276–7.
4. Ibid., October 1828, p.557.
5. Clements MS (Lockhart–Croker correspondence), 26 May 1845, III, ff.39–42. See also I, Lockhart to Croker, 3 September 1831: ' I rely on your kind assistance to keep the *Quarterly* in the right [political] tune', f.46.
6. Brightfield, *John Wilson Croker*, p.403.
7. W.E. Broughton (ed.), *The Wellesley Index to Victorian Periodicals*, 5 vols (Toronto, 1965–74), vol. I, p.709; and see Brightfield, *John Wilson Croker*, p.403.
8. Robert Blake, *The Conservative Party from Peel to Major* (London, 1998), p.6. See also Sack, *Jacobite to Conservative*, pp.5–6. Sack believes Miller to have been the author and cites the *Journal of Thomas Moore*, III, p.1287. William Thomas, *Quarrel of Macaulay and Croker*,

p.105: that the *Quarterly* was 'without any political guide until Croker was brought in', during the summer of 1831.

9. Clements MS, Lb. 21 contains a letter from Croker responding to one from Murray concluding: 'P.S. I shall look over those proofs again', dated 1 January 1828, f.2. Some other items referring to Murray at this time are to be found in Clements MS, Lb. 21, Croker to Charles Knight, 18 April 1828, f.284 and Croker to Murray, 7 May 1828, ff.330–1, and 22 May 1828, f.22.

10. *Wellesley Index*, pp.707, 709 and 712. The reference to proofs is cited above, and probably refers to the March 1828 article.

11. National Library of Scotland, MS 4027, Lockhart to Blackwood, 30 January 1830, f.268. I am indebted to James Sack for this citation. See also J. Keen, E. Screider and I. Griggs, 'Lockhart to Croker on the *Quarterly*', *PMLA*, 60, 1 (March 1945), pp.175–98. As early as March 1826, after the *Representative* conflict, Lockhart was discussing some review with Croker; probably on architecture, see p.177. With regard to Fullarton there is a letter from Lockhart to Croker, December 1831: 'I still hope that when Fullarton has forwarded his paper you may have the goodness to look at it in the slips', p.179.

12. Hill Shine and Helen Chadwick Shine, *The Quarterly Under Gifford* (Chapel Hill, 1949), p.xviii and see also pp.iv–xx.

13. Ibid., pp.vii–xx.

14. See Roy Benjamin Clark, *William Gifford: Tory Satirist and Editor* (New York, 1948), pp.177–81 and Smiles, *John Murray*, II, pp.45–8.

15. See, Keen, Schreider and Griggs, 'Lockhart to Croker', p.177–9.

16. Clements MS (Lockhart–Croker correspondence), I, 19 December 1831, f.55. The article was on the history of the House of Commons.

17. *Wellesley Index*, pp.704–5.

18. Edmund Burke, *Reflections on the Revolution in France*, ed. Conor Cruise O'Brien (London, 1968 [Penguin edn]), p.106.

19. Sack, *Jacobite to Conservative*, pp.4–5.

20. Ibid., p.67, and the reference Professor Sack uses is taken from the *Anti-Jacobin Review*, September 1805.

21. *Quarterly Review*, 'Friendly Advice to the Lords', July 1831, note p.518.

22. White, *The Conservative Tradition*, pp.10–11.

23. Clements MS, Lb. 25, 30 November 1830, ff.62–9 and 77–8, and part cited in *Croker Papers*, 30 November 1830, II, pp.77–80.

24. Ibid., 21 November 1830, letter to anonymous recipient, f.56.

25. *Croker Papers*, Croker to Doyle, 22 November 1830, II, p.78.

26. Clements MS, Lb 25, Croker to O'Donoghue, 27 December 1831, f.191.

27. Ibid., Croker to Hertford, ff.131–4.

28. Henry, Earl Grey (ed.), *Correspondence with William IV and Sir Herbert Taylor* (London, 1867); Grey to Taylor, 14 January 1831, I, pp.58–9.

29. Clements MS, box 12, Lowther to Croker, 4 January 1831.

30. Ibid., Lb 25, Croker to Hertford, January 1831, f.145.

31. Ibid., Croker to Lowther, 26 January, f.182, and part cited in *Croker Papers*, II, p.105.

32. *Croker Papers*, 28 January 1831, II, p.104.

33. 'Ellenborough Diary', 28 January 1831, in Aspinall, *Three Diaries*, p.43.

34. Carlisle MS, D. Lons. L1/2/116, Croker to Lowther, February 1831, *Croker Papers*, 21 February to Lord Hertford, II, p.108.

35. Clements MS, Lb. 25, Croker to Hertford, 1 March 1831, ff.234–5; *Croker Papers*, II, p.109.

36. Ibid., ff.238–43.

37. Blake, *The Conservative Party from Peel to Major*, p.16. See also Brock, *Reform Act*, pp.148–52; Ian Newbould, *Whiggery and Reform: 1830–41* (London, 1990), pp.314–16: that there was little idealism in the Whig motives; Michael Turner, *Age of Unease*, examines some other interpretations, pp.218–21.

38. Hilton, *A Mad, Bad and Dangerous People*, p.425.

39. Russell, *Recollections and Suggestions*, p.73.

40. *Hansard*, 3 March 1831, II, cols 1334–56.

41. Ibid., 4 March 1831, III, cols 84 –96, part reprinted in *Croker Papers*, II, pp.94–5. For Jeffrey's relationship with Whigs see John Clive, *The Scotch Reviewers* and Henry Cockburn, *The Life and Times of Lord Jeffrey with a Selection of his Correspondence* (London, 1852), pp.104–5.

42. Ibid., cols 84–96.
43. Hilton, *A Mad, Bad and Dangerous People*, pp.432–3. For a more extensive study of Macaulay's politics and influences on the Whigs and 'whiggery' see Joseph Hamburger, *Macaulay and the Whig Tradition* (Chicago, 1976), *passim*, and Thomas, *The Quarrel of Macaulay and Croker*.
44. *Hansard*, 2 March 1831, II, cols 1204–5.
45. Ibid., III, 4 March 1831, cols 95–105.
46. Thomas, *Quarrel of Macaulay and Croker*, pp. 1–31, 158 and *passim*.
47. Cannon, *Samuel Johnson*, p.1.
48. Hugh Trevor Roper, *New York Review of Books*, XXII, 16 (16 October 1975), p.30.
49. *Hansard*, III, 4 March 1931, col. 107.
50. *Croker Papers*, II, p.111.
51. Duke MS, box 3, 16 March 1831.
52. Brougham, *Life and Times*, III, p.498.
53. Clements MS, Lb 25, Croker to Hertford, 15 March 1831, ff.259–62.
54. Ibid., 5 and 12 April 1831, ff.330 and 353.
55. Add. MSS 40320, Croker to Peel, 10 April 1831, ff.175–6, and Clements MS, Lb. 25, f.345.
56. Brougham, *Life and Times*, III, p.115.
57. Clements MS, Lb. 25, Croker to Hertford, 22 April 1831, f.383. See also Brock, *Reform Act*, pp.188–92 for an account of events.
58. Stewart, *Brougham*, p.266.
59. Clements MS, box 13, Lowther to Croker, 8 May 1831.
60. Turner, *Age of Unease*, p.232; Brian Hill, *Early Parties and Politics in Britain* (Basingstoke, 1996), p.193; Brock, *Reform Act*, p.198, see also pp.196–9; Robert Stewart, *The Foundations of the Conservative Party: 1830–1867* (London, 1978), pp.77–80.
61. Stewart, *Foundations*, pp.79–82.
62. *Quarterly Review*, 'Progress of Misgovernment', January 1832, pp.602–3.
63. Ibid., pp.603–6.
64. Aspinall, 'Social Status of Journalists', p.221.
65. Bob Clarke, *Grub Street to Fleet Street*, p.227.
66. Aspinall, *Politics and the Press*, Arbuthnot MS, 29 January 1831, cited p.334.
67. Add. MSS 57404 (Herries Manuscripts), Herries to J. McTaggart, 26 December 1830, ff. 5–7.
68. 'Ellenborough Diary', in Aspinall, *Three Diaries*, p.23 and Aspinall, *Politics and the Press*, p.329. See also Clements MS, box 12, file for January 1831, loose uncatalogued letters, 4 and 12 January 1831, from Lowther to Croker referring to Hook and their cause; Brightfield, *Croker*, p.201 citing a *Blackwood's* MS, NLS, 25 November 1830.
69. *Blackwood's*, 'Reform', February 1831, pp.235–8.
70. Ibid., p.238.
71. Ibid., pp.247–8.
72. Stephen Koss, *The Rise and Fall of the Political Press in Britain* (London, 1981), p.42. After a long career in the press, the unfortunate Byrne was murdered in 1833, see pp.41–2.
73. Clements MS, box 12, 20 February 1831. See also Lowther to Croker, boxes 12 and 13, 1831–3 for numerous other items of their correspondence.
74. 'Ellenborough Diary', 16 April 1831; Aspinall, *Three Diaries*, p.79.
75. Aspinall, *Politics and Press*, p.334; see also Stewart, *Foundations*, pp.75–7.
76. Clements MS, Lb. 26, Croker to Newcastle, 1 January 1832, ff.201–3.
77. Ibid., Lb. 25, 21 January 1831, ff.167–8.
78. Ibid., 9 February 1831, f.199.
79. *Fraser's*, May 1831, p.531. See also Lockhart's letter to Croker asking him to read it when 'Fulllarton has finished … in its slips', Keen, Schreider and Griggs, 'Lockhart to Croker', p.179.
80. *Quarterly Review*, 'Reform in Parliament', April 1831, pp.279–83.
81. Ibid., April 1831, pp.279–83.
82. Ibid., pp.283–6.
83. See Thomas, *Quarrel of Macaulay and Croker*, pp.104–5.
84. Brightfield, *Croker*, citing a Lockhart MS, NLS, p.403.
85. *Quarterly Review*, 'Friendly Advice to the Lords', July 1831, pp.505–6.
86. Ibid., pp.507–8.

87. *Quarterly Review* [mainly written by George Poulett-Scrope], 'The Political Economists', January 1831, pp.1–52; 'Poor Law for Ireland', February 1831, pp.511–54; 'Malthus and Sadler', April 1831, pp.97–145; 'The Archbishop of Dublin on Political Economy', November 1831, pp.46–54, and for the specific quotations: 'Senior's *Letter on the Irish Poor*', January 1832, pp.391–410.
88. *Standard*, 4 January 1831; see also Sack, *Jacobite to Conservative*, p.182.
89. *Blackwood's*, 'Mr Sadler and the Edinburgh Reviewers', February 1831, pp.393–4 and 428.
90. *Fraser's*, 'Mr Sadler and the *Edinburgh Review*', March 1831, pp.209–21; and Thrall, *Rebellious Fraser's*, pp.129–45.
91. *Fraser's*, 'Parliamentary Reform', April 1831, pp.269–75.
92. Ibid., pp.274–80.
93. Gambles, *Protection and Politics*, p.57.
94. Ibid., 'To *Petrus Maximus* on the Ejectment of Jeffrey', April 1831, pp.391–2.
95. Add. MSS 40319, Croker to Peel, 30 June 1825, f.152.
96. *Fraser's*, 'The *Quarterly Review* on Reform', May 1831, p.528.
97. Thrall, *Rebellious Fraser's*, p.14.
98. Ibid., pp.133 and 187.
99. *Standard*, 2 and 3 March 1831.
100. *Croker Papers*, 15 April 1831, II, p.114.
101. *Standard*, 22 and 23 April 1831.
102. See *Blackwood's*, 'Reform', February 1831, pp.235–8 and 247; 'A Word from the Wise Old Christopher', May 1831, p.726 and for a fuller representation of *Blackwood's* 'conservative' arguments see the rest of the February article, written by David Robinson, pp.235–54.
103. Ibid., May, pp.726–31.
104. *Fraser's*, 'The *Quarterly Review* on Reform', May 1831, p.532.
105. Ibid., 'The Dissolution of Parliament', pp.512, 515 and 518.
106. Thrall, *Rebellious Fraser's*, p.155, citing *Fraser's*, 1833, IX, pp.314 and 370.
107. *Fraser's*, May 1831, 'The *Quarterly Review* on Reform', pp.529–31. See also June 1831, p.638.
108. *Croker Papers*, Peel to Croker, 28 May 1831, II, pp.116–17. The letter Peel referred to is missing.
109. Jenkins, *Goulburn*, p.229; see also pp.244–9.
110. Angus Hawkins, 'Parliamentary Government and Victorian Political Parties, c.1830–c.1888', *English Historical Review*, vol. CIV (1989), p.652.
111. Stewart, *Foundations of the Conservative Party*, p.71. In this instance Stewart is criticising Donald Southgate's *Conservative Leadership*, p.2. Norman Gash remains the most famous modern proponent of Peel's central role; see 'The Founder of Modern Conservatism', in *Pillars of Government* (London, 1986), pp.153–6; Douglas Hurd, *Robert Peel: A Biography* (London, 2007). For some more critical assessments: Duncan Watts, *Tories, Conservatives and Unionists: 1815–1914* (London, 1994), p.93; Hilton, 'Peel: A Reappraisal'; Ian Newbould, 'Peel: A Study in Failure'.
112. See John Thomson, *Armchair Athenians* (London, 2003), pp.6–9 and *passim*.
113. Aspinall, *Politics and the Press*, p.336; and Stewart, *Foundations*, p.72.
114. Ibid., p.330, citing a Lonsdale MS, 7 May 1831.
115. Duke MS, folder for 1831, Planta to Croker, 5 and 11 June 1831.
116. Parker, *Peel Correspondence*, II, 5 June 1831, p.187.
117. For Peel's letter see Parker, *Peel Correspondence*, II, pp.99–122; also part cited in Gash, *Sir Robert Peel*, pp.38–9. For similar arguments see Stewart, *Foundations*, p.61.
118. Clements MS, Lb. 26, Croker to Peel, 8 July 1831, f.32.
119. 'Ellenborough Diaries', 23 July 1831, in Aspinall, *Three Diaries*, p.109.
120. Ibid., 12 July 1831, p.103.
121. Aspinall, *Three Diaries*, note, p.103.
122. See *Hansard*, as per index references for Croker in vols. IV and V for June to December session 1831.
123. Brock, *Reform Act*, pp.204–5.
124. Grant, *Recollections and Suggestions*, p.96.
125. *Hansard*, 12 July 1831, IV, col. 1130.

126. Ibid., cols 1227–36, for both Croker's full speech and Althorp's response.
127. Brougham, *Life and Times*, III, p.498.
128. See Brock, *Reform Act*, pp.220–1 and Le Marchant, *Life of Althorp*, p.400.
129. Cannon, *Parliamentary Reform*, p.245.
130. John A. Phillips and Charles Wetherall, 'The Great Reform Act and the Political Modernization of England', *The American Historical Review*, 100, 2 (April 1995), p.427; James Vernon, *Politics and the People: A study in English Political Culture, 1815–1867* (Cambridge, 1993), disagrees with some of this theory, believing that electors paid more interest to local issues, loyalties and leaders, pp.90–164.
131. Russell, *Recollections and Suggestions*, p.92.
132. *Croker Papers*, Elgin to Croker, 15 July 1831, II, pp.127–8; see also Duke MS, box 3, 28 July 1831.
133. Clements MS, Lb. 26, Croker to O'Connell, 16 July 1831, f.35. See also Clements MS, loose folder files and letter-book entries for this period and Duke MS, box 3, for letters praising Croker for his role.
134. *Standard*, 14 and 22 July 1831; see also 21, 27, 29 July for similar remarks.
135. Ibid., June 1830, pp.587, 581, 588 and *passim*.
136. *Fraser's*, 'The New Parliament', June 1831, p.638.
137. Ibid., 'Right Hon. John Wilson Croker', September 1831, p.240.
138. *Blackwood's*, August 1831, p.412.
139. Add. MSS 40313 (Peel Manuscripts), Hardinge to Peel, 12 September 1831, ff.156–9.
140. Clements MS, Lb. 26, Croker to Hertford, 12 and 19 September 1831, ff.50 and 61.
141. See *The Times*, for 11, 13, 15 October and 2 November 1831 for an extensive report on events, and most days until 2 December.
142. Turner, *Age of Unease*, p.238; Brock, *Reform Act*, pp.248–50.
143. *The Times*, 2 November and 2 December 1831.
144. See Brock, *Reform Act*, pp.248–58 for a condensed account of the violence and demonstrations. The quotations are taken from *The Globe*, 12 October; *The Poor Man's Guardian*, 8 October 1831; the Whig *Morning Chronicle*, 26 October, calling for a fusion of both groups into a National Guard. Grey officially proscribed such organisations on 17 November.
145. *The Times*, on 6 December 1830, objected to the use of the term 'conservative' by the new opposition, and mocked their new title: '"the Conservatives" (as they call themselves)' for proposing that they represent 'order and authority in Britain'. On 7 August 1830 it had advocated a 'representative government that is Conservative and progressive', and on 27 October 1830 celebrated the enactment of the 'great conservative measure of Catholic Relief inspired the enlightened advocates of civil and religious liberty with hope' for a future measure of Reform. On 27 October 1831 it called for a 'Conservative Guard' to protect society from the mob, and on 3 March 1831, and argued Russell's bill was an 'ameliorating' measure between 'two extreme parties', one opposed to all Reform and the other proposing the 'worst species of Reform with a view to subvert the existing institutions and the gradations of all the ranks of society. Between the two extremes the only safe path was the conservative principle.' On 7 March 1831: 'If ever there was a measure Conservative and protective ... that scheme has been exhibited in the present bill of Reform.'
146. Add. MS 40320, Croker to Peel, 1 [or 3] November 1831, ff.186–7.
147. Ibid., Peel to Croker, 10 November, p.190.
148. Clements MS, Lb. 26, Croker to Peel, 11 November 1831, part cited in *Croker Papers*, II, p.136.
149. Add. MSS 40320, Croker to Peel, 18 November 1831, ff.189–91.
150. *Quarterly Review*, 'The State of Government', November 1831, pp.303–8.
151. Clements MS, Lb. 26, Croker to Hertford, 12 December 1931, ff.161 and 166.
152. Cannon, *Johnson*, pp.1–3.
153. *Hansard*, IX, 16 December 1831, cols 392–8.
154. Ibid., cols 396–402.
155. Ibid., cols 404–9.
156. Ibid., cols 408–18.
157. Clements MS, Lb. 26, Croker to Hertford, 26 December 1831, ff.183–6.
158. Ibid., Lb. 26, ff.184–6. For an account of O'Connell's negotiations with the Whigs during

1831–2 and his conflict with Stanley, see Angus Macintyre, *The Liberator: Daniel O'Connell and the Irish Party, 1831–1847* (London, 1965), Chapters 2 and 3.

159. Ibid., Croker to Hertford, 12–13 December 1831, f.161.
160. *Hansard*, IX, 17 December 1831, col. 539.
161. Ibid., cols 527–8.
162. Ibid., cols 528–33.
163. Ibid., col. 544.
164. Clements MS, Lb. 26, Croker to Hertford, f.161, 12–13 December 1831, and part cited in *Croker Papers*, II, p.141. For details of some of these amendments see Brock, *Reform Act*, p.264 and Norman Gash, *Politics in the Age of Peel: A Study in the Technique of Parliamentary Representation, 1830–1850* (New York, 1953).
165. Ibid., ff.162–4, and part cited in *Croker Papers*, II, p.141.
166. Ibid., Croker to Hertford, 23 December 1831, f.183, and 26 December, ff.184–6.
167. Clements MS, Lb. 26, Croker to Hertford, 17 April 1832, ff.319–20.
168. 'Ellenborough Diaries', in Aspinall, *Three Diaries*, 1 to 3 April 1832, pp.218–19.
169. Duke MS, folder for 1832, Ellenborough to Croker, 3 April 1832.
170. Add. MS 38078, Wellington to Croker, 24 April 1832, f.5; see also f.6 and *Wellington New Despatches*, VIII, p.271 and *Croker Papers*, II, pp.173–4 for other correspondence in the affair.
171. Add. MSS 40320, Croker to Peel, 22 April 1832, f.204; see also Clements MS, Lb. 26, Croker to Peel, ff.326–7 and Croker to Wellington, ff.324–5. A version of this with sections deleted is in *Croker Papers*, II, p.175; see also pp.173–4, and Add. MSS 38078, f.6.
172. *Croker Papers*, Peel to Croker, 23 April 1832, II, p.175. A number of letters on this subject may be found at Duke MS, box 3, files for April and May 1832, no cat. numbers. In June 1832 Croker published a pamphlet containing some details of the events and the plan entitled *A Letter to a Noble Lord who Voted for the Second Reading of the Reform Bill, on the Amendments which it May be Expedient to Make in Committee* (London, 1832). He reviewed it along with some other publications in the *Quarterly*, 'Stages of Revolution', July 1832, pp.559–89, commenting in a footnote that it was written, 'we are informed, by Mr Croker', p.572.
173. Ibid., Wellington to Croker, 29 April 1832, II, pp.173–4 and at Add. MS 38078, f.6.
174. Duke MS, box 3, Ellenborough to Croker, 30 April 1832.
175. *Croker Papers*, Wellington to Croker, 1 May 1832, II, pp.174–5. See also *Wellington New Despatches*, VIII, p.292.
176. Turner, *Age of Unease*, p.246; Brock, *Reform Act*, pp.290–1.
177. Clements MS, notebook handwritten by Croker entitled 'Notes of what passed about = Change of Ministry = May 1832'. An almost complete transcript is also available in *Croker Papers*, II, pp.153–70.
178. Clements MS, 'Change of Ministry', 9 May 1832.
179. *Wellington New Despatches*, Wellington to Lyndhurst, 10 May 1832, VIII, p.304.
180. Clements MS, 'Change of Ministry', 10 May 1832.
181. Ibid.
182. Add. MSS 40320, Croker to Peel, 11 May 1832, ff.207–8. Copy of same in Clements MS, Lb. 26, ff.346–50 and part cited in *Croker Papers*, II, pp.177–9, and Parker, *Peel Correspondence*, II, pp.204–5, but incorrectly dated 4 May 1832.
183. Ibid., ff.208–9, and *Croker Papers*, II, pp.177–9.
184. Clements MS, 'Change of Ministry', 12 May 1832; also in *Croker Papers*, II, pp.157–8. This account and Croker's long-stated plan to resign office is largely confirmed by Ellenborough in his diary; see Aspinall, *Three Diaries*, 12 May 1832, p.250 and Longford, *Wellington*, pp.274–7.
185. Ibid., and partly cited in *Croker Papers*, Peel to Croker, 12 May 1832, II, pp.179–80. Part of this letter is also reproduced in Parker, *Peel Correspondence*, II, pp.205–6, but the section where Peel says he had made 'a hundred declarations' against Reform is omitted.
186. Ibid., p.180.
187. Clements MS, Lb. 26, Croker to George Robinson, 17 May 1832, f.362.
188. Gash, *Sir Robert Peel*, p.33.
189. Kitson Clarke, *Peel*, p.62.

190. Brougham, *Life and Times*, III, pp.196–7.

191. Gash, *Sir Robert Peel*, pp.30–2.

192. Aspinall, *Three Diaries*, Ellenborough Diary, 12 May 1832, p.250 and 14 May 1832, pp.254 and 258–60; see also Duke MS, box 3, Ellenborough to Croker, 19 May 1832.

193. See Newbould, *Whiggery and Reform, 1830–1840*, pp.93–4; Hilton, *A Mad, Bad and Dangerous People*, pp.426–8; and E.J. Evans, *The Forging of the Modern State* (London, 1996).

194. *The Times*, 12, 18 and 22 May 1832.

195. Turner, *Age of Unease*, p.249.

196. Gash, *Sir Robert Peel*, p.39.

197. Clements MS (Lockhart–Croker correspondence), I, Lockhart to Croker, 20 June 1832, f.61.

CHAPTER FOUR

The First Reformed Parliament and Press Campaign for the First Conservative Ministry: 1833–5

> The leader of a party though elected no doubt into high station for very superior qualities becomes, by accepting such a confidence only the first partner in the concern ... As the parliamentary party represents one portion of public opinion, so the leader represents the party; and cannot, in any rational theory of constitutional connections, hold himself independent of those whose *foreman* he is, and without whom the greatest orator or statesman can be, in our present political system, no more than a unit – whose utility and value must depend, in a great measure, on the number that follow it. (J.W. Croker, *Quarterly Review*, September 1846, p. 566)

Croker's status among Tories and Conservatives in Ireland and Britain had never been higher. He was praised by the dignitaries of a number of English and Irish constituencies and invited to represent them as their MP. He refused them all, including his old Dublin Collegians and a highly flattering appeal from the Dean, Corporation and Clergy of Wells offering him a safe seat.[1] On 11 August he wrote to Wellington as 'one to whose partiality I owe my first success in public life and by whose personal friendship I have been in private life, so long and so much gratified', that he 'would not offer myself for the new Parliament' because it represented an 'usurpation' liable to lead to 'as complete a subversion of our ancient constitution as the Long Parliament'.[2] Wellington had also said he would never sit in the Lords following Reform,[3] but he replied with a terse three lines. 'I have received your letter. I am very sorry that you do not intend again to be elected to serve in Parliament. I cannot conceive for what reason.'[4] Croker's rather grand statement of principles was perhaps seen by Wellington as an affectation, given that he had always advocated the importance of politicians pragmatically adapting to circumstances and had compiled a Conservative Reform bill. Furthermore, Croker told many of his Irish friends that his main reasons for retiring were weariness and ill-health. 'Be assured you will never see me in office again – I dislike it, Mrs Croker and Nony dislike it,' he wrote to Major in May, 'and I do not see that I am obliged to resign my private happiness to the views of any other.'[5]

The Fellows of Dublin University continued to press him. Not only old supporters like Lloyd and Elrington, but also Charles Boyton, a leading supporter of Lefroy, and Dr Joseph Henry Singer, who told Croker he must accept or 'the conservative interest will be so broken'.[6] By this time most members of the two main rival groups at the college had acknowledged their shared interests, and in the spring of 1832 founded the Irish Protestant Conservative Society. In doing so, as Joe Spence describes, they 'pre-empted Peel's call for a new emphasis on party organisation, therefore understanding that the battle for the constitution, which they believed they defended more tenaciously than he, could only be won at the registries'.[7] This is true, but as we have seen, some of their associates and compatriots in Britain had also been pre-empting Peel for some time. At the inauguration of the Conservative Society, Boyton announced that 'the time had come to reduce the sectarian content of his appeal to Irish Protestants and to promote national interests instead.' One of its first products would be a new addition to the press circle, the *Dublin University Magazine*. It too called for a range of unitary legislative, social and economic reforms such as proposals for the prohibition of duties and laws detrimental to Ireland; measures to stimulate a monetary economy and encourage agricultural improvement; public works and for preference given to Irishmen in Irish appointments. 'As soon as people see that they have a ready avenue to the public mind for whatever they have to complain of,' Boyton argued rather ambitiously, 'I consider we shall have the whole country with us in a month.'[8]

In August Croker sent Peel a morbid letter expressing his fears at the advance of 'Democracy' and that they would be lucky to pick up a quarter of the seats in the coming election. He was pleased to be out of the Commons, but he would miss the 'private society and intimate intercourse' of those 'whom I have lived the intelligent part of my life' and have 'the pain of seeing them tost on a tempestuous sea, while I stand – perhaps not out of danger, but out of sight – on the shore'.[9]

Not surprisingly, Croker would be far from politically marooned: his work for the *Quarterly* would greatly increase; he was a house-guest of Wellington at Walmer Castle and of the Duke of Dorset at Kew, and he regularly met and dined with other politicians and pressmen in London.[10] Peel encouraged him to visit him at Drayton in October, but he refused to 'bring you bad spirits and gloomy anticipation – I know not whether my mind grows morbidly despondent, but certain it is that every day increases my terror, if it were not so [awful] I would bury my despair'.[11] Croker was a keen angler and shot, and in a kind-hearted attempt to cheer him up and entice him to change his mind, Peel wrote again saying he had 'cherished some wild partridges for you', and he could also come trolling 'for Pike on the Tame or the Wimble ... but I suppose fly fishers despise all other fishing'. Although he normally closed his letters 'yours affectionately', on this occasion he used the more emphatic 'ever most affectionately yours, my dear Croker, R.P'.[12] Croker submitted and visited from 22 to 27 October, where he found Peel 'in high force and thinking better than any one I have yet met of the probabilities of salvation'. Goulburn, Herries and Holmes were fellow guests, and while pike and partridge absorbed some of their time, politics almost certainly monopolised most of their conversation.[13]

In helping plan their election campaign for the coming December, Croker argued that it was of the greatest importance they keep Radicals and ultra-Whigs out of the Commons by seeing that as many Whig 'conservatives' were returned if 'Conservatives' stood no chance of winning.[14] This meant that if necessary, those radical or ultra-Tories who were liable to be less moderate or manageable should also be excluded. As has been seen, Michael Sadler was greatly admired by the press circle, but he was running as a candidate in Leeds against Macaulay and certain to propose extensive measures of reform on behalf of the poorer classes and alienate many of the moderate reformers among the mercantile and middle-class electorate. On 7 October Croker wrote to Peel saying Sadler had not only 'refused to submit to pledges', but also conveyed his refusal 'in a long letter in which he pledges himself to a series of principles which must inevitably lead him to the very votes which he effects not to engage for'. Despite his rival being a political and literary enemy, Croker argued that the party should, therefore, support the moderate Whig candidate, because 'I really have no doubt that Macaulay will be more of a conservative than Sadler.'[15] The character of the reformed Commons would lend itself to this practical policy. The number of electors had only increased by about 80 per cent; the overwhelming majority of MPs were still closely associated with property, and a third of them still with the landowning aristocracy. They were naturally predisposed to conserve the status quo, and as scholars argue today, the 'fundamental aim of the Reform Act was to strengthen the power of government' and 'thereby to entrench the position of virtuous local gentlemen'.[16]

The Conservatives suffered a substantial defeat in the election, but the 'conservative' result was largely 'to my satisfaction', Croker wrote to Hertford: 'the Radicals are everywhere beaten by the Whigs' and although Conservatives liable to act together would only be 149, the Whigs had won 320 seats against the Radicals and 'Irish Repealers' 190.[17] Goulburn agreed, telling Peel that the 'conservative principle has gained great strength in the educated classes of the community', and attempted to convince him of 'the importance of the perfect union and complete concert with all who called themselves Conservative'. Peel, however, still refused to 'unite cordially with' any 'Tory Ultras',[18] or to make any public statement of policy. As Herries complained, 'throughout the whole body of the party' there was eagerness 'to learn the determination or disposition of the two leaders', but their followers remained 'in a state of torpor, listlessness and waiting upon display by the Conservative party'.[19]

Six month earlier, Stanley Lees Giffard had written to Croker criticising the continued failure of their leaders to promote their party and principles, and that they should look to Croker to be 'their fitting and peremptory instructor':

> I think of the highest possible importance to lay it before
> you to whom your party – if they are not even greater fools
> than I and the world think them – will look to you as their
> fitting and peremptory instructor in all that concerns the
> literary and intellectual department of the causes in which
> you are engaged ... I have no personal motive in this
> advice, as thank God, I have hope soon to be done with
> newspapers.[20]

By that time the *Standard* was effectively the Conservatives' daily newspaper; and promoted the merits of the 'Conservative party', advertised 'Conservative dinners', 'Conservative societies' and spoke of the 'Conservative interest' in most editions.[21] *Blackwood's* did much the same every month, arguing in an article following the Reform Act entitled 'Duties of the Conservative Party' that the 'battle of order against anarchy, of property against spoliation must now be fought in every town and village of England'. In anticipation of the election, it frankly declared that in contrast to 'the culpable, incredible supineness of the Conservative' leadership's neglect of the press and their supporters in the past, 'let the Conservative party, in every county, town and village in the Empire immediately assemble'. A concerted effort must be made 'by the Conservative committees over the whole country, and a fund provided by general subscription' to support their party in the coming election.[22] Despite the failure to win many seats, like Croker, they praised the success of their tactic 'where none but the "destructive" candidate came forward ... the Conservatives gave them no support. Where a Radical was opposed by a Ministerialist, the Conservatives, as the least of the two evils, gave their votes to the latter.'[23]

By November 1832, *The Times*, still the moderate ministerial press mainstay, was using the capitalised term 'Conservative' to describe the party assembled around Wellington and Peel, and the lower case 'conservative' to express its approval of Whig moderates who should keep those it denounced as the 'Destructives' out of the Commons.[24] That same month in a *Quarterly* article, Croker had predicted the post-election character of the reformed parliament, arguing that the 'immense majority of rank, property and education will no doubt contribute to the return of the least objectionable candidates' and substantial number of 'members absolutely *conservative* will be returned'.[25] He reinforced this point by differentiating between Whigs with 'conservative' political views by using the lower case, and declared 'Conservative' supporters, with the upper, emphasising their affinities and arguing that both must unite against the ultras:

> Hated and despised as the Ministers and their adherents are by the two great parties which divide the state, many of them will find their way back to Parliament through the determination of the *Conservatives*, where the contest is between a Whig and Radical, to support the ministerialist as the less evil of the two ... And in many cases electors, by no means well disposed to conservative, or even Whig principles, are content to adopt men whose *names are known to them* and whose rank and talents give them, even in the eyes of the £10 householders, a consideration which obscure demagogues and nameless adventurers have not yet been able to attain.

For all these reasons we expect to see in the House of

Commons many conservative names and many Minister-
ialists who, having sat in former Parliaments, will bring
with them at least the tradition of the constitution.[26]

He warned his readers that parliament must check 'the gigantic spirit
of innovation' or anarchy and violent revolution would grow,[27] and
that many leading Whigs were now 'obliged to talk language more conservative than any real Conservative has dared to use'. The *'Edinburgh
Review* expresses distinctly enough the altered views and feelings of
"fanners of the sacred flame"', and 'even *The Times* newspaper, hitherto the most effective and unhesitating advocate of the Bill, has been
forced to designate those whom it formerly glorified as *Radicals* by the
more appropriate and emphatic title of the *Destructives*'.[28] If the latter
ever held sway in the Commons then the popular voice would not be
heard but subsumed by 'mobs and demagogues whose nature it is to
usurp the name and abuse the power of the real people' to elevate
themselves and their deadly ambitions.[29]

Although they shared most of the same views on these issues, *The
Times* aggressively defended the ministry in anticipation of stiff opposition to Whig plans for Church reform, in particular of the Irish
Church. 'Let the "Conservatives" but act with common foresight and
whatever is most valuable or excellent in the venerable Church of both
islands will be scrupulously protected.' But if they play the 'Wellington
game of decrying all [Church] reforms as needless and pernicious' ...
such as the removal of 'bloated pluralists, who never visit a flock but at
shearing time', then the edifice will not be 'cleaned and repaired – it
will be barbarously re-roofed and gutted', and the 'Conservatives' will
play into the arms of the 'Destructives'.[30] In January 1833, Croker once
again noted that the Irish chief secretary, 'Lord Stanley, and Lord Grey
have been at variance, all seems to tend to his separation',[31] and that 'the
Conservatives, a few by pledges, many by professions, will find themselves obliged to vote for popular measures' to maintain the ministry.[32]

By this time the disturbances in Ireland were worse than ever despite
the government having been, by their standards, 'well meaning, well
informed and determined to take advantage of the goodwill which they
hoped had been created by emancipation'. They had 'advanced nine-
teen bills for solving the country's social and economic problems';
funded non-denominational education as a major concession to the Irish
Catholic hierarchy; created a large fund for public works; a tithe commission in anticipation of further reform, and proposals for subsidising
agricultural reform and various reclamation projects.[33] All of the press

circle would argue that these attempts at practical Irish reforms were at best inadequate, and that as they had predicted, Emancipation had produced neither peace nor tangible benefit for the poorer classes. In fact the disfranchising five-sixths of poorer Catholics, as Croly argued, had even dispossessed most of them of the value of their only political right and asset. Lauded as 'the sovereign remedy for all the diseases of Ireland', Croker wrote, Emancipation had proved 'absolutely worthless', and further attempts by the 'Whig engine of *Concession* ... their grand expedient' 'to render all coercion unnecessary, has been followed by disturbances more frightful than ever', eventually forcing them to implement an Irish Coercion Act 'ten times more severe, and a hundred times more unconstitutional' than any measure of the Tories.[34]

Another bad harvest in 1830 had triggered a revival of Rockite and Whiteboyism exceeding any since 1798.[25] 'I can only say that I believe that the Church of Ireland will not be tolerated,' Croker argued in December 1831, 'I tremble for the Protestants of Ireland – I expect to hear of a Popish insurrection, but I fear we shall have no Londonderry.'[36] Not surprisingly, all the press circle continued to argue that the Catholic leaders were diverting popular disaffection onto religious and associated issues such as Church tithe and Repeal of the Union, and although they were unlikely to see merit in any O'Connellite or Catholic campaign, it was true that those organising the movement were 'generally the substantial farmers, who formed the bulk of the tithe payers'.[37] The new wave of disturbances was energised mainly by material concerns, however, and although many of the Catholic larger farmers and middling orders were also under attack, the Protestant community in the southern provinces had good reason to live in a higher state of alarm.[38] There were huge Catholic meetings, some reputedly a few hundred thousand strong, and incidents of riotous assembly, murder and reported night-time attacks doubled.[39] Something the press made abundantly clear in Britain, as it did that some disturbed districts of Ireland were effectively under the control of violent local Catholic factions. In December 1832 Wellington privately expressed his own fears in much the same manner as a Maginn or Giffard editorial:

> You are quite right in what you say about the Repeal of the Union. The Protestants of all classes will soon discover that like the rebellion of 1798 it must become a religious affair ... I confess I have always considered O'Connell as the personification of the Roman Catholic religion in Ireland ... He and the Roman Catholic church get together,

whether he or others lead I cannot tell ... There is no end
to our troubles in Ireland, we shall have to fight for
possession of the country.[40]

That January prior to the new session, *Blackwood's* argued that Ireland was suffering 'not because of the tyranny of England, but the
tyranny of her own demagogues'. If the energy they expended could
only be directed at improving the state of Ireland, then she would be
as 'rich and prosperous as she is populous – instead of being overspread
with the most wretched and squalid population in Europe'. But let a
'Catholic Republic be established in Ireland; let O'Connell be its pres-
ident', then 'it would speedily fall into an abyss far greater than that
which already overwhelms it'.[41] In the *Quarterly Review*, Mortimer
O'Sullivan reiterated much of what he had said in 1825: that the
'disaffection of the people had its origins in real grievances', but the
Catholic leaders 'laboured for notoriety' while the 'people demanded,
or desired relief ... from the dreadful enormities of the incendiary and
the assassin' and 'the pressure of the most intolerable distress'. The
government should have been 'the guardians of the people; but ...
Captain Rock, in conquering the people, and Counsellor O'Connell in
bullying the parliament were performing each his allotted part'. The 'proprietors of landed estates' and the 'absentee, who is removed from the
annoyance of squalid huts, and all the other characteristics of wretchedness, physical and moral' were doing theirs. As were, of course, as the circle never failed to point out, the Roman Catholic priests, who could have
been the 'instrument of tranquillising and improving a country', but knew
that this they could never do, for whenever 'agitation ceases in Ireland
the inevitable hour of the Roman Church has come'.[42]

While aggressive anti-Catholicism would be a significant part of the
press circle's writing on Ireland in the 1830s, it would be a mistake to
see it as the main feature of their work or to separate it from their
political ideas and let it obscure a better understanding of their more
extensive arguments. *Blackwood's* spoke for them all when insisting
that tithe should be paid by landlords, but as all the circle had argued
for some years, it also wearily reiterated that in practice this would play
no part in 'improving the condition of the farmers, or satisfy the desires
of the abolitionists', because the real ambition of the Catholic movement was 'the resumption of the tithes to the Catholic clergy, of the
estates to Catholic landlords, and of government to Catholic leaders'.[43]
They cared little for practical reforms, which if implemented earlier,
'would already have had a great effect in the sufferings of Ireland' and

'prevented the terrible discord which has lately taken place'. The 'great object of Irish legislation', Samuel O'Sullivan argued again in March, should 'be the establishment of a judicious and enlightened system of Poor Laws for the relief of the sick, the aged and those who, though willing, can find no employment', together with government works 'on a great scale' such as development of 'the fisheries and neglected harbours and waste lands of Ireland'. When this much had been done for the 'welfare and happiness of Ireland – having strained every nerve for the real benefit and prosperity of its numerous inhabitants, Government could deliver them from the worst curse which desolates their land – that of their own priests and demagogues'.[44] In that same January number, *Blackwood's* praised a 'brilliant speech lately delivered by "Mr Cummings" at a Cork meeting of the "Conservative society" calling for "a union on moderate principles of all men of all … a union of Whig and Tory upon sound Conservative and Protestant principles". We rejoice at having the opportunity of drawing closer the bonds of union between the great Conservative party in this country and their intrepid supporters on the other side of the channel.'[45]

All the members of the press circle would continue to campaign for extensive practical reforms to be part of the unitary policy of the Conservative party they were all now promoting. And although few of them would be implemented in their lifetimes, as Angus Macintyre has described, the simple argument of 'No Church, No Union' would be successfully 'used against all the enemies of the Irish Church', whether Radicals, Irish Catholics or Whigs.[46] Furthermore, Croker's prediction when attempting to rouse Peel at the start of the Reform battle, that the new reformed Commons would become a polarising contest between the 'two parties', would be increasingly fulfilled. For Croker and the circle, on the one hand were the 'conservative forces of moderation', and on the other, a 'coalition of *Destructives*', and the 'question of the Irish Church, serious enough in itself', becomes 'a thousand times more so … by its being the field of battle in which we are to fight for all property and all institutions'.[47]

THE IRISH CRISIS AND THE GROWTH OF CONSERVATIVE POPULAR SUPPORT

In opening the first session of the reformed parliament, the moderate Scottish Whig, the Earl of Ormelie, made a conciliatory appeal to 'that portion of the State which, with mistaken notions and feelings, had arrogated to itself the exclusive title of Conservatives'. He asked them to yield up 'party feeling and spirit by joining hand in hand with those who now looked to the course which opinion was taking the country'. He then introduced the first feature of the ministerial proposals for the session, an Irish Coercion bill designed to repress disturbances in that part of the empire 'where lawless violence prevailed and that the grossest outrages were daily committed'. Its people 'had been long oppressed by serious ills and grievances ... The Government not only admitted the fact', but was also 'sincere in its sympathy for Ireland'. At this point Daniel O'Connell interjected with shouts of 'No! No!', but Ormelie ignored him and expressed his deep regret at the failure of the Union to produce the peaceful and productive relationship that existed between Scotland and England, and that the pressing need to alleviate the misery of Ireland's people was being lost almost entirely due to those who exploited disaffection. O'Connell attempted to intervene once more, and Ormelie rounded on him: 'Long oppressed as that country had been by centuries of mismanagement, [it was] oppressed still further by those fomenters of evil discord who live and fatten upon the ills of their country – oppressed by those harpies, or birds of prey ... ready to pierce their destructive talons into its side.' [48] [49]

Stanley rose next to give the details of his Coercion bill for Ireland, and in justifying it also criticised O'Connell's part by agitating the people of Ireland that 'there should be a Parliament sitting in Dublin' and pledging that 'he alone could relieve them from the yoke of the *Sassenach*'. O'Connell attempted to intervene again by shouting denials, but Stanley responded that they were on record, and castigated him for playing an opportunist double-game promoting Repeal inIreland while pretending not to in the Commons. Stanley then moved on to justify the need for what Croker would describe as the most repressive Irish legislation enacted since 1798. 'It would almost surpass belief if I were to read the record of crimes committed in Ireland': in Kilkenny alone, not the most disturbed of the counties during the last twelve months, 'there had been thirty-two murders and attempts at murder; thirty-four burnings of houses, 519 burglaries; thirty-six houghings of cattle and 519 serious assaults':

> In Queen's county [Laois] the number of murders was still greater – namely sixty; of burglaries and attacks 626 ... injuries to property 115, serious assaults 209 ... The list, formidable as it was, contained only the crimes of which notice had been given to the police, and constituted only a

small portion of the offences really committed ... So complete was the system or organisation established by midnight murderers and disturbers of the public peace that their victims dare not complain ... and submitted to the despotic commands which they imposed upon them, because they knew that they carried the means of death.[50]

O'Connell responded with a long and passionate speech describing the proposals as 'a bloody and brutal address ... a declaration of civil war, and that declaration would be echoed by many a wail and many a lament throughout Ireland'. More blood had been shed in Ireland during the Whig administration 'than during that time of the Earl of Strafford, the peasantry were slain by day – assassinated by night – openly by groups of soldiers and policemen'. A description, according to reports, was received with angry retorts and hoots of ironic laughter.[51] Only five members other than O'Connell's own party would vote against the bill on the first reading, and as Le Marchant, a Whig Emancipist and no friend of Stanley, argued, the 'fierce deportment and baseless assertions' of his supporters 'at length heartily wearied the House, and several Members who had on the first night supported O'Connell subsequently became his most violent adversaries'.[52] In expressing the views of almost all the moderate Whigs, Macaulay, having won the contest in Leeds, denounced him for having raised tensions in Ireland 'with so much vehemence and accompanied with so much of personal invective and abjuration', and made the portentous point that if, as O'Connell had argued, Catholics cannot get fair treatment other than in a 'Hibernian Republic' due to the 'difference of religion', then this logically warranted 'the separation of Protestant Ulster' and one 'domestic legislature in Dublin', and another 'in Derry or some other large town in the north of Ireland'.[53]

A number of Irish Protestant members described their personal experiences of what they attributed to Catholic violence and 'persecution', and judging by responses in the House and the press they appear to have had the greatest effect. The new MP for Trinity College and leader of the Irish Conservatives, Frederick Shaw's long speech was dramatically featured not only in the Conservative press, but also in Whig papers and *The Times* in sensationalised detail. He ridiculed O'Connell's proposed alternatives to the Coercion bill as cynically calculated to further empower the violent Catholic gangs responsible for most of the violence. New judges were to be 'regulated and assisted by the Roman Catholic priesthood; the police and the constabulary were to be altogether got rid of and the "armed volunteers" of the hon. and learned Member to keep the peace'. In the meantime, the Irish police must be armed 'with his constables staff alone'. Why? Because with 'pain and sorrow he must bear that testimony against his poor deluded countrymen, that in nine cases out of ten … it would lead to the single destruction of the man that bore it'. O'Connell's justice would be 'the mad tyranny of an ignorant and deluded democracy, and the torturing inquisition of a Roman Catholic priesthood in the full plenitude of its power'. The O'Connellite member for Drogheda, Andrew O'Dwyer, had angrily called out: 'destroy the Protestant Church Establishment, nothing else will satisfy me', permitting Shaw to exploit what he acknowledged was the naïve interjection of a tyro, but nevertheless an accurate glimpse of the sinister purpose of the Catholic leaders despite taking an oath on entering parliament not to 'subvert' the Anglican Church.[54]

Shaw's post brought him daily news from Ireland, where many lived in daily fear 'of the mid-day murderer and the nightly burglar and assassin'. One letter recounted a 'brutal murder in Waterford, of an old man dragged from his bed, and because he refused to give up two acres of land, his brains were shot out', and many Irish Protestants no longer thought of their property, 'their lives alone were now their object'. A few weeks earlier he had arranged a meeting with a friend, but 'the coach he was to have travelled [in to Dublin] conveyed the news of his being murdered … on the public road in broad daylight, his head so battered with stones his own friends could not recognise him'.[55] Shaw did not name the man, but *The Times* did, and enlarged upon the incident as grimly as any of the press circle. The victim was an elderly Anglican pastor named Ferguson who had been stopped on the road and 'in the presence of several hundred of the peasantry, dragged from his gig, knocked prostrate on the road, and a large flag [stone] was then thrown upon his head, so as to crush it to mummery and render it impossible for his friends to recognise his features'.[56]

Charles Walker, MP for Wexford, a Protestant member of O'Connell's party, accused Shaw of having 'not said one word with regard to those oppressions which had driven the people to madness'. This was partly justified, but most of the examples he gave of repression were so comparatively moderate that they would perhaps have been better left unsaid. Even if a man were arrested for a 'trifling offence he was put in handcuffs so tight that the hands swelled in a manner which rendered it impossible for the poor victim to use them for weeks', and he then told the story of a policeman recently brought to court in his constituency that raised more ridicule and laughter than sympathy from the members:

> It appeared that he [a policeman] went in the night to arrest a man; he broke open the door of the House, and directly he had done so a naked man started out and ran. The policeman asked if that was the man, levelled his piece at him, and shot him dead, by the light of the moon, as he was getting over the stile. The man, it was true, was charged with rape; but there was no charge of which persons were more frequently committed in Ireland; and at any rate the policeman had no right to shoot him.[57]

Shaw's dramatic accounts of ostracised Anglican pastors and their families living in fear and penury were mocked by Feargus O'Connor: had they been concerned when the 'last blanket [was] stripped from the widow and orphan', and the case of the clergyman who had been pulled to the road and had his head 'smashed with a flagstone, ... it was a melancholy event', he agreed, 'but not more than 11 or 12 persons were privy to it'.[58]

As Angus Macintyre says, it was not surprising that the O'Connellites rapidly lost the sympathy of many new members, who turned 'overnight from friends to violent adversaries'.[59] Croker knew the Conservatives would gain the most from the parliamentary and public response to these debates, and within the first week his spirits had risen considerably:

> For two nights and a half the vehemence and disorder were so great that people began to think that the National Convention was begun. Peel told me that it was 'frightful – appalling'. This induced him to rise late the third night and read the House a most able, eloquent and authoritative lecture ... He expressed his determination to support their Conservative dispositions, and he deprecated these idle and violent debates. The fate of the Government was, and he knew it, in his hands ... The storm moderated, the English Members got time to reflect on the insanity of the Irish, the debate was conducted next night with decency, and the Ministers had 438 to 40 ... I am surprised the Radicals were not stronger. That is to be attributed to O'Connell's

violence, and the shame which Peel's speech produced in some of their minds.[60]

Members on all sides praised Peel's role during the debate, and noted that at one point he took the opportunity to 'flatly deny that he had ever been an enemy of gradual and temperate reform' when it was done 'dispassionately and deliberately'. Ellenborough recorded that Peel 'astonished the new Members, Irishmen and lawyers', and that even 'Cobbett had said to Holmes: "that is a handy fellow, that leader of yours, if he would place himself at the head of the Movement we would turn these fellows out in twenty four hours."'[61]

Peel defended the Irish Church from 'the attempts that are made to charge the Clergy of Ireland with exaction and rapacity, and to represent tithe as the crying grievance of Ireland', but also gave details of the burdens placed on the poorer farmers and cottiers by 'intermediate landlords' [middlemen] and the lack of proper leases 'which leaves them entirely at the mercy of the landlord'. When he had been chief secretary many tenants 'complained to me' that they were charged tithe, but 'got no credit for it in the accounts of their landlords'. On an unusually personal note, he said he was 'still haunted by the recollections of the scenes of atrocity and suffering with which I was once familiar'. He asked the House's permission to add an account of an incident he had experienced so as 'to prove the truth of what I say, both as to the misery that is endured and the fortitude that is exhibited'. A child of nine years of age had been hidden by her mother in a turf stack and then witnessed both her parents beaten to death outside their home by a local agrarian gang. Despite the terrors she had endured and the ostracism of her neighbours, when rescued 'she remembered the faces and every motion of the assassins' and in court nothing could shake her from testifying 'against the men she had seen that night: Such are the romances of real life!' In a society where 'laws are powerless; all the moral restraints and checks on crime seem to have lost their force', and unless firm measures were taken, 'the contagion of depravity will rapidly extend; the places yet healthy will become infected; the whole land will become a moral wilderness ... and every rule of justice will be reversed – in which there will be no punishment except for innocence.'[62]

Croker wrote to Peel that his speech had even won the support of Francis Burdett, who 'had a mind to make a direct attack on the ingratitude of the Roman Catholics ... I ventured to implore him not to say so now, that it could do no good, that he was a great card in the Conservative hand and ought not to be prematurely played'. 'Talk of you and me as Conservatives! I wish you could have heard his eulogy of the Protestants of Ireland and the [necessity] of supporting and encouraging them.'[63] Near the end of the debates, *John Bull* expressed itself delighted with the union of 'conservatives' in the Commons and the 'spirited exposé of Mr Stanley (which roused the enthusiasm of the House into the extreme measure of hooting down Mr O'Connell) and the luminous and constitutional speech of Sir Robert Peel'.[64]

The Coercion bill would raise constitutional concerns among some members, and approximately a hundred would vote against it on the final reading a few weeks later, but it passed with an overwhelming majority, and the Irish Church and Anglican community 'in danger' was firmly established as the issue to rally 'conservatives' and Conservatives. In that same session, the government presented a fairly moderate 'Irish Church Temporalities Bill'. It attempted to avoid any controversial proposals, but many believed the inclusion of a clause enabling some 'lay appropriation' of its income for local reform and relief meant it would end up in the hands of the Catholic clergy. This exacerbated the growing division between the 'conservative' Whigs, represented by Stanley, and what Croker called the 'ultra-Whigs', increasingly dominated by Russell. And as Peter Mandler describes, 'Ireland was to be the pivot of the struggle between the Foxite and moderate wings of the party', for although few in Britain were opposed to any reform 'which would redirect revenues from an overpaid Protestant Clergy to some other Church sponsored ends', they were 'violently opposed to any appropriation of Church fisc, because this would appear to reward agitators and sanction the "spoliation" of private property'.[65]

Most MPs were in favour of Church reform, but as Peel said, most were unwilling to see the 'Church's position weakened and its property impounded by the legislature which had ceased to be even a Protestant, let alone an Anglican assembly, [and] which openly numbered in its ranks Catholics, Dissenters, Utilitarians and free thinkers'.[66] In the *Quarterly* in October 1833, Croker argued that the Whigs had made no attempt to arrest or defeat the 'active conspiracy against the tithes' and that even their 'minor measures' to reform the Church in Ireland 'seem calculated to plunder and *destroy* it'. One of the first duties of any government was to protect property, but an exception was to be made for the Church, and even the Coercion Act had included a surreptitious clause to exclude tithes from protection.[67] Croker and Peel would be more guarded in their public declarations and commitments as they tactically evaluated developments in parliament, but the *Standard*,

Blackwood's and the circle's other publications waged a much more aggressive public campaign.[68] *John Bull* suggested that Irish Church Reform accompany the Coercion bill 'so that conciliation and coercion may go hand in hand', but denounced the Whig programme as an 'Irish Church Spoliation Bill' designed to 'impoverish and degrade' the Church. Its actual income from tithes was 'in practice five-sixths' of its entitlement, and the real purpose was 'the extinction of Protestants in Ireland' which has 'long been known to be the ulterior motive of O'Connell's party in all their movements, but the people in England cannot believe it, because they think it can never be accomplished'.[69] Maginn was now a dedicated advocate of building the Conservative party, and in *Fraser's* that March he appealed to Protestants in Ireland to sacrifice a portion, 'and perhaps a large portion' of their wealth to support the Conservative organisations then being established. The 'more Conservative candidates the better … the great object should be to keep up the spirits of the Protestants, to protect their rights, to redress their wrongs' and win wider support in Britain. The 'Irish Church' had long been under attack from the Catholics, but now it was to be 'robbed, not that the state may be benefited, but that absentee landlords may spend elsewhere the money that the Protestant Bishop or clergyman would spend in Ireland'.[70]

By that time many Irish Anglicans believed the Whig ministry had abandoned them. In January 1832, Frederick Shaw's election manager, William Long, had proposed that southern Protestants were 'so deserted and betrayed' by the government that now 'it becomes our duty to endeavour by repeal of the Union to recover the advantages we have lost'.[71] But tentative hopes that affiliation with O'Connell could provide any appealing alternative soon disappeared, and their *Dublin University Magazine* would be an earnest advocate of the urgency of building Conservative organisations, warning in May 1833 that the Conservative clubs would be of little use '*when the Protestant population has emigrated*'. In the last four years some 94,000 had left Ireland, and 'it was a melancholy fact that the whole Protestant population of the lower orders are in preparation to abandon this country'. It acknowledged that this was for a number of reasons other than being 'neglected by their landlords and persecuted by the Popish population', and that Catholics were also driven to leave. This, however, was also largely because their 'self-appointed leaders had near destroyed the economy by their agitation', and 'sick of the bondage which they suffer from their priests and the factions', large bodies of Catholics had also 'been induced to emigrate'.[72]

The *D.U.M.* would be the Irish equivalent of *Blackwood's* and *Fraser's*, and its leading early writers and organisers, Charles Boyton, Samuel O'Sullivan and Frederick Shaw, made sure that it was singing from the same hymn sheet as the press circle in Britain. The first number praised that 'noble periodical the *Quarterly Review*' for defending the Church, but criticised the parliamentary leaders for neglecting their supporters in the press, many of whom 'had laboriously and with great sacrifices advocated their cause for years'.[73] Reforms should be part of the agenda of the 'Conservative party in Parliament' in order 'to remove any obnoxious abuse', but only in a 'time of peace, tranquillity and leisure'. The 'Conservative party, though defeated' in the winter elections, 'has not been destroyed ... and it is to be hoped [that it] has gained wisdom by experience'; it only lacked determined leaders, and the *D.U.M.* illustrated the tradition and calibre of those it set as a standard:

> Burke was the great providential instrument by whom the designs of those arch-innovators were first detected ... whose penetrating intellect detected the sophistry, whose keen and cutting sarcasm, whose biting irony chastised and ridiculed ... that race of pseudo-patriots who rode for a season, upon the passions of a misguided and infuriate populace, and whose lofty eloquence (a voice from the shrine where reason and conscience maintained a joint supremacy) ... Such are the trophies which encircle his venerable name and ... If there existed amongst us even one such mind as that of Burke, before three months you would see a party in England by whom even at this eleventh hour, the progress of revolution would be arrested.[74]

It would patriotically claim that the great Irish Whigs and Tories Swift, Grattan, Flood, Sheridan, Burke and Canning (who it claimed as Irish) were the political ancestors of modern conservatism.[75] In the May 1833 number, Samuel O'Sullivan defined their philosophy in much the same manner Croker had in the *Quarterly*, arguing that 'the principles of the old Whigs were essentially conservative, and were in fact precisely the same as those of modern Tories', and in a later number reiterated that the 'spirit of the old Whigs was purest Conservatism'.[76] As indicated by their solicitations for him to sit for the college, Croker's views were highly valued by the Irish Conservatives, and he also retained his influence with the Scots, sending William Blackwood the occasional 'political pieces ... worthy I think a page of your magazine'.[77] However,

Blackwood's main political articles were usually the work of its editor John Wilson or Archibald Alison, with George Croly and the O'Sullivan brothers writing on many Irish topics. As has been seen, Samuel was also a leading writer for the *D.U.M.*; Mortimer wrote for the *Quarterly*; Croly socialised with Crofton Croker, Giffard and Maginn; Hook with Maginn, Lockhart and Croker etc, and apart from clearly studying each other's work, these personal connections also encouraged a synthesis of arguments and policies.[78] As Joe Spence says of the *D.U.M.*, their concerns 'necessitated not only a reunification of those Tories divided over the Catholic question', but also securing of all Protestant support to 'what they conceded to be the "Conservative cause"'.[79] All the press circle were keen to heal any remaining rifts between the ultra-Tories and the Conservatives; most of whom also fraternised nationally in the same provincial associations and clubs where they discussed the news and debated their political ambitions, and to see the two as distinct sections has been over-emphasised.[80] As Croker later described, they looked to the *Quarterly* to be 'a kind of direction post to a large body of people … its chief use is to keep our friends on a right course and to furnish them with arguments in support of their opinions'.[81]

   In April 1833, Croker, who Giffard had called the 'instructor in all that concerns the literary and intellectual department',[82] provided his readers with what may be seen as the first substantial post-Reform guide to Conservative principles and policies. In an article entitled 'The Present and Last Parliament', Croker argued that the Commons had always been made up of 'a variety of interests and classes', and after calm and proper debate addressed popular concerns and reformed proven abuses. More significantly, he connected this with what he emphasised was the importance of '*Party*', if intemperate factions and pressure from Destructives were to be resisted and the 'equilibrium' of the constitution preserved. 'For "No men", as Burke observes, can act with effect who do not act in concert … who are not bound together by common opinions, common affections and common interest.'[83] The Whigs were being manipulated by dangerous Radicals and ultras who were threatening property and the constitution:

> Checks and controls must exist, but the supreme power must rest in one place … That place must be the House of Commons, and it was here that the influence of the Crown and the Peers were mingled in due proportions with the power of the people and public measures were there so prepared, manipulated and modified …[84]

MPs were necessarily alive to a 'greater or lesser degree of popular feeling', permitting safe reforms and 'the gradual adaptation of our constitution to the progress of society'. The other important influence 'intending to preserve the equilibrium in our constitution', he continued with emphasis, was *'Party in Parliament*, that honourable and powerful bond which held men together either in office or opposition, and without which a government with so much democracy as ours must soon become an anarchy'. This restricted 'individual presumption, and even the passion for popularity has been restrained by the predominant and salutary influence of *Party*'. Those who say this is 'theoretically unreasonable and at variance with principles of freedom, independence and individual conscience' ignore a more important and practical principle. Croker then presented a Conservative political philosophy and connected it with the importance of party:

> The theorist forgets that the object of all this complication of machinery is the government of mankind, and that man is himself an anomaly – guided by no steady laws, and liable to all the changes and shifts of human temper, all the errors and passions of human frailties; and that, if he is to be governed, it must be not by the rules of the Philosopher's square, but by means analogous to his nature, in unison with his feelings and which may enlist, as it were, his very frailties into the general cause of social order. We do not attempt a mere defence of party connexions – but we go a step further. The times in which Mr Burke wrote required no more than he should establish the expediency of political connexions – the times in which we live press upon us their necessity. A government may deliberate, and an assembly cannot exist without them [but] 'No men' as Mr Burke observes, can act with effect 'who do not act in concert ... who do not act with confidence; no men can act with confidence who are not bound together by common opinions, common affections, and common interest'. We add that no assembly of six or seven hundred men can be brought into any steady useful course of proceeding, but by some kind of discipline or subordination ... a union, which they feel to be not a surrender, but an amalgamation of individual opinions – a contract, voluntary and indefinite ... submitting its peculiar feelings and fancies, on individual points, to necessity

of having some common standard of manners, and some guide to action.[85]

This echoes the fear of factions he expressed in his letter on Walpole to Liverpool, and that many MPs were now 'representatives', not in the positive sense Burke had outlined to his Bristol electors, but having to respond constantly to the whims of their constituents and jostle for temporary alliances. The Whigs had a 'vast majority', but it had 'proved itself a rope of sand' and the country was only saved from anarchy by the support of the principled minority: 'those Conservatives whom they hate and persecute'.[86]

He concluded with a conciliatory appeal to moderates who had supported the Reform bill by acknowledging that they had acted to the best of their judgement, and that reform, when moved through the deliberative filters of the legislature, was necessary and beneficial.

> We are willing to believe that our new representatives are as upright and conscientious men as any of their predecessors ... Nor do we impune the good sense of the new constituency of England, nor undervalue it, except on considerations drawn from the imperfections of our state and nature. [But] large masses of men cannot be well informed on the intricate details of politics and statistics; and even those that are less imperfectly informed are liable to seductions, excitements and errors, which are often epidemic ... Representative government itself stands on the admitted principle that the people are not capable of exercising in primary assemblies political power; and as Lord John Russell truly said in his last work, this popular power is not fit for use till it has been strained and filtered by some more intermediate process.[87]

This article was issued by Murray as a pamphlet, and although similar on some points to his July 1831 and January and April 1832 articles, it appears to be the first substantial statement issued in a nationally acknowledged Conservative party publication on the importance of '*Party*' and promoting the firm defence of the Church and constitution, and the unity of moderates, yet accepting the need for the reform of proven abuses, in much the same way Peel's *Tamworth Manifesto* would almost two years later when purportedly 'inventing' modern Conservatism. In his article, however, Croker was considerably more assertive on the importance of *Party* than Peel would ever be; and as significantly for this study, he was clearly promoting the same political philosophy he had advocated all his life for a unitary alternative to 'ultras' and for good government to conciliate proven popular concerns.

In October 1833 he wrote another important political article, 'The Reformed Ministry and Parliament', in response to another promoting the principles of the ministry compiled by Brougham with the close collaboration of Althorp, Palmerston, Stanley, Macaulay and Nassau Senior. The success of the Whig article, then pamphlet, has been described as 'enormous and almost unprecedented, with substantial sections from it republished in most newspapers and periodicals'.[88] Although Croker's response has received almost no attention, it may reasonably be assumed that it was also seen as a rival statement of their party's principles by Conservative supporters, and a national discussion document for them prior to the new session of 1834.

Croker consulted a number of leading Conservative figures,[89] but does not appear to have received the same sort of assistance Brougham had for his article. Following a query for his views, Peel replied:

> Strange as it may seem I have not read, nor have I seen, the Ministerial pamphlet. I saw some extracts from it in the newspapers, which sated my appetite for such reading. I cannot see much ground for triumph on the part of the promoters of the Reform Bill in the results of the last session ... it was only got through because that which we prophesised took place; namely, that the popular assembly exercised tacit power, that the House of Lords – to avoid the consequences of collision – declined acting upon that which was notoriously the deliberate conviction of the majority. I allude particularly to the Irish Church Bill.[90]

Wellington was more enthusiastic, replying 'that the object of the answer ought to be to show that the Parliament which has been formed [was] delegated for the purpose of pulling down the antient [sic] constitution and institutions of the Monarchy'. Croker should also show the danger the Whigs were posing to foreign policy and economic reform, and deal with 'the Irish Church bill, together with the other measures above referring to Tithes', for it must 'destroy the Church of England in Ireland'.[91]

Croker covered all of these issues extensively, and dealt with each point of policy in the Whig pamphlet by restating much of what he had said in his earlier *Quarterly* articles and argued in the Commons. 'A spirit of innovation, said Mr Burke, is generally the result of a selfish temper and confused science [and] flies to every expedient', and the Whig ministry 'has touched nothing which it had not disturbed ... but we find no traces of anything like mental attention, like grave consideration, like balancing of counter-ponderant interests, like the conciliation of antagonists' interests'.[92] They may mock what they call 'the "terrors" and the "prophecies" of the Conservatives', but the evidence of the disrupted Commons illustrates that as the

> ... Conservatives foretold from the disorganisation of the old political system ... the irregular passions and illegal power of the turbulent are increased, while moderate and sober minded men – the friends of good order and good government retire in despair ... Government is, we are convinced, prepared to prolong its precarious existence by the sacrifice of the Church ... and for a season they may succeed, by the abolition of church taxes and tithes, and when after a humiliating series of concessions they have nothing else to surrender, they will be swallowed up; not alas the only victims of anarchy ...[93]

Together with his earlier articles and those of the press circle, there must have been a widespread general acceptance by now that the Conservatives were presenting themselves as moderate reformers as well as firm defenders of Church, property and the constitution. Croker's *Quarterly* articles could, of course, only appear every three months, and they were more moderate than his old allies, but the press circle clearly drew upon his work, albeit making more radical reformist demands which failed to meet with the approval of the parliamentary leaders. In May 1833, Lord Melville wrote to Peel:

> I am shocked and provoked at the radical doctrines and language of some of our ultra-Conservative newspapers, both in London and Edinburgh, from no other motive than hostility to the present Ministers, and totally forgetting that all those Doctrines and anti-governmental principles ... are much more at variance with our sound principles than with those of our Whig Ministers ... they will disgust all the really loyal and well-intentioned conservatives, who look only to the stability of the Monarchy and preservation of the Constitution.[94]

As one historian of the Conservative party remarked in 1959, the 'Conservative publicists' were much more enthusiastic about taking on the Whigs than the Conservative leaders, and they 'were mainly responsible for providing the party with its general arguments and intellectual inspiration'. Although Professor McDowell mentioned few of the circle or their publications by name, as he continued, in contrast to Peel, '"their cold parliamentary chief"', who was more concerned with preserving and increasing his reputation for political seriousness and administrative competence than elaborating his party's doctrine', the 'Conservative publicists were much more expansive'. But the 'vehemence with which they expressed their extraordinarily distorted view of the political situation in the years following the passing of the Reform Bill to some extent justified his reserve'.[95] Although he has the merit of being almost the only scholar to identify the press circle's influence on the early Conservative party, McDowell's purpose was to present a short narrative account of Conservative party history between 1832 and 1914, and he could only provide a few examples of some of their arguments. How 'extraordinarily distorted' were their views is disputable however, especially when the circulation of the publications and, as he acknowledges himself, the successful results they eventually helped produce for their party are considered. Furthermore, as another political historian argues, if their 'distorted' views on state welfare and economic and political interventionism are measured by today's standards of good government, many of their proposals could be thought of as considerably more 'modern' than those of their Whig and 'Liberal Tory' rivals.[96]

Among the most celebrated of those 'Conservative publicists were men whose spirited Protestant conservative speeches set hats flying in Exeter Hall', and so full of Irish affairs were their publications that they frequently gave the appearance of 'being produced in Dublin rather than London'.[97] This emphasis on the belligerent Irish Protestant aspect of some of their writing, while accurate, has overshadowed their other ideas. One of the only other scholars to notice their work, Gilbert Cahill, defined the 'Tory' press at this time as largely reactionary 'no-popery' and 'anti-Catholic' 'bigotry',[98] and while all of these factors were present, they were a subordinate feature. As Croker emphasised, 'bigotry' was a political weapon exercised on both sides of the Irish religious divide, and in refuting the selective interpretations of the 'Causes of the French Revolution' developing at the time, he appropriately argued that to 'cull out ... all the bad men, or bad women, or bad actions, to mould them into one mass of iniquity', produces simple and satisfying narratives, but it was 'a common but great mistake in modern political writers to consider government with reference, not to public feeling of its own time, but of the public feelings of ours'.[99] Religious identity was, as Linda Colley argues, 'still a crucial unifying force in most nations in Europe', and it is only to be expected that it still 'lay at the core of British national identity'. It would certainly be central to the rise in Conservative support that the press circle would win for their party,[100] but 'religion' was also a crucial unifying force for Irish Catholics, and it is clear that 'bigotry' was also redolent in many of their publications, speeches, ballads, etc. Unless one wishes to 'cull out' those on one side and mould them into a simple image of 'iniquity', then a wider examination of contemporary evidence presents problems for 'modern political writers' who pass simple predetermined judgments to prduce 'simple satisfying narratives' in accord with the public feelings of our own time.

Samuel O'Sullivan was correct when he angrily criticised O'Connell in *Blackwood's* for having 'never attempted to regulate rents or obtain for the poor farmer permanency of possession [and] he has invariably opposed enactment of the Poor-Law'.[101] In his first year in the Commons O'Connell opposed Sadler's advocacy of a Poor Law for Ireland, arguing that Anglican tithes should meet their needs. He was won over for a short time in 1831 by the forceful arguments of Bishop Doyle, but in the following session he 'completely reneged on his pledge to Doyle and reverted to his fundamentalist antagonism towards poor laws on principle'. This was, he said, because his 'minute and patient investigating ... convinced him that compulsory laws inevitably destroyed the morality of the poor, stoked class antagonisms'. Other qualifications were little more plausible: 'my system of poor laws for Ireland – the Repeal of the Union!'; Poor Laws were 'calculated to destroy the feelings of humanity ... in the hearts of the people and the voice of revealed religion'; it implied 'slavery on the part of those who thus obtained relief'; a right to relief was 'prejudicial to the national interest'.[102] O'Connell 'could perhaps', as Peter Gray suggests, 'afford to shrug off the waves of hostility and allegations of heartless cruelty [this] provoked from British radicals and tories'.[103]

Most scholars of this period also appear to have shrugged them off too, but the press circle's arguments that the Catholic movement was largely motivated by anti-Protestantism in order to elevate its leaders locally and nationally, rather than any ambition to improve the state of

Ireland and condition of the Irish masses was not shrugged off so easily by their British and Irish readers. By this time *Fraser's* was one of the most popular monthly magazines of the period, and while Maginn wove his ambitions for Ireland with attacks on 'Popery', it was almost always related to his much more extensive attacks on both the O'Connellite movement and successive British governments for neglecting and exploiting the Irish peasantry. In the Commons, Maginn accurately argued in March 1833, that O'Connell and Whigs such as Spring-Rice and Lord Oxmanton had told 'English gentlemen to remember the great advantage they derived from the *absence of poor laws* in Ireland', because 'England was supplied with *labourers at so low rate*!' But the 'mainstay of these objectors is found in the abuses of the English poor-laws ... and since when was it deemed allowable, with men of sincerity and common sense, to plead the *abuses* of a system against its *use*?' 'Nothing more insulting was ever attempted by O'Connell himself', although he 'has also used the same arguments'. No-one, however, *Fraser's* continued, can doubt his 'real, but concealed objection', and this was that if 'once justice were done to the whole population of Ireland, the game of agitation would no longer answer'. He puts forward 'the Repeal panacea', because poor laws 'would put an end to the state of things which gives to Daniel O'Connell all his power'. He would, perhaps, 'himself propose a Poor law in an Irish Parliament – nay, as we would not believe him a fiend, or a political economist, we rather expect that he would. But in the meantime, while all his political chicane is going forward, the wretches in Connaught are dying by their thousands!'[104]

What is 'the government doing in this matter? Just nothing; and that for two very good reasons': the first being because 'they have among them such a strong admixture of political economists', and 'secondly, by the absurd impunity they yield to O'Connell ... and this is not the vice of present rulers of Ireland merely; it has equally been the character of past administrations'.[105] 'In proportion then, as England has diminished the influence of her natural supporters in Ireland, has she increased that of her enemies' and the 'combined influence of the physical force, the parliamentary tail, and bigotry of its Irish enemies' has forced the ministry to rely on physical coercion:

> The power of Irish agitation arises from the existence of two old and one new element. 1st, the misery of the people; 2dly, the popish priesthood, 3dly, the parliamentary influence of Irish hostility to England. It is not easy to approach the discussion of the state of the labouring classes of

Ireland with that temper and forbearance which every such discussion requires; because it is not easy coolly to contemplate the mass of misery which it discloses ... the intensity and extent of privations, sufferings and temptations of those unfortunate beings ... in whose name fancied wrongs are substituted for actual wants, whose degradation has never yet been attributed to its true source ...

The 'march of the intellect men', the 'spirit of the age', 'liberal opinions', the 'schoolmaster abroad', the 'principle of self-government', 'reform not revolution', etc. etc. are all so many phrases of unmeaning cant, which must stink in the nostrils of every man who is intimately acquainted with the details of the Irish peasant's life, and who still sees those who utter them with so much self-complacency, leaving this degraded and defrauded creature a prey to all the horrors of the most abject penury. The Irish peasant is incorrigibly idle, says one party. Idle!!! Is he an idler, who, with perhaps no other earthly support than a thin cake of oaten bread, leaves his family and his home, traverses on foot the breadth of his native country, crosses the channel in search of work ... then returns with his hard earned wages; and for what to gladden and rejoice the hearts of his ragged and wretched family? – no such thing ... As he returns, he must visit his landlord or the agent; every farthing is transferred to him – not a penny is brought to the cabin ... and in return for all his toils and privations is the miserable produce of some bog or swamp or mountain.[106]

Maginn quoted from the Whig paper the *Morning Chronicle* in order to crow that even O'Connell's foremost English allies were now agreeing that the primary cause of wretchedness in Ireland was the exaction of excessive rent, and that access to land lay at the heart of 'the outrages and disorders of the Irish'. Measures were urgently required to make landlords responsible and to break the power of the middleman: 'The tenant is the paymaster not the landlord and it is the connection between the tenant and the labourer which requires vital and radical correction.' The labourer is paid 'in truck or barter in land', and 'the cost is so usurious and the competition so great that his exploitation is inevitable.' Keen to see old-style Poor Law introduced to Ireland, Maginn argued that it must be accompanied by legislation to control the price paid to lease land or the 'poor rates would only go to pay the rents of the worst set of landlords, at the expense of the best'. Another necessary reform would be to 'secure to the labourer a bona fide ready-money payment', for they 'are kept in a state of the greatest misery by the fraudulent system which prevents their labour from being fairly remunerated', and easily raised to a 'high degree of excitement by the Priests and the lay leaders of agitation ... distress must be removed as a means of reclaiming them'. If parliament fails in this, then it will be the 'public disturber and nuisance – the destroyer of public harmony, parent of convulsion, and ally of rebellion'.[107]

He never changed his view that 'Reform is continually needful, and a free government exists in no small degree to make it.' The 'people' must make their voice heard, and the 'Conservative leaders' must listen to the 'voice of the real people';[108] and Maginn had better knowledge of 'real people' than most. He regularly socialised with Spitalfield weavers, drank in the working-class areas of London, and despite earning at least £1,000 p.a., he was personally profligate and often in debt. Not least because, Elizabeth Thrall argues, 'destitution in others ... he could not witness without trying to relieve it.' Between 1832 and 1835 he sometimes took refuge from his debtors in some of the worst London slums where his fluent Irish enabled him to survive in the worst 'stews' of St Giles.[109] Among Peel's papers is a letter written in 1833 from Giffard to an anonymous recipient, almost certainly Croker, who forwarded it to Peel seeking a contribution to free Maginn from a spunging house. Despite the abuse Peel had received, he wrote on the back that he would give 'a hundred pounds distinctly without reference to any political intentions whatever; but to be considered as part of a subscription to a literary man of distinguished talent in difficulties and imposing no sort of personal obligation'.[110]

Perhaps another reason why the leaders wanted to keep the likes of Maginn at arm's length was that the commission enquiring into what would be the New Poor Law of 1834 was coming to its conclusions at this time, and all the press circle would be dedicated opponents of it as cruelly designed to deny the poor their traditional rights. Peel would be a firm supporter, writing to Croker later that he doubted 'whether any [Whig] minister took upon himself more responsibility for passing the Poor Law than I did, or more frankly avowed [it] upon the hustings'.[111] Croker would, accordingly, be more guarded in his public criticisms, but in October 1833 he argued in the *Quarterly* that, given Nassau Senior's influence on the Commission, no good could be expected from it.[112] Three months later the *Quarterly* agreed that the old Poor Laws needed reform, but 'where parochial dependence has become common, it has been *forced* upon [the poor] by the persevering efforts of the administrators of the poor-laws, who, conspiring with the employers of labour to lower the rate of wages, have prevented the labourer from obtaining employment ... *except on the condition of becoming a pauper*'.[113]

Where Ireland was concerned, not another session of parliament must be permitted to pass without measures being taken to compel

> ... Irish landowners to relieve the infirm and employ the destitute population of their estates; which estates are notoriously as in much want of expenditure of labour in their improvement, as the miserable beings dragging out their miserable existence in idleness and beggary upon them are in want of employment. But we will not be tempted to diverge into this topic, which we have elsewhere fully treated. It is enough to repeat our conviction that the extension of the [old] Poor-Law to Ireland, in its principle and most important provisions, is a first and indispensable step towards any effectual improvement of the working of that law in Britain.[114]

Extensive measures of Irish reform were needed: among them subsidised voluntary emigration, with assistance upon arrival in settler colonies; free access to 'garden allotments'; the instigation of public works where the workers would be paid more than paupers in projects designed to reclaim land for their own benefit as well as improvement of the national infrastructure. In order to encourage employers to take more responsibility, the *Quarterly* even advocated an early form of social security. A tax should be levied on employers 'creating a fund for assuring labourers from destitution, and would throw the expense of maintaining the aged, impotent, and sick poor precisely where it ought by justice to fall – *viz*, on the persons who have profited by their labour'. Infirm labourers would be guaranteed a weekly allowance 'of ten shillings bed lying, and five shillings walking', with an 'annuity of five shillings weekly after the age of sixty-five, and a payment of ten pounds to his relatives on his death'.[115]

There would be little support in the Commons for such radical measures, but as we will see, opposition to the New Poor Law would help win support for the Conservatives, particularly from one highly influential old press ally of Croker's. In the meantime other reforms occupied the members, notably the abolition of slavery, the most famous achievement of the reformed parliament. Some of the press circle were ambiguous on the issue, mainly because it was a potent political one. The *Quarterly*, *Blackwood's* and the *Monthly Magazine* generally in favour of abolition, *John Bull* and *Fraser's* usually opposed, and in this, as James Sack describes, 'it represented a substantial break from its humanitarian tradition', and 'one suspects (and these things are always difficult to trace) that some money was changing hands.'[116]

This is highly possible where Maginn and Hook were concerned, but another factor and a common accusation was that the campaign had been hijacked as a political tool, and they ridiculed the 'sanctimonious hypocrisy' of the same opponents of slavery who ruthlessly exploited and abused what he called the 'White Slaves', their industrial workers. In Croker's rather obsessional partisan view, 'the clamour' was 'the hobby-horse of Dissenters and Quakers', and he was worried that it might bring down the Whig ministry before the Conservatives had the strength to replace them.[117] It would, however, be the issue of Irish Church tithe reform more than any other that would split the Whigs and force the Conservatives into office.

THE FALL OF THE WHIGS AND THE FIRST CONSERVATIVE MINISTRY

On 6 May 1834, when Stanley proposed another motion for Irish Church Reform the controversial clause for lay appropriation of its funds for secular use had been removed. O'Connell had been marginalised, Angus Macintyre has argued. In 1834 during five days of debates on Repeal of the Union he 'made no impression ... on a wholly Unionist Parliament' and 'his motion defeated by 523 votes to 38'. Making 'no impression' in the 'positive' sense from an O'Connellite perspective perhaps, but given the nature of these debates, the extent of the defeat, and that he had further reinforced the negative impression the press circle promoted of his intentions for Ireland as sinister and sectarian, for them it was a positive one. By May he had to change his tactics, and as Macintyre continues, he would support the Whigs on major issues while 'seeking to exploit the well known divisions inside the Cabinet by maintaining a constant pressure on Appropriation'.[118] He made a moderate and conciliatory proposal on Irish Church tithe: essentially that the cost be divided into five portions with the landlord paying one fifth, the occupier two, the Crown one and the Church absorbing the other.[119] There was some confusion interpreting the exact details, but

Stanley congratulated him on the 'moderate tone and temper' of his speech and hoped it would be 'reciprocated by all who sat behind him' given that he too now accepted the money raised from Irish Church tithe was relatively small.[120] By this time, as Croker and the circle had argued, the tithe composition payment was on average between one thirtieth and one fiftieth of the productive capacity of a piece of land, of which by 1833 'only £12,316 was recovered at a rough cost of £26,000', and by 1835 only 12 per cent of the entitlement would be paid in the whole of Ireland, most of it, presumably, by Anglicans.[121]

Russell praised O'Connell's 'eloquent speech', but he still attempted to introduce the divisive issue of lay appropriation again, complaining that 'a tone exists in the House to disregard Irish feelings or Irish interests' and 'if ever there was just grounds of complaint on the part of any people' it was that 'of the people of Ireland against the present appropriation of tithe'. As Macintyre says, 'Russell's outburst may well have been directly caused by the apparent improvement in the relations between Stanley and O'Connell';[122] either way he was being deliberately provocative in raising the issue again and talking of 'justice for Ireland' in the face of his colleague, the Irish secretary. Stanley scribbled an angry note to his ally James Graham: 'Russell has upset the coach,' and that 'if ever a nation had the right to complain of any grievance it is the people of the Church of Ireland.'[123] Within weeks, Stanley and his own 'tail', nicknamed the 'Derby Dilly' by O'Connell, had resigned on the grounds that they were unable to 'accept that the property and the status of the church and similar institutions were to be allocated by the shaky judgement of the fleeting parliamentary majority'. The circumstances of his departure, according to Jonathan Parry, defined a 'great turning point in whig history' and might be seen as having initiated the later bi-party definition, of what was to become Conservative versus Liberal.[124]

Although Croker would have concurred, and was pleased at this further alienation of Whig moderates, he was concerned that with Stanley and most of the cabinet's 'conservative' element gone, the 'ultra-Whigs' would fill their places and the government obtain 'mischievous force from this decomposition'.[125] However, any hopes that Russell and his allies had held for a more radical ministry were spoiled when Althorp brought other moderates forward, and the Irish Church bill continued its progress without any clause for lay appropriation. Some other changes were made to make it amenable to the Radicals and O'Connellites, and these manoeuvres behind the scenes led to a further disintegration when O'Connell, having pledged they would be kept secret, transmitted the details to the *Dublin Register* and the *Pilot*.[126] This created an outcry in parliament, with the opposition demanding an enquiry. Althorp 'refused to be dragged any further through the dirt', resigning on 7 July, followed by an equally disgusted Grey.[127] The first Reform Ministry had ended in disarray and O'Connell could claim with some justice that 'it was I, in fact, that turned out the Administration', and that they were on the way 'from a half Whig, half Tory Government to one half Radical, half Whig'.[128]

Melbourne was summoned, but he was left facing weakening Commons support and the problem that he should seek to appeal with an election, the Conservatives would greatly improve their representation and force him into a closer alliance with Radicals and O'Connellites. Wellington controlled the Lords, and while he permitted the Irish Coercion bill to be renewed on 11 August, he threw out the amended bill on Irish tithe reform because he believed it still contained the lay appropriation clause. Peel made few interventions; in fact his last speech that year was made on 4 July,[129] and as Norman Gash describes, it was an 'odd feature of Peel's behaviour during the events of late July and August that he did nothing'; perhaps 'because he may have been reluctant to overstrain his credit by intervening on an issue less vital than the Irish Church bill'.[130] Other reasons may have been that Wellington was becoming ascendant over the increasingly cordial amalgamation of ultra-Tories and Conservatives, and as Croker commented, many of them were concerned that Peel's support for the Whigs had gone too far.[131] Another important factor was that Stanley's popularity was rising among the moderates on both sides of the House, and he not only had the ability 'to rally the House of Commons by the sheer force of his oratory', but he was 'personally congenial to the Members who made up the backbone of the Conservative party'.[132]

Once again there is a gap in Croker's correspondence for the period that may have revealed more on Peel's motives, but in the *Quarterly* of February 1835 Croker's overly earnest rebuttal of any idea that Stanley could ever replace Peel perhaps suggested the opposite: 'Could there be no other Conservative government than that of Sir Robert Peel? – might not, for instance, Lord Stanley be placed at the head ... the theory of such a combination is absurd *ex-hypothesi*, ... utterly impracticable.'[133] His future with the Conservatives could only be in service with Peel, and when accomplished 'we shall hail with great satisfaction their union in official responsibility.'[134] Whatever his reasons,

Peel was not only absent from the centre of political affairs when the Melbourne ministry was crumbling but preparing to go to Europe for the winter. Croker wrote to him that October just prior to his departure. 'Why should you hurry yourself? Will you not be in full time by Easter?' but he concluded with a typical loaded query, 'who will know where to send letters to you? One might have occasion to write to you.'[135]

On 10 November Althorp was raised to the House of Lords following the death of his father, and Melbourne was obliged to recommend Russell's promotion as leader of the Commons.[136] Croker wrote that the king considered 'Johnny, who was Melbourne's first horse, quite incapable', because he had 'pledged to act in the spirit of the Commission of Enquiry, issued in the summer, namely to spoliate the Protestant Church in all the parishes where the Roman Catholics should be in the majority'. Melbourne 'waited while the King wrote to the Duke' of Wellington, and then 'offered to convey the letter, which he did'. When Wellington arrived he 'advised his majesty to name Sir Robert Peel as First Minister [but] undertook to conduct the Government till Peel's arrival ... and that he (the Duke) would serve with him, or under him, or not at all, as might be thought best. The King gladly acceded.'[137]

On 17 November Croker wrote to Rosamund assuring her that a report in the *Standard* that he would join the cabinet was untrue.[138] He returned to Molesey in order to escape 'being summoned, which would have been awkward' if offered a place, because 'even under the Duke, I should have been most reluctant to do so, and should only have done at the last extremity of necessity':

> But no power shall ever force me to serve under Peel. We are excellent friends, and shall remain so, which would assuredly not be the case if we sat in the same Cabinet ... Nor am I at all swayed by any difficulty about getting into Parliament, for I have been already apprised that nothing but my declaring I will take the Chiltern Hundreds will prevent the Dublin University electing me, as I am informed, without one dissenting voice; but neither in office, or out, will I enter Parliament.[139]

Croker refused another offer from Charles Boyton to represent Dublin University 'despite the temptation to rejoin the private friends and companions of my whole life',[140] and expressed his concern that they had been forced to form a ministry while they were still too weak to maintain it.[141] Two messengers were sent to search for Peel in Italy. When found, he responded with alacrity, reaching London on 8 December after a remarkably rapid journey from Rome. He wrote to Croker the same day:

> My Dear Croker
> Though I have only been one night in bed since I left Lyons, and I have found anything but repose since my arrival here this morning, I must write you one line to certify to you that I am here ... I shall be very glad to see you. It will be a relief to me from the harassing cares that await me.
> Ever affectionately yours,
> Robert Peel.[142]

Croker thanked Peel, but wrote back: 'I am confined by a cold', and would try to 'come to town to-morrow'. In the meantime:

> One word of advice I will venture to you; don't suffer your-self to be hampered with the *veilleiurs* – the 'Monmouth Street men' of former Administrations. Get, if you can, new men, young blood – the ablest and the fittest – and throw aside boldly the 'mediocrities' with which we were over-laden in our last race.[143]

When Croker met Peel two days later, Lady Peel told him that he was the first person Peel had written to on his return, and Peel asked him whether he adhered to his resolution not to sit in the Commons. He replied that he did, and Peel then 'put into my hands his letter to Stanley, and Stanley's answer declining (on behalf of self and friends) to take office'. 'This now meant that he would make offers to Lord Chandos, Knatchbull and Baring', and then Peel 'twice over said, with a querulous tone, that it would be only the Duke's old Cabinet'. Croker told Rosamund that he emphasised that Peel must recruit new men for his government and that 'a great many seats will be lost if the Ministry shall assume an entire anti-Reform colour'.[144]

Like Croker, Peel was concerned that the new ministry would appear 'anti-Reform', but given Stanley's and his 'conservatives' decision to remain on the cross-benches he had to include more old ministerial figures than he had hoped. He brought forward a few talented new men such as his young admirer, twenty-five-year-old William Glad-stone; but he hardly represented a 'liberal' element, sitting for Newark as a client of the ultra-Protestant Duke of Newcastle, and having spoken against the immediate emancipation of slaves and almost all the Whig reform proposals.[145] Few thought the ministry could last long, and perhaps not surprisingly, Croker believed that the image they presented to the public was of greater importance than preserving office. A highly significant new ally in this would be *The Times*, by then on the verge of abandoning the Whigs and supporting the Conservatives. Most accounts identify this as having been initiated on 20 November, when the editor, Barnes, sent Wellington terms for supporting them. There was to be no interference with the Reform bill, no change in foreign policy, and any tithe commutation and municipal reform already sanctioned by the Commons should be ratified. Wellington was delighted, and agreement was reached by 5 December, with formal ratification to be approved by Peel following his arrival.[146] However, there is compelling evidence that Croker had been secretly involved in discussions with the proprietor, John Walter, since late August, and that it was Walter's affinity with the press circle's views on social reform and, to a lesser extent, threat to the Irish Church that first stimulated the decision to align his paper with the Conservatives.

As has been shown, *The Times* had been concerned with the growing influence of what it described as the 'Destructives' for some time, and before the election had tentatively advocated the unity of 'conservatives' and 'Conservatives'. An advocate of Church reform, it noticeably became more sympathetic to the argument that the Irish Catholic campaign was unjust and sectarian during the debates of 1833, but the main stimulus for its break with the Whig ministry was because Walter was 'passionate in his hostility to the "cruel" New Poor Law'. Although he received little sympathy or support 'from Peel on that subject',[147] he would, however, as Robert Stewart has argued, from 'a small band of Tories, heirs to a tradition of rural paternalism, who had condemned the harsh illogic which underlay the Whig law'.[148] According to a modern historian of the Whig party, the drastic measures proposed in the New Poor Law bill of 1834 made it 'so direct and so potentially savage in its effects that no pre-Reform government would have dared pass it'.[149] The commission of inquiry had been part-led and organised by the lord chancellor, Henry Brougham, who became obsessively determined that it should succeed and fervently hostile to any critic.

In October 1833 Croker had remarked in the *Quarterly* that Brougham's growing eccentricity and ambitions were bringing the office of chancellor into disrepute. Furthermore, given the Whig planners' adherence to the ideas of political economy and 'sciolist' theories, he was confident that the Poor Law commission had not been established 'for any general investigation of truth, but expressly for the purpose of finding only a preconceived class of facts, and recommending a predetermined line of opinions'.[150] In July 1834, in an animated address to the Lords on behalf of the proposed New Poor Law, Brougham quoted from the work of Malthus who had arisen to 'enlighten mankind' as designed to counter 'the monstrous progeny of the unnatural system' whereby the 'pauper ... listless and unsettled – wearing away the hours restless ... needy, yet pampered', had no incentive to work. As Brougham's biographer described, 'to speak in those tones was to speak not from experience of the lives led by the poor, but from knowledge gained from the library', and from now on the able-bodied unemployed would be denied relief unless they accepted confinement in the planned new workhouses and separation of their family.[151] As recent researchers have argued, the reports used to qualify such reforms were often 'highly ideologically charged' and as time would prove, 'profoundly shaped by disputable assumptions' rather than compassionate or common sense practicalities.[152]

The Poor Law bill was of great personal importance to Brougham; he was a highly accomplished debater and brilliant politician, but as both a parvenu and loose cannon, he had been manoeuvred into the Lords by the Whig leaders after his 1830 Yorkshire election campaign. He soon regretted this, and in his frustration was unable to disguise his 'vaulting ambitions or to behave with the dignity that aristocratic reformers expected'.[153] Afer 1833 he became increasingly excitable, parading publicly, and sometimes drunkenly, in his chancellor's robes, publicly criticising his party leaders and intriguing with various political factions.[154] By the summer of 1834 he was an easy target for the press circle; in particular Maginn, who portrayed him in *Fraser's* as a clown to rival Grimaldi. 'Bridlegoose Brougham ... the most illustrious buffoon that was ever exhibited ... highly applauded at Brook's and Billingsgate ... a clever sayer of absurd things' when sober, and when not 'a clever sayer of tipsy absurdities'.[155]

In the summer of 1834, John Walter one of the first pressmen to be elected an MP, spoke against the New Poor Law in the Commons. He declared it cruel and unjust, an especially abhorrent feature being that in the new workhouses husbands would be separated from their wives, parents from their children and the elderly from their communities.[156] His objections had little effect on the progress of the bill, and although there was substantial public as well as parliamentary concern, it passed with an overwhelming majority.[157] There was little threat of failure, but despite *The Times* having long been the ministry's most important press ally, Brougham made an 'amazing blunder' when he launched a series of personal attacks upon John Walter.[158] On 21 August *The Times* responded by accusing Brougham of being out of control, his 'mind being in a perpetual fever'. Over the next few days he was described as a 'mountebank' who 'not only disgraced the Cabinet of which he formed a part' but 'dragged the Great Seal through the kennel'. Unlike the lord chancellor of England, *The Times* had never been 'guilty of any fraudulent or base manoeuvres' in pursuit of power; 'nor lied for it, nor fawned, nor slandered, nor betrayed'. Concluding that '*The Times* for fifteen years ... praised, supported, or if you will patronised his Lordship ... We did by every possible exertion, through evil report and good, zealously, boldly, indefatigably' in order to 'maintain the influence of Lord Brougham'.[159]

No longer would that be the case, nor would *The Times* ever support his party again. Five days later John Walter wrote to Croker saying he was coming to London and 'if next Tuesday or Wednesday will fit [for] you to receive me I shall be happy to wait upon you.' The subject he intended to discuss was presumably associated with Walter's complaints in the letter that 'the Chancellor's enmity towards me can only spring from my opposition to his poor-law project. I never spoke to him more than twice in his life.' 'Some of my friends [Barnes] indeed have been on a more intimate footing with the C[abinet] and they begin to fear, with you, that he is not quite right in the mind.'[160] That same month, the *Quarterly* had published a strong criticism of the New Poor Law, condemning the likes of Harriet 'Martineau and her disciple Lord Brougham' for having 'exaggerated the abuses of the old system' because their 'predetermined object', regardless of their findings, was 'the adoption of the workhouse system'. The 'severe system of indoor relief will be costly and cruel ... the whole country must be studded with district workhouses, or rather work gaols, for their management and discipline is to be precisely similar to that of the penitentiary.' The principle 'is clearly vicious', whereas the 'true and only principle by which parish relief, whether to the infirm or the able bodied, must be determined, is the natural wants of the pauper'.[161] In England, a problematic but humane standard had long existed, but recently, as 'in Ireland, the extortion and oppression to which, without a safeguard, the lower classes are necessarily subject from those who alone possess the soil of the country' has 'ground them down to the very lowest means of poverty – to a state of hopeless irredeemable misery'.[162]

These were, as we have seen, the same arguments the press circle had made for some years when campaigning for what they believed were practical and compassionate inclusive social and economic reforms in opposition to 'political economists' and ministers who were denounced for putting abstract theories before people. As at least one study of the 'History of Irish Thought' has recently suggested, such conservative arguments 'against the selfish philosophers' were perhaps something of an Irish tradition in the work of Swift, Molyneaux and Burke. 'Nothing can be conceived more hard than the heart of a thoroughbred metaphysician,' Burke had famously argued in his intemperate attack upon an ancestor of Lord Russell's, and the 'philosophes [who] consider men in their experiments no more than do mice in an air pump' are 'like the principle of evil himself ... pure unmixed defecated evil'.[163] Croker and the circle's writing emphasises this same hostility to abstract theorists in similarly indignant language, and they would have fully concurred with the guiding principle a modern Conservative thinker applies to rationalism in politics: 'so far from political ideology being the quasi-divine parent of political activity, it turns out to be its earthly step child.'[164] Regardless of the complexity and appeal of such theories, or what Maginn called 'metaphysical intertwistings' and theoretical 'quackery', they were for him and the circle inevitably the product of 'subjective predilection and profane ambitions'. The labours of the 'present race of economists' may help pave 'the way for more successful inquiries and sounder conclusions', he argued in another article calling for Irish Poor Laws, 'but when they hold up their feeble glimmering lamp to guide the rulers of nations through the most intricate paths of legislation and government ... they be the blind leaders of the blind; and if the blind shall lead the blind both shall fall in the ditch.'[165]

Although certainly not opposed to all political thought, the only solid possible guide for good government was custom and precedent: 'A plague on opinion I may wear it on both sides like a leather jerkin', would remain another Burkeian principle, if something of a 'sciolistic' argument itself, that Croker and the circle would apply to rationalist theorists, *philosophes*, and 'literary caballers' who believed their 'gifted revelations' made them the unacknowledged legislators for mankind. They were, for the most part, two sides of the same self-appointed and self-aggrandising conceit evident in all history. The 'aim and the object of all oratory [was] leading the mind of others', Croker argued and the theorist forgets 'the government of mankind, and that man is himself is an anomaly – guided by no steady laws, and liable to all the changes and shifts of human temper, all the errors and passions of human frailties; and that if he is to be governed, it must be not by the rules of the Philosopher's square'.[166]

None of which, of course, was ever likely to appeal to successive generations of writers and intellectuals who naturally empathised with the grand political plans for ordering society according to the 'rules of arithmetic' that would dominate the later nineteenth and twentieth century. Russell's insistence on forcing the lay appropriation clause and dividing his party may have been principled resolve, but Croker and the circle could not believe he was unaware that tithe was a tool of religious politics, or that it raised relatively little revenue. Furthermore, if he wished to improve the state of Ireland, then rent and other practical reforms like Poor Laws would be much more efficacious. In 1833 he described Russell's motives as the product of his 'personal monomania – that *he alone* must be the *reformer* of the age ... and his single voice propound it',[167] and thought the same applied to Brougham's less orderly presented ambitions. An overly cynical view perhaps, but despite the latter's dedication to the New Poor Law, he appears to have taken no interest in its application following its enactment and never visited a workhouse.[168] Much later he would write to Croker frankly declaring that he believed all political motive were driven by the personal 'desire of power and plunder'. Croker responded with a slightly more positive theory, that the choice of a cause and one's political view of the world were largely determined by innate predisposition and character. '*Place*, would, I think, better express your meaning' than plunder, 'but I differ from your definitions altogether'. Brougham's scale was like that 'of an ordinary thermometer, graduated as high as is necessary for the ordinary uses of life, but not calculated for the philosophical extremes of political science':

> There are two great antagonistic systems at the root of all government – stability and experiment. The former is Tory, and the latter is Whig; and the human mind divides itself into these classes as naturally and as inconsiderately as to personal objects as it does into indolence and activity, obstinacy and indiscretion, temerity and versatility, or any other contradictory moods of the mind. Which, without believing in Spurzeim's occipital or sincipital bumps [sic],

one may be satisfied are inherent in human nature. Burke's intellect was Tory, Lord Chatham's Whig, and neither place, nor power, nor Opposition, nor Ministry, could have destroyed this, though they often did restrain and modify the original predisposition. I don't believe any circumstances could have made you a Tory or me a Whig ... You might have attached yourself to Pitt, and I might have been a humble follower of Fox, but amongst our more homogenous associates we should have been considered as 'crotchety, troublesome fellows', always hankering after the opposite direction. Look at Canning; look at Windham. What an unsatisfactory Tory was the former. What an imperfect Whig was the latter. And this I take it was the cause in those anomalies in Burke's character which Goldsmith (unconscious to their cause) so admirably sketched:

Tho' equal to all things, for all things unfit.
Too nice for a Statesman, too proud for a wit.
For a Patriot too cool, for a drudge disobedient.
And too fond of the right, to pursue the expedient.

But besides those innate pre-dispositions which your scale does not include, ... I mean acquired principles and personal convictions, these are generally the fruits of the natural pre-disposition. (But they may be occasionally, though rarely, independent of it.) How many honourable instances could I give you, I dare say, give me, in which party, place, power, have been sacrificed to the pure sense of right and justice. Depend upon it, bad as we are, your views of party make us blacker than the reality.[169]

Whatever may or may not be the merits of such speculation on personal propensities and motives, although there was a substantial parliamentary majority in favour of the New Poor Law this did not reflect widespread un-represented concerns, which almost certainly played a significant part in further undermining the Whigs' popular support.[170] In September, *The Times* was pleased that the 'judgement of the press' was 'all but complete' in sharing its opposition to the New Poor Law bill, and while this was an exaggeration, it was certainly true with regard to the Conservative and many early working-class and Radical publications.[171] Neither the press circle nor Walter would receive much satisfaction from Peel on this issue, but as Alexander Baring wrote

to Croker when unsuccessfully trying to convince him to stand in the
election that December: 'please let me know you are to be the member
for Dublin University', reminding him that even *The Times*, 'aware that
popular feeling is with us' has joined their ranks. Croker would still
refuse to sit for Trinity but, like him, *The Times* would remain a dedicated and influential Conservative supporter and at the forefront of
their press campaign.[172]

Croker remained in close contact with Peel, and told Lowther he may
have saved Peel from a difficult choice. Given his part in battling the Whig
Reform bill, 'I am in public opinion too notorious an anti-Reformer to
have suited the colour which he is forced to give to his administration.'[173]
After Peel had agreed to terms *The Times* had laid down, Croker wrote to
him that the opposition had 'placarded London with a notice that I had
been at Walter's house and bought him and *The Times* for only two
millions; I only wish I had kept £100,000 to myself.' On a more serious
note, he emphasised once again that, although 'things seem on the whole
to look better than I expected to see them ... who is to manage the press
– manage it must be, and by a Cabinet minister too ... Pray think – soon
and deeply on this subject, always important, now vital.'[174]

Wellington admitted that he had neglected the newspapers in the
past,[175] but they would not repeat the same mistake again. Herries,
Holmes, Lyndhurst and Ellenborough all remained active in press management, and Giffard, perhaps fearing *The Times* would overshadow his
paper, wrote to Wellington formally offering to commit the 'service of
the *Standard* newspaper ... circulating more than all the other London
evening papers, of all parties put together'. 'Hitherto we have always
done our best for Conservative principles freely – and will continue to
do so' without 'favour, present or remote'. Wellington thanked him for
his 'determined' course, but candidly warned that the ministry was unlikely to last long. Peel received a similar letter from Giffard. 'I cannot
be ignorant, sir, that you have good cause for objections personal to
myself', but no other newspaper can bring to 'the aid of any Government which it supports a weight of character ... and a corresponding
claim upon the confidence of Conservatives'. However, so serious was
their cause that he would be willing to resign if his presence as editor
would 'embarrass' the formation or progress of the ministry. Peel responded generously that he retained 'not the slightest hostility or ill
will towards you' and 'being pleased to bear its occasional severities
upon myself' rather than 'forego the satisfaction of reading the able
and powerful eloquent comments upon public affairs'.[176]

That January Maginn published a long article in the form of an imagined meeting of 'Fraserians', among them Hook, Lockhart, Crofton Croker, F.S. Mahony, Southey, Hogg, Thackeray and Thomas Carlyle, where he made a formal speech declaring his allegiance to the Conservatives and to 'Sir Robert Peel' who 'we may justly look for our guidance'. I have not 'lost any of my feelings of 1829', but 'it is useless to endeavor to fight over a lost combat':

> That I deeply deplore the evils of my native land is true ... not a promised good has come to pass. No one is concili- ated; no agitator silenced; no howl of hatred checked. All that we predicted had occurred. The Church which was to have been secured by concession, is all but prostrate; the knife of the murderer is in more active requisition than ever. It is no pleasure for me as an Irishman to draw this picture of my native soil; it is with shame that I feel the country of Swift and Burke, and Goldsmith and Sheridan, fast sinking down to the intellectual degradation of Spain or Portugal ... But it is necessary, for the sake of the future, to look to the sad consequences of what has passed. I trust that Sir Robert Peel will face the real evils of Ireland ... He will see the misfortunes consist mainly in the want of provision for the poor. In the poor laws is to be found the panacea for the swindling quacks pretending to see Catholic Emancipation, and which to the leaders in that measure is hateful as death : *Care for the Poor* ....
>
> I may be excused perhaps for dwelling on Irish affairs, not only because I am Irish myself but because Ireland is the sore part of the empire ... [yet] I take the hint and shall cut my oration short. There are some measures anticipated of which I do not approve, and some men connected with the government whom perhaps I despise, but on the whole let us look forward with hope ... Let the gentlemen of England and her good yeoman shew themselves firm and zealous at the approaching election ... we may defy the malice of our enemies.[177]

Now that the Conservatives held office Croker lobbied for their press allies to be rewarded, and kept loyal. Peel told him to compile a list of literary supporters,[178] and among those Croker sought a small pension for were Southey on the *Quarterly*; Sharon Turner and Henry

Hallam the historians and James Hogg, *Blackwood's* and *Fraser's*.[179]
Lockhart wrote to Croker that despite Maginn having 'irreversibly disgraced himself by his low vices' and the 'infamous scoundrels in the
Age', 'his wife is the most excellent and unhappy woman' and perhaps
something could be done. Giffard, of the '*Standard* is a man of different cast and calibre' and 'he is really worth thinking of. He too is poor
... I believe if Brougham had remained in office there was a scheme for
placing his elder son in Govt. office.'[180] Croker rejected any reward for
himself, but suggested that if 'my old friend for years' John Barrow, the
second secretary at the Admiralty, who had written for the *Quarterly*
since 1809, was made a baronet, it would transfer to his son, and
thereby to his wife, Croker's adopted daughter Nony.[181]

Lyndhurst appears to have been delegated to do something for
George Croly, Croker telling him that Croly had a weakness for writing very bad poetry, but he had written a serialised biography of Burke
for *Blackwood's* between March 1833 and August 1834 as well as other
pro-Conservative articles, and Brougham had been trying to win him
over: 'I most strongly urge you to do the thing. It is right in itself, and
I should have pressed it.'[182] Lockhart noted that Theodore Hook was
put forward as 'Censor of plays', but the Conservatives were forced
from office before it could be formalised.[183] Although there is some
confusion with the dates of this correspondence, Lockhart also wrote
to Croker complaining of Maginn, that 'neither I, nor, I believe, anyone of those who subscribed have received any token of his thankful-
ness' but he needed bailing out again. Croker told Peel that he could not
recommend the 'respectability' of 'Dr Maginn – but he is a powerful
writer', and I think 'he has some claim to be warmed by the sunshine,
short and wintry as it may be, that now exhilarates his party'. Peel
appears to have sent another £100.[184] Perhaps because he needed little
encouragement, Giffard appears to have received nothing. Lockhart
sought a Board of Trade appointment for himself through Croker, but
it was too controversial, and he would remain the *Quarterly*'s efficient
if never entirely contented editor for the rest of his working life.[185]

THE TAMWORTH MANIFESTO: PARTY POLICY AND PRINCIPLES

Following the formation of his cabinet, Peel called an election and issued
what became his famous *Tamworth Manifesto* in the form of an election
address to his constituents. Although written by Peel, the eight-page
document was almost certainly hatched in the offices of *The Times* and

compiled under pressure from a number of Peel's colleagues who convinced him to make a statement of principles in order to reassure electors that his ministry would be different to the pre-1830 Tories.[186] On 17 December copies were sent to all the leading papers: there would be no interference with the Reform Act; the Conservative administration would act in the spirit of reform and be willing to address proven grievances with corrective reforms, while at the same time conserving the now adapted constitution. It was the 'creed of moderate Conservatism', as Robert Stewart says, but not at all original in its proposals, for most of them had been used in Conservative election addresses since 1833.[187] More pertinent to this study is that this 'creed of modern Conservatism' had been promoted by Croker and the press circle, whose publications had provided many of the arguments used in those election addresses and constituency discussions.

The *Manifesto* argued that Peel had never been the 'defendant of abuses, or the enemy of judicious reforms ... I took a great part in the reform of the currency ... the whole system of Trial by Jury and other branches of jurisprudence.' Few would have denied the truth of these remarks, and although cautious in saying he was a franchise reformer, he now considered the Reform bill

> ... a final and irrevocable settlement of a great constitutional question – a settlement which no friend to the peace and welfare of this country would attempt to disturb. If the spirit of the Reform Bill implies merely a careful review of institutions, civil and ecclesiastical, undertaken in a friendly temper, combining with the firm maintenance of established rights the correction of proved abuses and the redress of real grievances in that case I can, for myself and my colleagues, undertake to act in such a spirit and with good intentions ...[188]

He would support an enquiry into municipal reform, the reform of government pension allocations, and reform of the Church Establishment in Ireland with an 'improved distribution of the revenues of the Church', but not the 'alienation of Church property in any part of the United Kingdom'. He wished to 'place all the King's subjects, whatever their religious creeds, upon a footing of equality with respect to any civil privilege'. The object of his ministry would be 'the maintenance of peace', 'the support of public credit, the enforcement of strict economy, the just and impartial consideration of what is due to all interests, agricultural, manufacturing, and commercial'.[189]

There was no specific reference to a 'party', nor was the word 'Conservative' ever used, and Peel would avoid using both for the next few years. Nevertheless, the *Manifesto* was 'waved from innumerable hustings and ... cited as an authority by countless party candidates' and this has, as Norman Gash says, 'obscured both its character and purpose'. Peel did not consider it a statement of government, and when Croker submitted his proofs 'for a review of the *Manifesto* for the *Quarterly Magazine*' [sic] Peel criticised Croker for ascribing too much importance to the necessities imposed by the Reform Act, rather than 'from the policy of aiding our friends at the election'.[190] This was a proposal that Croker should emphasise a more tactical policy to win them greater support from wavering Whigs, rather than any party line or principles, and as Angus Hawkins argues in challenging the promotion of Peel as 'the founder of modern Conservatism': Peel 'would never accept the principle that organised party opinion constituted a legitimate source of executive authority'. Furthermore, he would play 'little part in the organisation of the Conservative party during the 1830s, it was sufficient that he supplied an executive ethic ... herein lays the paradox of the Conservative victory of 1841. It was a great party triumph for an anti-party view of executive authority.'[191]

This verdict is broadly correct, but this did not mean that Conservatives in the press and their national readers shared an anti-party view of executive authority or their ambitions. Peel's *Manifesto* contained little original for Conservative supporters, but great attention was given to it and it was 'waved from innumerable hustings' because they welcomed their reluctant leader's belated official acknowledgment of the policies and principles they had been familiar with and championing for some time. What made the document more important than just an election address was, as Boyd Hilton says, that 'it signalled Peel's willingness to lead his party', and it publicly 'indicated that the Conservative leadership would pursue liberal Tory, rather than Ultra-Tory, policies'.[192] As this study has sought to show, if 'liberal Tory' may be seen as representing moderate reforming government addressing proven popular concerns rather than primarily ideas of political economy, then Croker and his press circle, most of whom would be designated 'Ultra-Tory', had been at the forefront of promoting these principles. Furthermore, they would continue to insist that they should be the policy of Peel's ministry before he arrived from Italy and during and after the election.

Croker could not respond to the *Tamworth Manifesto* in the *Quarterly* until the next number was due in early February. When he did he would expand upon it in an article five times longer than the document itself, but in the meantime he continued to influence the contents of the other publications. On 21 December *John Bull* justifiably responded to the *Manifesto*: 'we had distinctly and clearly foretold what the principle would be' and 'unflinchingly maintained' what we knew 'must, and what would, be the course of Conservative Ministry'.[193] This was equally true for all the circle's publications. *Blackwood's* had insisted that those who wished to preserve the Church and state must accept the Reform Act as a final measure and 'give his cordial support to the Conservative candidate on every occasion'. In this the Conservative was 'not acting in opposition to former principles and professions; he is, on the contrary, giving them their just and fair application'.[194] While Peel was still in Italy, *Blackwood's* told its readers 'the Reform bill is a matter of history ... we assume the changes to be irrevocable and to form the foundation, be it good or be it bad, of the new constitution.'[195] *The Times* argued on 22 November: 'If the proposed government of those hitherto passed for Conservatives [is] to strengthen itself in Parliament it must be conscious that the spirit of reform pervades the nation and to create the slightest chance of a return favourable to an embryo Cabinet of Mr Peel and Wellington the whole country must have satisfactory proof of the measures about to be adopted on reform in Church, State, England and Ireland.'[196]

On 26 November, when Peel was en route from the Continent, Maginn wrote an article for the December number of *Fraser's* mocking those who accused the Conservative party of being 'downright anti-Reform'. 'Sir Robert Peel ... grounds half his fame on various reforms', and long before the Reform parliament, the Tories had been 'quite as earnest and serviceable in the cause of reform' as the Whigs. While Maginn would certainly not have said this of Peel two years earlier, he was justified in arguing that *'Fraser's Magazine* in England, *Blackwood's* in Scotland, the *Standard* newspaper ... had warmly urged on Reform when scarcely a Whig in either country had wagged a finger.' He then dictated rather than recommended the policy Peel must adopt; whether any 'declaration of its views and intentions be made or not', the new Conservative ministry 'ought to be most full and explicit on these *two great points*':

1. That practical reform will be honestly and earnestly carried into effect in every department.
2. No tampering with *fundamental principles* will be tolerated under the pretence of reform. On the first

point we must again remark that the main effort of the
Whig-Radical party at the present moment is to force
upon the Tories that character which they have never
knowingly and voluntarily assumed or deserved, of being
anti-reformers. But nothing can be more dishonest ...

3. Let the [new] Cabinet resolve to meet the House of
Commons with such measures as may carry with them
their own recommendation, and the good wishes of the
country. Opposition will thus be neutralised ... Com-
mence then with propositions, which may be at once
Conservative and ameliorating. Prove to the country, by
acts, that the Tories are not *Anti-Reformers*; and then if
a factious and carping opposition rears its head, dissolve
without a moment's hesitation, and the country will do
its duty.[197]

As he announced through the words of Hook in another *Fraserian*
scenario that January, Peel's 'address to the folks in Tamworth' was
'vague' in comparison to the policies presented by the assembly of
pressmen long before it appeared.[198]

In deference to Peel's wishes, Croker was obliged to be a little vague
himself, but all of his readers would have been familiar with the principles of the *Tamworth Manifesto* from his earlier *Quarterly* articles.
Any serious editorial or political comment in *John Bull* at this time was
almost certainly influenced by Croker, and on 30 November, like all
the others it reiterated the arguments that the choice was now between
the 'Conservatives and the Destructives' and that 'Conservatism does
not necessarily imply Toryism, and that there exists a vast and increasing body of Conservative Whigs.' As with their supporters nationally,
Bull continued that it was waiting for 'a manifestation of principles
from Sir Robert Peel'. However, until he returned from Italy, the arguments made by Mr Sergeant Spankie, a former Whig but now a 'Conservative', best illustrated the principles by which 'we believe the
country will be saved from the ruinous inroads of the revolutionary
party'. *Bull* dedicated a full page to his speech: 'Imperfections [were]
to be corrected and improvements to be made in both Church and
State, and blemishes to be removed which at present deform our institutions.' Reforms should be the 'subject of quiet discussion, of candid
explanation, of mutual concessions', not the dictate of 'a few turbulent
demagogues ... I see no ground, however, to apprehend that just and
reasonable reform in any department will necessarily be sacrificed by

the change of Ministers.' The Whigs can no longer 'carry even safe reforms without risking at almost every step the convulsion of the State'. A government of unity was required: 'neither high Churchmen, nor Dissenters, nor Tories, nor Whigs, nor Aristocrats, nor Democrats can be permitted to carry every measure to the extent of their prejudices and our Constitution affords the opportunity for all to live in peace.'[199]

In late January Murray wrote to Croker referring to *Bull*'s 'Spankie address' when referring to 'THE article' Croker was preparing, that was of greater importance 'than to any other since the establishment of the "Quarterly Review"'.[200] When Croker finished it he sent the proofs to Peel saying that 'his sole object was to do good' and 'you are the best judge of <u>how</u> good is to be done.' Peel should 'scribble the margins freely, for this copy no eye but mine shall ever see, and no-one can tell that you and I are in any communication about it'.[201] Peel replied that he was so busy he had hardly time to read it, but suggested that he was not greatly concerned with the details. His manifesto had been primarily designed 'from the policy of aiding our friends at the election', and 'our main hope must be in the adhesion of moderate men, not professing adherence to our politics. Do not therefore discourage their adhesion by an attack on their party, or enable their leaders to throw scruples of honour and feeling in the way of their withdrawal from old connections.'[202]

Considering that winning the moderate Whigs had been one of Croker's main ambitions since he began his Commons campaign in 1831, it was perhaps rather unnecessary to emphasise this. Of equal early significance had been the arguments he made, such as the one in January 1832, that it had 'never been denied by any person professing to belong to the conservative party, and certainly not by us' that Reform 'as on all other subjects of the moment, public opinion (by which we mean, the prevailing opinion of persons competent to form a sound judgement on such matters)' would 'sooner or later overcome all obstacles'. The only condition was that 'time be afforded in all cases for the opinion being deliberately formed and clearly ascertained'.[203] In December 1832 he had appealed to moderate Whigs, acknowledging that a substantial number of 'members absolutely *conservative* will be returned', emphasising their affinity with the '*Conservatives*' and that 'we expect to see in the House of Commons many conservative names' and that they should unite against the ultras.[204] In the same number, as well as in April 1833, he warned of the revolutionary threat offered by the combined

Destructives, the need for moderates to unite and of the importance of 'Party'. Reform, he continued, when proven by the deliberative filters of the legislature was constructive, and added that in a conciliatory appeal the great majority of 'our new representatives' in the reformed Commons were 'as upright and conscientious men as any of their predecessors'.[205]

One of the first things Croker acknowledged in his review of the *Manifesto*, was that Peel 'must accept as FACT – the changes which the Reform Bill has made in the practice of the constitution and ... avail himself of all the good of which its friends consider it susceptible, and palliate its mischiefs.' There 'was no other commonsense mode of dealing with any of the fluctuating affairs of mankind',[206] and the Conservatives were better qualified to protect the reformed Commons because their ministry would be dedicated to preserving the constituted structures from further depredations. He reminded his readers that Peel had protected and preserved the Whig ministry and 'justly says that the whole of his political life evinces a sincere, though not blind, deference to *public opinion*' but 'by the paramount consideration of what may be really and permanently beneficial to *public interests*'. No minister ever stood against public opinion, and in 'that *principle* the Reform bill has made no change', but in the past it acted 'slowly through Parliament and upon the government ... examining, correcting and improving *itself*'. This was the principle of good government managing corrective reform, and Croker continued by using the same fluid metaphors he had used since July 1831.[207] 'The first burst from that popular spring is naturally somewhat turbid and requires to be filtered, before it becomes fit for use, by various salutary impediments of the old system.' 'Purified in its quality, [it] was rendered not eventually less powerful, but more regular in its supply, and more wholesome in its effects.'[208]

Those who argued that Peel was anti-reform forget that he had made 'an important concession to Public Opinion' in the 'the case of Catholic emancipation', when he was 'applauded by every liberal in the country', and 'a statesman, to be, in the true spirit of the word, consistent, must adapt his judgment to the fluctuation of events in which he is destined to live.' This was the political philosophy Croker rather than Peel had promoted and used unsuccessfully when trying to convince Peel and some other Tory leaders to support Emancipation and moderate Reform before they created a crisis. He continued nevertheless, that 'Sir Robert Peel' means to continue 'in perfect consistency with the whole tenor of his public life' and 'to conduct his government in ... "the correction of proved abuses and the redress of real grievances" ... and the conservation of the great principles of the constitution of the Church and the State'.[209] Those 'Whigs who see the danger of coalition with the Radicals as strongly as we do' were reluctant 'to be dragged by men they despise into an alliance with men they distrust'. They should consider the urgency of the situation and not be 'forgetful of the old principles' of the Whig party:

> We have always had great respect for fidelity to party connexions. We are in that – as in everything else – disciples of Mr Burke. Party was in our old system one of the safeguards of the constitution; but even under the old system, there were occasions when honour and patriotism not only allowed, but required the sacrifice of party feelings. Witness the cases of the Duke of Portland, Lords Fitzwilliam and Spencer, Mr Windham and of Mr Burke himself ... Witness Lord Goderich and Palmerston ... not to mention Lord Melbourne – all recent from an alliance with the Duke of Wellington and Sir Robert Peel.[210]

The most important issue hanging 'in the balance of debate is no longer Whig and Tory – of this party or that – of individual men – or even particular measures – the question is shall we maintain the *British Constitution* – YES or NO? ... The Conservatives need no more expressive watchword – no safer rallying point' against those who demand 'change for its own sake'. '*The Church*, we need not say what is intended for her. Her property is to be the first battlefield ... the *Laws*, civil, criminal and ecclesiastical, all are themselves arraigned' and the rights of other property would follow. '*Land, Manufacturers*, menaced with a deluge of foreign produce', and parliament is 'threatened with a radical subversion ... and a majority, we are told, of the Irish representatives are pledged to attempt to repeal the Union!'

> Finally, and most fearfully of all, the Protestant religion itself is to be stripped of its established rights – its connexion with the state, coeval with the state itself, is to be forcibly dissolved. ... These are the prospects of the *Movement* system [that] have been openly stated, avowed and advocated by one class or other of that *now united and unanimous body*, which has arrayed itself against Sir Robert Peel's Administration.[211]

The only safe alternative was a strong government led by Sir Robert Peel informed by the principles of Croker's own Irish political hero:

> The abuse of the word reform is about to be corrected. For the last four years [reform] has been synonymous with subversion and revolution; we have now a prospect that it may return to its more proper sense – of remedy and reparation. [Peel's] letter to his constituents, and subsequent speeches ... show that he places his administration on the basis laid by the wisest of statesmen – 'a disposition to preserve, and an ability to improve'. That wisest of statesman, that patriarch of rational reform, has left us in a few clear and beautiful words the safe rule of conduct – the authentic canon of the reformation: 'We shall find,' says Mr Burke, 'employment enough for a truly patriotic, free and independent spirit, in guarding what we possess from violation. I would not exclude alteration either – but even when changed, it should be to preserve. I should be led to my remedy by a great grievance. In what I did I should follow the example of our ancestors. *I would make the reparation as nearly as possible in the style of the building.* A politic caution, a guarded circumspection, a moral rather than a constitutional timidity, were the ruling principles of our forefathers.'
>
> The first great question now about to be decided is whether the House of Commons is actuated by a like spirit of moderation, discretion and justice; or is it to strike without hearing and to rush at once into the chaos of general innovation? – which, in short, does it intend – REFORM or REVOLUTION ...[212]

Those eminent 'Whigs whose late secession from the *Destructive* ministry seemed to afford a rational hope ... might see no inconsistency in joining a *Conservative* one'. The 'circumstance of the times are such that the Whigs of the school of Walpole, Pelham, Burke, Windham or even Grattan or Fox ought in fair construction and application of the principles of those great men to be now Conservatives'.[213] For Croker, these were the two parties he had predicted were being formed in 1831, and 'if Sir Robert Peel fulfils his professions – as no one doubts that he will – by correcting all acknowledged abuses, and operating salutary reforms, he will leave no man any resting place between him and Mr O'Connell.' Furthermore, given that 'Lord Stanley has given of his resolution to maintain the Constitution in Church and State, we cannot bring ourselves to doubt whatsoever of the side on which influence and his talents will be eventually employed.'[214]

Croker's article would appear too late to have any influence upon the elections, but the others continued to promote the same policies and the importance of organising the 'Conservative party'. In January *Blackwood's* heralded that the Conservatives would 'SEPARATE REVOLUTION FROM REFORM' and rather than 'dam up the streams of improvement, they will only direct it into safe and fertilizing channels'; society 'is dividing into two classes, and two classes only, Conservatives and Destructives', and moderates must unite in 'conservative amelioration'.[215] *Fraser's* proclaimed that the Reform bill 'was *final* as regarded the constitution of Parliament', but the policy of reform should continue. The choice for 'Conservative Whigs was Reformers' or '*Destructives*', and 'if you commit the empire to the care of Durham, Hume and O'Connell' you will precipitate 'your native land into the gulf of Revolution and civil war'.[216]

THE MINISTRY OF A HUNDRED DAYS

Croker wrote to Wellington on 11 January predicting that although they would win a substantial number of seats, their ministry could not last long, 'but I will not worry you with my croakings'.[217] The Whigs and Stanleyites won roughly 218 seats, the Radicals and O'Connellites 150, and the Conservatives 290 reliable supporters. This made them the largest single party in England and the Commons, and while pleased at the result, young Gladstone expressed the common view that they still only entertained a small 'deliberate and reasonable hope ... that we have now some prospect of surviving the Reform Bill without a bloody revolution', but they were all determined to put up the best possible fight.[218] Just before the beginning of the new session Peel wrote to Croker:

> I doubt whether the Whigs *can* turn me out on the Address, but I cannot tell you how little all this disturbs of disquiets me. I have done my best. I will leave nothing undone to succeed ... If I fail, having nothing to reproach myself with, no man was ever installed in office with half the satisfaction to his own personal and private feelings as I shall retire from it, and sit with you in the new library at Drayton manor after a day's shooting ...[219]

The Commons assembled on 19 February, and the first point of business produced a minor defeat for the Conservatives when Manners-Sutton lost the Speakership to Abercromby by 316 votes to 300. This was something of a test of a new secret alliance between the Whigs and some Radicals; and most importantly the O'Connellites, made at Lichfield House on 18 February.[220] It rapidly became clear that Peel's ministry could not survive more than a few weeks, but the Lichfield pact and the fear many believed it posed for the future of the Irish Anglican Church and community remained a growing popular concern in Britain. As John Wolfe has shown, 'the general election of January 1835 marked the culmination of the process by which Protestantism returned to the status of a central issue in politics after the hiatus following Emancipation.' The 'situation of the Irish Protestants was attracting widespread and emotive attention', and to 'emphasise this aspect of public opinion is to complement, but not to contradict, conventional attention to the *Tamworth Manifesto* and moderate Conservatism'. Many who had traditionally 'despised Toryism' would give increasing support to the Conservatives as the cry of 'Protestantism in Danger' raised the concern of many former Anglican critics; both Whig moderates and Radicals such as Burdett, as well as Irish Presbyterians and English, Welsh and Scottish Dissenters.[221]

The press circle could take some satisfaction in seeing this as largely the fruition of their efforts. *Fraser's* pronounced itself 'satisfied beyond expression' with Peel's proposals for Church Reform: the 'object being not to destroy, but save the Church', and while keen for funding to be used to educate or relieve the poverty of Irish Catholics,[222] Maginn remained fervently opposed to any Church or public funds being given to the Catholic clergy who he deemed were 'blinded by hereditary or imbibed hatred of the Established Church' and sought to destroy it.[223] Like Croker, *Blackwood's* was not opposed to them receiving a government stipend, but only saw a slim chance of it having any positive effect. 'By all means introduce general commutation of tithes, remove the evils of non-residence and pluralities ... increase the efficiency of the Clergy – none of which will help the poor', although it may 'help disarm the Catholic priesthood and the Great Agitator'. But if the government really wished to improve the state of Ireland and relieve the sufferings of its people, then let the 'Conservative Reformers introduce, and that right speedily, a general system of Poor Laws divested of the evils which disfigure the English system [and] set in foot great public works'.[224]

By this time, as Brendan Cahill has pointed out, *The Times* had become as vociferous in its denunciations of the Irish 'Popery' and defence of the Irish Anglican Church and community as any of the press circle.[225] However, as with the rest of the circle, the main feature was its passionate defence of the Irish poor and demands for radical Irish reforms. 'Nothing is easier than to inflame the suffering wretch,' and 'the great majority of the people of Ireland are suffering under the most cruel wrongs that bad laws and bad usages can inflict.' The 'two great evil' obstructing improvement, however, were the 'demagogues' and those who direct 'the monstrous outrages which defy the laws and invest human nature with the characters of demons'.[226] 'Poor laws to relieve the destitute poor of Ireland had long been a favourite and earnest object of this journal', and however many 'improvements might be effected by Popery or tithe laws, they would have no effect'. What did 'Emancipation accomplish for the relief of the Irish Peasantry ... for the poor – for the distressed – for the naked and the starving ... Literally! – Rigorously! – Nothing!', and Daniel O'Connell is 'called a "Liberator" never having moved his little finger to assuage the sufferings'.[227] Throughout the year *The Times* continued to condemn the 'heartless New Poor Law Act' in Britain, 'that unchristian Law – really in fact more horrible than Shylock's bond', and called for 'Poor laws for Ireland ... founded on the principle of the 43rd Elizabeth', which would 'accomplish more for the repose of Ireland than any effort of political economy'.[228]

Despite their growing Conservative support, retaining their authority in a disruptive Commons would prove increasingly difficult, and when the cabinet met on 27 February Peel was 'noticeably depressed'.[229] On 10 March they won the vote on Malt Tax and he recovered his spirits, with Croker writing that he was 'resolute, and so I may say are his friends'. Unfortunately, 'power has no solid basis to enable it to stand', he told Hertford, and teased him for having 'prudently adopted O'Connell's livery' by using green notepaper.[230] A week later the ministry proposed a motion for Irish Church tithe reform similar to the one Grey and Stanley had approved. Few doubted that Russell would wreck it by moving a motion for lay appropriation, and Peel suffered a barrage of daily abuse from the opposition backbenches as the day approached. He wrote to all the cabinet members saying it was pointless to continue, but Wellington encouraged him to 'bear with the evils of your position, till the conviction will be general that you cannot any longer maintain it.'[231] Croker reinforced this by emphasising that how they fought the fight was of greater importance:

The utter prostration of the Conservative Party which will attend your resignation make it necessary that every man should be satisfied that you did not abandon the ship so long as two planks stuck together ... I would push on public business every day and at all not unreasonable hours. I would bring obstacles and impeding arguments to a nightly division; if necessary more than one. The vulgar and disorderly palavering of the House disgusts the people out of doors, they will be more disgusted to find the business is impeded, this you must show. I know how irksome to your feelings ... it is to hold on against a majority ... but I <u>also think that the principles in which you undertook your task, and the spirit you have hitherto professed to act, have pledged you not to be put out by abstract affront</u> ... some people who affect to know something of Stanley think that a junction with him is now possible ... certainly it would be well for you, for him and the Conservative interest that you would be united at least in the future Opposition ... All the world talks of you with admiration.[232]

Peel responded resolutely that Russell's anticipated motion would be resisted on 'principle and by direct opposition'. It 'was no abstract one. It means the destruction of the Church in Ireland', and Lord Stanley 'approves of our course and will cordially act with us on this discussion'. It 'would not save us long – perhaps not a day – but it would make the Conservative Party so strong in Opposition as to afford us some little hope and security for persons and property'.[233] On 1 April Stanley attacked the Whigs for allying themselves with O'Connell, and Peel joined him in denouncing amendment to appropriate Irish Church income as a pretence: 'an unprofitable right to apply an imaginary surplus to an unexplained purpose'.[234] But the Whig alliance won the vote, and what Croker would have considered the first Conservative ministry was defeated by a majority of thirteen and Peel handed his resignation to a disappointed king on 8 April.

His short tenure of power 'saw a remarkable increase in Conservative strength and no doubt helped efface the bitter Tory memories of the "betrayals" of 1829 and 1832'. The O'Connellite majority had been the guarantee of the Whigs' success, Angus Macintyre continues, for the week before the vote, 'at a dinner given for Russell on 28 March, O'Connell had formally affiliated his faction under the Whigs' leadership, declaring that "it was the most delightful evening he ever passed in his life".'[235] On the other side, unity would develop between the Conservatives, Stanley and most Whig 'conservatives' and old ultra-Tories. This 'sealed the fate of the centre party' that Stanley and Graham had hoped to establish, Robert Stewart suggests, meaning that if the Whig ministry were to survive it would have to remain 'tied to its Radical tail'.[236] While Croker would have agreed with the second part of this assessment, rather than 'seal the fate of the centre party', in his view it had helped consolidate and establish the Conservatives as the moderate *via media* of British politics.

Many years later, when Croker's reputation as a reactionary 'enemy of reform in every shape' was becoming firmly established, in contrast to Peel's continuing to rise as a lost 'liberal' among the Tories, Croker remarked in a sarcastic and resentful *Quarterly* article that Peel may have secretly been a 'liberal', but he could hardly believe it. 'The Tories were satisfied and the Whigs dissatisfied at seeing him an avowed supporter of Lord Eldon's [ultra-Protestant] section of the Liverpool Cabinet, and from him, they in their respective views neither feared nor hoped for a conversion to liberalism.' Peel only gave 'one great warning' of any actual political liberality, and this had been when 'he suddenly fell in love with the *bête noir* of his whole preceding life and embraced Catholic Emancipation' having helped divide the Tory party and earned the enmity of his old 'Ultra-Protestant' allies. After 1829 'there existed in many quarters a strong feeling of dislike and distrust of Sir Robert Peel' that would only be 'allayed, if not obliterated' five years later 'by the energy and apparent sincerity of his opposition to Lord Melbourne's Ministry in 1834'.[237] As Angus Hawkins argued more recently, Peel had been reluctant to promote the early Conservatives before Melbourne took office, after which, however, he would play an important part in decking out the new party in its 'rhetorical livery'.[238]

Careful historian that he was, Croker was well aware that although a 'great man' may commonly receive the greatest accolades, it was often those relegated to the wings or behind the scenes of history who had first produced the 'rhetorical livery', managed the production, and won most of the audience. By the mid-1830s, the religious and political conciliation, the unitary *via media* he had campaigned for in his homeland since he was a student at Dublin University, had been largely lost. If he felt bitter at the failure of his ambitions for Ireland and the decline of his own reputation and the elevation of Peel and O'Connell, the two old rival 'ultra' champions, as national political icons, there was perhaps some patriotic consolation in seeing something of an Irish tradition of thought at the centre of his new party's political philosophy. As he had argued in his *Quarterly* articles, some Conservatives had a long history of fidelity to party and to the unitary principles of corrective reform and conciliation, and they were 'in that – as in all things – the disciples of Mr Burke'.[239]

NOTES

1. Add. MSS 40320, Croker to Peel, 7 August 1832, ff.210–12. See also Duke MS, box three, no cat. nos, random dates between August and December for invitations.
2. Duke MS, box 3, Croker to Wellington, 11 August 1832, part cited in *Croker Papers*, II, pp.183–4.
3. Longford, *Wellington*; on 24 March 1831 Wellington said: 'I certainly never will enter the House of Lords if it shall pass', p.278.
4. *Croker Papers*, Wellington to Croker, 14 August 1832, II, p.184.
5. Clements MS, Lb. 26, Croker to Major, 17 May 1832, f.361, and box 12 for other letters.
6. Ibid., box 12, Boyton to Croker, 12 July 1832, and from Singer, Duke MS, box 3. See also Clements MS, Lb. 26, Croker to Boyton, f.384, to Lloyd, f.386.
7. Spence, 'The Philosophy of Irish Toryism', p.72.
8. Ibid., p.72 and also citing letter from Boyton to Lord Farnham, 29 February 1832.
9. *Croker Papers*, Peel to Croker, 10 August 1832, II, p.188 and 15 August 1832, p.190.
10. See Clements MS, Lb. 27, August to November, ff.20–65 and Add. MS 40320, Croker to Peel, ff.214, 217 and 220.
11. Add. MSS 40320, Croker to Peel, 11 October 1832, f.217; and see Clements MS, Lb. 27, f.25.
12. Duke MS, box 3, Peel to Croker, 14 October 1832.
13. See Add. MSS 38078, Wellington to Croker, f.14 and *Croker Papers*, Croker to Hertford, II p.192.
14. See also *Quarterly Review*, 'How Will It Work', for this policy, December 1832, pp.542–4.
15. Add. MSS 40320, Croker to Peel, 17 October 1832, f.222.
16. Parry, *The Rise and Fall of Liberal Government*, p.87; John Derry, *Politics in the Age of Fox, Pitt and Liverpool* (Basingstoke, 1990), pp.195–7; Bentley, *Politics Without Democracy*, p.55 and the early work of F.S. Nowley, 'The Personnel of the Parliament of 1833', *English Historical Review*, vol. LIII (1938).
17. Clements MS, Lb. 27, Croker to Hertford, 11 and 13 December 1832, ff.64–5, part cited in *Croker Papers*, II, p.196. The figures are taken from a later undated report cited by Jennings, p.198.
18. Jenkins, *Goulburn*, pp.240–1, citing Add. MS 40333, 5 November 1832; see also Add. MS 57401.
19. Edward Herries, *J.C. Herries: A Memoir of a Public Life* (London, 1880), pp.163–6.
20. Duke MS, folder for 1832, Lees Giffard to Croker, 11 June 1832.
21. *Standard*, 12 March 1833. For some more examples of reports and advocacy of a variety of 'Conservative' organisations in early 1833, see 2 ,7, 9, 18, 28 February and 1, 5, 7, 12 March.
22. *Blackwood's*, July 1832, pp.140–3. See also 'The Late Conservative Dinner in Edinburgh', in February 1833, pp.260–74.
23. Ibid., February 1833, 'The Late Conservative Dinner', pp.270–1.
24. See *The Times* for 17, 29 November 1832; see also 1, 3, 6, 7, 8 December, 11 January 1833 for the use of the term Conservative at this time.
25. *Quarterly Review*, 'How Will it Work?' December 1832, p.544.
26. Ibid.
27. Ibid., p.545.
28. Ibid.
29. *Quarterly Review*, December 1832, p.552.
30. *The Times*, 11 January 1833.
31. Ibid., Croker to Hertford, 6 January 1833, ff.67–9.
32. Clements MS, Lb. 27, Croker to Hertford, 6 January 1833, ff.67–9.

33. Hilton, *A Mad, Bad Dangerous People*, p.194.
34. *Quarterly Review*, 'The Reform Ministry and the Reform Parliament', October 1833, p.223.
35. See Stanley H. Palmer, *Police and Protest in England and Ireland: 1780–1850* (Cambridge, 1988), pp.318–45 for a statistical account of events in Ireland and government responses at this time.
36. Clements MS, Lb. 26, Croker to Mr Bishop, 21 December 1831, ff.172–3.
37. Virginia Crossman, *Politics, Law and Order in Nineteenth-Century Ireland* (Dublin, 1996), p.52.
38. See Bowen, *History and Shaping of Irish Protestantism*, p.241; Crossman, *Politics, Law and Order*, pp.49–71; O'Ferrall, *Catholic Emancipation*.
39. Palmer, *Police and Protest*, pp.322–6, and see pp.338–41 for statistical graphs and details.
40. *Wellington New Despatches*, Wellington to Maurice Fitzgerald, 16 December 1832, VIII, pp.486–7.
41. *Blackwood's*, 'Ireland', January 1833, pp.67, 72.
42. *Quarterly Review*, 'State and Prospects for Ireland', January 1832, pp.414–15, 439–41 and 456–60.
43. *Blackwood's*, 'Ireland', January 1833, p.79.
44. Ibid., pp.78–81. See also 'Tithes' by Samuel O'Sullivan, March 1833 and *Fraser's*, March 1833, pp.283–91 for similar arguments.
45. *Blackwood's*, January 1833, pp.86–7.
46. Macintyre, *Liberator*, p.37.
47. Ibid.
48. *Hansard*, XV, 5 February 1833, cols 140–3.
49. Ibid., col. 143.
50. Ibid., cols 184–6.
51. Ibid., O'Connell, cols 148–61, and see Russell, col. 161.
52. 'Le Marchant Diary', in Aspinall, *Three Diaries*, p.295.
53. *Hansard*, XV, 6 February, cols 250–2, 256, 259 and 264.
54. Ibid., 7 February, cols 435–43, and see *The Times*, 8 and 9 February 1833; O'Dwyer's speech, cols 419–24.
55. Ibid., cols 444–8, and *The Times*, 8 February 1833.
56. *The Times*, 8 February 1833. The elderly rector of Golden, near Cashel, had also been found in a field with his head smashed in by rocks, and other such incidents were reported in detail by the circle, and in the case of *Fraser's* hugely exaggerated; see 'Church Reform: The Irish Althorpeans', April 1833, p.430.
57. *Hansard*, XV, cols 448–51; *The Times*, 9 February 1833.
58. Ibid., pp.452–3. *The Times*, 9 February 1833, contains a longer report, designed to make O'Connor's account appear more trivial and callous than in *Hansard*.
59. Macintyre, *Liberator*, pp.46–7.
60. *Croker Papers*, Croker to Hertford, [9] February 1833, II, pp.201–2.
61. 'Ellenborough Diary', in Aspinall, *Three Diaries*, p.298; see Gash, *Sir Robert Peel*, pp.45–6 for a full account.
62. *Hansard*, XVI, 1 March 1833, cols 75–99.
63. Add. MSS 40320, Croker to Peel, 1 and 3 March 1833, ff.232–4.
64. *John Bull*, 4 March 1833.
65. Mandler, *Aristocratic Government*, p.152. For another perspective see A.D. Kriegel, 'Whiggery in the Age of Reform', *The Journal of British Studies*, 32, 3 (July 1993), pp.290–8.
66. Gash, *Sir Robert Peel*, p.48.
67. *Quarterly Review*, October 1833, 'The Reform Ministry and the Reform Parliament', pp.224–5.
68. See *Blackwood's*, 'Ireland (no. IV): The Coercive Measures – Church Spoliation', pp.561–82; 'The 'Progress of the Movement: Incipient Plunder and Subversion of the Irish Church', pp.651–67, both in the April 1833 number.
69. *John Bull*, 18 February, 15 July and 16 December 1833.
70. *Fraser's*, 'Ireland and the Priests', March 1833, pp.264–6.
71. *The Times*, 13 January 1832; for a short account of O'Connell's attempt to obtain Protestant support for Repeal in Dublin, see MacDonagh, *The Emancipist*, pp.69–70.
72. *Dublin University Magazine*, 'On the Emigration of Protestants', May 1833, pp.470–1, 482, 479.
73. Ibid., 'The Present Crisis', January 1833, pp.8–10 and 3–5; see also 'A Brief Discourse on General Politics', February 1833, p.113, and April 1833, p.384.
74. Ibid., p.5.

75. Spence, 'The Philosophy of Irish Toryism', pp.181–4. They especially acknowledged Burke's *Appeal from the New Whigs to the Old*, and argued that it was 'precisely' the same philosophy. Canning was included posthumously for having declared himself 'proud to be an Irishman', and a 'Tory of the present hour'. This was tantamount to being a 'Whig of the old school of Mr Burke ... thus all glory was kept within the Irish Tory family', pp.182–3.

76. *Dublin University Magazine*, 'Ancient Whigs and Modern Tories', May 1833, p.508 and see also 'What is a Radical', September 1836, p.289, both written by O'Sullivan. Both are also part cited in Spence, 'The Philosophy of Irish Toryism', p .183. Croker had said the same in *Quarterly Review*, 'Friendly Advice to the Lords', July 1831, p.518 and as has been seen in Chapter 8, the Irish pressmen associated themselves with what is normally seen as the Whig tradition of the Glorious Revolution.

77. Clements MS, Lb. 27, 10 April 1833, Croker to William Blackwood, f.152.

78. Almost every number of the Conservative/Tory publications contained similar articles on the Church and the state of Ireland from this period on, as well as directives for 'Conservative' policy and tactics to its readers. Some are quoted in the general text, but see in particular *Blackwood's*; 'Tithes' by Samuel O'Sullivan, pp 321–7 and 'Ireland: The Administration of Justice', by Archibald Allison, pp.338–57, both in March 1833; 'Ireland: The Coercive Measures – Church Spoliation', by A. Alison, pp.561–82; 'The Progress of the Movement: Incipient Plunder of the Church', by S. O'Sullivan, pp.651–67, both in April 1833; 'A Letter to the King on the Irish Church Bill', by George Croly, pp.705–36, May 1833; 'The Rev. Charles Boyton of Trinity College Dublin', pp.171–2, August 1833; 'The Irish Union', by Croly, pp.569–93, October 1833; 'The Irish Union (II)', by Croly, pp.204–27, February 1834; and 'The Irish Union (III)', pp.386–404, March 1834; 'The Present State of the Parties', by John Wilson, pp.883–98, June 1834; 'The Church and its Enemies, letter from a Liberal Whig', by J.H. Merivale, pp.954–60, June 1834; 'The Fall of Earl Grey', by A. Alison, pp.246–57, August 1834; 'The Character of the Reform Parliament', by A. Alison , pp.661–73, November 1834; 'Ireland', V, by A. Alison, pp.747–67, December 1834; ' Ireland: A Deputation from the Irish Protestants to the People of England', by S. O'Sullivan, pp.210–24, February 1835; February 1835, 'Ireland' pp.211–24 containing extracts of the arguments of Boyton and O'Sullivan on Irish affairs. For similar arguments in the *Quarterly Review* see 'The Reform Ministry and the Reformed Parliament', by Croker, pp.224–6; October 1833, 'State and Prospects of Ireland', by Mortimer O'Sullivan, pp.410–61, January 1832; 'The Church and the Voluntary System', pp.175–213, February 1834. In *Fraser's* see 'Ireland and the Priests', pp.251–66 and 'Church Reform', pp.346–9; March 1834 and 'Ireland and the Progress of the Repeal Question', pp.253–67, March 1833; 'Church Matter', pp.379–98, April 1834; 'The Rev. Mr Croly ...', pp.711–25, December 1834; 'Church Reform', pp.247–58, March 1835, all by Maginn.

79. Spence, 'The Philosophy of Irish Toryism', pp.64–5.

80. B.T. Bradfield, 'Sir Richard Vyvyan and the Country Gentlemen', *English Historical Review*, vol. LXXXXIII (1968), pp.729–43. See also Stewart, *Foundations*, pp.128–75, and *Party and Politics*, pp.102–4.

81. Add. MS 40502, Croker to Peel, 20 February 1842, ff.326–7.

82. Duke MS, folder 1832, Lees Giffard to Croker, 11 June 1832.

83. *Quarterly Review*, 'The Present and Last Parliament', April 1833, pp.272–4.

84. Ibid., pp.271–2.

85. Ibid., pp.272–4.

86. Ibid., pp.274–80.

87. Ibid., pp.279–81.

88. Aspinall, *Politics and the Press*, pp.158–9.

89. *Croker Papers*, II, pp.214–20. Jennings had access to many of the notes from Peel and Wellington, prior to the dispersal of the *Croker Papers* and reprints a four-page section of one long memorandum from Wellington and a shorter letter from Peel as examples. Other opinions and contributions were made by Goulburn, Lockhart Sugden and G.R. Gleig, a writer for *Fraser's* and *Blackwood's* and, later, Wellington's biographer; see also miscellaneous letters for October and November, Duke MS, box 3, for the period.

90. *Croker Papers*, Peel to Croker, 28 September 1833, II, pp.214–16.

91. Ibid., pp.216–20.

92. *Quarterly Review*, 'The Reform Ministry and the Reform Parliament', October 1833, pp.218–20, 234, 235–49.

93. Ibid., pp.270–1.

94. Add. MSS 40403, Melville to Peel, 22 May 1833, f.252; Gash, *Sir Robert Peel*, p.59.
95. R.B. McDowell, *British Conservatism 1832–1914* (London, 1959), pp.17–18.
96. See Blake, *The Conservative Party: From Peel to Major*, pp.20–3. Blake is referring to Tory Protectionists generally, although he does cite extracts from *Blackwood's* and some other publications. See also Perkins, *Origins*, pp.241–50; Gambles, *Protection*, parts II and III.
97. R.B. McDowell, *British Conservatism*, p.24.
98. Gilbert A. Cahill, 'Irish Catholicism and English Toryism', *The Review of Politics*, 10, 1 (January 1959), pp.62–88; see particularly pp.68–70 for his terms describing the pressmen.
99. *Quarterly Review*, 'Lord John Russell's *Causes of the French Revolution*', April 1833, p.157.
100. Colley, *Britons*, p.369; see also pp.321–75.
101. *Blackwood's*, 'Ireland', December 1834, pp.753–4.
102. Gray, *Irish Poor Law*, pp.87–91.
103. Ibid., p.90.
104. *Fraser's*, 'National Economy: Poor Laws for Ireland', March, 1833, pp.286–91; for *Hansard's* debates, O'Connell and Spring-Rice opposition, see, for example, vol. XIII, cols 831–73.
105. Ibid., p.291.
106. Ibid., April 1833, pp.460–1.
107. Ibid., pp.418–25.
108. Thrall, *Rebellious Fraser's*, pp.155–7 citing from published arguments of Maginn and *Fraser's*, February 1834, pp.324 and 314.
109. Ibid., pp.133, 185–6.
110. Add. MSS 40403 (Peel Manuscripts), no date, but catalogued for 1833, f.305; this may be related to a later contribution, in 1835, see below and 40321, f.186.
111. *Croker Papers*, Peel to Croker, 29 October 1839, II, p.337.
112. *Quarterly Review*, 'The Reformed Ministry', October 1833, p.251.
113. Ibid., 'The Poor Law Question', January 1834, pp.350–62 and 367. This article was almost certainly influenced or approved by Croker, but the greater part the Whig MP for Stroud, George Poulett-Scrope.
114. Ibid., p.367; see also *Quarterly Review*, 'The New Poor Laws', August 1834, pp.258–61.
115. Ibid., pp.368–72.
116. Sack, *Jacobite to Conservative*, pp.174–8.
117. Clements MS, Lb. 27, 6 and 30 May 1833, ff.164 and 171.
118. Macintyre, *Liberator*, p.129.
119. *Hansard*, XXIII, 6 May 1834, cols 650–4 and see also col. 666.
120. Ibid., cols 662–3.
121. See Macintyre, *Liberator*, pp.184–9, p.85 note, and p.182.
122. Ibid., p.132, and see Add. MSS 37307, ff.26–9.
123. See Bentley, *Politics without Democracy*, p.53.
124. Parry, *The Rise and Fall of Liberal Government*, p.109; see also pp.108–12.
125. Add MSS 40320 June (no date but evidently June 1834), ff.14–15. Unfortunately, this is one of the fewer than ten letters between Croker and Peel dealing with political matters for the period April and early November 1834 that appears to have survived, and there is also a gap in Croker's letter-book entries for this period.
126. Aspinall, *Brougham and the Whig Party*, pp.196–7, citing Hatherton's Memoirs and Althorp MS. See Macintyre, *Liberator*, pp.133–4; Aspinall, *Politics and the Press*, pp.282–3; Dublin *Pilot*, 27 July 1833.
127. *Hansard*, XXIV, 7 July 1834; for O'Connell and Littleton's response and some others see cols 1222–54. For the Althorp quotation see Gash, *Sir Robert Peel*, p.70. For O'Connell's insulting Grey see Macintyre, *Liberator*, p.134; Jenkins, *Goulburn*, pp.252–5.
128. MacDonagh, *The Emancipist*, p.104.
129. *Hansard*, XXIII, 4 July 1834, col. 1199. The last speech Peel made that year was on 30 July, its main topic that landlords should be responsible for the collection of tithes and that it should be made integral to the rent, XXV, col. 761.
130. Gash, *Sir Robert Peel*, p.74.
131. Ian Newbould, *Whiggery and Reform, 1830–41: The Politics of Government* (Stanford, 1990), p.136.
132. Stewart, *Foundations*, p.112, citing a letter from Londonderry to Buckingham, 25 March 1833.
133. *Quarterly Review*, 'Sir Robert Peel's Address', February 1835, pp.285–6.
134. Ibid., p.286.

135. Add. MSS 40321, October 1834, ff.18–19 and 20–1.
136. Ziegler, *Melbourne*, p.182.
137. Clements MS, Lb.27, Croker to Hertford, 24 November 1834, ff.295–9. Croker compiled his letters to Hertford in daily segments, and the date given probably indicates his final contribution prior to posting.
138. Ibid., box 13, Croker to Rosamund, 17 November 1834: 'Dearest Love, Do not be afraid, I am not likely to take office if I can refuse without the deepest disgrace, and I hope I shall not be pressed, don't mind what the *Standard* says.'
139. Ibid., Lb 27, ff.300–3, and part cited in *Croker Papers*, II, pp.243–5.
140. Clements MS, box 13, Ferns to Croker, 20 November 1834, and Clements MS, Lb. 27, Croker to Boyton, 21 November 1834, f.313.
141. Ibid., Lb. 27, Croker to Vesey Fitzgerald, 19 November 1834, f.294.
142. *Croker Papers*, Peel to Croker, 9 December 1834, II, p.247.
143. Clements MS, Lb. 27, Croker to Peel, 10 December 1834, ff.315–16, part cited in *Croker Papers*, II, pp.248–9.
144. *Croker Papers*, Croker to Rosamund, 12 December 1834, II, pp.248–9.
145. John Morley, *William Ewart Gladstone: His Life and Times*, 2 vols (London 1908 [Lloyd popular edn]), I, pp.60–72 and 78 for his voting record in the Commons; Philip Magnus, *Gladstone* (London, 1963), pp.15–16. Newcastle's son, Lord Lincoln, was a college friend and had proposed him to his father. Robert Inglis, the ultra-Tory Oxford MP and ally of Newcastle had probably seconded the request.
146. See *Greville Diary*, 19 November 1834, III, pp.144–51; Aspinall, *Politics and the Press*, pp.261–3; Fox Bourne, *English Newspapers*, pp.79–80; Stevens, *History of The Times*, I, pp.343–8.
147. Hilton, *A Mad, Bad, Dangerous People*, p.501. See also Wolffe, *Protestant Crusade*, p.91.
148. Stewart, *Henry Brougham*, p.309. Stewart, however, does not identify the members of the 'small band'.
149. Parry, *The Rise and Fall of Liberal Government*, p.126. Parry illustrates some of the benefits of the Poor Law, as well as its failings. As a guide to some of the extensive debates on the various interpretations of the attitudes to the New Poor Laws, see Anthony Brundage, David Eastwood and Philip Mandler, 'Debate: The Making of the New Poor Law, *Redivivus*', *Past & Present*, no. 127 (1990), pp.183–201. Both of the former deny that there was a general consensus of support among the county gentry for the New Poor Laws.
150. *Quarterly Review*, 'The Reformed Ministry and the Reformed Parliament', October 1833; for Croker's criticism of Brougham, pp.235–49, and the citation on Poor Law commission, p.251.
151. Stewart, *Henry Brougham*, pp.306–7, citing Brougham's speech to the Lords on 21 July 1834.
152. See Innes and Burns, *Rethinking the Age of Reform*, pp.50–1 and *passim*.
153. Parry, *The Rise and Fall of Liberal Government*, p.112.
154. See Aspinall, *Brougham*, pp.203–10.
155. *Fraser's*, 'Bridlegoose Brougham', April 1834, pp.500–3.
156. *Hansard*, XXIII, 9 May 1834, cols 830–1, and XXIV, July 27, cols 915–18.
157. Ibid., XXIII, 19 May 1834, col. 842.
158. See Aspinall, *Brougham*, pp.205–12; Clements MS, box 13, Walter to Croker, 28 August 1834, cited in more detail below.
159. *The Times*, 19, 21 and 23 August 1834; see also Aspinall, *Brougham*, pp.208–9.
160. Clements MS, box 13, Walter to Croker, 28 August 1834.
161. *Quarterly Review*, 'The New Poor Laws', August 1834, pp.233–41.
162. Ibid., pp.242–53 and 261.
163. Thomas Duddy, *A History of Irish Thought* (London, 2002), pp.124–208; the Burke quotation is from *A Letter to a Noble Lord* (London, 1796).
164. Michael Oakeshott, 'Rationalism in Politics', in J.S. McLelland (ed.), *A History of Western Political Thought* (London, 1996), p.777; see also John Gray, *Black Mass: Apocalyptic Religion and the Death of Utopia* (London, 2007).
165. *Fraser's*, 'The Poor Laws into Ireland', December 1831.
166. See *Quarterly Review*, April 1833, pp.272–4 and 156; this was co-written with Lord Mahon.
167. Ibid., 'The Reform Bill', p.559.
168. Stewart, *Brougham*, p.308.
169. *Croker Papers*, Croker to Brougham, 14 March 1839, II, pp.350–1.

170. See Nicholas Edsall, *The Anti-Poor Law Movement, 1834–44* (London, 1971); Peter Mandler, 'Tories and Paupers: The Christian Political Economy and the Making of the Poor Law', *The Historical Journal*, 33, 1 (1990), pp.81–103; Richard Brent, *Liberal, Anglican Politics: Whiggery, Religion and Reform, 1830–1841* (Oxford, 1987).
171. *The Times*, 8 September 1834.
172. Clements MS, box 13, folder 8, Baring to Croker, 12 December 1834.
173. Carlisle MS, D. Lons. L1/2/116, Croker to Lowther, 14 January 1835.
174. Add. MSS 40321, Croker to Peel, 17 December 1834, ff.28–9. See also *History of The Times*, vol. 1, pp.344–5 for an account, and Aspinall, *Politics and the Press*, p.262; Croly is wrongly transcribed as 'Kelly' in both of these.
175. Aspinall, *Politics and the Press*', p.261.
176. Griffiths, *Plant Here the Standard*, pp.53–5; see also Aspinall, *Politics and the Press*, pp.340–1.
177. *Fraser's*, 'The Fraserians', January 1835, pp.22–3.
178. *Croker Papers*, Peel to Croker, 21 January, II, p.259, and Add. MSS 40321, 23 January, f.61.
179. Add. MSS 40321, Lockhart to Croker (Croker sent the original on to Peel), ff.66–75, and Croker to Peel, 1 February 1835, ff.66–75.
180. Ibid., 40231, Lockhart to Croker, 26 January 1835, ff.66–75.
181. Ibid., f.58.
182. Clements MS, Lb. 27 Croker to Lyndhurst, 3 February 1835, also part cited in *Croker Papers*, II, pp.259–61. Croly's articles on Burke appeared in *Blackwood's* between March 1833 and August 1834; some of the other more specifically political articles he wrote for it are 'The Irish Union' '(No. 1)', October 1833, '(No. 2)', February 1834, and '(No. 3)', March 1834; On 'Mirabeau', May 1834 and 'William Pitt', January 1835.
183. Newton-Dunn, *John Bull*, p.297.
184. Add. MSS 40321, Croker to Peel, 15 January 1835, ff.53–7, part cited in *Croker Papers*, II pp.257–8, but incorrectly dated as 18 January; a copy is also in Clements, Lb. 27, ff.368–72.
185. Add. MSS 40321, Croker to Peel, 2 February 1835, f.91, and Peel to Croker, 8 February 1835, f.96.
186. Gash, *Sir Robert Peel*, pp.94–5.
187. Stewart, *Foundations of Conservative*, p.96.
188. Robert Peel, *Address to the Electors of the Borough of Tamworth* (London, 1835), pp.2–5.
189. Ibid., pp.7–9.
190. Gash, *Sir Robert Peel*, pp.96–7; see also *Croker Papers*, Peel to Croker, 26 January 1835, II, pp.256–7. The *Manifesto*, as Ian Newbould has made clear, was for Peel primarily a promotion of a political tactic rather than a political principle; see his 'Sir Robert Peel ... A Study in Failure', pp.529–57.
191. Hawkins, 'Parliamentary Government', pp.652–4. His reference is to a chapter entitled 'The Founder of Modern Conservatism', in N. Gash, *Pillars of Government* (London, 1986), pp.153–61.
192. Hilton, *Mad, Bad, Dangerous People*, p.497.
193. *John Bull*, 21 December 1834. See 1 and 7 December for 'Conservatives' versus 'Destructives' and 29 December for more of the same, and reports of what it described as 'Conservative dinners and meetings which have taken place during the last month in every part of the country'.
194. *Blackwood's*, 'Present State of Parties', June 1834, pp.896–8. See also 'The Fall of Earl Grey', August 1834, and 'The Influence of the Press', September 1834.
195. Ibid., 'The Character of the Reform Parliament', November 1834, p.674.
196. *The Times*, 22 November 1834.
197. *Fraser's*, December 1834 (article dated 26 November), 'Our Closer for the Month', pp.742–7. See also 'The Last News of the Ministry' in same number, p.736, 'State and Property of Toryism', January 1834, pp.1–25, and an article with the same title, September 1834, pp.257–63.
198. Ibid., *Fraser's*, 'The Fraserians', January 1835, pp.22–3.
199. *John Bull*, 1 December 1834 (editorial dated 30 November); see also 7 and 14 December, where Bull emphasised the need to consolidate the Conservative interests on common principles.
200. Iowa MS, MsL. M9826c, Murray to Croker, 22 January 1835, f.218.
201. Add. MSS 40321, Croker to Peel, 25 January 1835, ff.64–5.
202. *Croker Papers*, Peel to Croker, 26 January 1835, II, pp.256–7.

203. Ibid., January 1832, 'Progress of Misgovernment', pp.602–3.
204. *Quarterly Review*, 'How Will it Work?' December 1832, p.544.
205. *Quarterly Review*, 'The Present and Last Parliaments', April 1833, pp.279–81. See also July 1831, pp.506–8 and 514–15; December 1832, pp.542–50; and January 1832, pp.603 and 621. Ibid., pp.279–81.
206. *Quarterly Review*, 'Sir Robert Peel's Address', February 1835, pp.261–2.
207. See *Quarterly Review*, 'The Present and Last Parliaments', April 1833, pp.280–1: 'Popular power is not for use till it has been strained and filtered by some intermediate process ... The Reform bill has broken all our strainers and filtering machines, and has sent us back to drink, as we may say, in a turbulent stream.' See also July 1831, pp.506–8 and 514–15; December 1832, pp.542–50; and January 1832, pp.603 and 621.
208. Ibid., 'Sir Robert Peel's Address', February 1835, pp.263–4.
209. Ibid., pp.264–5.
210. Ibid., pp.268–70.
211. Ibid., pp.274–5.
212. Ibid., pp.278–9.
213. Ibid., pp.280–1.
214. Ibid., pp.285–6.
215. *Blackwood's*, January 1835, 'Fall of the Melbourne Ministry', pp.46–8.
216. *Fraser's*, 'A Few Words to the Supporters of Earl Grey's Administration', January 1835. pp.113–19. See also February 1835, 'The Politics of the Month', pp.235–45.
217. Clements MS, Lb. 27, Croker to Wellington, 11 January 1835, f.388.
218. Morley, *W.E. Gladstone*, I, p.90.
219. *Croker Papers*, Peel to Croker, 10 January 1835, II, pp.255–6.
220. See Macintyre, *Liberator*, pp.135–51.
221. Wolfe, *Protestant Crusade in Britain*, pp.82–3. See also D.H. Close, 'The General Election of 1835 and 1837 in England and Wales', unpublished DPhil. thesis (Oxford, 1966), pp.141–52; Bew, *The Glory of Being Britons*, pp.127–55; and Bowen, *History and the Shaping of Irish Protestantism*, pp.249 and 253–4.
222. *Fraser's*, February 1835, 'The Politics of the Month', pp.241–3. See also 'Church Reform', March 1835, pp.248–59 and 'The Irish Church', April 1835, pp.491–6; *Blackwood's*, 'Fall of the Melbourne Ministry', January 1835, pp.47–8. *Quarterly Review*, 'The Church and the Voluntary System', February 1835, pp.174–215. It should be noted that there were variations in the arguments made by different writers within the same journal, in *Fraser's* especially, but I have not found any that argue against the need for reform.
223. *Quarterly Review*, 'The Church and the Voluntary System', February 1835, pp.194–5.
224. *Blackwood's*, 'Fall of the Melbourne Ministry', January 1835, pp.46–7. See also 'Deputation of the Irish Protestants to the People of England', in the same issue, pp.210–24.
225. See Cahill, 'Irish Catholicism and English Toryism', *passim*.
226. *The Times*, 29 January and 15 February 1833.
227. Ibid., 18 December 1835.
228. Ibid., 9 February 1835 and 18 December 1835.
229. Gash, *Sir Robert Peel*, p.110.
230. Clements MS, Lb. 27, Croker to Hertford, 10 March 1835, ff.397–9.
231. Parker, *Peel Correspondence*, Peel memo dated 26 March 1825, II, pp.292–4, and letter from Wellington, pp.294–5.
232. Add. MSS 40321, Croker to Peel, 26 March 1835, ff.118–21. A slightly different version of this letter, probably copied from a draft, rather than the copy taken from the Peel Manuscripts and actually received by Peel, and cited above was published by Jennings in *Croker Papers*, II, pp.268–9.
233. Add. MS 40321, Peel to Croker, 30 March 1835, ff.126–7; Croker to Peel, 31 March, ff.128–9. Part cited in *Croker Papers*, II, pp.270–1, an identical copy of Croker's letter is also available at Clements MS, Lb. 27, f.415.
234. Gash, *Sir Robert Peel*, pp.115–18.
235. Macintyre, *Liberator*, p.144.
236. Stewart, *Foundations*, pp.116–17.
237. Ibid., 'Peel Policy', June 1847, p.283 and see also pp.282–5.
238. Hawkins, 'Parliamentary Government', pp.639–69, and p.652 for quotation.
239. *Quarterly Review*, 'Sir Robert Peel's Address', February 1835, p 269.

Conclusion

John Wilson Croker did not disappear into political obscurity after
1835 as he had feared; on the contrary, the years between 1835 and
his death in 1857 were marked until near the end by a remarkable
output of writing, particularly essays for the *Quarterly Review*. He
continued to play a role as an advisor and writer for his old party leaders,
remaining on close terms with Peel until 1846, and Wellington until his
death in 1852. After 1835, the Whig alliance would slowly lose popular and parliamentary support, but Peel would, as he said, take care not
to bring down their ministry until he was confident there was no chance
he would 'be the instrument of carrying other men's opinions into
effect'. In the 1841 election the Conservatives won a Commons
majority of roughly eighty MPs, much of this as a result of increasingly
efficient and powerful local Conservative party organisations and the
dedicated efforts of the press circle. The main issues once again were
the defence of the Irish Church and 'Protectionism', in particular agricultural protection. However, after 1841 many Conservatives justifiably feared Peel was weakening on these issues by implementing tariff
reform, eroding the Corn Laws, and conceding to Irish Catholics on education and endowments to Maynooth. Croker loyally campaigned to
convince the *Quarterly*'s readers that this did not represent a creeping
free trade policy or the adoption of weak Whig policies, and on the
ministry's failure to implement the social reforms that many of his circle had hoped for, he adopted Peel's arguments that those who think
governments 'can feed the hungry without labour' are deluding themselves. 'Governments can have no more power over these matters than
... over the wind and waves.' All of which combined to put the *Quarterly* 'increasingly at odds with the opinion of the bulk of the party',
and as William Thomas astutely remarks, probably provoked the attack in 1844 from an increasingly ambitious Disraeli upon 'Croker as
Peel's *éminence grise* in *Coningsby*'.[1]

Not surprisingly, Croker's defence of Peel would also put him at
odds with most of his press circle; although by then two of its most

colourful members had died before they could launch any major assault. Maginn in 1842, from alcoholism and tuberculosis contracted in debtors' prison, but a few weeks before he died he took one last swipe by publishing a resentful verse in the *Age* entitled the 'Familiar Epistle to John Wilson Croker': 'In order then to change your caper, you next got up a Sunday paper, *Id est*, you took in hand the reins, and wielding Hook's prolific Brains and Hertford's purse of ingots full, You boldly issued forth *John Bull*.'[2] Hook had died almost exactly a year earlier, and despite his own increasingly dissolute life being one of intermittent penury and binges after 1835, Croker and Rosamund continued to make him welcome at their home where 'Mrs Croker', a kind and 'rather formidable religious lady, frequently tried her hand at reforming him'.[3] She never succeeded, but following his funeral, his far more respectable nephew, the Reverend W.F. Hook, wrote to Croker:

> I cannot refrain, as the eldest of his surviving relatives, from writing to say that I remember with gratitude that he was indebted to you for almost everything in life. When he was under circumstances of deepest depression, you were the person who helped him; and when all the world was frowning upon him, in you he found a patron and a friend ... and I know he loved you; and you will be glad to hear he died penitent and praying.[4]

Hook was probably the only member of the circle to have had any certain knowledge of Croker's part in the establishment of *John Bull*, and perhaps repaid him by taking any secret he may have had to his grave. John Walter resigned his Commons seat in 1837 from 'disgust and dissatisfaction', he told Croker, 'and not the least with the Conservative powers' over the Poor Law and associated issues, but *The Times* continued to be a loyal if critical supporter. Stanley Lees Giffard remained in control of the *Standard*, as well as *The Morning Herald* after 1840, celebrating the Conservative party election success they had all campaigned for by telling Peel that all the papers under his control 'were unreservedly at your command'. *Blackwood's* and *Bull* concurred; although since the late 1830s, George Croly and the O'Sullivans had become much more fervently hostile to the Irish Catholic movement, writing passionate polemics and touring ultra-Protestant venues like Exeter Hall making fiery speeches warning of the evil ambitions of 'Popery' in Ireland.

John Walter's satisfied assessment after the election that all the 'Government journals ... *The Times*, the *Standard*, the *Post* and the *Herald* were on the same footing' would, however, prove short-lived. The *Standard* would become increasingly concerned with what Disraeli famously described as Peel 'stealing the Whigs' clothes' by eroding Protectionism and wavering on defence of the Irish Church. It would violently disagree with Peel and Croker on the issue of the Maynooth grant, and indicative of Gifford and some of the others' increasing obsession with the Irish Catholic clergy, by May 1845 the *Standard* was even denouncing *The Times* – itself still no friend of Catholicism – for publishing extracts from the 'filthiest part of the most filthy book by which Roman Catholic Priests are made to prepare themselves for the duties of the Confessional'.[5]

It would, however, be the looming horror of famine following the potato blight in Ireland and Peel's purported need to address it with the repeal of the Corn Laws that would finally rupture the Conservative party in parliament, in the constituencies and in the press. In late October *The Times* pre-empted Peel by responding to early reports of Irish famine: 'once we might not have declared for a free trade in corn, now we must', and a week later it attacked Peel for not repealing the Corn Laws and accelerating the approaching catastrophe. But by 4 December it confidently assured its readers that they would be repealed when the new session opened in January. The *Standard* responded with a defence of its 'champion' evocative of 1828 by refuting it as 'an atrocious fabrication'. But Peel was preparing another apostasy, having already told his ministers that this was his intention and irreparably dividing the cabinet and his parliamentary support. He resigned, but returned to office when Russell was unable to form a government, informing the Commons on 22 January that he was firmly resolved to repeal the Corn Laws as the only way the appalling consequences of the famine could be relieved.[6]

In response to Peel's repeated assurances between 1841 and 1845, Croker had used the *Quarterly* to convince party supporters that the Conservative ministry was firmly committed to agricultural protection right up until, as he complained to Wellington on 13 December, 'the bomb burst'. He would, perhaps, have accepted some arguments on the necessity for it, but 'neither I nor the Review can change opinion which two years ago we published under Peel's sanction' because the 'Conservative party have looked to it, and could not now with decency and safety desert its colours.' More importantly, he became increasingly convinced that there was no plausible practical reason for full repeal, and soon discovered that Peel had probably been moving towards this decision before any sign of famine and made up his mind at least as early as October. Wellington agreed with Croker that it had been a deceit and that the 'decision founded upon the potato disease was erroneous', but he reluctantly supported Peel because he feared that no government opposed to it could be maintained in the Commons. On 25 June the bill passed through the Lords. The same evening the Conservative ministry was defeated on another Coercion bill by 292 votes to 219, and John Russell took office and would hold it until 1852.[7]

Croker would formerly break off any fraternal or political connection with Peel, and over the next two years published extensive arguments in the *Quarterly* qualified by statistical research to prove that Free Trade and repealing the Corn Laws will 'not, and could not, and cannot by any possibility, relieve the Irish famine, which is not a famine of corn, but of the means to buy it'. He fully supported the relief of distress, but argued that Peel's policy would have long-lasting destructive consequences in Ireland, because rather 'than the produce of their own soil, which their own labour has contributed to raise, and the whole value which is distributed among themselves and their neighbours', the supposed 'great moral revolution, which was to regenerate Ireland' was basically buying cheap 'American corn'. We 'have heard much of the misery of Ireland attributed to absenteeism', but to 'remove all the agriculture of Ireland to the banks of the Mississippi' is the 'most gigantic scheme of absenteeism that ever entered the mind of man'.[8]

Peel had 'solicited and obtained the confidence of the country in the general election of 1841' by opposing 'the whole scheme of Free Trade'. This was a betrayal in itself, and contrary to the arguments that cheaper bread in Britain will improve the lot of the poor, it will lead to the lowering of wages. The 'sophism' of the Anti-Corn Law leaguers, who were effectively the representatives of the mercantile interest, had swayed Peel, despite there being no sensible reason to believe that foreign rivals would also opt for free trade. Much of Croker's analysis would be proven broadly correct in the long term, but despite his scathing criticisms of his old friend and resentment at the betrayal, unlike most of the old press circle he also argued that Peel was not motivated by any 'sordid or unworthy' motives. It was rather the product of his 'over-cautious and over sensitive ratiocination'; his susceptibility 'to the delusions and plausibilities of theorists' and fear of 'the menaces of popular agitation'. He might, 'as we once hoped he was destined to do, have stayed the revolution', and, quoting Burke, Croker continued that a 'leader of a party is not fit to be in such a position if he is not able to guide the party to unity of opinion by his superior tact and judgment, upon mutual explanation and concession'. Its supporters would not necessarily be hostile to reforms of the Corn Laws, if after careful consideration such reforms were proven a practical corrective. 'It is the main use of Party' that measures may 'be modified and ripened and rendered generally acceptable':[9]

> A party is a kind of republic, of which the leader is only the President – owing to his party the same, or indeed rather stricter allegiance ... in direct proportion with the eminence to which the confidence of the party may have raised him ... The Party raises the man, or, which is nearly the same thing, affords him the same footing and the force to raise himself to great political distinction ... What would be thought of the Minster who, or on any pretence whatsoever should turn against the sovereign – for the Party has been the earlier and greater benefactor.[10]

Like most of the press circle, after breaking off relations with Peel, Croker, joined with Edward Stanley, Lord Derby, and served as one of his close advisors. He adapted, but did not see himself as surrendering his Conservative principles, continuing to argue that all government must ultimately be 'based on property – the land', for 'nothing else can afford any fair prospect or even chance of stability to the national institutions'. This is 'the great fundamental truth that Conservatives should never forget'; but the protectionist corollary of this was that it placed obligations on Conservatives to promote social responsibility and conciliatory reform. Although he would always argue that it was delusion to believe government could or should ever effectively intervene to the extent of most of his press allies, 'it was clearly right, both in principle and practice, that the place which had benefited by the labour of the young and strong should have the burden of maintaining him', and that the 'Cotton Lord in Manchester' having made a 'gigantic fortune' from their labour must share that burden. Putting himself at odds with most of the old press circle, however, he also continued to press Stanley to support legislation to pay the 'Irish priests ... that I have thought for over fifty years as the only measures that could pacify and civilise Ireland'.[11] 'We entreat our friends to ask themselves who were the founders of Maynooth – *William Pitt and Edmund Burke*, the immortal guides and glory of Conservatism!', he argued in the *Quarterly*, and those who fear this may have no beneficial result, forget that 'education is the only missionary: you must teach people to read before they can think', and furthermore, that 'we are not a Protestant people. We are an Anglican and Presbyterian and Roman Catholic people.' The 'great axiom of practical politics … without which the world cannot be governed', is that all 'the wisest or even the boldest statesman can do is endeavour to moderate and guide impulses, which he could not avert'. To steer 'the bark through dangerous rapids into which current events has brought it and to act in public as a wise man does in private life – make the best of bad bargain'.[12]

Croker would continue to dedicate himself to guiding those he believed should be the state's political pilots in his correspondence and within his *Quarterly Articles* until three years before his death. But by the late 1840s his tone of commentary on political developments would increasingly reflect his Jeremiah's view that the damage done to the fabric of the old constitutional structures by the Reform Act would eventually bring about the collapse of social order. He never again made any attempt to return to the parliamentary theatre, and although he supported many of the social changes taking place in the early Victorian years, his political influence within the readership of the *Quarterly* noticeably diminished by the late 1840s. As we have seen, his predisposition to see the gloomier alternative had long been a feature of his politics. Perhaps because, as Thomas says, 'despite his own rise to respectability and affluence he remained the anxious, restless, rootless immigrant, who found a kind of luxury in the indulgence of pessimism and in using his sharp powers of observation and analysis to remind the ruling classes … how insecure the foundations of their authority were'.[13] Yet his maudlin predictions could be politically positive and influential, often shared by his leaders, and usually appreciated. As Lord Stanley wrote to him in 1850, he could give him 'Jeremiad for Jeremiad', and asked Croker to 'take the field in the *Quarterly* … in almost Cassandra like strain, endeavouring to rouse the gentlemen of the country' who hold 'Conservative principles' to the exertions 'which might yet place them at the head of a powerful party'.[14]

In his dealings with his political leaders Croker appears to have always offered his advice and his service in good faith and remained unusually consistent in his principles and political philosophy. The imprint of his Irish origins, the intellectual debt to a tradition of patriotic conciliation carried forward from Swift to Burke, and the example of Revolutionary France and Ireland in 1798 are central to understanding Croker's ideas and the propagandist energy and the urgency by which he sought their dissemination and practical application. The past generation has seen a welcome stirring of scholarly interest in the varieties of nineteenth-century Irish unionism and 'Protestant' history. The simplistic characterisation of the dynamics of Irish political debate and conflict in the Union era in terms of an implacable opposition between, on the one hand, a broad reformist Irish nationalist and overwhelmingly Catholic movement (whether incrementalist or revolutionary) and, on the other, a reactionary unionist resistance to conciliations or reforms has been slowly giving way to a more nuanced and sophisticated representation of the aspirations among the political and 'thinking' classes of all denominations in nineteenth-century Ireland. Much more remains to be done before any balance is achieved however, particularly given the overwhelming dominance of the Catholic nationalist tradition and its revived predominance in Irish cultural and literary studies. To a lesser extent modern British political and literary history still needs to pay greater attention to the influence and writing of less high-profile conservative press writers and politicians, and Croker and his circle's work straddles many of the critical junctions of debate within both of these areas of both Irish and British historiography. In particular, this work has proposed that Croker is pivotal to any examination of the junction between the nature and intellectual tradition of a constructive conciliationist Irish unionist disposition, or what might be called early 'Constructive Unionism' and the origins of a British, and Irish, conservative political ethos and party.

Croker's reputation for political dealing, together with his opposition to the Reform bill and the vilification of a few literary enemies, provides the best key for why Croker's political career has remained so neglected despite the valuable light it can shine on the careers and the characters of his more famous peers. In 1851 he re-read his review of Macaulay's 'mischievous parody of history', and wrote telling John Murray III that he was 'more and more convinced' of its negative influence and that he 'would like to leave behind me an antidote in the same shape as the poison which it is meant to counter react'.[15] He never would, nor would he write the political history of his period that many anticipated, leaving instead a clear field for the enduring vilifications of Whig historians and political and literary enemies like Macaulay, Lady Morgan or Harriet Martineau, who Disraeli permitted to denigrate in the *Daily Press* as a reactionary 'old man' with the 'malignant ulcer of the mind' on the day of Croker's funeral in 1857.

Croker the publicist and political thinker may have been too versatile and talented, and too sharp with his pen and tongue for his own good, but the evidence presented here illustrates that, whatever his flaws, he was more often the opposite of his enemies' caricatures. In closing this study therefore, it is unlikely that any injustice has been done to his reputation as a political figure of consequence, a thinker, writer and politician whose intellectual influence upon his contemporaries was substantial, and deserving of closer attention and respect than it has received. In 1854 he wrote to his old rival of many years Brougham, who was by then his equally conservative friend: 'I dare say you know better than I in my deep retirement', that the 'Reform Bill in establishing the broad principle of representation' had erected into 'omnipotence what was formerly a valuable subordinate agent, now called public opinion'. She had 'been the old queen of the world; she has now become its tyrant, and the newspapers her ministers; that is they assume to represent public opinion'.[16] The irony being, of course, that since he had been a young boy writing 'spin' for Lord Shannon in County Cork, Croker had played a more active part in this than almost anyone.

NOTES

1. Thomas, *Quarrel of Macaulay and Croker*, pp.112–16; the quote from Peel's speech, p.110.
2. *The Age*, 28 August 1842. See also David E. Latane Jr. 'Perge, Signifer – or, Where did William Maginn Stand', in James H. Murphy (ed.), *Evangelicals and Catholics in Nineteenth-Century Ireland* (Dublin, 2005), and also his 'Charles Molloy Westmacott and the Spirit of the *Age*', *Victorian Periodicals Review*, 40, 1 (2007), pp.44–72, at pp.50–6.
3. Myron Brightfield, *Theodore Hook and his Novels* (Harvard, 1928), p.210.
4. *Croker Papers*, 27 August 1841, I, p.261.
5. Griffiths, the *Standard*, pp.63, 73; *Croker Papers*, Walter to Croker, II, p.316; the *Standard*, 5 May.
6. Ibid., quoting from the *Standard*, 10 December 1845; *The Times*, 29 October, 4 December 1845.
7. See *Quarterly Review*, 'Policy of Ministers', September 1843; 'Repeal Agitation', December 1844; 'Ministerial Resignations', December 1845; and *Croker Papers*, III, pp.41, 126, and see pp.27–102 for fuller account.
8. *Quarterly Review*, 'Close of Sir Robert Peel's Administration', September 1846, pp.540–2, 561–5.
9. Ibid., pp.560, 552, 571.
10. Ibid., pp.566–7.
11. *Croker Papers*, III, pp.104, 106.
12. *Quarterly Review*, 'Peel Policy', June 1847, p.311; and 'Ireland', June 1845, pp.267–8, 281.
13. Thomas, *Quarrel of Macaulay and Croker*, p.208.
14. *Croker Papers*, III, p.221.
15. Ibid., III, pp.228, 250.
16. Ibid., III, pp. 342.

Bibliography

PRIMARY SOURCES

Unpublished Manuscript Sources

The British Library Additional Manuscripts, London
Anglesea Manuscripts
Canning Manuscripts
Croker Manuscripts
Halsbury Manuscripts (John Giffard and S.L. Giffard)
Herries Manuscripts
Liverpool Manuscripts
Peel Manuscripts
Wellesley Manuscripts
Annotated items from Croker's French Revolution collection

Clements Library, University of Michigan, Ann Arbor
Croker correspondence, diaries and letter-books
Brougham Manuscripts
Canning–Croker correspondence
Lockhart–Croker correspondence

Cumbria Public Records Office, Carlisle
Croker–Lowther correspondence (Lonsdale papers)

Hammersmith and Fulham Public Record Office, London
Theodore Hook diary and letters

Iowa University Library, Iowa City
Murray–Croker correspondence

National Library of Scotland, Edinburgh
Croker–J.G. Lockhart correspondence
Croker–William Blackwood correspondence
National Library of Ireland, Dublin
Annotated pamphlets by Croker and others

Perkins Library Duke University, Durham, North Carolina

Croker correspondence
Miss Godman's diary

Regenstein Library, University of Chicago
Croker–Theodore Hook correspondence

Smathers Library, University of Florida, Gainseville
Croker–Thomas Casey correspondence

Trinity College Dublin
Minute books and records of the Historical Society: 1796–1800
Croker correspondence

University College London
Brougham–Croker correspondence
Brougham–O'Connell correspondence

Newspapers and Periodicals

Anti-Jacobin or Weekly Examiner
Ballina Impartial
British Review
Courier
Dublin Correspondent
Dublin Evening Post
Dublin University Magazine
Edinburgh Review
Ennis Chronicle
Fraser's Magazine for Town and Country
Freeman's Journal
Guardian
Mayo Constitution
Morning Post
New Monthly Magazine
Pilot
Political Register
Quarterly Review
St James Chronicle
Standard
The Age
The New Times
The Poor Man's Guardian
The Times

British Parliamentary Papers and Reports

The Parliamentary Debates, ed. T.C. Hansard (London)

First Report From the Select Committee on the Employment of the Poor In Ireland (London, 1823)

First and Second Report From the Select Committee on the State of Ireland (London, 1825)

The Parliamentary Acts

The Eighth Report of the Commissioners of Irish Education Inquiry (London, 1827)

Parliamentary Sessional Papers (Newspaper Advertising and Stamp Duty Returns 1827–1831)

The History of Parliament: The House of Commons, 1790–1820, ed. R.G. Thorne, 5 vols (London, 1986)

British Parliamentary Papers, Select Committee Reports of returns and other papers relating to Newspaper Duties (Papers Weekly) 1814–88 (Shannon, 1972)

History of the Irish Parliament 1692–1800, ed. E.M. Johnston-Liik, vol. III (Belfast, 2002)

The Act for the Relief of His Majesties Roman Catholic Subjects (10 April 1829), 10 George IV

Other Printed Sources, Memoirs and Correspondence

Arbuthnot, Charles, *The Correspondence of Charles Arbuthnot*, ed A. Aspinall (London, 1941)

Arbuthnot, H. *The Journal of Mrs Arbuthnot*, ed. F. Bamford and the Duke of Wellington, 2 vols (London, 1950)

Aspinall, A. (ed.), *The Letters of George IV*, 3 vols (Cambridge, 1938)

Aspinall, A. (ed.), *Three Early Nineteenth Century Diaries* [Ellenborough, Le Marchant and Littleton] (London, 1852)

Brougham, Henry, *The Life and Times of Henry Lord Brougham, Written by Himself*, 3 vols (Edinburgh 1871) Broughton, Lord (John Cam Hobhouse), *Recollections of a Long Life, with Additional Extracts from his Private Diaries*, ed. Lady Dorchester, 6 vols (London, 1909)

Broughton, Lord (John Cam Hobhouse), *Recollections of a Long Life, with Additional Extracts from his Private Diaries*, ed. Lady Dorchester, 6 vols (London, 1909)

Burke, Edmund, *The Correspondence of Edmund Burke*, ed. T.W. Copeland, 10 vols (Cambridge, 1958–70)

Burke, Edmund, *The Writings and Speeches of Edmund Burke*, ed. P. Langford, 6 vols (Oxford, 1981–90)

Burke, Edmund, *On Empire Liberty and Reform: Speeches and Letters of Edmund Burke*, ed. David Bromwich (Yale, 2000)

Burke, Edmund, *Reflections on the Revolution in France*, ed. C.C. O'Brien (London, 1968 [179])

Clinch, J.B. and Dr Dromgoole, *Letters on Church Government* (Dublin, 1812)

Clinch, J.B. and Dr Dromgoole, *An Inquiry, Legal and Political Into the Consequences of Giving to his Majesty a Negative on the Appointment of Irish Catholic Bishops* (Dublin, 1810)

Cooke-Taylor, W. *The Life and Times of Sir Robert Peel*, 2 vols (London, 1851)

Creevey, Thomas, *The Creevey Papers*, ed. Sir H. Maxwell, 2 vols (London, 1903)

Crofton Croker, T. *Portraits of Eminent Conservatives* (London, 1840)

Crofton Croker, T. *The Queen's Question Queried: A Pedantless Phillippic Production by an Irish Barrister* (London, 1820)

Croker, John Wilson, *The Opinions of an Impartial Observer on the Late Transactions in Ireland* (Dublin, 1803)

Croker, John Wilson, *Familiar Epistles to Frederick E. Jones Esq., on the Present State of the Irish Stage* (Dublin, 1804)

Croker, John Wilson, *An Intercepted Letter from J—T—, esq., Writer at Canton, to his Friend in Dublin, Ireland* (Dublin, 1804)

Croker, John Wilson, *The History of Cutchacutchoo* (Dublin, 1805)

Croker, John Wilson, *Sketch of the State of Ireland, Past & Present* (London, 1822)

Croker, John Wilson, and Robert Peel and Henry Palmerston, *The New Whig Guide* (London, 1819)

Croker, John Wilson, *Substance of the Speech of John Wilson Croker Esq., in the House of Commons, 4th May 1819; On the Roman Catholic Question* (London, 1819)

Croker, John Wilson, *A Letter from the King to His People*, 7th edn (London, 1820)

Croker, John Wilson, *The State of Ireland: Letters from Ireland on the Present Political, Religious and Moral State of that Country, republished from the 'Courier' Newspaper* (London, 1825)

Croker, John Wilson, *The Life of Samuel Johnson LLD, Including a Journal of a Tour of the Hebrides by James Boswell, Esq: A New Edition with Numerous Additions and Notes, By John Wilson Croker, LLD, FRS* (London, 1831)

Croker, John Wilson, *Military Events of the French Revolution of 1830* (London, 1830)

Croker, John Wilson, *A Letter to Noble Lord who Voted for the Second Reading of the Reform Bill* (London, 1832)

Croker, John Wilson, *The Reform Ministry and the Reform Parliament* (London, 1832)

Croker, John Wilson, *Essays on the Early Period of the French Revolution* (London, 1857)

Croker, John Wilson, *Correspondence between R. Hon. J.W. Croker and R. Hon. Lord John Russell on Some Passages in 'Moore's Diary' With a Postscript by Mr Croker* (London, 1854)

Croly, George, *Popery and the Irish Question: Being an Exposition of the Political and Doctrinal Opinions of Messrs. O'Connell, Keogh, Dramgoule, Gandolphe etc.* [sic] (London, 1825)

Croly, George, *Englishman's Polar Star* (Preston, 1828)

Croly, George, *A Slight Sketchbook* (London, 1813)

De La Hogue, Dr, *Tractatus de Theologia* (Dublin, 1795)

Dictionary of National Biography (Oxford, 1968 [1917])

Doyle, James Warren (J.K.L.), *Letters on the State of Education in Ireland and on the Bible Societies* (Dublin, 1824)

Doyle, James Warren (J.K.L.), *Letters on the State of Ireland Addressed by J.K.L. to a friend in England* (Dublin, 1825)

Drennan, William, *The Drennan–McTier Letters: 1802–1819*, ed. Jean Agnew, 3 vols (Dublin, 2006), vol. II

Dromgoole, Dr Thomas, *The Speeches of Dr Dromgoole Against Surrendering the Government of the Catholic Church in Ireland* (Dublin, 1814)

Ellenborough, Lord, *A Political Diary 1828–30*, ed. Lord Colchester (London, 1881)

Gordon, Mary, *Memoir of John Wilson* (New York, 1963 [re-print])

Grant, J. *The Great Metropolis*, 2 vols (London, 1836)

Grant, J. *The Newspaper Press: Its Origins, Progress, and Present Position*, 2 vols (London, 1871)

Grey, Henry, Earl, *Correspondence with William IV and Sir Herbert Taylor* (London, 1867)

Greville, Charles, The Greville Memoirs: A Journal of the Reign of King George IV, King William IV and Queen Victoria, by Charles Greville, ed. H. Reeves, 8 vols (London, 1888)

Herries, Edward, *J.C. Herries: A Memoir of a Public Life* (London, 1880)

Holland, Henry Edward, *The Memoirs of the Whig Party During My Time*, ed. Lord Richard Holland, 2 vols (London, 1952–4)

Hook, Theodore and Croker, J.W. *(Vicesimus Blinkinsop) Tentamen, or and Essay Towards the History of Whittington, Sometime Lord Mayor of London, by Vicesimus Blinkinsop* (London, 1820)

Jennings, Louis J. (ed.), *The Diaries and Correspondence of the Right Honourable John Wilson Croker, LLD, FRS*, 3 vols (London, 1886)

Kenney, A.H. *Memoir of the Late Right Reverend William Magee* (Dublin, 1842)

Knight, Charles, *Passages of a Working Life*, 3 vols (London, 1864)

Lang, Andrew, *The Life and Letters of John Gibson Lockhart*, 2 vols (London, 1898)

Lloyd, Bartholomew, *An Inquiry Whether the Disturbances in Ireland have Originated in Tithes* (Dublin, 1823)

Lloyd, Bartholomew, *Miscellaneous Observations on J.K.L.'s Letter to Marquis Wellesley* (Dublin, 1824)

Lockhart, Gibson John, *The Life of Sir Walter Scott* (London, 1937 [Everyman edition])

Lockhart, Gibson John, *Theodore Hook: A Sketch* (London, 1842)

MacHale, the Rev. John, *The Letters of the Most Rev. John MacHale, Archbishop of Tuam* (Dublin, 1888), including 'The Hieropholis Letters' (1820)

MacHale, the Rev. John, *The Rev. John MacHale's Testimony to the Maynooth Commission to The Eighth Report of the Commissioners of Irish Education Inquiry* (London, 1827)

Magee, William, *A Charge Delivered at his Primary Visitation in St Patrick's Cathedral, on Thursday the 24th of October 1822* (Dublin, 1822)

Maginn, William, *Miscellaneous Verse and Prose* (London, 1885)

Maginn, William, *Ten Tales by Dr. William Maginn*, ed. R. Montague (Manchester, 1933)

Mahony F.S. *The Reliques of Father Prout* (London, 1873)

Moore, Thomas, *The Journal of Thomas Moore*, ed. W.S. Dowden, 6 vols (Delaware, 1984)

Moore, Thomas, *The Memoirs of Captain Rock, The Celebrated Irish Chieftain with Some account of his Ancestors. Written by Himself* (London, 1824)

Morgan, Lady, *Lady Morgan's Memoirs*, 2 vols (London, 1886)

Newcastle, Duke of, *Unrepentant Tory: Political Selections from the Diary of the 4th Duke of Newcastle-under-Lyme, 1827–1838*, ed. R.S. Grant (Suffolk, 2006)

Newport, Sir John, *The State of Borough Representation in Ireland in 1783 and 1800* (London, 1832)

O'Connell, Daniel, *The Correspondence of Daniel O'Connell*, ed. M.R. O'Connell, 8 vols (Dublin, 1972–80)

O'Connell, Daniel, *Correspondence between Daniel O'Connell and the Rev. Dr Blake, Catholic Vicar Apostolic of Dublin* (Dublin,1822)

O'Sullivan, Mortimer, *Captain Rock Detected, or the Origins and Character of the Recent Disturbances, by a Munster Farmer* (London, 1824)

Oliphant, Margaret, *Annals of a Publishing House: William Blackwood and his Times*, 2 vols (New York, 1897)

Owenson, Sydney, *Dublin Run Mad! Or Remarks on Cutchacutchoo and its History* (Dublin, 1805)

Owenson, Sydney, *A Few Reflections Occasioned by the Perusal of a Work Entitled Familiar Epistles to Frederick J——s Esq. on the Present State of the Irish Stage* (Dublin, 1804)

Owenson, Sydney, *Cutchacutchoo, or the Jostling of the Innocents* (Dublin, 1805)

Patterson, M.W. *Sir Francis Burdett and his Times: 1770–1844*, 2 vols (London, 1831)

Peel, Robert, *Sir Robert Peel from His Private Papers*, ed. C.S. Parker, 3 vols (London, 1899)

Peel, Robert, *Address to the Electors of the Borough of Tamworth* (London, 1835)

Peel, Robert, *The Private Letters of Sir Robert Peel*, ed. George Peel (London, 1920)

Peel, Robert, *Memoirs by the Right Hon. Sir Robert Peel*, eds Lord Mahon and E. Cardwell, 2 vols (London, 1857)

Phelan, Margaret, *The Remains of William Phelan, with a Biographical Memoir* (Dublin, 1832)

Phelan, William, *The Bible, Not the Bible Society* (Dublin, 1817)

Phillips, Charles, *Curran and his Contemporaries* (London, 1850)

Romilly, Samuel, *Memoirs Written by Himself with a Selection of his Correspondence* (London, 1840)

Russell, Lord John, *Recollections and Suggestions* (London, 1875)

Sheil, R.L. *Sketches, Legal and Political*, ed. M.W. Savage, 5 vols (London, 1855)

Smiles, Samuel, *A Publisher and his Times:The Memoirs and Correspondence of the Late John Murray*, 2 vols (London, 1891)

Wellesley, Arthur, *Civil Correspondence and Memoirs: Ireland of Field Marshal Arthur Duke of Wellington, KG, Ireland*, ed. 2nd Duke of Wellington (London, 1860)

Wellesley, Arthur, *Supplementary Despatches, Correspondence and Memoranda of Arthur, Duke of Wellington*, ed. 2nd Duke of Wellington, 8 vols (London, 1880)

Wyse, Thomas, *Letters on the Organisation of Liberal Clubs* (Dublin, 1827)

Wyse, Thomas, *A Historical Sketch of the Late Catholic Association*, 2 vols (London, 1829)

SECONDARY SOURCES

Books

Acheson, Alan, *A History of the Church of Ireland, 1691–1996* (Dublin,2002)

Akenson, D.H. *The Irish Education Experiment: The National System of Education in Nineteenth-Century Ireland* (London, 1970)

Aspinall, Arthur, *Lord Brougham and the Whig Party* (Manchester, 1927)

Aspinall, Arthur, *Politics and the Press:1780–1850* (London, 1949)

Bartlett, Thomas, *The Fall and Rise of the Irish Nation: The Catholic Question 1690–1830* (Dublin, 1992)

Bentley, Michael, *Politics Without Democracy: 1815–1914* (Oxford, 1984)

Bew, John, *The Glory of Being Britons: Civic Unionism in Nineteenth-Century Belfast* (Dublin, 2009)

Blackstock, Allan, *An Ascendancy Army: The Irish Yeomanry, 1796–1834* (Dublin, 1998)

Blackstock, Allan, *Loyalism in Ireland: 1789–1829* (Belfast, 2007)

Blake, Robert, *The Conservative Party From Peel to Major* (London, 1998)

Bourne, Kenneth, *Palmerston: The Early Years: 1748–1841* (London, 1982)

Bowen, Desmond, *The Protestant Crusade in Ireland: A study of Protestant–Catholic Relations between the Act of Union and the Disestablishment* (Dublin, 1978)

Bowen, Desmond, *History and the Shaping of Irish Protestantism* (New York, 1995)

Bowen, Desmond, *Souperism: Myth or Reality* (Cork, 1970)

Boyce, G.R. and O'Day, Alan (eds), *The Making of Modern Irish History: Revisionism and the Revisionist Controversy* (London, 1996)

Boyce, G.R. and O'Day, Alan (eds), *Nineteenth-Century Ireland* (Dublin, 1990)

Brent, Richard, *Liberal Anglican Politics: Whiggery, Religion and Reform 1830–1841* (Oxford, 1987)

Briggs, Asa, *The Age of Improvement* (London, 1962)

Brightfield, Myron, *John Wilson Croker* (Berkeley, 1940)

Brightfield, Myron, *Theodore Hook and His Novels* (Harvard, 1928)

Brock, Michael, *The Great Reform Act* (Hampshire, 1993 [revised edn])

Broeker, Galen, *Rural Disturbances and Police Reform in Ireland: 1812–36* (London, 1970)

Butler, J.R.M. *The Passing of The Great Reform Bill* (London, 1914)

Butterfield, Herbert, *George III and the Historians* (London, 1957)

Cannon, John, *Parliamentary Reform 1642–1832* (Cambridge, 1973)

Cannon, John, *Samuel Johnson and the Politics of Hanoverian England* (Oxford, 1994)

Chenivix-Trench, Charles, *The Great Dan* (London, 1984)

Clark, J.C.D. *English Society: 1688–1832* (Cambridge, 1985)

Clark, J.C.D. *Samuel Johnson: Literature, Religion and English Cultural Politics from the Restoration to Romanticism* (Cambridge, 1994)

Clark, Roy Benjamin, *William Gifford: Tory Satirist and Editor* (New York, 1948)

Clarke, Bob, *From Grub Street to Fleet Street* (Aldershot, 2004)

Clarke E., *Benjamin Disraeli* (London, 1826)

Clarke, George Kitson, *Peel and the Conservative Party: 1832–1841*, 2nd edn (London, 1964)

Clarke, Samuel, *Social Origins of the Irish Land War* (Princeton, 1979)

Clifford, Brendan, *The Veto Controversy* (Belfast, 1985)

Clive, John, *The Scotch Reviewers: The Edinburgh Review, 1802–1815* (London, 1957)

Colley, Linda, *Britons: Forging the Nation, 1707–1837* (Reading 2005 [new paperback edn])

Collini, S., Winch, D. and Burrow, J.W. *The Noble Science of Politics: A Study in Nineteenth-Century Intellectual History* (Cambridge, 1983)

Collini, S., Whatmore, R. and Young, B. (eds), *History, Religion and Culture: British Intellectual History, 1750–1950* (Cambridge, 2000)

Connolly, Seán, *Priests and People in Pre-Famine Ireland:1780–1845* (Dublin, 2001)

Cookson, J.E. *Lord Liverpool's Administration: The Crucial Years 1815–1822* (Edinburgh, 1975)

Copisarow, Alcon and Thompson, John, *Armchair Athenians* (London, 2000)

Corish, Patrick J. *Maynooth College: 1795–1995* (Dublin, 1995)

Crossman, Virginia, *Politics, Law and Order in Nineteenth-Century Ireland* (Dublin, 1996)

Crowe, Ian, *Edmund Burke: His Life and Legacy* (Dublin, 1997)

Deane, Seamus (ed.), *The Field Day Anthology of Irish Literature*, 3 vols (Derry, 1991)

Deane, Seamus, *Celtic Revivals: Essays in Modern Irish Literature, 1880–1980* (London, 1985)

Derry, John, *Politics in the Age of Fox, Pitt and Liverpool* (Basingstoke, 1990)

Dixon, Peter, *Canning: Politician and Statesman* (London, 1976)

Duddy, Thomas, *A History of Irish Thought* (London, 2002)

Edsall, Nicholas, *The Anti-Poor Law Movement, 1834–44* (London, 1971)

Elliott, Marianne, *Robert Emmett: The Making of the Legend* (London, 2003)

Evans, E.J. *Britain Before the Reform Act: Politics and Society, 1815–32* (London, 1989)

Evans, E.J. *Sir Robert Peel: Statesmanship, Power and Party* (Suffolk, 1991)

Evans, E.J. *The Forging of the Modern State* (London, 1996)

Fleming, Fergus, *Barrow's Boys: A Stirring Story of Daring, Fortitude and Outright Lunacy* (London, 1998)

Foster, R.F. *Paddy and Mr Punch: Connections in Irish and English History* (Middlesex, 1995 [paperback edn])

Fraser, Flora, *The Unruly Queen: The Life of Queen Caroline* (London, 1996)

Friendly, Alfred, *Beaufort of the Admiralty* (Essex, 1997)

Gambles, Anna, *Protection and Politics: Conservative Economic Discourse, 1815–1852* (Suffolk, 1999)

Garvin, Tom, *The Evolution of Irish Nationalist Politics* (London, 2004)

Gash, Norman, *Sir Robert Peel: The Life of Sir Robert Peel After 1830* (London, 1972)

Gash, Norman, *Sir Robert Peel* (Harlow, 1986 [new paperback abridged edn])

Gash, Norman, *Reaction and Reconstruction in English Politics: 1832–52* (Oxford, 1965)

Gash, Norman, *Mr Secretary Peel* (London, 1985 [paperback edn])

Gash, Norman, *Pillars of Government, and other Essays on the State of Society, c. 1770 to c. 1880* (London, 1986)

Gash, Norman, *Politics in the Age of Peel: A Study in the Technique of Parliamentary Representation, 1830–1850* (New York, 1953)

Geoghegan, Patrick, *King Dan* (Dublin, 2008)

Gibbons, S.R., *Captain Rock, Night Errant: The Threatening Letters of Pre-Famine Ireland, 1801–45* (Dublin, 2004)

Gilmour, Ian, *Riots, Risings and Revolution: Governance and Violence in Eighteenth-Century England* (London, 1995)

Gittings, Robert, *John Keats* (Aylesbury 1971 [Pelican edn])

Gough H. and Dickson, D. *Ireland and the French Revolution* (Dublin, 1990)

Gray, John, *Black Mass: Apocalyptic Religion and the Death of Utopia* (London, 2007)

Greene, Donald J. *The Politics of Samuel Johnson* (Connecticut, 1960)

Griffiths, Dennis, *Plant Here the Standard* (London, 1996)

Halévy, Elie, *The Liberal Awakening: 1815–1830* (London, 1949 [revised edn])

Halévy, Elie, *The Triumph of Reform: 1830–1841* (London, 1950 [revised edn])

Hamburger, Joseph, *Macaulay and the Whig Tradition* (Chicago, 1976)

Harling, Phillip, *The Waning of Old Corruption: The Politics of Economical Reform in Britain, 1779–1846* (Oxford, 1996)

Herzog, Dom, *Poisoning the Minds of the Lower Orders* (Princeton, 1999)

Hibbert, Christopher, *George IV: Regent and King, 1811–1830* (Devon, 1975)

Hill, Brian, *The Early Parties and Politics in Britain, 1688–1832* (Basingstoke, 1996)

Hill, Jaqueline, *From Patriots to Unionists: Dublin Civic Politics and Irish Protestant Patriotism, 1660–1840* (Oxford, 1997)

Hill, R.L. *Toryism and the People: 1832–46* (London, 1927)

Howe, Stephen, *Ireland and Empire: Colonial Legacies in Irish History and Culture* (Oxford, 2002)

Hilton, Boyd, *A Mad, Bad and Dangerous People* (Oxford, 2006)

Hilton, Boyd, *Cash, Corn and Commerce: The Economic Policies of the Tory Government 1815–1830* (Oxford, 1977)

Hilton, Boyd, *The Age of Atonement: The Influence of Evangelicism on Social and Economic Thought, 1795–1895* (Oxford, 1988)

Hinde, Wendy, *George Canning* (London, 1973)

Hobsbawm E.J. and Rude, G. *Captain Swing* (Oxford, 1969)

Hobsbawm E.J. *Nations and Nationalism Since 1780* (Cambridge, 1992)

Hobsbawm E.J. and Ranger, T. *The Invention of Tradition* (Cambridge, 1984)

Holme T., *Caroline* (Edinburgh, 1979)

Hoppen, Theodore K. *Elections, Politics and Society in Ireland: 1832–1885* (Oxford, 1984)

Hoppen, Theodore K. *Ireland Since 1800: Conflict and Conformity* (London, 1989)

Hoppit, J. *Parliament, Nations and Identities in Britain and Ireland* (Manchester, 2003)

Howe, Stephen, *Ireland and Empire: Colonial Legacies in Irish History and Culture* (Oxford, 2002)

Hudson, David, *The Ireland That We Made* (Ohio, 2003)

Inglis, Brian, *The Freedom of the Press in Ireland 1784–1841* (London, 1954)

Jenkins, Brian, *Henry Goulburn, 1784–1856: A Political Biography* (Liverpool, 1996)

Johnson, Paul, *Birth of the Modern: World Society 1815–1830* (London, 1991)

Jones, Aled, *Powers of the Press: Newspapers, Power and the Public in Nineteenth-Century England* (Aldershot, 1994)

Jones, Peter, *The French Revolution in Social and Political Perspective* (London, 1996)

Jupp, Peter, *British Politics on the Eve of Reform: The Duke of Wellington's Administration, 1828–1830* (New York, 1995)

Jupp, Peter, *British and Irish Elections: 1784–1831* (Newton Abbott, 1973)

Kelly, Ronan, *Bard of Erin: The Life of Thomas Moore* (Dublin, 2008)

Kenealy, Arabela, *Memoirs of E.V. Kenealy* (London, 1908)

Keogh, D. and Furlong, N. (eds), *The Mighty Wave: The 1798 Rebellion in Wexford* (Dublin, 1996)

Larkin, Emmet, *The Historical Dimension of Irish Catholicism* (Dublin, 1997)

Larkin, Emmet, *The Pastoral Role of the Roman Catholic Church in Pre-Famine Ireland* (Dublin, 2006)

Leerssen J. *Remembrance and Imagination: Patterns in the Literary Representation of Ireland in the Nineteenth Century* (Cork, 1996);

Leerssen J. *Hidden Ireland, Hidden Sphere* (Galway, 2002)

Lloyd, C. *Mr Barrow of the Admiralty* (London, 1970)

Lochhead, Marion, *John Gibson Lockhart* (London, 1958)

Longford, Elizabeth, *Wellington: Pillar of State* (London, 1972)

LoPatin, Nancy, *Political Unions, Popular Politics and the Great Reform Act* (New York, 1999)

MacDonagh, Oliver, *The Hereditary Bondsman: Daniel O'Connell, 1775–1829* (London, 1988)

MacDonagh, Oliver, *The Emancipist: Daniel O'Connell, 1830–1849* (London, 1989)

Machin, G.I.T. *The Catholic Question in English Politics, 1820–1830* (Oxford, 1964)

Macintyre, Angus, *The Liberator: Daniel O'Connell and the Irish Party, 1830–1847* (London, 1965)

Magnus, Philip, *Gladstone* (London, 1963)

Mandler, Peter, *Aristocratic Government in the Age of Reform* (Oxford, 1990)

McBrien, Richard P. *The Lives of the Popes* (New York, 2000)

McDowell, R.B. *Public Opinion and Government Policy in Ireland, 1801–1846* (London, 1952)

McDowell, R.B. *British Conservatism, 1832–1914* (London, 1959)

McDowell, R.B. *Historical Essays, 1938–2001* (Dublin, 2003)

McGrath, Thomas, *Politics, Interdenominational Relations and Education in the Public Memory of Bishop Kames Doyle of Kildare and Leighlin, 1796–1834* (Dublin, 1999)

McManus, Antonia, *The Irish Hedge Schools and Their Books, 1615–1831* (Dublin, 2002)

McWilliam, Rohan, *Popular Politics in Nineteenth-Century England* (London, 1998)

Milner, Gamaliel, *The Threshold of the Victorian Age* (London, 1934)

Mitchell, Austin, *The Whigs in Opposition, 1815–1830* (Oxford, 1967)

Mitchell, Leslie, *Holland House* (London, 1980)

Moneypenny, W.F. and Buckle, G.E. *The Life of Benjamin Disraeli, Earl of Beaconsfield*, 2 vols (London, 1910)

Morley, John, *William Ewart Gladstone: His Life and Times* (London, 1908 [Lloyd popular edn])

Newbould, Ian, *Whiggery and Reform, 1830–41* (Stanford, 1990)

Newcomer, James, *Lady Morgan the Novelist* (London, 1990)

Newman, Gerald, *The Rise of English Nationalism: A Cultural History, 1740–1830* (New York, 1987)

Newton-Dunn, Bill, *The Man Who Was John Bull* (London, 1996)

Ó Buachalla, Breandán, *Aisling Ghéar* (Dublin, 1996)

Ó Ciosáin, Niall, *Print and Popular Culture in Ireland, 1750–1850* (London, 1997)

O'Ferrall, Fergus, *Catholic Emancipation: Daniel O'Connell and the Birth of Irish Democracy, 1820–1835* (Dublin, 1985)

O'Gorman, Frank, *The Emergence of the British Two-Party System, 1760–1832* (London, 1982)

O'Gorman, Frank, *Voters, Patrons and Parties: The Unreformed Electoral System of Pre-Hanoverian England, 1734–1832* (Oxford, 1989)

O'Reilly, the Rev. Bernard, *John MacHale, Archbishop of Tuam: His Life and Times*, 2 vols (New York, 1890)

Ó Tuathaigh, Gearóid, *Ireland Before the Famine, 1798–1848* (Dublin, 2001 [revised edn])

Palmer, Stanley H. *Police and Protest in England and Ireland, 1780–1850* (Cambridge, 1988)

Parry, Jonathan, *The Rise and Fall of Liberal Government in Victorian Britain* (Yale, 1996)

Pearce, Edward, *Reform! The Fight for the 1832 Reform Act* (London, 2004)

Perkin, Harold, *The Origin of Modern English Society, 1780–1880* (London, 1969)

Philpin, C.H.E. (ed.), *Nationalism and Popular Protest in Ireland* (Cambridge, 1987)

Pocock, J.G.A. *Politics, Language and Time: Essays in Political Thought and History* (London, 1971)

Prior, James, *The Memoirs and Character of the Right Hon. Edmund Burke* (London, 1824)

Quennell, P. *Byron: A Self Portrait, Letters and Diaries*, 2 vols (London, 1950)

Ramsay, A.A.W. *Sir Robert Peel* (London, 1928)

Reynolds, J.A. *The Catholic Emancipation Crises in Ireland, 1823–1829* (New Haven, 1954)

Ridley, Jane, *The Young Disraeli, 1804–1846* (London, 1995)

Robbins, Jane, *The Trial of Queen Caroline* (New York, 2006)

Roberts, M. *The Whig Party* (London, 1939)

Sack, James, J. *From Jacobite to Conservative: Reaction and Orthodoxy in Britain, 1760–1832* (Cambridge, 1993)

Shattock, Joanne, *Politics and the Reviewers: The Edinburgh and the Quarterly in the Early Victorian Age* (Leicester, 1989)

Shine, Hill and Shine, Helen Chadwick, *The Quarterly Under Gifford* (Chapel Hill, 1949)

Southgate, Duncan, *The Passing of the Whigs, 1832–1886* (London, 1961)

Stanlis, P.J. *Edmund Burke and the Natural Law* (Michigan, 1958)

Stevens, F.G. *The History of 'The Times': The Thundered in the Making, 1785–1841*, vol. I (London, 1936)

Stewart, Robert, *The Foundations of the Conservative Party, 1830–1867* (London, 1978)

Stewart, Robert, *Henry Brougham: His Public Career, 1798–1868* (London, 1986)

Summerson, John, *Georgian London* (Middlesex, 1969 [paperback edn])

Thomas, William, *The Quarrel of Macaulay and Croker* (Oxford, 2000)

Thomas, William, *Philosophical Radicals* (Oxford, 1979)

Thompson, E.P. *The Making of the English Working Class* (London, 1968 [Penguin edn])

Thrall, Elizabeth, *Rebellious Fraser's* (New York, 1934)

Turner M.J. *The Age of Unease: Government and Reform in Britain, 1782–1832* (Stroud, 2000)

Vernon, James, *Politics and the People: A Study in English Political Culture 1815–1867* (Cambridge, 1993)

Wahrman, Dror, *Imagining the Middle Class: The Political Representation of Class in Britain, c. 1780–1840* (Cambridge, 1995)

Walker, B.M. *Parliamentary Election Results in Ireland, 1801–1922* (Dublin, 1978)

Ward, A.W. and Waller, A.R. *Cambridge History of English and American Literature*, vol. XII (Cambridge, 1907–21)

Watts, Duncan, *Tories, Conservatives and Unionists, 1815–1914* (London, 1994)

Weintraub, Stanley, *Disraeli: A Biography* (London, 1993)

Whelan, Irene, *The Bible War in Ireland: The Second Reformation in Ireland and the Polarisation of Protestant–Catholic Relations, 1800–1840* (Dublin, 2006)

Whelan, Kevin, *The Tree of Liberty, Radicalism, Catholicism and the Construction of Irish Identity: 1760–1830* (Cork, 1996)

White, R.J. *The Conservative Tradition* (London, 1964)

Wolfe, John, *The Protestant Crusade in Britain, 1829–1869* (Oxford, 1991)

Zamoyski, Adam, *Holy Madness: Romantics and Revolutionaries, 1776–1871* (London, 1999)

Ziegler, Philip, *Melbourne: A Biography of William Lamb, 2nd Lord Melbourne* (London, 1978)

ARTICLES AND CHAPTERS

Aspinall, Arthur, 'The Social Status of Journalists at the Beginning of the Nineteenth Century', *The Review of English Studies*, 21, 83 (July 1945)

Cahill, Gilbert A. 'Irish Catholicism and English Toryism', *Review of Politics*, 10, 1 (January 1959)

Bentley, Michael, 'The Ripening of Sir Robert Peel', in Michael Bentley (ed.), *Public and Private Doctrine: Essays in British History Presented to Maurice Cowling* (Cambridge, 1993)

Bradfield, B.T. 'Sir Richard Vyvyan and the Country Gentlemen', *The English Historical Review*, vol. LXXXXIII (1968)

Bradhurst, A.C. 'The French Revolutionary Collection in the British Library', *British Library Journal*, vol. 2 (1976)

Bric, M.J. 'Priests, Parsons and Politics: The Rightboy Protests in County Cork, 1785–1788', in C.H.E. Philpin (ed.), *Nationalism and Popular Protest in Ireland* (Cambridge, 1987)

Brown, Thomas N. 'Nationalism and the Irish Peasants: 1800–1848', *Review of Politics*, vol. 15 (October 1953)

Brown, S.J. 'The New Reformation Movement in the Church of Ireland, 1801–1829', in S.J. Brown and D.W. Miller (eds), *Piety and Power in Ireland, 1760–1869* (Belfast, 2000)

Brundage, Anthony, Eastwood, David and Mandler, Philip, 'Debate: The Making of the New Poor Law *Redivivus*', *Past & Present*, no. 127 (1990)

Davis, R.W. 'The Tories, the Whigs and Catholic Emancipation, 1827–9', *The English Historical Review*, no. 382 (1982)

Donnelly, J.S. 'Pastorini and Captain Rock: Millenarianism and Sectarianism in the Rockite Movement of 1821–4', in S.J. Clark and J.S. Donnelly (eds), *Irish Peasants: Violence and Political Unrest 1780–1914* (Manchester, 1983)

Donnelly, J.S. 'The Rightboy Movement', *Studia Hibernica*, no. 18 (1978)

Dunne, Tom, 'Tá Gaedhil Bhocht Cráidhte: Memory, Tradition and the Politics of the Poor', in L.M. Geary (ed.), *Rebellion and Remembrance in Modern Ireland* (Dublin, 2001)

Dunne, Tom, 'The Best History of Nations: Lady Morgan's Irish Novels', *Historical Studies*, no. 16 (1987)

Dunne, Tom, 'Ballads, Rhetoric and Politicisation', in H. Gough and D. Dickson (eds), *Ireland and the French Revolution* (Dublin, 1990)

Eastwood, David, 'Robert Southey and the Intellectual Origins of Romantic Conservatism', *English Historical Review*, vol. CIV (1989)

Evans, Eric, 'Some Reasons for the Growth of English Rural Anti-Clericalism', *Past & Present*, no. 66 (1975)

Gambles, Anna, 'Rethinking the Politics of Protection: Conservatism and the Corn Laws', *English Historical Review*, 113, 453 (1998)

Hamilton C.H. 'John Wilson Croker: Patronage and Clientage at the Admiralty', *The Historical Journal*, 43, 1 (2000)

Hawkins, Angus, 'Parliamentary Government and Victorian Political Parties, c. 1830–c.1888', *English Historical Review*, vol. CIV (1989)

Hilton, Boyd, 'Peel: A Reappraisal', *The Historical Journal*, 23, 3 (1979)

Hilton, Boyd, 'The Ripening of Sir Robert Peel', in Michael Bentley (ed.), *Public and Private Doctrine: Essays in British History Presented to Maurice Cowling* (Cambridge, 1993)

Jupp, Peter, 'Government, Parliament and Politics in Ireland', in J. Hoppitt (ed.), *Parliament, Nations and Identities in Britain and Ireland: 1660–1850* (Manchester, 2003)

Keen, J., Schreider, E. and Griggs, I. 'Lockhart to Croker on the *Quarterly*', *PMLA*, 60, I (March 1945)

Kelly, James, 'Conservative Political Thought in Late Eighteenth-Century Ireland', in S.J. Connolly (ed.), *Political Ideas in Eighteenth-Century Ireland* (Dublin, 2000)

Kingon, Suzanne T. 'Ulster Opposition to Catholic Emancipation, 1828–9', *Irish Historical Studies*, XXXIV, 134 (November 2004)

Kriegel, A.D. 'Whiggery in the Age of Reform', *Journal of British Studies*, 32, 3 (July 1993)

Laqueur, T.W. 'The Queen Caroline Affair: Politics as Art in the Reign of George IV', *Journal of Modern History*, 54, 3, (September 1982)

Larkin, Emmet, 'Before the Devotional Revolution', in J.H. Murphy (ed.), *Evangelicals and Catholics in Nineteenth-Century Ireland* (Dublin, 2005)

Latane, David E. Jr. 'Perge, Signifer – or, Where did William Maginn Stand', in James H. Murphy (ed.), *Evangelicals and Catholics in Nineteenth-Century Ireland* (Dublin, 2005)

Lee, Joseph, 'The Ribbonmen', in T.D. Williams (ed.), *Secret Societies in Ireland* (Dublin, 1973)

Leighton, C.D.A. 'Gallicanism and the Veto Controversy: Church, State and the Catholic Community in early Nineteenth-Century Ireland', in R.V. Comerford (ed.), *Religion, Conflict and Coexistence in Ireland* (Dublin, 1990)

Macarthy, B.G. 'Contentions of Maginn', *Studies: An Irish Quarterly Review*, 32, 127 (September 1943)

Machin, G.I.T. 'The Catholic Emancipation Crises of 1825', *The English Historical Review*, vol. LXXVIII (1963)

Mandler, Peter, 'The Making of the New Poor Law, *Redivivus*', *Past & Present*, no. 117 (1987)

McDowell, R.B. 'Trinity College Dublin and Politics', in McDowell, *Historical Essays: 1938–2001* (Dublin, 2003)

Mitchell, L.G. 'Foxite Politics and the Great Reform Bill', *The English Historical Review*, 118, 427 (1993)

Moore, D.C. 'The Other Face of Reform', *Victorian Studies*, vol. 5 (1961)

Nickerson, C.C. 'Disraeli, Lockhart and Murray: An Episode in the History of the *Quarterly Review*', *Victorian Studies*, vol. 15 (1972)

Nockles, Peter, 'Church or Protestant Sect? The Church of Ireland, High Churchmanship and the Oxford Movement', *The Historical Journal*, 41, 2 (1998)

Nowley, F.S. 'The Personnel of the Parliament of 1833', *The English Historical Review*, vol. LIII (1938)

Noyce, Karen A. 'Wellington and the Catholic Question', in Norman Gash (ed.), *Wellington: Studies in the Military and Political Career of the First Duke of Wellington* (Manchester, 1990)

Oakeshott, Michael, 'Rationalism in Politics', in J.S. McLelland (ed.), *A History of Western Political Theory* (London, 1996)

Ó Tuathaigh, Gearóid, 'Political History', in L. Geary and M. Kelleher, *New Views of Nineteenth-Century Ireland: A Guide to Recent Research* (Dublin, 2004)

Ó Tuathaigh, Gearóid, 'Gaelic Ireland, Popular Politics and Daniel O'Connell', *Journal of the Galway Archaeological and Historical Society*, vol. 35 (1975)

Phillips, John A. 'The Structure of Electoral Politics in Unreformed England', *Journal of British Studies*, 19, I (1979)

Phillips, John A. 'Popular Politics in Unreformed England', *The Journal of Modern History*, no. 52 (1980)

Phillips, John A. and Wetherall, Charles, 'The Great Reform Act and the Political Modernization of England', *The American Historical Review*, 100, 2 (April 1995)

Roberts, Paul E.W. 'Caravats and Shanavests', in S. Clark and S.J. Donnelly (eds), *Irish Peasants, Violence and Political Unrest, 1780–1914* (Manchester, 1983)

Rude, George, 'English Rural and Urban Disturbances, 1830–1', *Past & Present*, no. 37 (1967)

Sack, James, 'The Memory of Burke and Pitt: English Conservatism Confronts its Past, 1806–1829', *The Historical Journal*, 30, 3 (1987)

Sack, James, 'Wellington and the Tory Press', in N. Gash (ed.), *Wellington: Studies in the Military and Political Career of the First Duke of Wellington* (Manchester, 1990)

Sack, James, 'Burke and the Conservative Party', in Ian Crowe (ed.), *Edmund Burke: His Life and Legacy* (Dublin, 1997)

Sack, James, 'The Memory of Burke and the Memory of Pitt', *The Historical Journal*, no. 30 (September 1987)

Shipkey, Robert, 'Problems of Irish Patronage During the Secretaryship of Sir Robert Peel', *The Historical Journal*, 10, 1 (1965)

Shunsuke, Katsuta, 'The Rockite Movement in County Cork in the Early 1820s', *Irish Historical Studies*, XXXIII, 131 (May 2003)

Stevenson, Lionel, 'Vanity Fair and Lady Morgan', *PMLA*, 48, 2 (June 1933)

Strout, Alan Lang, 'Lockhart and Croker's Correspondence', *Times Literary Supplement*, 30 August 1941

Thomas, William, 'Religion and Politics in the *Quarterly Review*: 1809–1853', in Stefan Collini, R. Whatmore and B. Young, *History, Religion and Culture: British Intellectual History, 1750–1950* (Cambridge, 2000)

Watson, E.A. 'The Great Whigs and Parliamentary Reform: 1809–1880', *Journal of British Studies*, 24, 4 (1985)

UNPUBLISHED THESES

Bradford, R.E. 'Sir Richard Vyvyan and Tory Politics with Special Reference to the Period 1825–1846' (PhD thesis, University of London, 1965)

Breiseith, Christopher Neri, 'British Conservatism and the French Revolution: John Wilson Croker's Attitudes to Reform and Revolution in Britain and France' (DPhil. thesis, Cornell, 1964)

Simes, D.G.S. 'Ultra-Tories in British Politics, 1824–1834' (DPhil. thesis, Oxford University, 1974)

Spence, J.A.F. 'The Philosophy of Irish Toryism: A Study of Reactions to Liberal Reformism in Ireland in the Generation Between the First Reform Act and the Famine, With Especial Reference to the National Feeling Among the Protestant Ascendancy' (DPhil. thesis, Birkbeck College, University of London, 1991)

Index